AMERICAN POLITICS

AND ITS INTERPRETERS

AMERICAN POLITICS
AND ITS INTERPRETERS

Louis C. Reichman *and* **Barry J. Wishart**
Fullerton Community College

WM. C. BROWN COMPANY PUBLISHERS
Dubuque, Iowa

ACKNOWLEDGMENTS

Richard K. Doan, "What are the Pollsters Themselves Saying?" *TV Guide,* October 26, 1968, pp. 7-8. Reprinted by permission of the publisher.

Melvin Maddocks, "Knowledge is Power," *The Christian Science Monitor,* March 8, 1969. Reprinted by permission of *The Christian Science Monitor.* © 1969, The Christian Science Publishing Society, all rights reserved.

Edith Efron, "The 'Silent Majority' Comes into Focus," *TV Guide,* September 27, 1969, pp. 6-9. Reprinted by permission of the publisher.

Jack Rosenthal, "The Cage of Fear in Cities Beset by Crime," *Life,* July 11, 1969, p. 17. Reprinted by permission of the publisher.

William H. Stringer, "Whose Facts do You Read?" *The Christian Science Monitor,* December 26, 1967. Reprinted by permission of *The Christian Science Monitor.* © 1967, The Christian Science Publishing Society, all rights reserved.

Jesse P. Ritter, Jr., "Nightmare For the Innocent in a California Jail," *Life,* August 15, 1959. Reprinted by permission of the author.

Michael Harrington, "The Other America Revisited," *The Center Magazine,* January 1969. Reprinted by permission of *The Center Magazine,* a publication of the Center for the Study of Democratic Institutions, Santa Barbara, California.

The Christian Science Monitor, "Those on Welfare," April 24, 1967. Reprinted by permission of *The Christian Science Monitor.* © 1967 The Christian Science Publishing Society, all rights reserved.

Eldridge Cleaver, "Requiem for Nonviolence," Copyright © 1968 by Eldridge Cleaver. Reprinted from ELDRIDGE CLEAVER: POST-PRISON WRITINGS AND SPEECHES, edited by Robert Scheer, by permission of Random House, Inc. and the author.

A Group of Alabama Clergymen, "Letter to Martin Luther King."

Martin Luther King, "Letter From a Birmingham Jail," April 16, 1963. Reprinted by permission of the publisher, Harper & Row, Inc.

Stewart Alsop, "The Wallace Man," *Newsweek,* October 21, 1968, p. 116. © Newsweek, Inc., 1968.

Newsweek, "In Politics, It's the New Populism," October 6, 1969, p. 60. © Newsweek, Inc., 1969.

95913

Yale Kamisar, "Assessment of Chief Justice Warren," *Los Angeles Times,* Opinion Section, June 15, 1969. Reprinted by permission of the author.

Herbert McClosky, "Implanting the Democratic Idea," *California Teachers Association Journal,* January 19, 1965, p. 12. Reprinted by permission of the publisher.

Time, "A Professional for the High Court," May 30, 1969, p. 16. Reprinted by permission from *Time,* The Weekly News Magazine; © Time Inc., 1969.

Nicholas De B. Katzenbach, "Law and Order—Has the Supreme Court Gone too Far?" *Look,* October 29, 1968, p. 27. © 1968 by Cowles Communications, Inc. Reprinted by permission of the editors.

Richard Dougherty, Joseph D. Lohman, "Crime and Society's Obligation," *Los Angeles Times,* Opinion Section, February 19, 1967. Reprinted by permission of the publisher.

Yale Kamisar, "Effective Crime Fighting is Costly," *Los Angeles Times,* Opinion Section, June 15, 1968. Reprinted by permission of the publisher and author.

L. H. Whittemore, "A Hard Cop and His Patient Partner on a Menacing Beat," *Life,* June 20, 1969, pp. 52-63. © 1969 by L. H. Whittemore.

James E. Clayton, "F.B.I. Report Makes Our Insecurities Understandable," *Los Angeles Times,* Opinion Section, September 7, 1969. (Reprinted from The Washington Post.) Used by permission of The Washington Post.

Seyom Brown, "The Unbalance of Our Times," *Saturday Review,* May 17, 1969. © 1969 Saturday Review, Inc. Reprinted by permission of the author and publisher.

Herbert J. Teison, Book Review of *The Selling of the President 1968,* by Joe McGinniss, *Saturday Review,* October 18, 1969, p. 38. © 1969 Saturday Review, Inc. Reprinted by permission of the publisher.

Chris Welles, "Newsweek (A Fact) is the New Hot Book (An Opinion)," *Esquire,* November, 1969, p. 152. Reprinted by permission of the publisher.

Newsweek, "Agnew's Complaint: The Trouble With TV," November 24, 1969, pp. 88-92. © Newsweek Inc., 1969.

League of Women Voters, "It's Your Party," Reprinted by permission of The League of Women Voters.

Edward Kennedy, "Text of a Brother's Funeral Eulogy," *Los Angeles Times,* June 9, 1968. Reprinted by permission of United Press International.

John F. Kennedy, "We Face . . . A Moral Crisis . . . As A People," *Newsweek,* June 24, 1963, p. 30. © Newsweek Inc., 1963. Reprinted by permission.

Philip Semas, "Reeducate 'Affluent Peasants' Young Tells Colleges," *The Chronicle of Higher Education,* November 25, 1968, p. 3. Reprinted by permission of the publisher.

Wilfred Laurier Husband, Book Review of *Theft of the Nation: The Structure and Operations of Organized Crime in America,* by Donald R. Cressey, *Saturday Review,* March 22, 1969. Reprinted by permission of the author.

Herbert J. Gans, "Equality Revolution of the 60's," *The New York Times Magazine,* November 3, 1968. © 1968 by The New York Times Company. Reprinted by permission.

Eric Sevareid, "The World Still Moves Our Way," *Look,* July 9, 1968, p. 27. © 1968 by Eric Sevareid. Reprinted by permission of Harold Matson Company, Inc.

PREFACE

It is very easy for beginning students of politics and inexperienced political onlookers to oversimplify what politics is all about. Through rose-colored glasses politics is always high drama, the competition of lofty ideals and convictions against cynicism and narrow self-interest, a noble joust between good and evil. Others with much darker hued glasses see politics as a series of crafty, below the surface deals and manipulations tolerated by the put-upon citizenry until the incumbent rascals are found out and turned out by new self-seekers who, in time, will follow the same path. Real-life politics is somewhere in between.

There are various methods of finding out about real-life politics. A student of politics could begin by participation in one or a variety of political activities. Informative and interesting books on politics abound. There is no scarcity of political "experts"—some of whom actually know what they are talking about —who will lecture, discuss, castigate, laud or otherwise elucidate the dilemmas of politics; but quite often the most difficult problem for the beginning and inexperienced student of politics is to find a "handle" by which he can make some sense from the confusing complexity of the competing political participants and their thoughts, words, and deeds.

The "handle" this book offers is political current events of interest and significance to the student taking his first college course centered around or relating to American politics. These political current events have been selected for their introductory readability and they are set in a framework of broad headings which organize the readings in a relatively simplified, orderly manner. These headings are "The Americans," "The Students," "The Politicians and Their Parties," "The Nonpolitical Influentials," "The Stakes," and "The Political Scientist's Perspective." The reasons for selecting the chapter headings as well as a brief overview of what politically related understandings each chapter attempts to accomplish are set out in the chapter introductions. Further introductions to each individual article aid the student in establishing continuity and perspective, as do the "Questions for Discussion and Dialogue" at the back of each article.

The outsider who is uninterested in or unconcerned with politics is beset by a cacophony of discordant noises and activities, "full of sound and fury, signifying nothing." This political "first book" is intended to offer that outsider a series of organized, interesting, and understandable vicarious exposures to the world of politics. These issues, challenges, and promises, together with the most publicized personalities who give them life, can usually be studied only through various interpreters. This book has been organized to sample some of the more important of these interpreters, including (but not limited to) the recently newsworthy communications media. Hopefully these exposures will be enough of a stimulant to help bring the politically uneducated and perhaps uninterested student to a serious consideration of the issues, challenges, and promises that infuse democratic politics.

The difference between articles and ideas used in class and editing a book of readings is vast. Both of us are indebted to many people who helped us bridge that gap.

Ed Cooney is the kind of editor with whom all fledgling writers should be fortunate enough to become associated. His confidence in us and especially in the idea we have shared that introductory books should be written for students rather than for academic peers have been major factors in our effort.

Our colleagues David Ibsen, Gary Graham, Larry Little, and Harry Weston have greatly aided us with suggestions, articles, and support.

As teachers who have not only taught us, but inspired us, Earl Pullias, John Francis Bannon, Jasper Cross, Louis Midgley, Kirk Hart, and Jerry Loveland have all demonstrated the talent of successfully blending a deep knowledge of subject matter with a real concern for their student's needs, abilities, and interests.

Peggy Reichman has patiently endured the fractured schedule demanded by one year of writing, organizing and editing this book.

And our most basic debt is to hundreds of students who have taught us that politics can be learned and appreciated on so many different levels in so many different ways.

Louis C. Reichman

Barry J. Wishart

Fullerton Junior College

CONTENTS

CHAPTER ONE

The Constituents: The Americans

CHAPTER TWO

The Students

CHAPTER THREE

The Politicians and Their Parties

CHAPTER FOUR

The Nonpolitical Influentials

CHAPTER FIVE

The Stakes

CHAPTER SIX

The Political Scientist's Perspective

The Constituents:
The Americans

Let us suppose that as students of political science we have been given our first assignment: Observe the governmental processes of the United States and describe in very general terms what you have observed about the constituency. What are people in the United States thinking, saying, and doing? What are their feelings? Even if we were novice observers, what conclusions could we draw?

As we study the Americans of the early 1970's, some answers to our questions begin to take shape. The selections presented in Chapter One show us the many faces of the Americans.

As Richard K. Doan describes them, many are in the mood for deep changes in governmental policy, but there is a very significant group of "No Change" advocates as well. Feelings are deep enough on each side to cause problems of polarization. Melvin Maddocks' concern is with implementation of the black-board motto, "Knowledge is Power" instead of the previous emphasis on making and doing. A television change is considered by Edith Efron who poses the question whether television is swinging to the right. Jack Rosenthal, relying on a poll by Louis Harris, concentrates on the influence fear has on the Americans. William Stringer reminds us of the necessity to attempt to find objective informa-tion about politics and government. The dissenting American who is suspected —for whatever reasons—of interfering with the majority is the concern of Jesse P. Ritter, Jr. The "poor" Americans are studied by Michael Harrington and *Christian Science Monitor.* Eldridge Cleaver discusses why nonviolence won't work for blacks in the U.S., and Martin Luther King offers a very different perspective to black anguish. "The Wallace Man" is considered next by Stewart Alsop, and Chapter One concludes with a *Newsweek* study of what it terms the "New Populism."

What Are The Pollsters
Themselves Saying?

Richard K. Doan

In summarizing the findings and interpretations of pollsters George Gallup and Lou Harris, this article discusses how American democracy is losing touch with the American people who are breaking with the old political voting patterns and explanations. The "New Politics" pits the "No Changers" against the "Change Coalition." Because it offers so many contrasts with the "Old Politics," it is very confusing.

... "We know what ideas the public would accept," he (George Gallup) said. "They (the public) would reform the whole electoral system. They'd throw out the electoral college. They'd set up direct primaries. They'd approve of shorter campaigns. They would as soon move Election Day to September. The only reason elections are held in November, you know, is that years ago the farmers had their winter crops in by then and had time to come to town for rallies."

As matters now stand, with the election in November and Inauguration in January, "we put an unprepared President in office," Gallup argued.

Even this isn't the worst of it, in his view. "Democracies all over the world are losing ground," he claimed, "for two reasons: (1) they're losing touch with the people, and (2) they do not have the right machinery for solving the social problems of our day. The members of our Congress have lost touch with the people. The people are 50 years ahead of Congress, and nobody listens to them. It's the Establishment that gets in the way. No priesthood, you know, ever initiates its own reform. That's our trouble.

He saw one ray of light: "I hope we'll soon have a whole new breed of young people who won't put up with these old ways."

Harris saw change coming, but he envisioned it being brought on not just by young people, but by two groups not mutually exclusive but new on the scene as potent political forces: "the educated" and the "Change Coalition", the latter a conglomerate of social and economic classes ignoring party lines.

Jabbing a finger against a bound stack of computerized demographic findings the size of a New York Phone book, the dapper, voluble opinion expert exploded: "Look at all this data! It's trying to talk to us! It tells us things. It says this is the most volatile, the wildest election year in polling history. ('68) But we're learning other important things too: it tells us the old economic issues don't have the same bite they once did.

"What we have surfacing now are these great areas of concern: (1) Viet Nam, a subject on which many people feel rather sad; (2) race, which is the more emotional issue; and (3) non conformity. And what we have is a commonality among people who want compromise in Viet Nam, and white people who feel a real accommodation should be made for the Negroes, and the people who see nothing wrong in boys wearing long hair, and girls in bell-bottom pants. All these people are in the same group and it cuts across all party lines."

Harris warmed to his theme. "We have two new coalitions—the No Changers and the Change Coalition. The No Changers are the older people, whites in the Deep South, lower-income whites in the Northern urban centers, and the conservatives, including Goldwater types, in the suburbs. The Changers are the young people, the blacks, the Spanish-speaking and the other minority groups, and the affluent, those making over $10,000.

"It's a completely mixed-up pattern by old standards.

"In another sense, we have two revolutions going on in America simultaneously, One is the revolt of the blacks, which we all know about. The other is a far more quiet one: the revolt of the educated people; that is, those with some college education. The professionals dominate this group. For the most part they have no roots in any corporate structure which might dampen their political views. They represent only about 25 per cent of the voting populace now, but by 1975 they will constitute about 45 per cent of it.

"It comes down to a case of the most privileged people being the ones who want change, and the least privileged, in many instances, *not* wanting change. It's Karl Marx upside down!"

Harris noted that neither Richard Nixon nor Hubert Humphrey appealed to the Change Coalition. "This coalition is fractionalized in its political leanings," he found. "Nixon and Humphrey are kind of the last residue of the Old Politics, interposed on an emerging structure of New Politics." Wallace, Harris observed, draws his support almost wholly from the No Changers. "It's entirely conceivable that Wallace may be the progenitor of the No Change candidate of 1972," he suggested. . . .

QUESTIONS FOR DISCUSSION AND DIALOGUE

1. How does Harris describe the "No Changers" and the "Change Coalition?"
2. What is your definition of the terms "Liberal" and "Conservative?" How do these definitions apply to the "No Changers" and the "Change Coalition?"
3. Are there historical precedents for this kind of political situation? Discuss.
4. Would you evaluate this kind of political situation as healthy and desirable for the United States or not? Why? Do you think your response makes you more a "Liberal" or a "Conservative?" Why?

Knowledge is Power
Melvin Maddocks

Melvin Maddocks discusses the new prominence and power of the "knowledge workers." He contrasts them with other influential groups in American history, and concerns himself with the question of whether we should separate the "learners and communicators" from the "makers and doers." These "learners and communicators" have their parallels to the Americans the previous article refers to as the "Change Coalition."

We are changing from a society of makers-and-doers to a society of learners-and-knowers. Ideas and information, not products, are the new form of wealth, and the professors are coming into their own as the knowledge elite—no longer just advisers at the elbow of power but policy-makers themselves.

The blackboard motto "Knowledge is Power," written in the best Palmer Method script, is coming true with a literalness our innocent old schoolteachers never dreamed of. Daniel Bell has put the matter bluntly:

"The university, which is the place where theoretical knowledge is sought, tested, and codified in a disinterested way, becomes the primary institution of the new society. Perhaps it is not too much to say that if the business firm was the key institution of the past one hundred years because of its role in organizing production for the mass creation of products, the university will become the central institution of the next hundred years because of its role as the new source of innovation and knowledge."

In other words, Mr. Bell is suggesting we are engaged in an astonishing, largely unrecorded revolution that is turning us from a nation of makers-and-doers to a nation of learners and communicators.

Buckminster Fuller was one of the first to point out: "The great industry of tomorrow will be the university, and everyone will be going to school."

The so-called "knowledge industries," which produce and distribute ideas and information rather than goods and services, will account in the late 1970's for one-half the gross national product, according to Peter F. Drucker: "Every other dollar earned and spent in the American economy will be earned by producing and distributing ideas and information and will be spent on procuring ideas and information."

In 1900, the largest single group of Americans—in fact, the majority—were farmers. By 1940, the largest single group consisted of industrial workers. By 1960, the largest single group included what the census describes as "professional, managerial, and technical people"—i.e., primarily "knowledge workers"—and by the late 1970's, they are expected to be the majority, as the farmer was at the turn of the century. (The farmer is now down to less than 6 percent.)

'Professorial Gothic'

The portrait subject of a new Grant Wood "American Gothic," one may assume, will be the professor and, of course, his professor-wife.

Teachers today make up the largest single vocational division in the American labor force. There are now around 80,000 public-school systems and 2,200 universities in the United States. Colleges are being founded at the rate of more than 20 a year. One economist has estimated that between now and 1975 twice as many buildings will have to be constructed as have been erected on campuses since Harvard was founded in 1636. Otherwise the No Vacancies sign will hang out for a number of the 10 million students anticipated.

No wonder Stephen Graubard has coined the phrase "university cities," foreseeing the time when the "knowledge industry" will dominate a community as, say, the automobile industry dominates Detroit today.

The standing complaint of the American intellectual always has been that he lacked the status and the influence of the European intellectual. With a measure of justice he called his society materialistic—i.e., anti-intellectual—implying that nothing really good could come of it so long as it ignored his leavening spirit.

Suddenly the academician has become everybody's darling, a new elitist. He may end up even richer than the Babbitts he has, by reflex, come to look down upon. Salaries of $100,000 are reported to lure "stars" from one faculty to another. Even poets are said to make $25,000 for becoming "resident"—for giving a campus a certain chic.

"Knowledge is power." One is told in copious biographies of scientists acquiring, willy-nilly, by their knowledge a degree of political, military, and economic power that precipitates problems of conscience. Anthropologists and physicists, economists and psychologists, linguists and historians—the whole faculty is "consulting" as much as teaching. Even Bible scholars, we are told, are valuable to both Israeli and Arab armies as consultants on such subjects as "hidden water resources."

The man of knowledge, one observer put it, is no longer on tap but on top. The intellectual sees himself escalating from the secondary role of adviser to the primary role of decision maker. For in an increasingly complex world he has become the indispensable man.

Alfred North Whitehead spoke years ago of the Specialists and the Integrators. The Specialists are the masters of 20th-century knowledge—ever more narrow, ever more exquisite. The Integrators are the practical leaders—the middle men who apply to everyday life what the Specialists learn, much as industry converts into new products the theoretical discoveries of research.

But, asked Whitehead, what if the new knowledge becomes so specialized, so refined that the Integrators cannot conceive of its application, its meaning for them and the community?

Jets to Washington

Our academicians—our Specialists—are not altogether sure that time has not come. A growing minority today might hold that even the Integrators would have to be part-Specialists—that, in an updated Platonic sense, the philosophers should be kings.

George Santayana once remarked acidly that if philosophers were made kings they would last about two weeks. Then the politicians, the soldiers, the businessmen would be sent for, quick. For, Santayana assumed, what is needed in the realm of action is not deep thinking but an almost reckless capacity for the instant decision—a physical drive to get on with it. Better to be wrong than to be Hamlet.

What Santayana may have discounted is that when philosophers are made kings they, too, tend to become less philosophical. In coming down from his proverbial ivory tower, the academician has landed in the arena with an almost frightening show of briskness. He jets to Washington. He writes off the top of his head for the popular magazines. He sits on any number of "activating" committees.

Our old figure of fun, the absent-minded professor, has suddenly remembered where he left his umbrella, and he is using it to stab his way down those corridors of power.

Contemplating their prospects as Specialists-cum-Integrators, the academicians have referred to themselves, without undue modesty, as "new Prometheans." They speak of the future as the private preserve of a "professoriate"—an "academic-scientist-intellectual complex." With every evidence of satisfaction they dub the university a "superheated cockpit."

'Utopias ... on the Agenda'

The "new Prometheans" may not be totally optimistic about the future. But they cannot help thinking it a good sign that it promises to rest in their hands. They have seen clearly that "power corrupts" in the cases, for instance, of politicians and businessmen. With the usual myopia that sets in when one looks at the mirror, they are more complacent about their own motives.

Dr. Glenn T. Seaborg, chairman of the Atomic Energy Commission, has placidly predicted "the dawn of a scientific-humanistic era, a quiet revolution that will prevail—simply because it speaks a prevailing truth."

"Utopias," another "new Promethean" exulted, "are on the agenda everywhere." In these Utopias "humanistic individualism" will be the norm. Institutions will "be constructed or reconstructed so as to enable everyone to 'do his own thing.' " And in this best of all possible "professoriate" worlds, there will be a "displacement of competitive egoism by humanist altruism"—just as at faculty meetings, no doubt.

Pragmatism Revisited

Certainly knowledge, not money, is the new form of wealth. Certainly the knowledge specialist will be more and more valuable to a society whose problems have become a problem even to articulate, to say nothing of solving.

But the notion that a "professoriate," by sheer intellectual competence, can bring in the millennium may be simply the latest example of the arrogance of American "know-how." One does not even trust the intellectual competence of people who think it is going to be all that easy.

It is a little disturbing to see just how unphilosophical the "new Prometheans" can be. Embarrassed by any ideology beyond pragmatism, they ask the same old question everybody else asks: Does it work? "Goals" are what they like to talk about rather than "purpose."

Involved up to their ears, how remote, how quaint they make the last generation of professors seem. Here was historian Carl Becker "On Being a Professor":

"Less than ever did I desire to return to the known world and tread in monotonous routine the dusty streets of Now and Here. . . . How fine not to have 'to do' anything! And one day it dawned upon me that this was precisely the case of my admired professors. . . . From that moment I was a lost man. I was bound to become a professor."

There are obvious disadvantages, of course, to being "out of it." But the pre-Prometheans had one supreme service to render. As truly free from self-interest as the "new Prometheans" pretend to be, they could make relatively detached judgments on the society which they were in but not of. Among other things, they could bring to bear those "scientific-humanistic" values that are severe on expediency and remind us of a sense of usefulness higher than the "Now" and "Here" can afford.

Who Will Man the Brakes?

It is precisely when the practical tasks of history seem most urgent, the German philosopher Josef Pieper once protested, that someone must ask *why*. The "unrealistic" mind, even the "otherworldly" mind—the mind that refuses to "see things" as the more active participants do—is invaluable. If it didn't exist, it would have to be invented to deliver us from the final insanities of too much common sense.

If our knowers, by a kind of irony, become makers-and-doers themselves, who will tell us that we are not always right about what we think is so immediate-attention important—that life has its own priorities beyond the man-made?

Revolutions, alas, have plenty of hands for the steering wheel, to say nothing of feet for the accelerator. What they really need is somebody to man the brakes.

QUESTIONS FOR DISCUSSION AND DIALOGUE

1. What relationships do you see between the "professional, managerial, and technical people" in this article and the "change coalition" discussed in the previous article?
2. Do you think the Americans should be optimistic or pessimistic about the academician becoming "a new elitist"? Why?

3. Do you think academic and intellectual activism are compatible with or contradictory to good teaching? Discuss.
4. What are the greatest advantages and the greatest shortcomings that you see in—"a nation of makers and doers," or "a nation of learners and communicators?"

The 'Silent Majority' Comes into Focus

Edith Efron

One of the most famous phrases of the 1968 Presidential campaign was "the Silent Majority." On many occasions and in a variety of ways Richard Nixon referred to how "fed up" most of the American public was with violence and radicalism. How much of this violence and radicalism was and is a new and troublesome phenomenon in the United States, and how much was exaggerated out of proportion by television coverage and interpretation? Is television responsible for changing the Americans by "profoundly (affecting) what we call the process of socialization," as Federal Communications Commissioner Nicholas Johnson says; or does television confuse, exaggerate, and distort our understanding of the Americans and their politics? (The reader might be interested in "Agnew's Complaint . . . " in Chapter Four at this point. It discusses Vice President Spiro Agnew's attack on the news reporting and editorializing of the three national television networks.)

"The Riots."
"Chicago."
They stick like giant burrs in the newsmen's minds—symbols of the clash between them and the majority of the public.

That clash has not yet been resolved. It still flares up at the slightest provocation and is a chronic issue at the networks, where top executives wait tensely for the day's mail and look back nostalgically at the days when five critical letters were a crisis.

The nature of the public's simmering anger is well understood. CBS's Bill Leonard says: "The right and the middle complain that we put on irresponsible people from the left." ABC documentary producer Steve Fleischman, too, says: "People feel we've given too much play to the radicals." And NBC News president Reuven Frank says: "The general view of the public is that we have too many radicals in the network news departments."

The newsmen's awareness of the seriousness of this situation was brought to a peak by the "conservative" electoral results—"conservative" being the odd "new politics" label for an amorphous antiradical coalition encompassing the spectrum from "Establishment Democrats" through the Nixon center to the far-right Wallace voters. This active antiradicalism of the majority has reoriented important aspects of the newsmen's professional thinking. As a result, something new is happening in programming. It is a development that will please many Americans and anger others.

What is happening results from a change in newsmen's thinking—so we'll start with that.

The most obvious change is the sudden emergence in strength of an attitude that has been commonplace among viewers for years. Namely, that there has been too much one-sided attacking of the United States, its institutions and its citizens, on the airwaves. This opinion, once viewed as "flag waving" by many newsmen, today is enunciated as follows:

ABC's Lester Cooper: "I want to do a show on what's *right* with America. We've heard so much about what's wrong. I'm not a chauvinist, but I am a patriot. There's a *great* America out there to cover."

CBS's Bill Leonard, on an upcoming documentary: "It will capture the spirit of America. We'll be showing *strengths* as well as weaknesses. It's a wonderful country *and* it's absurd. You'll be laughing *and* crying. That's what the U.S. is all about."

NBC's Eliot Frankel: "One of the themes in *First Tuesday* is to show what's *right* with America, as well as what's wrong. There's a *lot* that's right. Decent people, leading decent lives, knocking themselves out for others. . . . "

A good many men are also engaging in intensive soul-searching into the issue of biased reporting. NBC's documentary producer Shad Northshield says: "Bias is on everybody's mind. We've claimed we don't have it. And the viewers say, 'Yes, you do.' I was stunned by the public reaction to Chicago. We all were. I was stunned, astonished, *hurt*. It's the key thing that opened my eyes to the cleavage between newsmen and the majority. We didn't *know* 56 percent would have thought we were unfair. It raises enormous questions about journalism."

One of the issues it raises for Northshield and others is a pronounced bias in favor of minority coverage in past network operations. "In TV news departments," says Northshield, "we appear to know a lot about the black minority. It's the silent majority we must explore. We haven't done it. We didn't know it was *there!*" CBS's Phil Lewis says: "We're beginning to realize we've ignored the majority. America doesn't end at the Hudson!" CBS News star Joseph Benti says: "We spend so much time on angry blacks, angry youth. But what about that vast forgotten army out there? How many hard-working, law-abiding whites are mad as hell because *their* story isn't being told?"

Other men have taken their analyses further, in an attempt to get at the causes of this pro-minority emphasis. CBS's Desmond Smith is one of those who suspects that the newsmen have been politically used: "There's been a great deal of manipulation from the left. The left and SDS have been getting a great deal of play. Americans are getting to feel they're not getting the whole story."

Fred Freed of NBC goes further yet. He attributes the situation to the newsmen's own liberal ideology: "This generation of newsmen is a product of the

New Deal. These beliefs that were sacred to the New Deal are the beliefs that news has grown on. This is true of the networks, of *Newsweek,* of *The New York Times,* of all media. Men of like mind are in the news. It's provincial. The blue-and white-collar people who are in revolt now do have cause for complaint against us. We've ignored their point of view. It's *bad.* It's bad to pretend they don't exist. We did this because we tend to be upper-middle-class liberals. We think the poor are 'better' than the middle class. We romanticize them. The best thing that happened to me was a month I spent walking in Detroit slums after the riots. I stopped romanticizing the poor.

"I've come to understand that it's really the same with all classes. You've got to sit down with the cop, with the little storekeeper, and get their views. They're human beings like everyone else. Their attitudes emerge logically from their interests and their values. They should be covered that way."

There are those in top managerial positions who don't pour out such confessions. CBS's Bill Leonard, for example, claims objectivity for CBS News, and declares vehemently: "We have *nothing* to apologize for, *nothing*—and I personally include our coverage of Chicago." But, in the course of several hours of conversation, Leonard relaxes and launches into an attack on "bad reporting"—which turns out to be a powerful disquisition on bias: "Most reporting is *lousy.* It's lousy because people are lazy, because people don't think ahead, because they approach things in rote ways. We have these kinds of reporters here, unfortunately. The worst problem of all is the reporter who doesn't ask the next question —the *cheap, lousy* reporter who'll quote an attack but doesn't go to the other side, because the answer might kill his story. ... And these producers who develop and edit a broadcast from the point of view of the way *they* want it to turn out—with their own prejudices showing. That happens quite often. . . . If we could get rid of those people we'd be a lot closer to our goal of objectivity."

And finally ... there are those who are not theorizing about bias because they're too busy traveling back and forth between New York and Washington, coping with Congressional investigations into their alleged practice of it. CBS News producer Jay McMullen says the following: "We're getting a lot of flak from Congress and the FCC—a lot of harassment. The Congressional focus is on the news area. It has to do with this whole business of our coverage of the riots, of Chicago. Producers are being called down to Washington and asked to explain their news decisions."

With all of this ferment going on behind the scenes, what, precisely, is happening to news and public-affairs programming? The trends are exactly what you might guess: there is a shifting of coverage patterns at the polar ends of the usual spectrum covered by the networks. The basic coverage, which has a moderate-liberal orientation, will remain the same. But in network news there is a distinct deflation of the coverage of radical left and of radical-left causes, particularly those of a militant type.

Prime-time news, for example, which operates in a restricted time slot, is upping its coverage of the middle and lower-middle classes. CBS has inaugurated a polling service to be used in key controversial stories to check on nation-wide opinion. Regular coverage of suburbia and lower-middle-class areas in the environs of New York City is being stepped up by CBS and NBC New York stations.

These trends are far more visible, however, in the documentary realm, where subjects are few and where the selective process is readily apparent.

Much of the vigorous planned activity for the season's opening lies in the area of "exploring middle- and lower-middle-class Americans." Various broad-gauge sketches of the Nation are ready to go. Some may already have appeared before you read this. At CBS: "A Day in the Life of the United States of America"; "The Making of the President: 1968"; two on "The Generation Gap." At NBC: a two-and-a-half-hour "From Here to the Seventies"; "Election '69: What We Learned," and, on *First Tuesday,* says producer Eliot Frankel, one of the themes will be "the malaise in middle-class life."

As for ABC, there is a veritable outbreak of Americana—with a list of shows up for sale to sponsors with names like: "The American Dream," "Hemingway's Idaho," "Small Town Judge," "A Country Preacher," "American Farmer," "Forest Ranger," "The Marines" and "Sousa Sound"—14 or 15 of such projected shows, as compared to eight last year. According to documentary vice president Tom Wolf, this reflects the thinking of sponsors, who themselves are responding to "the shift of climate in this country, the new attitudes of viewers."

By contrast to this ferment of activity on the majority front, "problem coverage"—the kind that increasingly requires the inclusion of radical opinion white and black—is in decline. The same number of documentary hours is scheduled as last year—a significant proportion of them, however, now packed into two "magazine" formats at CBS and NBC, which, of necessity, have acquired a lighter, "variety" approach to coverage. The number of straight, hour-length documentaries has shrunk and with it has come a diminution of "hard" problem coverage.

Why is this happening? Because of political pressure—defined in its broadest sense, from Congress down to the smallest grass-roots hamlet. The most visible pressure is coming from Congress. Says McMullen: "The tendency, when Congress harasses, is for individual producers to pull in their horns. I think this whole Congressional thing might be affecting the documentary operation." ABC's Steve Fleischman, too, says: "The medium is generally frightened of the documentary realm."

The three network presidents are on record with strong statements that, for the past year or so—ever since some of the public started to blast away at the networks' featuring of radicals and radical issues—Congressional pressures have been threatening the medium's First Amendment rights.

On the national grass-roots level, which underlies Congressional pressure, there is evidence that resistance is building up to coverage of the radicals and radical issues at local broadcasting stations—for whom network news and documentary production is destined. A nation-wide survey conducted by Television Age indicates that programs on these issues are declining. "It may indicate," says Television Age, "that the public has been satiated with studies of . . . urban crises . . . racial tensions . . . dope addiction and poverty."

There are many students of the broadcasting world who believe that the networks, always fear-ridden in the realm of politico-economic coverage, can scarcely afford to become more so. ("We never did have more than four or five tough documentaries a year," concedes CBS's Bill Leonard, "and at that we had more than the other networks put together.") Protests are now surfacing from the left side of the political spectrum—from liberals, radicals and militant blacks who are beginning to charge that the news departments are going "conservative."

One prominent TV journalist describes the trend as "the Nixonization of the airwaves." *Variety,* the industry's trade paper, accused the networks of cutting back on "hard" issues. And FCC Commissioner Nicholas Johnson charged broadcasters with squeezing out radical thought and of censoring news of capitalist-caused "death, disease, dismemberment and degradation."

Some TV newsmen, too, view the trends in the news departments as "conservative." Says Steve Fleischman, who describes himself as "ABC's kept radical": "Television is reflecting the national trend. There's a conservative, know-nothing stream in this country. And there's a liberal-progressive-radical stream. And there's a great body of people in the middle. The majority of newsmen are in that middle group. Today, that middle group is swinging back to conservatism. It's all part of the white backlash."

Needless to say, many other newsmen actively repudiate the *Variety*-Johnson-Fleischman criticism.

CBS's Salant has already hurled an answer to Johnson into print (TV GUIDE, Sept. 20) in which he presents a long list of anticorporation stories aired by CBS; and, in answer to the charge that there is not enough "death, disease, dismemberment and degradation" on the air, says: "let [the Commissioner] drop into my office some time and see the viewers' mail that comes across my desk complaining that that is *all* we ever talk about."

And others too grow angry at being described as creatures of a reactionary "establishment."

Snaps Lester Cooper of ABC: "Such criticisms are made by self-conscious, self-righteous, guilt-ridden people who feel the only way they can say something is by attacking." NBC's Shad Northshield raps out: "Doctrinaire, dogmatic opinion!" And NBC's Reuven Frank groans, "Oh, it's so tendentious. Those people want so to be 'in.' The next thing you know, Nick Johnson will be wearing Pucci pants!"

What really seems to be happening is this: "Public-interest" programming—and, most of all, documentary programming—is adjusting itself in a jerky, impulsive yet fear-ridden way to the massive pressure of middle-class opinion, while straining to attain a journalistic perspective. By virtue of this trend, coverage of militant-radical groups will not be eliminated but it is decreasing. As a corollary, the view of America as one vast abscess is now being corrected.

QUESTIONS FOR DISCUSSION AND DIALOGUE

1. Do you think the shift in television reporting and interpretation is "squeezing out radical thought and . . . censoring news of capitalist-caused death, disease, dismemberment and degradation?" Why? How?
2. Do you think criticisms like the one above "are made by self-conscious,

self-righteous, guilt-ridden people who feel the only way they can say something is by attacking?" Why?

3. Do you think that, all things considered, television helps or hinders the Americans in their attempts to understand politics?

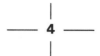

The Cage of Fear in Cities Beset by Crime

Jack Rosenthal

Fear, justified and unjustified, is studied by this article. Some of the political influences bred by fear are explored, and the reader might ask himself whether in the case of crime and fear of crime, there is truth to Alexander Pope's line "A little knowledge is a dangerous thing."

A stranger's footsteps echo in the darkened street and a mother stares out through her steel-caged window. She is afraid. Crime is increasing all over the U.S.—robberies up 22%, beatings up 8%—but most dramatically in the large cities and their suburbs where fear has turned the night into a prison. The fear of crime, combined with the apprehensions created by racial and campus turmoil, has made law and order a prime political issue in such cities as New York, Los Angeles and particularly Minneapolis, which last month elected a policeman as its mayor.

People build fences, mount floodlights, buy heavy-duty locks, install complex alarm systems, and then look for additional means of protection. Training and leasing guard dogs has become a booming business. Private protective services—the "rent-a-cop" business—now comprise more manpower than the combined police forces of the entire nation. The sale of guns is steadily increasing, especially flimsy new revolvers that retail for under $20 and are known as "Saturday night specials."

To determine the extent of fear in one urban area, *Life* undertook a six-week study in Baltimore, a city with a typical range of problems and unusually accurate police statistics. The polling firm of Louis Harris and Associates surveyed a 1,545-person cross section that was specially designed to permit comparisons between high- and low-crime areas. The findings reveal that in the daily lives of many citizens the fear of crime takes an even greater toll than crime itself.

Beneath the pleasant gloss of early summer, Baltimore is a city of silent terror. *Life's* Harris Poll shows that the increase in crime is the single most important concern of its citizens—more important than Vietnam, inflation or poverty. Indeed, the Harris Poll shows they are so concerned about the rising rates in robberies, assaults and murders that fear has changed their everyday lives.

But the poll findings also indicate that fear is rising even more sharply than crime, and that there is a marked contrast between the attitudes of those most afflicted by crime and those most afflicted by fear.

Baltimore is not a special case. Its crime rate is neither much better nor worse than that of other cities in its 900,000-population class. It has experienced riots, but so have dozens of other cities. Its young mayor, Thomas J. D'Alesandro III, is widely respected, and Police Commissioner Donald Pomerleau has generated public confidence in his force, And yet:

How many of those polled are more likely now to keep their houses locked even when someone is home? Fifty-five percent.

How many use the parks less at night? Forty-eight percent. Less in the daytime? Thirty-three percent.

How many go downtown less often to a restaurant or a movie? Forty-one percent. How many do so less in their own neighborhood? Thirty-nine percent.

How many have bought extra locks? Twenty-nine percent.

How many more now keep a loaded gun handy at home? Sixteen percent.

Hence, the first major finding of the Harris Poll: overall, nearly three fourths of those polled have changed their daily lives at least somewhat because of their fear of crime, and one fourth have changed their lives considerably.

When more than half the people of a city lock themselves into their own homes; when nearly half are reluctant to go downtown for entertainment in the evening; when some 40,000 families keep a loaded gun handy in the house, the fear of crime has eroded precisely those qualities that make urban life appealing.

Walk into the elevators of a parking garage under Charles Center, downtown's gleaming new $100 million business complex, and you find yourself watched by a "Teletector Synchroscan," a caged, closed-circuit television camera. Walk out into the plaza and you are eyed by K9 police dogs. Walk to the door of 2 Charles Center, a new apartment complex, and you are under the surveillance of a special guard force via yet another closed-circuit TV camera.

Sunday night church services are disappearing because parishioners are afraid to go out after dark. Nurses carry hatpins, even pistols. Suburban housewives headed for downtown drive 10 miles out of the way to bypass ghetto areas. So few suburbanites are willing to make the trip that merchants now offer "Downtown Discovery Tours." ("The people were so pleasant and friendly to us," one lady said of the tour, "that for a while we imagined we were in another country.")

"We now have a gun and I take my German shepherd with me when I go out," says Mrs. Carol Disney, a young white housewife. "We've taught him to attack." A middle-aged Negro woman refuses to say whether she has a burglar alarm or extra locks, fearing the information "might get into the wrong hands" and lead to her becoming a crime victim. A white widow moved her TV set out of her front room so "someone outside can't watch my every move."

Though Baltimore is known as "Nickel Town" because of its frugality, the fear business is booming. The owner of a large pet store says German shepherds and Doberman pinschers sell as fast as he can get them—some 90% of his shepherds are bought by Negro families. One chain of surplus stores sells 1,200 pocket tear-gas devices a month. Despite a new state registration law, pistol sales this year average 595 a month, twice the 1966 average.

A large burglar alarm concern reports it is eight weeks behind in installations in private homes, even though its systems are expensive ($800 and up, for invisible systems which emit sound-wave patterns). An increasing number of home-owners are renting powerful lamps for their backyards. The "rent-a-cop" business has more than doubled—some firms even offer armed escorts for bejeweled partygoers and utility company repairmen in "red circle" areas.

Many of those who can afford it simply flee the city. In the past, people moved to the suburbs because of the pull of open space. Now pull has yielded to push. Since 1960, the white population of Baltimore has decreased from 609,000 to 505,000, while suburban Baltimore County's white population has grown from 475,000 to 576,000. "I would say the fear of crime is the greatest stimulus to movement from the city," says William Boucher III, executive director of the Greater Baltimore Committee, the energetic urban action arm of the city's business establishment. "And Baltimore pays a terrible price for it. It leaves the city racially and economically imbalanced. It puts a tremendous burden on Baltimore County for schools and other services that already exist in the city. And it means we're destroying open space and generating urban sprawl."

Many residents feel they pay a tremendous price either way—staying or fleeing. Robert and Sandra Leaf live in a working-class neighborhood in a spotless two-family house which he completely remodeled not long ago. The Leafs told the Harris Poll interviewer their home had been broken into three times in the last year. The day after that interview an expensive tape player was pried out of their car. "We'll do anything we can to get out," says Leaf. "It will cost us twice as much out in the County and we'll really be strapped. But if we don't go, I know I'll get into trouble trying to deal with these problems myself."

For the rising black middle class the dilemma is even more acute. Uncertain about suburban attitudes, they move to better city neighborhoods. "When they finally can afford the move, they find crime follows them even then," says Joseph L. Smith, special assistant to the mayor. "That discovery breeds a frustration even worse then the grinding poverty of the ghetto."

Most black residents cannot afford to flee crime. Clarence Ringgold, a neighborhood leader in West Baltimore, says: "If I go out on the street at night, I slip something in my pocket—you'd be surprised how many folks down here feel the need to have a gun for protection. A fellow stops me for a light and I tell him, 'Buddy, stand right there, put your cigarette in your mouth, and I'll light it from here."

The racial factor cannot be minimized. The high-crime areas surveyed by the Harris Poll are 88% black, low-crime areas 81% white. "The majority of the violent crimes are being committed by youths of the black race—and that's no reflection on the race," says Police Commissioner Pomerleau. "The same is true of other ethnic groups as they have come to the city." Many whites readily equate race and crime. "The white-collar reaction, especially," says Dr. Herzl Spiro, the director of Johns Hopkins' Baltimore Community Mental Health Program, "is to use phrases like 'fear of crime' as code for 'fear of blacks.' "

But in fact, blacks are the victims of a heavy majority of crimes in Baltimore. This underlies the second finding of *Life's* study: many people's fear of crime is exaggerated, and—proportionate to the amount of crime in their area—the people *least* in danger are *most* afraid.

Among those polled, fear vastly exceeds the actual incidence of crime (see table). The crime of robbery offers a good gauge. According to police statistics for the 12 months ending May 31, there were 9,006 robberies in Baltimore—or 100 for each 10,000 people. Based on the results of the poll, the number of people very concerned about actually being robbed would exceed 340,000—or 3,800 for each 10,000 people. Nearly a third of those interviewed, 30%, are very concerned about actually being murdered. Yet the odds of being murdered are less than one in 3,000. (And the chances of being murdered by a stranger are far smaller, since three fourths of all murders are committed by relatives or acquaintances of the victims.)

Even more startling is the exaggerated fear expressed by those who live in the safest areas of the city. In such areas the odds of being robbed are one in 300; in high-crime areas, the odds for a resident are one in 50. If fear corresponded to fact, residents of high-crime areas should be six times more concerned than those in low-crime areas. Actually they are only half as afraid.

This does not mean there is too little concern in high-crime areas. Instead it suggests excessive fear in other areas. In a distant and relatively safe suburb, Ellicott City, John O'Day and his wife Pat bought a huge Rhodesian Ridgeback, a breed which earned renown as a watchdog for whites in South Africa. "I got shaky," says Pat O'Day. "In summer, with the kids running in and out so often, you just can't lock the door."

Another indication of inflated fear in safe areas is the professed first-hand knowledge of crime. Though burglary is three times more frequent in high-crime areas, a larger percentage of residents in low-crime areas claim they know burglary victims. The disparity is even more astonishing between college-educated persons, 70% of whom say they know a victim, and those with eighth-grade educations, of whom 29% say they know a victim. Since the college-educated generally earn more and live in better, safer areas, how can 41% more of them *know* burglary victims?

One explanation is that better-educated persons are more likely to be exposed to news reports. They are more likely to remember them longer. They are more likely to talk about them and assimilate such news into their personal awareness. Another explanation is that crimes stand out with greater clarity in low-crime neighborhoods precisely because they are less frequent.

This wide gap in perceptions explains the third major finding of the Harris Poll—the sharp differences in attitudes about the causes of crime and what to do about it. People who see crime often and at first hand put far heavier emphasis on practical, specific causes—narcotics, unemployment. Residents from low-crime areas stress quite different factors—Supreme Court decisions, lack of parental discipline.

What should be done? High-crime area residents put more emphasis on increasing the *number* of police and improving antipoverty programs. Low-crime area residents put heavier emphasis on increasing the *authority* of police and cracking down on black militants. In high-crime areas, 38% feel treatment of minorities should be improved; in low-crime areas only 18% think this is important. On the other hand, 58% in low-crime areas think harsher sentences for criminals would be effective; in high-crime areas only 42% agree.

Lou Harris concludes that "whites believe America is a peaceful society and that crime is a cancer which must be cured by surgery. Blacks are far less convinced of the peaceful nature of society and are more willing to recognize that crime is a way of making it in a hostile environment. More whites see crime as a major problem that government should attempt to solve, yet more blacks are victimized by it. For whites, in short, crime is a public issue. For blacks it is a personal problem."

This gulf was dramatized three weeks ago in the Baltimore City Council. At issue was an anti-loitering proposal. Weeks of public controversy had turned it into a symbol of law and order. Some thought it was vital to the fight against street crime. Others saw it as a device to harass blacks. "We pick up the press and we get goose pimples from some of the crime that occurs on the streets," said a white councilman, his voice trembling. A black councilman responded: "Certainly we want to do something meaningful about crime—and the black community is the major victim of crime—and therefore we should stop this kind of make-believe ordinance and *do* something meaningful." Law and order won, 14 to 5. A few days later, Baltimore received a $10.5 million Model Cities grant for rehabilitation of ghetto areas. As these two events suggest, the gulf of fact, fear and antagonism may in the end be bridged by doing the things each side so strongly endorses—neither law and order alone nor social programs alone, but both.

Fear of Crime vs. Reality

	Actual Crime Rate / 10,000 Population	Strong Fear of Being a Victim / 10,000 Pop.
Homicide	3	3,000
Rape	7	4,300
Robbery	100	3,800
Assault	110	4,300
Auto Theft	127	3,500
Larceny	137	3,400
Burglary	249	4,100

QUESTIONS FOR DISCUSSION AND DIALOGUE

1. If the Americans relied totally on objective evidence, who should be very afraid of crime and who should not? Why?
2. Summarize the three major findings of the Louis Harris poll on fear. How does this relate to the "Change" and "No Change" groups discussed in the first article? Discuss.
3. What is the difference in their views about how to fight crime between people who see crime often and people who don't see crime often? Which approach do you agree with and why?
4. Give examples of "excessive fear" practices mentioned in this article. Do you agree with the article's negative view of such practices? Why?

Whose Facts Do You Read?

William H. Stringer

Mr. Stringer points his answer to the question posed in the title to the young, but it seems worth consideration by all the Americans.

If a newspaperman has any special message for today's inquiring young people, he would say: Use the utmost care in ascertaining your facts. Remember that normal, honest individuals may differ, not only concerning the opinions and conclusions to be derived from today's facts, but concerning what are the facts themselves.

Don't accept only such facts as agree with your own preconceptions.

Suppose you were to note the facts—as regards Vietnam, China, hippies, the welfare state, the Pentagon—implicit in the articles in the *New Statesman* (London) or the *New Republic* (USA). Compare these with the facts on the same subjects as seen by *U. S. News & World Report* or *Time* magazine. You'd find a wide divergence. One needs to amend Marshall McLuhan to say, not that the medium is the message, but that the particular medium may, wittingly or unwittingly, color the message.

And what you accept as gospel truth will color your views and conduct.

For example, suppose you watched, last evening, a graphic TV documentary on Vietnam. It centered on the hardships and sufferings of the refugees, caused by bombings and uprootings. Suppose you supplemented this with an eye-witness story of refugee plight in your favorite news magazine or newspaper. I don't know about you, but after about three such encounters, I am ready to conclude: "This war is disastrous. Let's get out fast."

All right, but suppose instead you've watched a television documentary which zeroes in on American-Saigon victories, and some very worthy rehabilitation efforts among the rice paddies. And you've supplemented this with a dispatch detailing respected Ambassador Bunker's reasons why the war is going better, why constructive rebuilding is now possible. One may well come away from this experience with a belief that the struggle is worthwhile.

The point is, both sets of documentaries and dispatches could have been factual, accurate, from where the reporter, the cameraman, stood.

Recently a student came in to discuss a column. He had marched in a number of peace demonstrations. He told how TV cameramen had walked down the file of marchers, photographing only the long-haired, the hippie-dressed, the unkempt, avoiding the earnest, the neat, the middle-aged. This happens. The effort is not intentionally to deceive, but to catch the dramatic, the spectacular.

I recall two dispatches, appearing about the same time in the *New York Times* and a news magazine. Both concerned the over-all Vietnam picture. One reported the United States forces as thin-stretched, their strategies spoiled. The other said the American effort, at long last, was beginning to succeed. Which is one to believe?

Perhaps you are familiar with the well-known journalism class exercise. A simulated hold-up takes place; police burst into the classroom. Afterward, the students are asked to write their versions of what happened. Believe it or not, they differ markedly, and these students have been in training to become newsmen.

What's the answer? First of all, read a newspaper or news magazine that you feel you can trust. Next, read more widely. If the *New Republic* is your journal, read *U. S. News & World Report* as a countering force or vice versa. Distinguish between journals of opinion and newspapers. When you're watching a television newscast, ask yourself if you're seeing the whole picture.

Cultivate a healthy skepticism. I said healthy. Not hate-filled. Compassionate. Discerning. Remember that most newsmen are trying hard to "get it straight." So are most editors. And if some have built-in biases, maybe you have, too. Too often we seek out, take in, just what we want to believe.

Man has the gift of insight and intuition. "Seek and ye shall find." An accurately informed public opinion is a strong bulwark to any nation. You can help build that kind of opinion.

QUESTIONS FOR DISCUSSION AND DIALOGUE

1. Summarize Stringer's "formula" for deciding which version of the news to believe.
2. Discuss how facts, insight, intuition and healthy skepticism lead to an informed public opinion. Could any of these be left out?

Nightmare for the Innocent in a California Jail

Jesse P. Ritter

Jesse Ritter shares a chilling personal experience in this article. One of the key phrases of the U.S. Constitution is the fourteenth amendment's provision that no state shall "deny any person of life, liberty, or property without due process of law." Although the interpretation of the "due process clause" is extremely complex, it is obvious that the kind of treatment described by Ritter is not "due process of law."

When I moved my family to San Francisco last year to teach in the English department at San Francisco State College, I did so with misgivings. I knew that the educational atmosphere in California was far from tranquil—Governor Reagan was waging virtual war against student protesters, and the political polarization between the left and the right could only be described in terms of paranoia. Through the year, my fears were confirmed as I witnessed student and faculty strikes, bombings, brawls, police assaults, mass arrests. But none of those events —brutal as they were—prepared me for the nightmare that followed my recent chance arrest this spring in Berkeley. Overnight that experience, which can be verified by many reliable witnesses, turned a father of five, veteran of the Korean war and law-abiding citizen into a bitter man.

On Thursday morning, May 22, I left San Francisco State College with four other teachers to drive to Berkeley. We were beginning work on an environmental art project one of the teachers was directing. We planned to borrow a sailboat from a couple I knew in Berkeley and dump a small amount of nontoxic dye in the bay water at strategic points to observe the action of the currents.

We arrived in Berkeley about noon. After a pleasant lunch and a trip to buy supplies for the sail we walked toward Shattuck on Addison Street. There we were to meet my friend's wife, Nora.

The city of Berkeley was then in something like a state of siege because of the People's Park issue. On the streets, under the command of Alameda County Sheriff Frank Madigan, was a vast force of National Guard troops, county sheriffs, San Francisco Tactical Squad units. Madigan had authorized use of shotguns against demonstrators. One man had already been killed, and many others wounded. Demonstrators, workers and onlookers trapped in a plaza on the University of California campus had been sprayed from a helicopter with a virulent form of tear gas currently being used in Vietnam. To protest, approximately 2,000 students had now begun a spontaneous march from the university campus through downtown Berkeley.

We could see a concentration of National Guard troops, policemen and citizens several blocks east of us. I described what Nora looked like to the others and we stopped at the southwest corner of Shattuck and Addison to scan the crowd for her. We decided not to go any farther because we saw soldiers, police and people both to the east and south of us. The National Guard troops nearest were climbing into trucks and moving out. Small groups of people on each corner of the intersection watched the troops; others walked casually on the sidewalks.

Berkeley policemen and Alameda County deputies began moving our way. An officer leading four or five others approached our group of 12 to 15 people and said, "Let's move out; clear the area!" Everyone on our corner obediently started walking away. Suddenly, a Berkeley policeman ran in front of us, spread his arms and shouted, "Stay where you are!" Behind us, two other policemen kept repeating, "Keep moving, clear out of here!" We said we were leaving, and at this point a Berkeley police sergeant approached and began pointing to various people in our group saying, "Get that one, that one, that one."

An officer snapped handcuffs on me and joined me with the cuffs to a protesting youngster. I asked if we were under arrest and the officer said yes—we were charged with blocking traffic. We were not allowed to talk to the policemen after that. The sergeant who had us arrested taunted us, using obscenities and accusing us of being revolutionaries, rock-throwers and hippies. Those not fingered by the sergeant continued down the street and were not apprehended. While we were being herded into the paddy wagon, however, officers continued to arrest people at random—mostly young people, and particularly those with long hair, mustaches, sideburns. Three of the teachers with me were arrested; our fifth companion was not, and he immediately began calling friends and relatives to arrange our release.

Nineteen of us—17 men and two women—were packed into a paddy wagon. I was never able to identify myself or state my business; indeed, the policemen threatened anyone who talked at all. We sat in the wagon for about 20 minutes, then it backed up the street a block, where we were transferred to a large bus. We were all being taken to "Santa Rita," a place I had never heard of.

During the 45-minute ride our feelings were reinforced that it had been an indiscriminate bust. Aboard were students with books and notepads who had been on their way to and from classes at the university. There was a U.S. mailman (with long hair), still carrying his bag of mail, and a resident psychiatrist who had stepped outside his hospital for a short walk during a 30-minute break. Others included several young divinity students and five medical observers—young men in white smocks with red crosses—who had accompanied the student march down Shattack Avenue. The police blew it, I thought. They went too far this time. Most of us will be released when we get to wherever we're going.

The bus stopped inside the Santa Rita Rehabilitation Center and Prison Farm, an institution run by Alameda County. Prison guards who work under the jurisdiction of County Sheriff Madigan now took charge of us. We heard repeated orders through the frosted bus windows: "Unload single file and march. Anybody talks and he'll get a club up the butt!" As we filed off the bus the sight that greeted us was from a World War II movie—shabby wooden barracks, barbed-wire fences, rickety watch towers and rows of men lying face down in an asphalt-paved compound. We were marched into the compound and ordered to lie prone in rows. Those who looked around or stumbled or didn't move fast enough were prodded and hit with clubs. Frequently, men were dragged out of the marching lines and forced to kneel while being struck. The guards shouted and screamed, often giving conflicting commands and clubbing those unable to obey them. Our chief source of terror was not so much the beatings as the wild hysteria that had seized many of the guards. They walked up and down our rows of flattened men, striking us on the soles of our feet with clubs to make us lie in even rows. We were told we would be shot if we tried to escape. We were cursed continuously; we were called dope users, revolutionaries, filthy long-hairs. We would, they shouted, be taught such a lesson that we would never again cause trouble. All of us were identified as political troublemakers. No attempt was made to distinguish us by age, nature of charges or physical condition. Periodically we were ordered to turn our heads to the left or right. I experienced severe leg cramps and sharp twinges of pain from an arthritic elbow. From time to time we were forced to close up ranks by crawling across the asphalt, which was covered with sharp gravel. Those accused of speaking or looking around or moving slightly were dragged out and forced to kneel with their hands behind them in a separate group. Some remained kneeling for hours. There were some 300 men on the ground.

After a few of us asked to use the rest rooms (and were abused for it), guards began allowing small groups to go. At times, the guards said, "You'll have to wait another half hour." One kid near me identified himself as a diabetic in the rest room and was cruelly beaten.

This savage parody of prison discipline had an obvious psychology behind it. Humiliate the prisoners totally from the beginning so they will obey orders and accept punishment without resistance. Of course, we weren't prisoners— *we were simply being held for booking!*

During the time I was lying in the compound, from approximately 4 until 8:30 p.m., new arrestees were brought in and forced to lie in rows. It was cold when the sun went down, and men around me were shivering. At 8 we were allowed to stand and exercise in place for a few minutes. We then lay back down on our faces. They had taken our names when we were first arrested, and about every 20 minutes a guard would call out some names in alphabetical order. At 8:30 my name was called along with seven others, and we were taken into an adjoining barracks for booking.

Here we experienced new refinements. We were forced to sit in single file on the floor, knees together, while a squat, dark-haired guard waving a blackjack shouted that if we didn't do exactly as he said he would beat us until we couldn't walk. He had us face the wall, spread our legs and place our hands high on the wall. We then turned and threw our jackets, belts and the contents of our pockets into a pile. During this procedure, the squat guard struck prisoners in the back, stomach, face and legs with his fist or the blackjack. He struck me four times with the blackjack during the booking process—either for not having my heels tightly together or for not clasping my hands in front of me. He assaulted one of us—

a very young boy with long hair—by slugging him with his fist and then grabbing the boy's hair and slamming his face into the wall. Later, in the barracks, we saw that the boy's left eye had swollen badly and he could barely open his jaw.

After the booking and fingerprinting, we again had to sit on the floor with legs drawn up, heels together. We were then lined up and marched to Barracks B across the street. The guard in charge treated us firmly but decently, telling us that while we were in the barracks we could get together and talk, plan our bail procedures and wait our turn to use the telephone. He repeated what other guards had told us in the compound—that the regular prisoners were outraged at us because we were troublemakers, because we were responsible for the regular inmates' missing movies and other privileges. The inmates would beat us terribly, and the guards couldn't prevent it. We would be turned over to "hardened criminals and sex perverts."

At about 11:30, four lawyers from the People's Park Defense Committee appeared in the barracks. They told us they were trying to arrange bail procedures for as many people as possible, but they lacked funds and organizations for rapid release. We filled out forms giving information about our families and personal legal arrangements. We later were told that many of these forms were destroyed by prison guards who claimed they were "messages." At no time during our detention did anyone in my barracks have an opportunity to make a telephone call to relatives or lawyers.

During the night we were taunted and threatened by different prison guards. We left in small groups all through the night to have photos taken—I went in a group at 2:45 a.m. Few of us slept.

At 4:30 a.m., the door crashed open and three guards moved among the bunks rousting out people with curses, threats and blows. We were going to eat, they said, and we would eat what we took or it would be "shoved in your faces." Under continual threats, we were marched to the mess hall. Breakfast was Corn Chex and milk (no sugar), half-cooked prunes, white bread and artificial marmalade. We sat packed at the tables, ordered not to move or talk. Five men were dragged from their seats and forced to kneel before an empty table for such things as "looking around," "talking" or "moving." They were not allowed to eat. One boy was forced to lean his head on a post while the guards beat on the post. His nose began bleeding. Guards would prod him, pull him off the post and strike him, or kick his feet back farther until he was leaning at a severe angle to the post, his head and neck bearing the full weight of his body. After about 15 minutes of quivering spasmodically, the boy collapsed to the floor. Two guards dragged him over to the empty table and made him kneel, still twitching, with the others. After we finished eating, we were forced to kneel on the floor in columns of two and wait for about 15 minutes before being marched back to the barracks.

At 6 a.m. a new guard, a small man with reddish-blond hair on his neck, came into the barracks, yelling, "I had a good night's sleep and I feel like KILLING!" He announced that he was now in total control of us and said he needed a "boss" in the barracks. He grabbed my bunkmate, Professor Gary Oberbillig, by the shirt and dragged him out to the center of the floor. "Get out here," he said. "You're big; you want to take me? Come on, let's go outside. Want to go outside?" He then instructed Oberbillig that he, Oberbillig, was the "barracks boss" and was to "beat the ——— out of anybody who don't do right!"

At 7:30 a guard came in and read off a list of names. We lined up and marched outside into the street, where several other guards spent approximately 30 minutes giving us military marching commands, making those who did not execute the commands smartly do calisthenics. (Ironically, not one of them was able to give an accurate "about-face" command, and our ragged "about-face" maneuvers enraged them.) We marched at double-time, forced to yell "WE LOVE THE BLUE MEANIES!"

The guards were proud of this idea: I overheard one tell another, "Say, we've gotta do that Blue Meanies bit some more." We marched to what appeared to be the receiving center of the prison, where we were put in open-screen cells already occupied by new arrestees. It was here that we learned we would be released soon. While we waited in the cells, several men were dragged out and beaten in our presence and told that they were on the way to further beatings and a stay in the "quiet room."

My three companions and I were finally processed for release on bail by 8:30 a.m., Friday, May 23, nearly 18 hours after our arrest. All released prisoners had to catch rides out of the main gate, a distance of a half mile, with outgoing bail bondsmen.

The first thing I learned face-down on the Santa Rita asphalt was that I could make it without begging or breaking. This felt good; it was enough strength to counter the fears engendered by the heavy blue-black guards' shoes slowly crunching by my eyes six inches away. *But to be put to these tests in America!*

At a press conference, Alameda County Sheriff Frank Madigan admitted there had been "irregularities" at Santa Rita on that Thursday. He put the responsibility on his guards. Many of the deputies assigned there, he said, are young Vietnam war veterans and "they have a feeling that these people should be treated like Vietcong."

On July 2 Madigan suspended 10 of his officers at Santa Rita for "violating civil service and/or departmental rules" in handling the mass arrests. The officers, all of whom were told they had the right to appeal (only four choose to do so), included the commander, his two immediate assistants and a sergeant. By July 9, charges against all the people who had been arrested—a total of 480—had been dropped by the court.

Still, several hundred young men and women came out of Santa Rita believing there is no middle ground anymore—nowhere to stand to reconcile the growing polarities of our political lives. I am haunted by the bitterness brought forth by such assaults on our humaneness and human rights. When in the history of man have prisons and guards ever rooted out the ideas in which men really believe?

QUESTIONS FOR DISCUSSION AND DIALOGUE

1. In the concluding paragraph Ritter says . . . "Several hundred young men and

women came out of Santa Rita believing there is no middle ground anymore
..." Discuss the significance of this statement.
2. Discuss the response of Alameda County Sheriff Frank Madigan described in
the third last paragraph.
3. Develop an introductory paragraph in a political speech you might expect two
politicians to make. Both are speaking about the situation described in this
article. One wants to appeal to the "No Change Coalition." The other wishes
to appeal to the "Change Coalition."

—— 7 ——

The Other America Revisited
Michael Harrington

The most well known, and in many ways, the most influential student of
poverty in the United States discusses comparisons and contrasts between the
poor in 1962 and the poor in 1969. They make up a very large minority of
the Americans. Mr. Harrington offers statistics which are optimistic, and
gives interpretations which are not. Difficult questions are posed about the
difference between seeing the poor in quantitative or qualitative terms.

The Other America was published in March, 1962. Now, almost seven years
later, the condition that book described is objectively not quite as evil as it was;
politically and morally, it is worse than ever. For despite a long, federally induced
boom and an "unconditional" war on poverty, tens of millions of Americans still
live in a social underworld and an even larger number are only one recession, one
illness, one accident removed from it.

Ironically, perhaps the most dramatic single breakthrough of the government's anti-poverty effort is the increase in our official knowledge of the needless
suffering that we tolerate. President Johnson's program did not achieve full
employment for all nor provide impoverished children and aging people with an
income but it did generate a tremendous anount of research, seminars, discussions, and even mass-media reports. So, since the poor have become less invisible,
for we know they are there, the society has become even more guilty; now it
knows its callousness.

Revisiting the other America in 1969 is easier than going there in the late
fifties and early sixties. Now Washington has produced some revealing maps of
misery. In general, the official figures show some progress in eliminating poverty,
but the accomplishment is so modest that one economic downturn would annul
it—and the powerful voices urging a calculated increase in unemployment so that
the price stability of the affluent can be protected would bring just such a down-

turn. Even if that does not come to pass, there is a disturbing potential in the other America of 1969 that particularly menaces both the young and the black poor. In looking at these trends statistically, one must remember that, even though the definitions and the percentages are much more precise than in 1962, there is an enormous margin of error which usually favors understatement and over-optimism. Not very long ago, the government triumphantly announced that there had been a major decrease in deteriorated housing. Then in the summer of 1967 it turned out that the gains had actually been negligible or even nonexistent; and in the 1968 Report of the Council of Economic Advisers the Administration admitted that housing deterioration in big-city slums had actually increased. These inaccuracies were not the result of a conscious attempt to delude. They were honest mistakes—but they were often seized upon by those who want to minimize the problem of poverty in America.

More generally there is a real invisibility of the poor. The Bureau of the Census has only recently discovered that it had not counted a significant minority of the adult Negro males in the ghetto. Some years before this acknowledgement, Bayard Rustin had told me that there were more blacks in America than the government figured. He pointed out that there were special problems in a place like Harlem—for instance, people doubling-up in apartments, a fair number of individuals who feared any contact with The Man, even with the census-taker—which could lead the professionals to err. I thought that Rustin had created an amateur's fantasy until the hard data began to come in (for instance, the 1967 Manpower Report of the Department of Labor found an "undercount" of twenty per cent of the adult men in the slums). This means that there are several million Americans whose conditions of life are so mercurial that they do not even qualify to be a statistic.

With this understanding that the government's numbers are too sanguine, we should take a closer look at them. One of the most imaginative students of the "poverty line" is Mollie Orshansky of the Department of Health, Education, and Welfare. For some time now rightists, like William F. Buckley, Jr., have tried to discredit concern for the poor by arguing that all of the definitions are totally subjective and relative. There is unquestionably an historic element in the setting of such standards—hungry Americans are certainly better off than starving Indians—but it is Miss Orshansky's merit that she emphasizes the objective determinants of misery in the other America. She takes the Department of Agriculture's low-cost diet plan ($5.90 a week for a four-person family in January, 1964) and the "economy" plan (for "temporary or emergency use when funds are low" at $4.60 a week, or twenty-two cents per meal per person, in January, 1964) and puts them at the center of an imagined budget. Neither diet guarantees adequacy, but if a family falls below them it is certain that they will miss important nutrients.

Miss Orshansky then worked out the rest of the poverty budgets in relation to these food costs. In this way, anyone who falls below the poverty line will have less than a minimum diet for health or, more generally, will have to choose between necessities. (The 1968 Report of the Citizens' Board of Inquiry into Hunger and Malnutrition in the United States concluded that "malnutrition among the poor has risen sharply over the past decade.") Using the Orshansky approach, the Social Security Administration came up with a figure of $3,130 for an urban family of four as the upper limit of impoverishment.

By 1966, the poverty line had risen to $3,335. (While this index went up by nine per cent, the average income of four-person families in America had increased by thirty-seven per cent, so the new criterion meant that the poor had even less of a share of affluence.) As a result, 17.8 per cent of the people were under the line in 1966 as compared to twenty-four per cent in 1959. This statistic allows the celebrators of America to claim that the other America is disappearing at a reasonable rate. It is that claim which I want to challenge here.

There is no point in denying that there has been some progress. We are now in the seventh year of an unprecedented prosperity which was purchased, in considerable measure, with a twenty-billion dollar tax subsidy that disproportionately favored the rich individuals and corporations. At the same time, the official unemployment figures have been reduced to under four per cent—but have not gone down to the three per cent goal that John F Kennedy set as the mark of "full employment" when he became President. The first several years of this boom did not aid the unskilled workers and the hard-core unemployed, although eventually a few of the crumbs of good times trickled down to them.

Pride, in short, must be somewhat restrained. The poverty line, is after all, an artificial, if extremely useful, construct. Miss Orshansky herself has pointed out that millions hover just above the definition (Daniel Patrick Moynihan calls them the "at risk" population). In 1966, there were more than three million families with incomes between $3,000 and $4,000; most of them were not officially classified as poor but all of them were in danger of becoming so with one bad break in the national economy or in their private lives.

Indeed, as Robert C. Wood of the Department of Housing and Urban Development has pointed out, the "average" American who works and earns between $5,000 and $10,000 a year "owes plenty in installment debts on his car and appliances. He finds his tax burden heavy, his neighborhood services poor, his national image tarnished, and his political clout diminishing. This, too, is alienation." And the Bureau of Labor Statistics said that, in late 1966, it took $9,191 a year for a four-person family to maintain a "moderate standard of living." If life for the organized, theoretically well-paid working class is still this precarious, one is probably justified in including as well all Americans in 1969 with family incomes(for four, in a city) of less than $5,000 within the magnetic field of poverty. This has explosive implications if the proposal of the top corporate executives to "trade off" an unemployment increase for an inflation decrease are put into action. It also means that the ambiance, if not the precise dimensions, of the other America has changed little since 1962 even though the society has produced unprecedented wealth.

In two particularly tragic cases it is not necessary to speculate about the numbers. The children and the blacks among the poor are worse off than when the war on poverty began. "All told," writes Mollie Orshansky, "even in 1966, after a continued run of prosperity and steadily rising family income, one-fourth of the nation's children were in families living in poverty or hovering just above the poverty line." This fact, of course, has the most disturbing and dangerous implications for the future. On the one hand, poverty more and more becomes a fate because the educational, economic, and social disadvantages of life at the bottom become progressively more damaging; and, on the other hand, the poor still have more children than any other group. Present evidence points to the melancholy conclusion that the twenty-five per cent of the young who are poor, or near-poor, will have large families very much like the ones of which they are now members. If this is true, the current incidence of poverty among children will guarantee that, short of radical political decisions, the next generation in the other America will be even more numerous than this one.

With Negroes, the problem is more a relative position than an absolute increase in indignity, but this is still a politically explosive fact. In 1959 the Social Security Administration fixed the black percentage of the other Americans at twenty-five per cent; by 1966, the proportion had risen to thirty-three per cent. This, of course, still shows that the scandal of poverty actually afflicts more whites than blacks, but it also indicates that discrimination even applies to the rate at which people escape from beneath the poverty line. During these years of prosperity even the worst off of the white Americans have had a special advantage, compared to the Negroes.

It is important to add to this brief survey of the federally certified dimensions of needless economic and social suffering in this country the remarkable "sub-employment" index of the Department of Labor. The index was developed in order to get a more accurate picture of the working—and non-working—lives of people in the slums. Whereas the official definition of unemployment, which currently is fixed at about 3.5 per cent for the nation as a whole, only counts those who are out of work and looking for work, the notion of sub-employment is much more comprehensive. It gives weight to part-time unemployment, to the fact that many people have to toil for poverty wages, to the twenty per cent of the "invisibles" in the slums, and to those who do not look for a job because they are sure they will not find one.

On this basis, the Labor Department discovered sub-employment rates in November, 1966, that ranged from around thirty per cent in the New York ghettos to near fifty per cent in New Orleans. The full significance of this analysis did not become apparent until the winter of 1967 and the report of the National Commission on Civil Disorders. For it was then that the nation learned that the typical rioter was not the least educated, most impoverished, and chronically unemployed citizen of the ghetto. Rather, he was a high-school dropout and a teen-ager and he had worked—but at a menial job. In other words, the frustrations of sub-employment—most particularly of laboring long hard hours without any real hope of advancement—are perhaps more likely to incite a man to violence than the simple despair of having no job at all.

To sum up—by courtesy of the government's card file (and computer tapes) on outrages in this nation—there has been modest progress in the official figures: a drop in the poverty population from twenty-five per cent to around eighteen per cent. Nevertheless, those who crossed the line are still very close to the world of hunger and hovels. There are signs that the present-day children of the poor will become the parents of even poorer children in the immediate future. Black

Americans are falling further and further behind the whites. And the sub-employ-ment statistics indicate a depression while the official jobless rates are cited to show that there is full employment.

What of the quality of life among the poor? Here, I think, the reality is more optimistic, but it is very easy to visualize a reversal of the positive trends.

The war on poverty was never more than a skirmish and the provisions for "maximum feasible participation of the poor" were quickly subverted by hysteri-cal mayors. In theory, the country wants the disadvantaged to stand up and fight for their rights as all the immigrant groups did; in practice, we have knocked people down for taking that pious myth seriously. And yet, there has been a significant growth in local insurgency. It was given an impetus, a public legitimacy, by the anti-poverty effort of recent years. To a degree, then, the other America has become less passive and defeated, more assertive. This is an enor-mous gain, for it is the psychological precondition for political and economic advance.

In saying this, I do not wish to suggest for a moment that the poor constitute a latter-day proletariat in the socialist sense of the term (a group goaded to solidarity and struggle by the common conditions of working life). Romantics who held such a theory have been shocked by the seemingly low rates of participa-tion in various community elections. The industrial plant, which assembles large groups of people under a single discipline and with similar grievances about wages and working conditions, is very different from a slum. The company and its assembly line provide an institutional spine for union organizers, but in the world of the tenements there is no such unifying experience and people turn upon one another more than they join together. As the President's Crime Commission reported, the main victims of violence by the black poor were the black poor.

Once this crucial point is understood, the militancy of recent years becomes important. In the South, the dramatic struggles of a mass movement in the street have led to the registration of more than a million new black voters. In the ghettos of the North, where the enemies of Negro freedom are more subtle than Governor Wallace and the disintegrative power of poverty more compelling, there have been urban *Jacqueries,* spontaneous, unplanned riots, and the emergence among the ghetto young of a new pride of race. No one knows how deep these organiza-tional efforts go (my impression is that the black militants have still to reach the majority of the black poor in any systematic fashion) and yet there is no doubt that there is more movement and thought and less despairing acceptance of social wrongs.

The Negroes are not alone in their insurgency. In California, some Mexican-Americans have organized economically in unions and exercised powerful politi-cal impact during the 1968 Democratic primary. In New York, Puerto Ricans have provided a mass base for unions in hospitals and public employment, and so have Negroes. Throughout the country, there are organizations of mothers on welfare demanding an end to the bureaucratic humiliations that are carefully structured into public assistance in America. And in Appalachia, poor whites have even had some limited success in the struggle against strip mining.

Yet, as I argued at some length in the book, *Toward a Deomocratic Left,* even if these rebellious movements grow in size and cohesion, even if they reach out to a majority of the poor, they will not be able to transform the society by themselves. Therefore the future of activism in the other America depends, in a considerable measure, upon what the non-poor do. This is certainly true if one thinks in terms of the need to create a vast majority coalition, for only such a movement would be capable of initiating the radical changes that are required if poverty is to be abolished in America. Paradoxically, the more fundamental and thoroughgoing an economic and social program, the more heterogeneous and inclusive must its supporters be. This is a truth not always appreciated by some of the sincerely self-righteous on the American Left. Even more immediately, insurgency among the poor is profoundly affected by the movement of the national economy. This fact leads to some larger generalizations about the dynamic of the other America in 1969.

When the Kennedy Administration began, the poor, with the exception of some Southern Negroes, were largely passive and pessimistic. This was partly a reflection of the daily life of the Eisenhower years: chronic unemployment and recession, official indifference, the invisibility of forty to fifty million people. The blacks made the first breakthrough below the Mason-Dixon line, and under the leadership of Martin Luther King, Jr., a general climate of hope developed. There was even the governmental policy of having the poor participate in the antipoverty program. The economic and political upswing and the success of the black freedom movement in the South created the base for the beginning of a new spirit in the other America.

But, as that spirit expressed itself in various forms of militant protest, a new period began in 1965. The war in Vietnam began to dominate American domestic politics and the thirty billion dollars or more invested annually in that tragedy precluded any serious attempt at an "unconditional" war on poverty. The modest impact of the new economics was felt at the bottom of the American economy but in every way the tax cut was inversely—and perversely—related to need; the rich got the most benefit and profit, the poor the least. So the demands for change did not end. There was a great danger in this situation and it came to the fore in the Wallace campaign of 1968. When the struggle against poverty was part of a broad strategy of domestic economic expansion, white workers and members of the lower middle class had a certain common interest with blacks and the rest of the other America, even if they did not lose their prejudices. But when, because of Vietnam, the fight against want seemed to take on the aspect of a competition between the have-nots and have-littles for scarce private and public goods, there were backlashers who feared that their own jobs, homes, and public places were being threatened.

At the beginning of 1969 it is uncertain what the next period will bring. In any case, I have no intention of indulging in prophecy. But it is not difficult to imagine how certain changes in government policy would affect the other America. If there is an economic downturn, the new activism of the poor—those tentative essays in hope which we have seen—will be turned into despair, most of it passive, some of it dangerously angry. If the talk of "trading off" a little unemployment in return for increased price stability becomes more than talk, and joblessness, as a result, rises to five or six per cent, the extremely modest employment gains of our recent efforts would be abolished and the nation would return to the *status quo ante,* or worse. Up to now, when the private sector has hired marginal workers, even with federal inducements, it has done so only because a relatively tight labor market had made it economically feasible to take a few— a very few—risks on the hard-core jobless; the moment the official unemployment rate hits five per cent it will become economically imperative for corporations to fire those men and women.

This would drastically affect the quality of life in the other America. It would deprive the poor of part of their already meager economic resources (the richer a union, or a community organization, the longer it can strike). It would confirm the suspicion, which is never dispelled in the minds of the poor, that the political order of the larger society is systematically rigged against those in it who are the worst off. And most terrible of all, it would teach those who had dared to be hopeful that America was only kidding and that cynicism is the better part of valor. Under such circumstances, a few would become even more militant; the many would sink back into apathy.

Sometimes, when I contemplate this possibility, I think the leaders of the United States have acted as Trotsky said the German Communists did before the rise of Hitler: they have infuriated all classes and won none. The poor were given promises that were not fulfilled, but the rhetoric made many workers and middle-class people fearful that they were being slighted, and the resulting political standoff alienated many of the most idealistic and active among the young. Politically, the entire society moved to the Right, and in the other America the fifth anniversary of the declaration of the war on poverty was a mockery.

The scenario need not be written this way. It is possible to make the massive planned social investments that would create the setting in which the poor would become more organized and determined to control their own political and economic destiny. But, as 1968 came to an end, the happy beginning was still not very imminent. It is not just that the statistical progress in abolishing poverty has been so modest or that the position of the "at risk" population of impoverished children and of blacks is so precarious and even explosive. It is more than that: there is a very real possibility that the spiritual gains of the poor—their new sense of dignity, their awareness that they need not forever be excluded from the democratic political process—are in danger. Looking back to the other America of 1962, it may be that in the years that have passed since then we have raised up the hopes of the most abused people of this land only in order to knock them down.

QUESTIONS FOR DISCUSSION AND DIALOGUE

1. The statement has been made that "The United States practices Socialism for the rich and advocates private enterprise for the poor." Does Harrington seem to agree or disagree with this statement? Why?

2. Outline the main points to be made on either side of this debate question: "Resolved, the poor in America have made definite progress from 1962—1969."
3. Harrington's approach to the Poor in America points up a consideration of key importance to the student of American politics. Objective, statistical data can be agreed upon by people with drastically different politically related interpretations. Discuss how Harrington's article demonstrates this. (Refer to question 2.)
4. What does Harrington mean by the term, "Romantics" in reference to the poor?

Those on Welfare

The Christian Science Monitor

This Christian Science Monitor editorial summarizes key results of a government study on earning potentials of relief recipients. It demonstrates the complexity touched on by question 3 at the end of the last article: It is relatively simple for educated people to agree on objective, statistical studies. The consequent interpretations are another matter!

Statistics may not tell the whole story—they rarely do—but without them it is impossible to weigh a situation and chart a proper course. It is important, therefore, for all who are concerned about the expansion of welfare in the United States to study what are called the first nationwide figures on earning potentials of relief recipients. These have just been made public by Joseph A. Califano Jr., an aide to President Johnson.

Are millions who could work for a living "taking it easy" on relief? Many would answer "yes." But Mr. Califano's report confirms what professional social workers have long maintained and what some city surveys have shown: Virtually all people receiving public aid are unable to get jobs.

Only 1 percent of the 7.3 millions on relief rolls presently qualify as "employables," according to this new government study. Of course even this 1 percent —73,000 persons—is too many to be on relief. Some could be trained for new occupations (as could also some of those listed as unemployable because of physical handicaps). And in the list of unemployables there's sure to be a handful of cheaters who evade detection. Unhappily, even a single known case of cheating tends to discredit the whole program in the eyes of many hard-working people who must pay for it through their taxes.

But a look at the categories of unemployables listed in the government study shows large groups of people who do not have what it takes to bring home a pay envelope.

What are these categories? For one there are the physically handicapped—700,000 of them. They cannot be dismissed as loafers. An even larger group is made up of the elderly, 65 years or older (median 72 years) who do not (with rare exceptions) qualify for jobs in a modern industrial society. There are 2.1 million persons in this classification. Last come the dependent children and their mothers —and in some cases their fathers. Three and a half million boys and girls are found in this dependent group, 900,000 mothers, 150,000 fathers.

True, most of these mothers would be employable if they could leave the care of their children to others, but they lack the money to do this even if they get jobs. That the majority do go to work when their children reach school age is indicated by other federal government studies. A recent national survey reported mothers of dependent children remaining on welfare rolls only about two years.

"Unemployable" is a relative term. One may argue about the criteria used by social workers to determine unemployability. But sound government policies can be shaped only on a basis of such figures as can be obtained. Those presented show the great majority of welfare recipients in need of the most intelligent and loving aid the nation can give them.

QUESTIONS FOR DISCUSSION AND DIALOGUE

1. Make a list of the categories of unemployed discussed in this article.
2. Outline some of the main points on each side of this debate question: "Resolved, virtually all people receiving public aid are unable to get jobs."

A. Requiem for Nonviolence
Eldridge Cleaver

B. Letter to Martin Luther King
A Group of Alabama Clergymen

C. Letter from Birmingham City Jail
Martin Luther King, April 16, 1963

As you read in Michael Harrington's article, the number of "poor" Negroes has increased during the 1962 to 1969 period from 25% to 33%. In the face of such realities as this it is difficult to intelligently dispute the conclusion that it is harder for a black than for a white man to live comfortably in the United States. In the light of these two related considerations— disproportionate poverty and racial discrimination—what path should the

Negro follow? King's or Cleaver's? Or is there some in between course? The answer is very important for all the Americans.

A. Requiem for Nonviolence

The murder of Dr. Martin Luther King came as a surprise—and surprisingly it also came as a shock. Many people, particularly those in the black community who long ago abandoned nonviolence and opted to implement the slogan of Malcolm X—"black liberation by any means necessary"—have been expecting to hear of Dr. King's death for a long time. Many even became tired of waiting. But that Dr. King would have to die was a certainty. For here was a man who refused to abandon the philosophy and the principle of nonviolence in the face of a hostile and racist nation which has made it indisputably clear that it has no intention and no desire to grant a redress of the grievances of the black colonial subjects who are held in bondage.

To black militants, Dr. King represented a stubborn and persistent stumbling block in the path of the methods that had to be implemented to bring about a revolution in the present situation. And so, therefore, much hatred, much venom and much criticism was focused upon Dr. King by the black militants. And the contradiction in which he was caught up cast him in the role of one who was hated and held in contempt, both by the whites in America who did not want to free black people, and by black people who recognized the attitude of white America and who wanted to be rid of the self-deceiving doctrine of nonviolence. Still, black militants were willing to sit back and watch, and allow Dr. King to play out his role. And his role has now been played out.

The assassin's bullet not only killed Dr. King, it killed a period of history. It killed a hope, and it killed a dream.

That white America could produce the assassin of Dr. Martin Luther King is looked upon by black people—and not just those identified as black militants —as a final repudiation by white America of any hope of reconciliation, of any hope of change by peaceful and nonviolent means. So that it becomes clear that the only way for black people in this country to get the things that they want— and the things that they have a right to and that they deserve—is to meet fire with fire.

In the last few months, while Dr. King was trying to build support for his projected poor people's march on Washington, he already resembled something of a dead man. Of a dead symbol, one might say more correctly. Hated on both sides, denounced on both sides—yet he persisted. And now his blood has been spilled. The death of Dr. King signals the end of an era and the beginning of a terrible and bloody chapter that may remain unwritten, because there may be no scribe left to capture on paper the holocaust to come.

That there is a holocaust coming I have no doubt at all. I have been talking to people around the country by telephone—people intimately involved in the black liberation struggle—and their reaction to Dr. King's murder has been unanimous: the war has begun. The violent phase of the black liberation struggle is here, and it will spread. From that shot, from that blood. America will be painted red. Dead bodies will litter the streets and the scenes will be reminiscent of the disgusting, terrifying, nightmarish news reports coming out of Algeria during the height of the general violence right before the final breakdown of the French colonial regime.

America has said "No" to the black man's demand for liberation, and this "No" is unacceptable to black people. They are going to strike back, they are going to reply to the escalation of this racist government, this racist society. They are going to escalate their retaliation. And the responsibility for all this blood, for all this death, for all this suffering . . . well, it's beyond the stage of assigning blame. Black people are no longer interested in adjudicating the situation, in negotiating the situation, in arbitrating the situation. Their only interest now is in being able to summon up whatever it will take to wreck the havoc upon Babylon that will force Babylon to let the black people go. For all other avenues have been closed.

The assassin's bullet which struck down Dr. King closed a door that to the majority of black people seemed closed long ago. To many of us it was clear that that door was never open. But we were willing to allow those who wanted to to bang upon that door for entry, we were willing to sit back and let them do this. Indeed, we had no other choice. But now all black people in America have become Black Panthers in spirit. There will, of course, be those who stand up before the masses and echo the eloquent pleas of Dr. King for a continuation of the nonviolent tactic. They will be listened to by many, but from another perspective. They will look back upon Dr. King and upon his successors with somewhat the emotions one feels when one looks upon the corpse of a loved one. But it is all dead now. It's all dead now. Now there is the gun and the bomb, dynamite and the knife, and they will be used liberally in America. America will bleed. America will suffer.

And it is strange to see how, with each significant shot that is fired, time is speeded up. How the dreadful days that we all somehow knew were coming seem to cascade down upon us immediately, and the dreadful hours that we thought were years away are immediately upon us, immediately before us. And all eternity is gone, blown away, washed away in the blood of martyrs.

Is the death of Dr. King a sad day for America? No. It is a day consistent with what America demands by its actions. The death of Dr. King was not a tragedy for America. America should be happy that Dr. King is dead, because America worked so hard to bring it about. And now all the hypocritical, vicious madmen who pollute the government of this country and who befoul the police agencies of this country, all of the hypocritical public announcements following the death of Dr. King are being repudiated and held in contempt, not only by black people but by millions of white people who know that had these same treacherous, political gangsters made the moves that clearly lay within their power to make, Dr. King would not be dead, nonviolence would prevail and the terror would not be upon us. These people, the police departments, the legislatures, the government, the Democratic Party, the Republican Party, those commonly referred to as the Establishment or the power structure, they can be looked upon as immediate targets and symbols of blame.

But it has been said that a people or a country gets the leaders and the government it deserves. And here we have at the death of Dr. King a President by the name of Lyndon Baines Johnson who has the audacity to stand before this nation and mourn Dr. King and to praise his leadership and the nonviolence he espoused, while he has the blood of hundreds of thousands of people and the slaughtered conscience of America upon his hands. If any one man could be singled out as bearing responsibility for bringing about the bloodshed and violence to come, it would be Lyndon Baines Johnson. But not just Lyndon Baines Johnson. All of the greedy, profit-seeking businessmen in America, all of the conniving, unscrupulous labor leaders of America, all of the unspeakable boot-lickers, the big businessmen of the civil rights movement and the average man on the streets who feels hatred instilled in his heart by this vicious and disgusting system—the blame is everywhere and nowhere.

Washington, D.C. is burning. My only thought at that is I hope that Stokely Carmichael survives Washington. Chicago is burning, Detroit is burning and there is fire and the sound of guns from one end of Babylon to the other.

Last night I heard Lyndon Baines Johnson admonishing his people, admonishing black people to turn away from violence, and not to follow the path of the assassins. And of all the corn pone that he spouted forth one thing struck me and I felt insulted by it. He was ringing changes on a famous statement made by Malcolm X in his speech, "The Ballot or the Bullet." Malcolm X had prophesied that if the ballot did not prevail in gaining black people their liberation, then the bullet would be made to prevail. And Lyndon Johnson said last night that he was going to prove to the nation and to the American people that the ballot and not the bullet would prevail. Coming from him, it was a pure insult.

Those of us in the Black Panther Party who have been reading events and looking to the future have said that this will be the Year of the Panther, that this will be the year of the Black Panther. And now everything that I can see leaves no doubt of that. And now there is Stokely Carmichael, Rap Brown, and above all there is Huey P. Newton. Malcolm X prophesied the coming of the gun, and Huey Newton picked up the gun, and now there is gun against gun. Malcolm X gunned down. Martin Luther King gunned down.

I am trying to put a few words on tape because I was asked to do so by the editor of this magazine, to try to give my thoughts on what the assassination of Dr. King means for the future, what is likely to follow and who is likely to emerge as a new or a prevailing leader of black people. It is hard to put words on this tape because words are no longer relevant. Action is all that counts now. And maybe America will understand that (but) I doubt it. I think that America is incapable of understanding *anything* relevant to human rights. I think that America has already committed suicide and we who now thrash within its dead body are also dead in part and parcel of the corpse. America is truly a disgusting burden upon this planet. A burden upon all humanity. And, if we here in America . . . (The tape from which this article was taken stopped here.)

B. Letter to Martin Luther King

Following is the text of the public statement on Negro demonstrations directed to Dr. Martin Luther King Jr. by eight Alabama clergymen.

April 12, 1963

We clergymen are among those who, in January, issued "An Appeal for Law and Order and Common Sense," in dealing with racial problems in Alabama. We expressed understanding that honest convictions in racial matters could properly be pursued in the courts, but urged that decisions of those courts should in the meantime be peacefully obeyed.

Since that time there has been some evidence of increased forbearance and a willingness to face facts. Responsible citizens have undertaken to work on various problems which cause racial friction and unrest. In Birmingham, recent public events have given indication that we all have opportunity for a new constructive and realistic approach to racial problems.

However, we are now confronted by a series of demonstrations by some of our Negro citizens, directed and led in part by outsiders. We recognize the natural impatience of people who feel that their hopes are slow in being realized. But we are convinced that these demonstrations are unwise and untimely.

We agree rather with certain local Negro leadership which has called for honest and open negotiation of racial issues in our area. And we believe this kind of facing of issues can best be accomplished by citizens of our own metropolitan area, white and Negro, meeting with their knowledge and experience of the local situation. All of us need to face that responsibility and find proper channels for its accomplishment.

Just as we formerly pointed out that "hatred and violence have no sanction in our religious and political traditions," we also point out that such actions as incite to hatred and violence, however technically peaceful those actions may be, have not contributed to the resolution of our local problems. We do not believe that these days of new hope are days when extreme measures are justified in Birmingham.

We commend the community as a whole, and the local news media and law enforcement officials in particular, on the calm manner in which these demonstrations have been handled. We urge the public to continue to show restraint should the demonstrations continue, and the law enforcement officials to remain calm and continue to protect our city from violence.

We further strongly urge our own Negro community to withdraw support from these demonstrations, and to unite locally in working peacefully for a better Birmingham. When rights are consistently denied, a cause should be pressed in the courts and in negotiations among local leaders, and not in the streets. We appeal to both our white and Negro citizenry to observe the principles of law and order and common sense.

Signed by:

C. C. J. Carpenter, D.D., LL.D., *Bishop of Alabama*

Joseph A. Durick, D.D., *Auxiliary Bishop, Diocese of Mobile-Birmingham*

Rabbi Milton L. Grafman, *Temple Emanu-El, Birmingham, Alabama*

Bishop Paul Hardin, *Bishop of the Alabama-West Florida Conference of the Methodist Church*

Bishop Nolan B. Harmon, *Bishop of the North Alabama Conference of the Methodist Church*

George M. Murray, D.D., LL.D., *Bishop Coadjutor, Episcopal Diocese of Alabama*

Edward V. Ramage, *Moderator, Synod of the Alabama Presbyterian Church in the United States*

Earl Stallings, *Pastor, First Baptist Church, Birmingham, Alabama*

C. Letter from Birmingham City Jail

April 16, 1963 My Dear Fellow Clergymen,

While confined here in the Birmingham City Jail, I came across your recent statement calling our present activities "unwise and untimely." Seldom, if ever, do I pause to answer criticism of my work and ideas. . . . But since I feel that you are men of genuine good will and your criticisms are sincerely set forth, I would like to answer your statement in what I hope will be patient and reasonable terms. . . .

I am in Birmingham because injustice is here. Just as the 8th century prophets left their little villages and carried their "thus saith the Lord" far beyond the boundaries of their home town, and just as the Apostle Paul left his little village of Tarsus and carried the gospel of Jesus Christ to practically every hamlet and city of the Graeco-Roman world, I too am compelled to carry the gospel of freedom beyond my particular home town. Like Paul, I must constantly respond to the Macedonian call for aid.

Moreover, I am cognizant of the interrelatedness of all communities and states. I cannot sit idly by in Atlanta and not be concerned about what happens in Birmingham. Injustice anywhere is a threat to justice everywhere. We are caught in an inescapable network of mutuality tied in a single garment of destiny. Whatever affects one directly affects all indirectly. Never again can we afford to live with the narrow, provincial "outside agitator" idea. Anyone who lives inside the United States can never be considered an outsider anywhere in this country.

You deplore the demonstrations that are presently taking place in Birmingham. But I am sorry that your statement did not express a similar concern for the conditions that brought the demonstrations into being. I am sure that each of you would want to go far beyond the superficial social analyst who looks merely at effects, and does not grapple with underlying causes. I would not hesitate to say that it is unfortunate that so-called demonstrations are taking place in Birmingham at this time, but I would say in more emphatic terms that it is even more unfortunate that the white power structure of this city left the Negro community with no other alternative.

In any nonviolent campaign there are four basic steps: 1) collection of the facts to determine whether injustices are alive; 2) negotiation; 3) self-purification; and 4) direct action. We have gone through all of these steps in Birmingham. There can be no gain-saying of the fact that racial injustice engulfs this community. Birmingham is probably the most thoroughly segregated city in the United States. Its ugly record of police brutality is known in every section of this country. Its unjust treatment of Negroes in the courts is a notorious reality. There have been more unsolved bombings of Negro homes and churches in Birmingham than any city in this nation. These are the hard, brutal, and unbelievable facts. On the basis of these conditions Negro leaders sought to negotiate with the city fathers. But the political leaders consistently refused to engage in good faith negotiation. . . .

As in so many experiences of the past, we were confronted with blasted hopes, and the dark shadow of a deep disappointment settled upon us. So we had no alternative except that of preparing for direct action, whereby we would present our very bodies as a means of laying our case before the conscience of the local and national community. We were not unmindful of the difficulties involved. So we decided to go through a process of self-purification. We started having workshops on nonviolence and repeatedly asked ourselves the questions, "Are you able to accept blows without retaliating?" "Are you able to endure the ordeals of jail?" . . .

You may well ask, "Why direct action? Why sit-ins, marches, etc.? Isn't negotiation a better path?" You are exactly right in your call for negotiation. Indeed, this is the purpose of direct action. Nonviolent direct action seeks to create such a crisis and establish such creative tension that a community that has constantly refused to negotiate is forced to confront the issue. It seeks so to dramatize the issue that it can no longer be ignored.

I just referred to the creation of tension as a part of the work of the nonviolent resister. This may sound rather shocking. But I must confess that I am not afraid of the word tension. I have earnestly worked and preached against violent tension, but there is a type of constructive nonviolent tension that is necessary for growth. Just as Socrates felt that it was necessary to create a tension in the mind so that individuals could rise from the bondage of myths and half-truths to the unfettered realm of creative analysis and objective appraisal, we must see the need of having nonviolent gadflies to create the kind of tension in society that will help men rise from the dark depths of prejudice and racism to the majestic heights of understanding and brotherhood. So the purpose of the direct action is to create a situation so crisis-packed that it will inevitably open the door to negotiation. We, therefore, concur with you in your call for negotiation. Too long has our beloved Southland been bogged down in the tragic attemp to live in monologue rather than dialogue. . . .

My friends, I must say to you that we have not made a single gain in civil rights without determined legal and nonviolent pressure. History is the long and tragic story of the fact that privileged groups seldom give up their privileges voluntarily. Individuals may see the moral light and voluntarily give up their unjust posture; but as Reinhold Niebuhr has reminded us, groups are more immoral than individuals.

We know through painful experience that freedom is never voluntarily given by the oppressor; it must be demanded by the oppressed. Frankly I have never yet engaged in a direct action movement that was "well timed," according to the timetable of those who have not suffered unduly from the disease of segregation. For years now I have heard the word "Wait!" It rings in the ear of every Negro with a piercing familiarity. This "wait" has almost always meant "never." It has been a tranquilizing Thalidomide, relieving the emotional stress for a moment, only to give birth to an ill-formed infant of frustration. We must come to see with the distinguished jurist of yesterday that "justice too long delayed is justice denied." We have waited for more than 340 years for our constitutional and God-given rights. The nations of Asia and Africa are moving with jet-like speed toward the goal of political independence, and we still creep at horse and buggy pace toward the gaining of a cup of coffee at a lunch counter.

I guess it is easy for those who have never felt the stinging darts of segregation to say wait. But when you have seen vicious mobs lynch your mothers and fathers at will and drown your sisters and brothers at whim; when you have seen hate-filled policemen curse, kick, brutalize, and even kill your black brothers and sisters with impunity; when you see the vast majority of your 20 million Negro brothers smothering in an air-tight cage of poverty in the midst of an affluent society; when you suddenly find your tongue twisted and your speech stammering as you seek to explain to your six-year-old daughter why she can't go to the public amusement park that has just been advertised on television, and see tears welling up in her little eyes when she is told that Funtown is closed to colored children, and see the depressing clouds of inferiority begin to form in her little mental sky, and see her begin to distort her little personality by unconsciously developing a bitterness toward white people; when you have to concoct an answer for a five-year-old son asking in agonizing pathos: "Daddy, why do white people treat colored people so mean?"; when you take a cross country drive and find it necessary to sleep night after night in the uncomfortable corners of your automobile because no motel will accept you; when you are humiliated day in and day out by nagging signs reading "white" men and "colored"; when your first name becomes "nigger" and your middle name becomes "boy" (however old you are) and your last name becomes "John," and when your wife and mother are never given the respected title "Mrs."; when you are harried by day and haunted by night by the fact that you are a Negro, living constantly at tip-toe stance never quite knowing what to expect next, and plagued with inner fears and outer resentments; when you are forever fighting a degenerating sense of "nobodiness" —then you will understand why we find it difficult to wait. There comes a time when the cup of endurance runs over, and men are no longer willing to be plunged into an abyss of injustice where they experience the bleakness of corroding despair. I hope, sirs, you can understand our legitimate and unavoidable impatience.

You express a great deal of anxiety over our willingness to break laws. This is certainly a legitimate concern. Since we so diligently urge people to obey the

Supreme Court's decision of 1954 outlawing segregation in the public schools, it is rather strange and paradoxical to find us consciously breaking laws. One may well ask, "How can you advocate breaking some laws and obeying others?" The answer is found in the fact that there are two types of laws: There are *just* laws and there are *unjust* laws. I would be the first to advocate obeying just laws. One has not only a legal but a moral responsibility to obey just laws. Conversely, one has a moral responsibility to disobey unjust laws. I would agree with Saint Augustine that "An unjust law is no law at all."

Now what is the difference between the two? How does one determine when a law is just or unjust? A just law is a man-made code that squares with the moral law or the law of God. An unjust law is a mode that is out of harmony with the moral law. To put it in the terms of Saint Thomas Aquinas, an unjust law is a human law that is not rooted in eternal and natural law. Any law that uplifts human personality is just. Any law that degrades human personality is unjust.

All segregation statutes are unjust because segregation distorts the soul and damages the personality. It gives the segregator a false sense of superiority and the segregated a false sense of inferiority. To use the words of Martin Buber, the great Jewish philosopher, segregation substitutes an "I-it" relationship for the "I-thou" relationship, and ends up relegating persons to the status of things. So segregation is not only politically, economically, and sociologically unsound, but it is morally wrong and sinful. Paul Tillich has said that sin is separation. Isn't segregation an existential expression of man's tragic separation, an expression of his awful estrangement, his terrible sinfulness? So I can urge men to obey the 1954 decision of the Supreme Court because it is morally right, and I can urge them to disobey segregation ordinances because they are morally wrong.

Let me give another example of just and unjust laws. An unjust law is a code that a majority inflicts on a minority that is not binding on itself. This is *difference* made legal. On the other hand a just law is a code that a majority compels a minority to follow that it is willing to follow itself. This is *sameness* made legal.

Let me give another explanation. An unjust law is a code inflicted upon a minority which that minority had no part in enacting or creating because they did not have the unhampered right to vote. Who can say the legislature of Alabama which set up the segregation laws was democratically elected? Throughout the state of Alabama all types of conniving methods are used to prevent Negroes from becoming registered voters and there are some counties without a single Negro registered to vote despite the fact that the Negro constitutes a majority of the population. Can any law set up in such a state be considered democratically structured?

These are just a few examples of unjust and just laws. There are some instances when a law is just on its face but unjust in its application. For instance, I was arrested Friday on a charge of parading without a permit. Now there is nothing wrong with an ordinance which requires a permit for a parade, but when the ordinance is used to preserve segregation and to deny citizens the First Amendment privilege of peaceful assembly and peaceful protest, then it becomes unjust.

I hope you can see the distinction I am trying to point out. In no sense do I advocate evading or defying the law as the rabid segregationist would do. This

95913

would lead to anarchy. One who breaks an unjust law must do it *openly, lovingly* (not hatefully as the white mothers did in New Orleans when they were seen on television screaming "nigger, nigger, nigger") and with a willingness to accept the penalty. I submit that an individual who breaks a law that conscience tells him is unjust, and willingly accepts the penalty by staying in jail to arouse the conscience of the community over its injustice, is in reality expressing the very highest respect for law.

Of course there is nothing new about this kind of civil disobedience. It was seen sublimely in the refusal of Shadrach, Meshach, and Abednego to obey the laws of Nebuchadnezzar because a higher moral law was involved. It was practiced superbly by the early Christians who were willing to face hungry lions and the excruciating pain of chopping blocks before submitting to certain unjust laws of the Roman Empire. To a degree academic freedom is a reality today because Socrates practiced civil disobedience.

We can never forget that everything Hitler did in Germany was "legal" and everything the Hungarian freedom fighters did in Hungary was "illegal." It was "illegal" to aid and comfort a Jew in Hitler's Germany. But I am sure that, if I had lived in Germany during that time, I would have aided and comforted my Jewish brothers even though it was illegal. If I lived in a Communist country today where certain principles dear to the Christian faith are suppressed, I believe I would openly advocate disobeying these anti-religious laws. . . .

In your statement you asserted that our actions, even though peaceful, must be condemned because they precipitate violence. But can this assertion be logically made? Isn't this like condemning the robbed man because his possession of money precipitated the evil act of robbery? Isn't this like condemning Socrates because his unswerving commitment to truth and his philosophical delvings precipitated the misguided popular mind to make him drink the hemlock? Isn't this like condemning Jesus because His unique God consciousness and never-ceasing devotion to His will precipitated the evil act of crucifixion? We must come to see, as Federal courts have consistently affirmed, that it is immoral to urge an individual to withdraw his efforts to gain his basic constitutional rights because the quest precipitates violence. Society must protect the robbed and punish the robber.

I had also hoped that the white moderate would reject the myth of time. I received a letter this morning from a white brother in Texas which said: "All Christians know that the colored people will receive equal rights eventually, but is it possible that you are in too great of a religious hurry? It has taken Christianity almost 2,000 years to accomplish what it has. The teachings of Christ take time to come to earth." All that is said here grows out of a tragic misconception of time. It is the strangely irrational notion that there is something in the very flow of time that will inevitably cure all ills. Actually time is neutral. It can be used either destructively or constructively. I am coming to feel that the people of ill will have used time much more effectively than the people of good will.

We will have to repent in this generation not merely for the vitriolic words and actions of the bad people, but for the appalling silence of the good people. We must come to see that human progress never rolls in on wheels of inevitability.

It comes through the tireless efforts and persistent work of men willing to be co-workers with God, and without this hard work time itself becomes an ally of the forces of social stagnation.

We must use time creatively, and forever realize that the time is always ripe to do right. Now is the time to make real the promise of democracy, and transform our pending national elegy into a creative psalm of brotherhood. Now is the time to lift our national policy from the quicksand of racial injustice to the solid rock of human dignity.

You spoke of our activity in Birmingham as extreme. At first I was rather disappointed that fellow clergymen would see my non-violent efforts as those of the extremist. I started thinking about the fact that I stand in the middle of two opposing forces in the Negro community. One is a force of complacency made up of Negroes who, as a result of long years of oppression, have been so completely drained of self-respect and a sense of "somebodiness" that they have adjusted to segregation, and of a few Negroes in the middle class who, because of a degree of academic and economic security, and because at points they profit by segregation, have unconsciously become insensitive to the problems of the masses. The other force is one of bitterness and hatred and comes perilously close to advocating violence. It is expressed in the various black nationalist groups that are springing up over the nation, the largest and best known being Elijah Muhammad's Muslim movement. This movement is nourished by the contemporary frustration over the continued existence of racial discrimination. It is made up of people who have lost faith in America, who have absolutely repudiated Christianity, and who have concluded that the white man is an incurable "devil."

I have tried to stand between these two forces saying that we need not follow the "do-nothingism" of the complacent or the hatred and despair of the black nationalist. There is the more excellent way of love and nonviolent protest. I'm grateful to God that, through the Negro church, the dimension of nonviolence entered our struggle. If this philosophy had not emerged I am convinced that by now many streets of the South would be flowing with floods of blood. And I am further convinced that if our white brothers dismiss us as "rabble rousers" and "outside agitators"—those of us who are working through the channels of nonviolent direct action—and refuse to support our nonviolent efforts, millions of Negroes, out of frustration and despair, will seek solace and security in black nationalist ideologies, a development that will lead inevitably to a frightening racial nightmare.

Oppressed people cannot remain oppressed forever. The urge for freedom will eventually come. This is what has happened to the American Negro. Something within has reminded him of his birthright of freedom; something without has reminded him that he can gain it. Consciously and unconsciously, he has been swept in by what the Germans call the *Zeitgeist,* and with his black brothers of Africa, and his brown and yellow brothers of Asia, South America, and the Caribbean, he is moving with a sense of cosmic urgency toward the promised land of racial justice. Recognizing this vital urge that has engulfed the Negro community, one should readily understand public demonstrations.

The Negro has many pent-up resentments and latent frustrations. He has to get them out. So let him march sometime; let him have his prayer pilgrimages to the city hall; understand why he must have sit-ins and freedom rides. If his repressed emotions do not come out in these nonviolent ways, they will come out in ominous expressions of violence. This is not a threat; it is a fact of history. So I have not said to my people, "Get rid of your discontent." But I have tried to say that this normal and healthy discontent can be channeled through the creative outlet of nonviolent direct action. Now this approach is being dismissed as extremist. I must admit that I was initially disappointed in being so categorized.

But as I continued to think about the matter I gradually gained a bit of satisfaction from being considered an extremist. Was not Jesus an extremist in love? "Love your enemies, bless them that curse you, pray for them that despitefully use you." Was not Amos an extremist for justice—"Let justice roll down like waters and righteousness like a mighty stream." Was not Paul an extremist for the gospel of Jesus Christ—"I bear in my body the marks of the Lord Jesus." Was not Martin Luther an extremist—"Here I stand; I can do none other so help me God." Was not John Bunyan an extremist—"I will stay in jail to the end of my days before I make a butchery of my conscience." Was not Abraham Lincoln an extremist—"This nation cannot survive half slave and half free." Was not Thomas Jefferson an extremist—"We hold these truths to be self evident . . . that all men are created equal."

So the question is not whether we will be extremist but what kind of extremist will we be. Will we be extremists for hate or will we be extremists for love; Will we be extremists for the preservation of injustice—or will we be extremists for the cause of justice? In that dramatic scene on Calvary's hill three men were crucified. We must never forget that all three were crucified for the same crime —the crime of extremism. Two were extremists for immorality, and thus fell below their environment. The other, Jesus Christ, was an extremist for love, truth, and goodness, and thereby rose above His environment. So, after all, maybe the South, the nation, and the world are in dire need of creative extremists. . . .

I hope the Church as a whole will meet the challenge of this decisive hour. But even if the Church does not come to the aid of justice, I have no despair about the future. I have no fear about the outcome of our struggle in Birmingham, even if our motives are presently misunderstood. We will reach the goal of freedom in Birmingham and all over the nation, because the goal of America is freedom. Abused and scorned though we may be, our destiny is tied up with the destiny of America.

Before the pilgrims landed at Plymouth, we were here. Before the pen of Jefferson etched across the pages of history the majestic words of the Declaration of Independence, we were here. For more than two centuries our foreparents labored in this country without wages; they made cotton "king"; and they built the homes of their masters in the midst of brutal injustice and shameful humiliation—and yet out of a bottomless vitality they continued to thrive and develop. If the inexpressible cruelties of slavery could not stop us, the opposition we now face will surely fail. We will win our freedom because the sacred heritage of our nation and the eternal will of God are embodied in our echoing demands.

I must close now. But before closing I am impelled to mention one other point in your statement that troubled me profoundly. You warmly commended the Birmingham police force for keeping "order" and "preventing violence." I don't believe you would have so warmly commended the police force if you had seen its angry violent dogs literally biting six unarmed, nonviolent Negroes. I don't believe you would so quickly commend the policemen if you would observe their ugly and inhuman treatment of Negroes here in the city jail; if you would watch them push and curse old Negro women and young Negro girls; if you would see them slap and kick old Negro men and young Negro boys; if you will observe them, as they did on two occasions, refuse to give us food because we wanted to sing our grace together. I'm sorry that I can't join you in your praise for the police department. . . .

It is true that they have been rather disciplined in their public handling of the demonstrators. In this sense they have been rather publicly "nonviolent." But for what purpose? To preserve the evil system of segregation. Over the last few years I have consistently preached that nonviolence demands that the means we use must be as pure as the ends we seek. So I have tried to make it clear that it is wrong to use immoral means to attain moral ends. But now I must affirm that it is just as wrong, or even more so, to use moral means to preserve immoral ends. . . . T. S. Eliot has said that there is no greater treason than to do the right deed for the wrong reason.

I wish you had commended the Negro sit-inners and demonstrators of Birmingham for their sublime courage, their willingness to suffer, and their amazing discipline in the midst of the most inhuman provocation. One day the South will recognize its real heroes. They will be the James Merediths, courageously and with a majestic sense of purpose, facing jeering and hostile mobs and the agonizing loneliness that characterizes the life of the pioneer. They will be old, oppressed, battered Negro women, symbolized in a 72-year-old woman of Montgomery, Alabama, who rose up with a sense of dignity and with her people decided not to ride the segregated buses, and responded to one who inquired about her tiredness with ungrammatical profundity: "My feets is tired, but my soul is rested." They will be young high school and college students, young ministers of the gospel and a host of the elders, courageously and nonviolently sitting in at lunch counters and willingly going to jail for conscience sake. One day the South will know that when these disinherited children of God sat down at lunch counters they were in reality standing up for the best in the American dream and the most sacred values in our Judeo-Christian heritage, and thus carrying our whole nation back to great wells of democracy which were dug deep by the founding fathers in the formulation of the Constitution and the Declaration of Independence.

Yours for the cause of Peace and Brotherhood
M. L. King Jr.

QUESTIONS FOR DISCUSSION AND DIALOGUE

1. Many Americans counsel the American Negro to practice more patience. Do

you think King and Cleaver would have different responses to this kind of advice? Explain.

2. Summarize how King's and Cleaver's approaches differ in tone and content.
3. Based on what you have read, how do you think Cleaver would respond to King's statement that, "One who breaks an unjust law must do it OPENLY, LOVINGLY, and with a willingness to accept the penalty. I submit that an individual who breaks a law that conscience tells him is unjust, and willingly accepts the penalty by staying in jail to arouse the conscience of the community over its unjustice, is in reality expressing the very highest respect for the law." How do you respond?

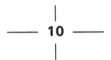

The Wallace Man

Stewart Alsop

The reader might compare Alsop's version of "The Wallace Man" to the "No Change Coalition." Race is certainly a key factor in the support Wallace received, but as Alsop points out, it is only the most obvious of factors, most of which are more complex than simple racism.

WITH WALLACE—You see him at every Wallace rally—a big, burly fellow who looks as though he drank his full share of beer at the local tavern on Saturday nights, and who shouts and cheers and stamps his feet when George Wallace denounces "the pointy-head pseudo-intellectuals who haven't got enough sense to park a bicycle straight." He is the Wallace man. Who is he, and why is he for Wallace?

Wallace says he is "the autoworker or the steelworker or the taxi driver," and he is confident that the Wallace man is going to make him President, in 1972 if not in 1968. He just might be right.

The Wallace man himself, if you ask why he is for Wallace, is likely to mumble something about how Wallace "has some pretty good ideas." Anti-Wallaceites write him off as a simple racist. But if you take a statistical look at the Wallace man, you begin to see more complicated reasons why he is for Wallace. A main reason is that he thinks that he is being unfairly forced to pay the real price of the Negro social revolution. And he is at least partly right.

Suppose the Wallace man is an autoworker or a steelworker. He then earns base pay of around $8,000 a year, with maybe another thousand for overtime. He almost certainly owns a house, and the house is worth about $16,000, in which the Wallace man has an equity of about $9,000. He is thus one of the highest-paid workers in the history of this or any other country. That equity also makes him a member of the bourgeoisie. So he ought to be as contented as a well-fed milk cow. He isn't.

Income

That income is illusory. Take away taxes and the monthly payments to the finance company, and the Wallace man's real spendable income is probably under $6,000 a year. That is not much on which to run a house and a car, and to support a wife and between two and three children (statistically, 2.3 children). The Wallace man works hard, but he doesn't have much left over for beer on Saturday night. And if you consider his situation, you can see why he is for Wallace.

He cannot afford to live in the safe and affluent far-out suburbs. He lives in or near the central city, and the statistics tell the story of the appalling rise in the crime rate in the central cities all over this country. When Wallace says that "your wife can go to the supermarket without fear of molestation when I am President," that empty promise means a lot to the Wallace man.

Another Wallace promise also means a lot to him—that "a man who works 25 years to own his own house ought to be able to sell it to whoever he wants to," which is really a promise to end open housing. The Wallace man fears that Negroes will move into his neighborhood, and that he will be forced to sell his house at panic prices. His house is his capital, and any threat to his capital makes him as unhappy as it might make a Mellon or a Rockefeller—and maybe more so.

School

There is a third Wallace promise that means a great deal to him—that Wallace will support "the inalienable right of a parent to decide where his children go to school," which is, of course, a promise to end integrated schooling. The Wallace man's children do not go to the well-financed, almost lily-white schools of affluent suburbia, and he doesn't have the money to send them to private schools. The schools in the central cities are for the most part very bad schools—again, the statistics tell the story. In some of them, vandalism and violence are daily facts of life, and the children learn little or nothing.

It may be illiberal of the Wallace man not to want to send his children to bad schools in the name of integration, but it is not at all unnatural. And it is not unnatural either for him to worry about the "molestation" of his wife, or about losing his equity in his house, which is all he has. The irony is that George Wallace's South helped to create the situation which has in turn created the Wallace man.

When millions of poor rural blacks from the Deep South flooded the cities of the North, the South had its revenge on the North for winning the Civil War. For the blacks were educated according to the South's "separate but equal" doctrine—and thus hardly educated at all. The inevitable results of this invasion of the cities by poor, and illiterate people were the high crime rates, the pressure on housing, and the terrible schools which have converted millions of formerly staunch Northern Democrats to Wallace's racism.

But it is important to note that Wallace says very little to stir up whites against blacks—he never says a derogatory word about "our Niggra citizens." He says a great deal to stir up whites against whites—the uneducated against the educated, the "average man in the street" against "the elite power groups." Wallace is, in fact, the leader of a revolt of the working people who drink beer in bars against the "elite" who drink Martinis at cocktail parties. And the Martini-drinkers will ignore the revolt at their peril.

For what makes Wallace so immensely effective a demagogue is that there is a lot of truth in what he says. What he says, again and again, is that "the pseudo-intellectuals" and "the guideline writers" and "the ivory-tower editorialists," who are for integrated schools and open housing and restrictions on the police power and so on, are forcing the working man to pay the real price of their liberalism.

Children

"There are 535 members of Congress," he says, "and a lot of these liberals have children, too. You know how many send their kids to the public schools in Washington? Six." It would be rather surprising if there were as many as six successful Washington journalists or upper civil servants who send their children to the integrated public schools. And in very truth, there is something a bit contemptible about the affluent liberal who lives in the safe suburbs, and reserves all his sympathy for the Negro militants and the radical young, with none at all left over for the hard-pressed, hard-working Wallace man.

One of these days—maybe in 1972—the Wallace man may get his revenge. Then the American free society which has miraculously survived all these years may die, four years short of its 200th birthday, to be replaced by some uniquely American form of the police state.

QUESTIONS FOR DISCUSSION AND DIALOGUE

1. Do you think Alsop in this article has actually taken the side of "The Wallace Man?" Discuss.
2. How does Alsop criticize the "Liberals" in this article? Do you agree with him? Discuss.
3. What is a "demagogue?" Why does Alsop think Wallace is such an effective one?

— 11 —

In Politics, It's The New Populism

Newsweek

This concluding article of the American's chapter points out the paradox of the previously discussed "No Change Coalition" striving for "change." The key question is change toward what? "The New Populism" that has an appeal for so many of the "silent majority" seems to be a "wistfulness for the old values, for traditional varieties and styles of life that somehow seem to have gone awry."

In Minneapolis, a policeman named Charles Stenvig becomes mayor by rolling up an astounding 62 per cent of the vote against the experienced president of the City Council. In New York, Mayor John Lindsay and former Mayor Robert Wagner, both liberals of national stature, bow to obscure interlopers in their parties' mayoral primaries. In Boston, grand-motherly Louise Day Hicks, whose crusade for the "forgotten man" and against school busing carried her within an inch of City Hall two years ago, leads a big field in the upcoming City Council elections. And in Newark, a onetime construction worker named Anthony Imperiale, master of karate, the bowie knife and a fleet of 72 radio cars that regularly patrol the city's white neighborhoods, confidently maps his campaign to win next year's race for mayor and "get rid of every quisling" in sight.

This is the year of the New Populism, a far-ranging, fast-spreading revolt of the little man against the Establishment at the nation's polls. Middle America, long counted upon to supply the pluralities on Election Day, is beginning to supply eye-opening victories from coast to coast. The over-all political cast of the country remains mixed, to be sure. The freshman crop of U.S. senators elected just last year, for example, includes a significant share of conventional liberals and moderates. Only a fortnight ago, a Negro candidate topped the field in the Detroit mayoral primary, and progressive Lindsay may yet eke out a victory in New York next month. But—especially in close-to-home city politics—the frustrated middle-class majority has increasingly been turning to newfound champions drawn from its own ranks.

The seeds of popular rebellion have been long implanted beneath the surface of liberal hegemony. Even as John Kennedy and Lyndon Johnson held sway in Washington, Barry Goldwater astounded the political pros with his temporary seizure of the GOP, Ronald Reagan carried the banner of the "citizen politician" from the movie lots to the California Statehouse, and George Wallace and Lester Maddox found that fulminations against "those bureaucrats" was a sure path to popularity both in the South and, to some extent, in the rest of the nation.

But this was the year that the phenomenon finally broke the surface with a series of municipal victories impossible to dismiss as regional aberrations. And this was the year that the New Populism began to be seen more clearly for what it really is.

It is not, most politicians now agree, simply a burst of racist backlash. Though sheer bigotry has certainly played a part in fueling the little man's revolt, part of his resentment of the black man is traceable to his sense of desertion by a government that appears preoccupied with Negroes' needs and inattentive to his own. Liberals who have shouted "racism!" at white response to the black revolution are now beginning to realize that this oversimplifies the impulses involved and bolsters Middle America's mounting impression that liberals neither understand nor sympathize with lower-middle-class whites.

And it is not simply a swing to the political right. Though the New Populists have unquestionably turned conservative on law enforcement, they show few signs of wanting to scrap the social reforms—medicare, aid to education, and social security improvements—wrought by the liberal left. "It's a swing against anarchy," says liberal Congressman Allard Lowenstein, and indeed the disgruntlement with the progressives seems to stem far more from their permissiveness than from their programs.

Perhaps, most of all, the New Populism is a quest for recognition. "People felt that nobody was representing them and nobody was listening," says Minneapolis's Charlie Stenvig. "They felt alienated from the political system, and they'd had it up to their Adam's apples on just about everything. So they took a guy like me—four kids, and average home, a working man they could associate themselves with. They just said, 'Lookit, we're sick of you politicians'."

Stenvig was, indeed, a paragon of Middle America: the son of a telephone company employee, a Methodist of Norwegian stock, a graduate of a local high school and a local college (Augsburg), and an up-through-the-ranks detective on the police force. His opponent, by contrast, was almost pure Establishment: the son of an investment banker, a graduate of Stanford and Harvard Law, and a resident of the fashionable Kenwood suburb.

In his campaign, Stenvig pounded away at the privileged bastions of suburbia —he pledged to "bring government back to the citizens of Minneapolis and away from the influence of the golden West out there in Wayzata"—a privileged enclave on the city's fringes. To low-income whites, the suburbs are where the liberals live. "The liberal preaches from his lily-white suburb," explains United Auto Workers official Paul Schrade, "while the worker usually lives on the borderline of the ghetto. The workers are on the front lines of the black-white conflict and resent the advice of rear-echelon generals."

Minneapolis's workers relished Stenvig's assault on the suburbs—"He told those rich guys to go suck a lemon," chortles one local auto mechanic—and as mayor he has kept up the attack. He has protested the financing plan for a new hospital on the ground that the suburbs would not pay enough of the tab, and he has staffed city jobs with what he calls "just average working people."

A few of these appointments have aroused the only controversy in what most people in Minneapolis agree has been an extremely hard-working, well-intentioned municipal administration. Antonio G. Felicetta, vice president of the regional joint council of the Teamsters union, created a citywide sensation recently when he delivered some pungent remarks in his new role as a member of the city Commission on Human Relations. "I'm not going to take any bull s---," he announced to a local journalist. "If there are any grievances, I sure as hell would want to see them taken care of. But I sure as hell wouldn't want to give'em [welfare recipients] half of my goddam paycheck when I'm working and they're sitting on their asses." Felicetta was promptly denounced as a "card-carrying bigot" by a group of Minneapolis blacks, but he also received a torrent of phone calls saying "That's the way, Tony, sock it to'em."

Middle America's radical right has always delighted in such tough words—and deeds. Newark's Tony Imperiale became an instant folk hero in these circles when he organized a band of white vigilantes in the wake of the disastrous summer riots in 1967. And last week, as he looked ahead to the day when he becomes mayor, he made plain that official investiture will not change his tune. "If any militant comes into my office, puts his ass on my desk and tells me what I have to do," he vowed, "I'll throw his ass off the desk and throw him out the door."

There is little question that Tony—38 years old, 5 feet 6 3/4 inches high and 260 pounds thick—is capable of doing just that. As he drove his volunteer ambulance—part of his vigilante patrol—past the corner of Mt. Prospect Street and Bloomfield Avenue in Newark's rugged North Ward one evening recently, he recalled an example of the sort of direct action he favors: "We came down here one night with eight guys and kicked the crap outa 22 junkies. Each time we came back to slap them around they lessened in ranks and finally took the hint." Imperiale keeps an arsenal of about 40 serviceable guns in his house, including a 14-inch-barrel scatter-gun stowed behind the couch (there have already been two attempts on his life).

Imperiale is a bit too rough-and-ready for the taste of most other politicians of the New Populism. And outside the South, most of them would disclaim any ideological kinship with Dixie's two most prominent contributions to the movement, former Alabama Gov. George Wallace and incumbent Georgia Gov. Lester Maddox. But Wallace, whose Presidential campaigns of 1964 and 1968 featured attacks on "pointy-headed intellectuals" and "briefcase-toting bureaucrats" that gave his appeal a dimension beyond sheer racism, claims paternity for much of the movement. "My vote was only the tip of the iceberg," he says. "There's others I'm responsible for: Stenvig, Mayor Yorty of Los Angeles, two mayoral candidates in New York. They were making Alabama speeches with a Minneapolis, Los Angeles and New York accent. The only thing they omitted was the drawl."

One of the things that draws the Populists together is their common wistfulness for the "old values," for traditional verities and styles of life that somehow seem to have gone awry. Lester Maddox, for example, likes to think of himself as part of "the mainstream of the thinking of the American people: the achievers, the success-makers, the builders, the individuals who like to set their own goals and accept the challenges." A number of Middle America's politicians also like to brandish the crusader's cross. "God is going to be my principal adviser," declares Charlie Stenvig, and Mary Beck, a 61-year-old Detroit councilwoman who placed a strong third in last month's mayoral primary, dedicated her campaign newspaper "to the laws of God and man."

When Populists brood on the agonies of contemporary society, a certain nostalgia for a simpler life is never far from the surface. "I was born in a little town of 6,000 people," recalls Democrat Mario Procaccino, who appears to be leading Lindsay and a conservative Republican in the New York mayor's race. "We respected our parents, our teachers, and our priest or man of the cloth. We had respect for men in public office. We looked up to them . . ."

Procaccino frequently exhibits another characteristic of this new political breed: emotionalism. He wept when he announced his candidacy. Occasionally he takes his wife, Marie, and his daughter, Marierose, for an evening visit to the top of the Empire State Building. "I look out over the city and say to myself, 'What's the matter with these people? Why can't they get together?' " Many middle-class voters seem to warm to these displays of feeling, perhaps because they themselves are so upset, perhaps because they sense that their government has been run recently by soulless technocrats spouting bureaucratic jargon or political cant. "I like him because he's so emotional," beamed one housewife to her neighbor as Procaccino campaigned through Queens last week. "Any tears he sheds, you know he has heart. He doesn't fear to shed them and they bring the people closer to him."

Mayor Sam Yorty of Los Angeles is another extremely warm-blooded politician, endowed with a coloratura stumping style that ranges between acid vituperation and passionate enthusiasm. Ever since the Watts riots of 1965, he has concentrated the former on militants and the latter on guardians of law and order. This approach proved immensely popular in last spring's mayoral election, when he won an upset victory over Negro challenger Thomas Bradley. "Personally, I like the way Yorty shoots off his mouth too much," said one white-haired old man at Los Angeles's recent 188th birthday party at the Hollywood Bowl. "He'll do a better job for me than the other guy keeping down crime and taxes."

Yorty is an interesting case history in the shifting course of Middle America's mainstream. During the 1930s, he was a New Deal liberal, espousing such progressive programs as a 30-hour workweek. In the '40s, he took up the cause of zealous anti-Communism, and now he is sounding the alarms of law and order. He is no political newcomer—he has been running for office ever since 1936— but today's disgruntled voters seem willing to reward the old pros provided they step to the new beat.

More often, however, Middle America is turning to new political faces, even when they don't look exactly like the one in the mirror. Its latest champion, S.I. Hayakawa, the feisty little professor of English who is now president of San Francisco State College, is not by nature a man of the people. "I've been, all my life, the kind of intellectual highbrow I disapprove of," he admits. But his uncompromising suppression of radical disruption at San Francisco State last fall suddenly vaulted him into political prominence: he began being mentioned as a possible opponent next year of Republican Sen. George Murphy, he started a statewide round of speech-making, and a recent Field Poll gave him a higher popularity rating than either San Francisco Mayor Joseph Alioto or California's former Democratic Assembly Speaker Jesse Unruh.

The yawning gap between the intellectual and the common man, between the governors and the governed, lies at the heart of the New Populism, and one of the first to discern it was Louise Day Hicks of Boston. A 50-year-old attorney from the predominantly Irish wards of South Boston, she pitched her 1967 mayoral campaign toward "the forgotten man," stressed the school-busing issue —and very nearly won. "I represented the alienated voter," she said last week in the midst of her new City Council campaign, "and that's who I'm representing now, except that the number has grown." Busing is no longer her main issue— some of her liberal opponents, in fact, now agree with her that the state busing law is unworkable. Now she concentrates her fire on higher taxes, declining municipal services and a government that, she contends, "is only concerned about the rich and the poor" and not about the man in the middle who pays the bills.

"The only thing saving this country," Mrs. Hicks says, "is the affluence that the middle class is feeling. But they don't realize the purchasing power is gone. When they do realize that, we're in for real trouble. There'll be a revolt—not violence, because the American people won't resort to violence, but they are going to speak up in a way to be heard."

In fact, they are already speaking up, and there is no reason to believe that November's elections will show a muting of their voices. "These people today are in revolt," warns Chicago Congressman Roman Pucinski. What's more, the middle class has become keenly aware of its political muscle and how to apply it. "The public is so much smarter than when I first started in politics," marvels Ken O'Donnell, JFK's special assistant who is running for the 1970 Democratic nomination for governor of Massachusetts. "Then it was no issues: just vote Democratic, vote Republican, and how to help your friends. What Gene McCarthy did was open the eyes of the people that they are the country. Before, it had been assumed that you couldn't bring a President down, that you couldn't fight the system. The McCarthy movement showed that you could do it after all."

The New Populism, as a matter of fact, seems to some analysts part of the same phenomenon as the New Politics. Eugene McCarthy and Robert Kennedy were trying to achieve on a national scale essentially the same goal that Charlie Stenvig and Louise Day Hicks have set on the municipal level: to bring new faces and new forces into play in the political arena, to mobilize the amateurs against the political pros, to return power to people whose interests and whose voices, they believed, had been too long ignored. Of course, the McCarthy-Kennedy movement was headed in a liberal direction, while the New Populism is exhibiting a rightward bent. And the fact is that several of its new champions seem to be helping to foment, not just reflect, the public's bitterness. Still, the two movements share some common impulses, which may explain the startling number of voters who felt a kinship with both Bobby Kennedy and George Wallace during last year's campaign.

It is still much too soon to say how long the New Populism may last or what direction it may take. It has cast itself loose from the traditional political parties, neither one of which seems to hold its favor, and it has lost faith in the programs and pieties of traditional liberalism. As George Wallace puts it, "The great pointy heads who knew best how to run everybody's life have had their day." Frustrated, fearful and confused, Middle America is stirring itself to seek out new pathways, and the nation has already begun to reverberate with the commotion of its search.

QUESTIONS FOR DISCUSSION AND DIALOGUE

1. How can politicians practicing the "New Populism" make an appeal to Americans who are saying, "Lookit, we're sick of you politicians?"
2. Does this article give you more or less confidence in "democracy?" Discuss.
3. What kind of difference do you think there is between an American who would support Tony Imperiale of Newark and Charlie Stenvig of Minneapolis? Is this an important difference? Discuss.
4. Compare and contrast the "New Politics" of Eugene McCarthy and Robert Kennedy and the "New Populism" of George Wallace and Charlie Stenvig.
5. After reflecting back over the articles in this chapter on the Americans, develop a written or oral statement about the prevailing politically related mood of "The Americans in the early 1970's."

CHAPTER TWO

The Students

In Chapter One the reader was introduced to the Americans in somewhat broad, general terms. There were some specific groups singled out, but the emphasis was on relatively large groupings. Here the reader is offered a specific group of Americans for a more detailed study and understanding.

The views of many students about "the corrupt draft system" are explored by Stewart Alsop's article. *Newsweek* considers " 'A Whole New Minority Group' " represented by the some 400,000 young people in attendance at the Woodstock Music and Art Fair whose goal of relating to each other seems a far cry from the "work ethic" which is so much a characteristic of most of the non-young Americans. A different kind of "revolutionary," James Kunen, is described by Henry S. Resnik in reviewing Kunen's book, *The Strawberry Statement: Notes of a College Revolutionary.* Leo Rosten offers colorful advice and criticism for an "angry young man" and an "angry old man." A special section of *The Chronicle of Higher Education* offers the observation by S. I. Hayakawa that "Alienation Is Being Taught by Professors." George Wald, a famous Harvard biology professor, states in a speech that he thinks he knows what is bothering students—they are not sure they have a future, and he advises that if the United States does not drastically alter its ways we might not have a future. The three concluding articles by Edgar Z. Friedenberg, K. Ross Toole, and Kenneth Keniston give different interpretations of the Students.

Does this study of one select and especially significant group of Americans —the Students—leave us with optimism or pessimism about American politics? Students of politics might well find reasons for both conclusions.

Yale Revisited

Stewart Alsop

Mr. Alsop, though tempted to dismiss the Yale students he has observed as "young jerks terrified of the draft (who were) Spocked when they should have been spanked," discerns very real cause for their dissent in the unfair draft system.

Kingman Brewster, president of Yale, addressing a mass rally of students on a proposal to banish the Yale ROTC: "I happen to respect and even admire those who serve their country in the military services."

Yale students: "BOOOOO!"

Old Blue, scribbling furiously in his notebook: "Young jerks terrified of the draft. Spocked when they should have been spanked."

The Old Blue in question was this reporter, who had returned to the scenes of his youth to try to understand something of what the current campus uproar is all about. Later, after talks with President Brewster, deans and professors, and a fair sampling of the "young jerks," another, less Pavlovian note was scribbled in the notebook:

"Collectively, these kids are not very attractive, with their attitudinizing and their inadequately fertilized facial shrubbery. But individually, they have a genuine idealism, a sort of searching innocence, and also a kind of good-hearted nuttiness which is very appealing. There's something going on here our generation will never understand. But understanding begins, though it does not end, with the draft."

National Disaster

Kingman Brewster considers the present draft system, with its blatant inequities and its built-in invitation to legal cheating, a national disaster. Every boy in Yale knows two things—that young men of his age, less privileged or intelligent, are getting shot at and sometimes killed; and that if he is agile, he can probably escape the draft and certainly escape getting shot at. This knowledge is inherently corrupting.

One way to escape the draft is to hide, in Brewster's phrase, in the "labyrinths of higher education." After the mass rally, I met three leaders of Yale's militant left, intelligent and idealistic young men, who were hiding in the labyrinths.

They were in the Yale Divinity School. One was studying "New Left politics," another "the causes of campus unrest," and a third "revolution and theology." "You create your own curriculum," one explained. Did they mean to take orders, then? The question surprised them—no, they said, the divinity school was a way to avoid being drafted. But didn't this make them feel a bit guilty? There was a pause, and then one of them said that of course it did.

A lot of Yale boys are seriously thinking of refusing induction and going to jail, as the only honorable alternative to the draft. Tim Bates, an editor of the Yale Daily News (now largely captured by the campus left) is one of these. Bates, an intelligent young man, is articulate and even moving about the failings of American society. But his chief concern, quite naturally, is his own future. It is a "terrible responsibility," he says, to have to decide "whether to go to jail or to shoot and get shot at in a stupid war."

Corrupt Society

Tom Gerety, a leader of the New Left who looks like a beardless Saint Francis, has already decided—rather than compromise with a corrupt society, he says, he will go to jail. Gerety's conversation is mostly the standard New Left jargon, but I found him an oddly impressive young man. He comes from a deeply religious family—his uncle is a Catholic bishop—and his spiritual forebears are clearly the early Christian martyrs. Like them, he may be foolish, but he is not a coward.

The need among those who escape the draft to prove that they are not physical cowards may have a lot to do with campus violence. The draft and the Vietnam war combined have made patriotism itself suspect among the young, as those boos for Brewster suggest. On the Yale campus, no one argues about the war any more—it is simply "stupid," or, more often, "vile."

Hatred of the draft feeds hatred of the war, and vice versa. But the process does not end there. For in the youthful syllogism, only a vile government and a vile system could produce a vile draft and a vile war. The syllogism largely accounts for the fact that the Yale campus, like campuses all over the country, is far more radical today, in a period of great prosperity, than it was in the depths of the Depression.

There are other factors in the equation, of course. The reverse discrimination of the admissions systems at Yale, as elsewhere, has transformed the student body from a closed society of the privileged and complacent to a closed society of the bright and dissatisfied. The cheerful prep-school boys in tweed coats with C averages who once dominated the Yale campus have been replaced by brilliant high-school radicals with scraggly beards.

At the same time the power to suspend or dismiss, once exercised by hard-eyed deans, has been taken over by unwieldy faculty committees. The faculty has its share, and more, of fashionable Marxists and of the kind of liberal who wants to curry favor with the dominant leftist students. "The faculty is a little scared of us," says Jerry Adler, a brilliant "conservative" student. The result, he says, is a "do-your-own-thing college," lacking discipline and "moral and spiritual guidance."

Under the circumstances, it is really rather surprising that Yale, unlike Harvard, Cornell and other Ivy League colleges, has not "blown." The main reason is Kingman Brewster. After the Harvard blowup, Brewster warned that "violent intimidation" would be met by "interim suspension," and he implied that, if the faculty did not back him up, he would resign forthwith. He even appalled the more timid members of the faculty by passing the word that, if the militants stormed his office, he would do his best to distribute a few bloody noses, and he expected the faculty to behave likewise. This basic toughness has been matched by what Brewster calls "resilient response."

Gigantic Fraud

The militants angrily call Brewster a "co-opter"—meaning that he has co-opted their best issues. Required courses, required class attendance, course marking and "parietal supervision" (meaning girls in rooms) have been dropped, while "do-your-own-thing courses" on topics like "radical thought," a black-studies program and—above all—immediate coeducation, have all been approved by Brewster.

To many Old Blues, Brewster's response has seemed much too resilient. But you have to smell the atmosphere of Yale to understand what he has been up against—and what, for that matter, the United States is up against. What the United States is up against is a whole generation of its brightest and best-educated young men, who are sourly convinced that the American system is a gigantic fraud. That conviction derives as much from a fraudulent and corrupting system of military recruitment as from a tragic war.

QUESTIONS FOR DISCUSSION AND DIALOGUE

1. Do you see any significance for most of the Americans and for the students in particular to Alsop's "Pavlovian" response contrasted to his "less Pavlovian" response? Discuss.
2. Do you agree that those who escape the draft by going to college are sometimes inclined toward campus violence to prove they are not physical cowards? Discuss.
3. What is so "vile" about the draft in the minds of many college students?

'A Whole New Minority Group'

Newsweek

In the late summer of 1969, approximately 400,000 members of the rock generation assembled in White Lake, New York, at the "Woodstock Music & Art Fair, An Aquarian Exposition." As the *Newsweek* article indicates, this was indeed an unusual group. Perhaps the temptation to write it off as a bizarre, but politically irrelevant event should be overcome, even if, as Abbie Hoffman said, "Most of these kids don't really think in political terms ... more and more, you've got to talk about magic." Politicians can both promise "magic" and appeal to the fear stirred up by those who practice magic!

The last sweet-scented wisps of marijuana smoke dissipated in a freshening breeze out of the Catskill Mountains. The few remaining nakeds sadly put on their clothes—all but one young man whom police found hiking homeward in the buff. Cars, campers, microbuses, U-Haul trucks and columns of plodding youngsters clogged the roads out of tiny White Lake, N. Y. The half-moon hillside on Max Yasgur's dairy farm lay under a miry blanket of Coke cans, Gallo jugs, sandwich wrappers, mud-stiffened pants and blankets and sleeping bags—the detritus left behind by 400,000 of the rock generation after their biggest turn-on ever. An electric pot dream called the Woodstock Music & Art Fair, An Aquarian Exposition (*Newsweek,* Aug. 25), had—to its own apparent surprise—not only come true but survived to a more or less happy ending. Now that it was over, blues queen Janis Joplin said for all of the Aquarians: "There's lots and lots and lots of us, more than anybody ever thought before. We used to think of ourselves as little clumps of weirdos. But now we're a whole new minority group."

And so they were. It was not easy for over-30 America finally to judge whether Woodstock was an act of revolution or merely a picnic—whether it more closely resembled Chicago without the politics or Fort Lauderdale with marijuana and LSD instead of beer. The most probable answer was that there were elements of both. Four hundred thousand of the nation's affluent white young had for three days encamped in the alfalfa, grooved on acid-rock anthems they could hardly hear, smoked and sniffed and popped illegal drugs, shucked their clothes, blown their minds, dug each other, coexisted with cops and grown-ups—and put on a show of numbers and spirit that their elders could ill ignore. They did it all passively, enduring rain, wind, mud, bad trips, short rations, flooded field toilets, blistered feet, paralyzed traffic, foul smells and miscellaneous other tortures more exquisite than anything the Establishment has yet thrown at most of them. Yet their presence alone could be—and was—read as their judgment on straight America.

Reading It:

But how to read it? Woodstock as an event in U.S. social history was surely less cosmic than it looked to beat poet Allen Ginsberg (who called it "a major planetary event") and less revolutionary than it seemed to the Yippies' Abbie Hoffman (who saw in it "the birth of the Woodstock Nation and the death of the American dinosaur"). Yet adult America correctly saw something gently, amiably and profoundly subversive in it all. Sociologists pondered it. Editorial writers puzzled over it. *The New York Times* one morning called it "a nightmare of mud and stagnation," slept on that judgment overnight, then decided next day that it had been something like "the Tulipmania or the Children's Crusade ... essentially a phenomenon of innocence." Pundit Max Lerner commended it to historians as an event in "a cultural, not a political, revolution"—but a revolution nonetheless.

"Some of the festival-goers," reported *Newsweek's* John Garabedian after four days of watching the camp-in, "were fairly straight college kids—future business executives and accountants. But the lesson of Woodstock is that the hippie population of the U.S. has grown incredibly (and invisibly) and that, today, far more kids than anyone thought have a more radical vision about the American way of life than most of us imagined. They form a new constituency whose views go beyond the anger that produces picket lines and reform drives in Congress to the turned-on indifference that sets them questing after tangerine trees and marmalade skies. Most of these kids don't really think in political terms. 'It's hard to reach them, Abbie Hoffman once told me. 'More and more you've got to talk about magic.' Most came to White Lake for more personal reasons—getting high, going out of your head, being swept up by music, looking for ecstasy, enjoying the drug and electrically amplified *now.* That is closer to religion than to politics —an effort to put meaning into life."

Into the Red:

Not even the festival's promoters realized how many converts that religion has enlisted. "We were sitting around stoned one night last fall," said co-producer Mike Lang, 24, an NYU business-administration dropout known for his teased-out curls as Orphan Annie, "and then all of a sudden it was gonna happen." Lang and a pal, Artie Kornfeld, 26, were put in touch with Pycope-Polident heir John Roberts, 24, and a Long Island dentist's son, Joel Rosenman, 26, both well-fixed kids looking for something creative to spend their money on. Woodstock, N.Y., sent their partnership packing with a name but not a site, and they finally found a taker in White Lake—partly on assurances by one of their advance men that the festival would probably draw about 5,000 people a day. The promoters were actually planning on 120,000—a disastrous miscalculation that, in the event, left them woefully undersupplied and undermanned, turned tickets into worthless paper, brought the festival nearly to a ruin and plunged the venture into the red by a claimed $1 million. "I don't feel we've actually made mistakes," Kornfeld

said afterward. Not even the crowd estimate? "That mistake," he confessed,
" . . . was a mistake."

Yet the wonder of Woodstock was that it somehow survived all its mistakes.
For three days, the kids constituted the third-biggest community in New York
State, and, whatever the larger lessons of the experience, it did make some
discernible points:

*Drug laws become meaningless when the rock generation gets together in
sufficient numbers.* So pervasive was pot at White Lake, one youngster said "you
can get high just breathing," and 400 of the Aquarians were treated for bad LSD
trips. Sellers hawked their wares openly: "Grass, acid, mescaline . . . Grass, acid,
mescaline . . . " (Replied a freaked-out hippie: "Pears, carrots, avocados . . .
Pears, carrots, avocados . . . ") Police did collar a few of the most flagrant pushers,
but mostly they stood by and watched.

The rock generation can get along fine with the police—on its own terms.
"Police don't keep people from doing what they really want to do," said the
festival's security chief, Wes Pomeroy, 49, a veteran California and Federal
lawman. So they elected not to try; the hippies were allowed to do their things
unmolested, whether or not their things happened to be legal, and as a consequence the few feeble attempts by radical activists to provoke a confrontation got
nowhere. That the youngsters came in peace was attested by the medical statistics
alone: three deaths (by a drug overdose, a burst appendix, a tractor accident), two
births, 5,000 miscellaneous casualties ranging from cut feet to a skull fracture—
but no black eyes, bloody noses or other wounds of war. "I've never seen that
many people in so small an area act so peacefully," said Beverly Hills, Calif.,
police chief Joseph Kimble, who came as an observer and wound up conscripted
for duty as a security supervisor. "I found there's no correlation between a
clean-shaven cheek and morality—and there's no correlation between long hair
and immorality."

*Not all of over-30 America is implacably hostile to the rock generation's
thing.* The Aquarians did leave some hard feelings around White Lake, particularly on neighboring farms where chilled and hungry strays from Yasgur's place
pilfered vegetables, uprooted fence posts for firewood and improvised latrines.
Yet some of the warmth of the celebrants spread to the community and was
reciprocated. During the worst of Woodstock's travail, townspeople in nearby
Monticello organized clinics and put together 30,000 sandwiches to feed the
festival's hungry. "People say, 'Why are you getting thick with this crummy
bunch?' " said one farm wife. "Well, what should we do—hate them because
everybody else does?" Echoed a contractor: "This is a community builder. Next
year when you see the U.S. map, you'll see White Lake biggest of all."

It would certainly be written large on maps of hip America. The festival was
a disappointment to political activists who remembered the confrontations on the
steps of the Pentagon in 1967, in the streets of Chicago in 1968 and around
People's Park in Berkeley this year. Woodstock belonged instead in another,
parallel tradition born in San Francisco and the Monterey Pop Festival of 1967
—the first of the great tribal feasts celebrating the culture of rock, drugs and love

as an end in itself. Woodstock marked a turning inward not unlike the impulse that produced the beat generation of the Eisenhower '50s—a retreat by the young from politics into the sanctuary of their youth and their senses.

Yet it may prove to be a revolutionary happening indeed. Not even the most turned-on of the rock generation imagined that Woodstock would change the prevailing American antipathy to the pot culture—not enough, certainly, to lead to a relaxation of current drug laws. Yet the 400,000 Aquarians by their very presence certified that there are indeed lots and lots of them—not enough to conquer America (or even to seduce it) but perhaps enough to flavor the American life style. And few among them thought Woodstock would be the biggest very long. "I wish I could rent Utah," sighed hip Hollywood promoter Lou Adler. "You could fill any place with young people who want to relate to each other."

QUESTIONS FOR DISCUSSION AND DIALOGUE

1. What is your reaction to this statement from the article? " . . . the hippies were allowed to do their things unmolested, whether or not their things happened to be legal, and as a consequence the few feeble attempts by radical activists to provoke a confrontation got nowhere." Discuss.
2. Is there a political significance to this Woodstock "happening?" Discuss.

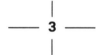

The Revolution Biz

Henry S. Resnik

In his book review and commentary on *The Strawberry Statement* by James Simon Kunen, Henry S. Resnik analyzes this "revolutionary" who is also "A contemporary Holden Caulfield, with strong overtones of Huck Finn . . . " Resnik's conclusions are more optimistic than pessimistic, but he has some important reservations about Kunen's "ability to join the action without a moment's thought."

In the spring and fall of 1968, nineteen-year-old James Simon Kunen was an undergraduate at Columbia College and a major participant in the political action that shattered the university and also forced a debate about the entire structure of American society. Strongly sympathetic to the goals of Columbia SDS, Kunen was even among the select few who occupied the office of university President Grayson Kirk. One thing led to another: Kunen wrote articles about Columbia for *New York* magazine, at first under a pseudonym, then openly; he went on radio and TV; finally, he became a more or less full-time revolutionary journalist writing a book about being a revolutionary journalist. *The Strawberry Statement* beautifully shows that being where-it's-at just about all the time can amount to a hell of an exciting education.

Liberals and moderates in major establishments throughout the country are going to like James Kunen and his book, for he is quite the antithesis of the obscenity-spouting revolutionary they are used to hearing about. Kunen is remarkably sane, level-headed, perceptive, thoughtful, and—somehow it is palpable in his book—clean. A contemporary Holden Caulfield, with strong overtones of Huck Finn, he was pretty much minding his own business, rowing crew with the jocks, and wondering about all the big questions of life as only a sensitive, literate graduate of Andover can, when the Columbia crisis erupted. Then suddenly a new kind of pop hero emerged from the din—Holden and Huck could link arms with Mark Rudd and march bravely into the uncertain future, at least confident of an audience. Kunen had found his moment, his medium, and an effective identity; he gave up crew after a while (he had left Kirk's office to attend practice one day) and began to spend a good deal of his time at political meetings, but he stayed clean. He even worked for McCarthy.

Like so many well informed college students today, Kunen cannot abide the injustices of American society. He is against the Vietnam war, racism, poverty, the destruction of the natural environment, and all the lesser evils perpetuated by a vast and brutal imbalance of power. It would be a mistake to base observations about his "generation" on this book, but he, for one, is willing to accept the American system if it can only show a sign of humanity. It is because of this willingness to accept change within the system that the liberals and moderates will find him such a tremendously appealing fantasy-archetype. Insisting throughout the book that he is opposed to violence, proving with his very style that he prefers rationality to ranting, Kunen will give hope to those who fear that an entire generation has lost its mind.

This is not to say, however, that Kunen doesn't support his convictions with action. He has a kind of cold-blooded fearlessness—spontaneous and unthinking, in contrast with his usual attitude of reflection—that the most ardent revolutionaries could well admire. Leaping to attack the hated fence that separates the Columbia gym from Morningside Park, dashing through barricades of angry jocks, or resisting the assaults of the Tactical Police Force, New York's special riot detachment, Kunen is as resolutely determined as the most uncouth of his confreres. There is something almost frightening, in fact, about his ability to join the action without a moment's thought. ("I am not privy to the secrets of my mind," he writes, recalling a peace demonstration in Times Square, "but for some reason at this particular juncture I was not afraid and jumped into the fray.") These actions may represent the vision of McLuhan in full flower—a sort of lust for participation—and in this respect the Kunen-archetype is anything but reassuring; thousands of James Kunens out for an afternoon's involvement could touch off a series of incredible disasters, their good intentions notwithstanding. But Kunen's occasional penchant for violence is sharply muted by the general tone of the book.

Kunen describes the wild factionalism of an SDS meeting, for example, with such clarity and objectivity that the result is flat, ironic distance. He continually discovers, pursuing his role of journalist-covering-the-revolution, that he *likes* his enemies when he confronts them for probing interviews. He is unconvinced that any of his fellow revolutionaries have come up with a workable program for social change, and in presenting a wide range of viewpoints, he blunts the case for any of them. Kunen is for revolution, all right, but although he is no more able than any other commentator to make sense of the incessant revolutionary babble, he will not accept a program of mindless destruction.

Moreover, the book is laced with a dry wit and humor that would have done Huck and Holden proud. During a phone call to his mother, for example:

For ten minutes we exchange mother-talk and revolutionary rhetoric. She points out that neither Gandhi nor Thoreau would have asked for amnesty. I admit I haven't read them. But Gandhi had no Gandhi to read and Thoreau hadn't read Thoreau. They had to reach their own conclusions and so will I.

Or commenting on the significance of long hair:

But as for bad vibrations emanating from my follicles, I say great. I want the cops to sneer and the old ladies swear and the businessmen worry. I want everyone to see me and say "There goes an enemy of the state," because that's where I'm at, as we say in the Revolution biz.

This superabundance of clever charm finally makes Kunen's revolutionary activities seem like just so much fun and games; one begins to wonder if even he knows the difference.

In truth, Kunen does not have his heart in revolution, however daring his revolutionary gestures. He is bitter, frustrated, and morally outraged, but the most pervasive evils of American society are too big and too boring for him. Once the action is over at Columbia and the basic points have been made, *The Straw-berry Statement* bogs down in repetitive diatribes against such mundane inevitabilities as advertising, cigarette manufacturers, the hypocrisy of organized religion, and the teen-music business. Kunen pretends to know the reality of social injustice and bloodshed, but finally such statements as "When I see statistics I practically throw up" and "Wars are silly," seem the merest collegiate palaver.

Like so many of the middle-class activists, Kunen simply cannot work up enough anger to get himself past his comfortable moderation. Realizing this, he even singles out a passage at one point for a savage outburst filled with obscenities, prefacing it with, "Reading over the book I fear I'm giving the impression that I'm hanging loose and bemused and don't overly care about anything. Well, how's this . . . " But when the anger does emerge, in this book at least, it's unconvincing.

One of the most incisive passages in *The Strawberry Statement* clearly indicates why those who agree with James Kunen will be much more willing to accept the patterns of history than to create them. Striking up a conversation with a perceptive girl in a restaurant one morning, Kunen gets to discussing the future and finally concludes: "We're the bridge generation. . . . We're the product of all the past and we'll determine all the future. . . . It's exciting. It's a challenge. It's up to us to keep future people human, assuming that's desirable." Here Kunen's usual irresolution vanishes; *The Strawberry Statement,* with its constant explanation of what "we youth" think about and its sophisticated, aloof coverage of the campus scene, resolves itself into a document addressed mainly to that older generation which could not possibly experience what it is like to be a college student in 1968 at firsthand. It is an attempt to explain where the "college generation" is "at," in the author's view, and in so doing to bridge chasms everywhere. More than a revolutionary outcry and a threat of violence to come, *The Strawberry Statement* is a desperate plea that the last vestiges of humanity be salvaged from a disintegrating society, that the generations and races live together in peace and harmony—but the plea cannot be made without the defensive snicker of one too often disillusioned: " . . . assuming that's desirable."

The source of the book's title—the public utterance of a Columbia dean in the early stages of the crisis—suggests why there is so little optimism:

"A university is definitely not a democratic institution," Professor Deane began. "When decisions begin to be made democratically around here, I will not be here any longer." Commenting on the importance of student opinion to the administration, Professor Deane declared, "Whether students vote 'yes' or 'no' on an issue is like telling me they like strawberries."

In the light of such attitudes—no doubt prevalent in high places, though rarely presented so unequivocally—a single individual's struggle for human dignity in a mass society that is just beginning to meet its practical and moral needs can only move us. There is something awful and sad about Kunen's last words on the matter, but they are a tacit admission of how little choice, how little power, he really has: "Since the First Republic of the United States is one hundred ninety-two years old and I am nineteen," he writes, "I will give it one more chance."

QUESTIONS FOR DISCUSSION AND DIALOGUE

1. Discuss the difference between the James Kunen that liberals and moderates can admire, and the Kunen who "is anything but reassuring," as Resnik describes him.
2. What kinds of appeals would a politician need to make to students like James Kunen? What would be the effect of such appeals on the majority of the Americans? See the article in Chapter One, "In Politics, It's the New Populism." Can you imagine a politician with an appeal to both groups? Discuss.
3. Resnik says the following statements by Kunen "seem the merest collegiate palaver": "When I see statistics, I practically throw up." "Wars are silly." What does Resnik mean? What does Kunen mean? With whom do you agree? Why?

To an Angry Young Man

Leo Rosten

Leo Rosten offers a no-holds barred polemic against "an angry young man." If the reader is tempted toward an intense reaction after reading this "letter," he might hold it in reserve until reading Rosten's letter "To An Angry Old Man" in the following article!

To an Angry Young Man

I HAVE BEEN GETTING lusty cheers and jeers for a rueful little paragraph I recently wrote about student riots. The most eloquent (and savage) letter ended: "Drop dead!!!" Another diatribe was signed "Columbia Senior." I wish I knew where to send this reply to both:

Dear (?!) Sir:

It will upset you to learn that I agree with many things you said. For instance: "Don't question our sincerity!" I don't. You are about as sincere as anyone can be. You are sincerely unhappy, sincerely frustrated and sincerely confused. You are also sincerely wrong about the few facts you cite, and sincerely illogical in the violent conclusions you reach. Besides, what does "sincerity" have to do with issues? Any insane asylum is full of sincere patients. Hitler was undoubtedly sincere. So are the followers of Voliva, who think the world is sincerely flat.

I sadly agree that your college courses have been "outrageously irrelevant to the times"—because your letter reveals that you could not pass a freshman exam in at least three fields in which you pass such sweeping judgments: economics, history, political theory.

You say, "Destroy a system that has not abolished unemployment, exploitation and war!" By the same reasoning, you should blow up all hospitals (and perhaps execute all doctors, biologists and researchers): they have not abolished disease.

Before you destroy a system, propose another that will solve (not hide, shift or disguise) unemployment, "exploitation," war. Anyone can promise Utopia—without specifying a program. Tom Hayden, idol of the New Left, has said: "First we'll make the revolution—then we'll find out what for." Would you employ a plumber who rips out all the pipes in your house before he learned how to repair a leak?

You say, "The mass media are not telling us the truth." Then how and from whom did you learn the "evils" you correctly deplore? After all, your information comes from one or another organ of—the mass media.

"This society is only interested in higher prices and profits!" You apparently do not understand this society, or a society, or the function of prices (and profits) in any economy. Has it never occurred to you that the marketplace is a polling booth? That buying is voting? That no economic system is possible without some form of pricing, without some measure of efficacy or worth? Has it never occurred to you that profits are a form of proof (that something gives satisfaction to those who pay for it)? Perhaps you should examine the public uses that we make of private profits—through taxation.

The countries that follow your platitude, "production for use," without exception produce far less for their people to enjoy, of much shoddier quality, at much higher prices (measured by the hours of work needed to buy something). Don't you know that "Socialist" countries are smuggling "capitalist" incentives into their systems? Has it not dawned on you that wherever and whenever there is no free market, there is no free thought, no free art, no free politics, no free life?

You rage against "a heartless country in which the poor get poorer." Alas, poor Yoricks: The decline in poverty in the U. S. is among the more astonishing and hopeful facts of human history. (In 1900, about 90% of our population was poor; in 1920—50%; in 1930—34%; in 1968—15%). You will cry that 15% is outrageous. Agreed. The question is: How best abolish it? (A negative income tax makes more sense than anything your colleagues propose.)

"The middle class exploits the unemployed." Please examine that cliche. Would the middle class be worse off or better off if all the unemployed magically disappeared? Obviously, much better off: Think of the enormous saving in taxes, the enormous improvement in public services, the enormous benefits from refocused energies now used to ameliorate poverty's abominable toll.

You say your generation "wants to be understood." Well, so does mine. How much have you tried to understand others? You pillory us for injustices not of our making, frictions not of our choice, dilemmas that history (or our forebears or the sheer intractability of events) presented to us. You say we "failed" because you face so many awful problems. Will you then accept the blame for all the problems that exist (and they will) when you are 20 years older? And how do you know that all problems are soluble? Or soluble swiftly? Or soluble peacefully? Or soluble, given the never-infinite resources, brains and experience any generation is endowed with?

I say that you are failing us—in failing to learn and respect discomforting facts; in failing to learn how to think (it is easier to complain); in using violence to shut down colleges; in shamefully denying the freedom of others to study and to teach; in barbarously slandering and abusing and shouting down those who disagree with you; in looting, stealing and defiling; in failing to see how much more complicated social problems are than you blindly assume; in acting out of an ignorance for which idealism is no excuse, and a hysteria for which youth is no defense. "Understanding"? You don't even understand that when you call me a "mother---" you are projecting your unresolved incestuous wishes onto me. The technical name for such projection, in advanced form, is paranoia.

Again and again, you say, "the American people want" or "demand" or "insist." How do you know? Every poll I have seen puts your position in a minority. You just say, "the American people demand"—then add whatever you prefer. This is intellectually sloppy at best, and corrupt at worst.

You want to "wreck this slow, inefficient democratic system." It took the human race centuries of thought and pain and suffering and hard experiment to devise it. Democracy is not a "state" but a process; it is a way of solving human problems, a way of hobbling power, a way of protecting every minority from the awful, fatal tyranny of either the few or the many.

Whatever its imperfections, democracy is the only system man has discovered that makes possible change without violence. Do you really prefer bloodshed to debate? Quick dictates to slow law? This democracy made possible a great revolution in the past 35 years (a profound transfer of power, a distribution of wealth, an improvement of living and health) without "liquidating" millions, without suppressing free speech, without the obscenities of dogma enforced by terror.

This "slow, inefficient" system protects people like me against people like you; and (though you don't realize it) protects innocents like you against those "reactionary . . . fascist forces" you fear: They, like you, prefer "action to talk." As for "security"—at what price? The most "secure" of human institutions is a prison; would you choose to live in one?

You want "a society in which the young speak their minds against the Establishment." Where have the young more freely, recklessly and intransigently attacked "the Establishment"? (Every political order has one.) Wherever "our heroes—Marx, Mao, Che" have prevailed, students, writers, teachers, scientists have been punished with hard labor or death—for what? For their opinions. Where but in "fake democracies" are mass demonstrations possible, or your bitter (and legitimate) dissent televised?

You rail against "leaders crazed with power," who "deceive the people." Your leaders are self-dramatizers who demand that power, which would craze them, and they deceive you in not telling you how they plan your "confrontations"—to force the police, whose excesses I hate more than you do, to use force. I, unlike you, want no one put "up against the wall." No "cheap politician" more cynically deceived you than fanatical militants did—and will. Your support feeds their neurotic (because extremist) needs. Washington's " 'Non-Violent' Coordinating Committee" has engaged in gunfire for three days as I write this.

You say Marcuse "shows that capitalist freedom actually enslaves." (He doesn't "show"—he only says.) He certainly does not sound enslaved. And does mouthing fragments of 19th-century ideology (Marx, Bakunin) really liberate? And is not Marcuse 40 years "older than 30," your cutoff on credibility? Incidentally, would you trust your life to a surgeon under 30—who never finished medical school?

Your irrationality makes me wonder how you were ever admitted into Columbia. You confuse rhetoric with reasoning. Assertions are not facts. Passion is no substitute for knowledge. Slogans are not solutions. Your idealism takes no brains. And when you dismiss our differences with contempt, you become contemptible.

Very Sincerely yours,
LEO ROSTEN

P. S. Please don't take any more courses in sociology, which seduces the immature into thinking they understand a problem if they discuss it in polysyllables. Jargon is not insight. Vocabulary is the opiate of radicals.

QUESTIONS FOR DISCUSSION AND DIALOGUE

1. Outline Rosten's criticisms of this kind of "Angry Young Man". With which do you agree and disagree?
2. Do you think Rosten means what he says in his postscript or is it a "put on"? Discuss.

—— 5 ——

To an Angry Old Man

Leo Rosten

Rosten, in this article, turns his concern from the "Angry Young Man" of the left—to the "Angry Old Man" of the right. As he indicates in his brief preface, his purpose is to defend rationality and democracy and he is not worried whether this might play into the hands of the right or of the left.

To An Angry Old Man

I COULD MASSAGE your heartstrings or curl your hair, depending on your politics, by quoting from the torrential reaction (laudatory, furious, flattering, venomous) to my evangelical letter "To an Angry Young Man" (LOOK, November 12, 1968). Before it was printed, a friend urged me to soften my stand, saying, "It may play into the hands of the Right!" And of the sermon you are about to read, others may say, "It will play into the hands of the Left!"

Both positions seem to me indefensible. Surely, the validity of an idea has nothing to do with who agrees or disagrees with it. To censor the expression of your thinking because of whom it may please or displease is simply to let others do your thinking for you. I detest thought control. Here, "sans" apology, is my answer to some overheated letter writers from the Right.
Dear Mr. X:

Thank you for writing—and that's about all the thanks you'll get from me. You say, "Let's throw all these young rebels out of college!" Over my dead body. Free speech does not stop at the gates of a campus. On the contrary, it should find a special sanctuary there, for it is indispensable to the search for truth. A student has a perfect right to protest, picket, petition, dissent. When students riot, set fires, throw rocks, stop others from attending classes, use bullhorns to disrupt the peace—they are acting not as students but as hoodlums. Let the law attend to them—the swifter the better.

But you want students "thrown out" simply for protesting, which is what the

Communists and Fascists do—from Russia to Spain, China to Cuba. They expel, intimidate or imprison those who question or complain. Don't emulate them.

You say, "Draft these college punks into the Army and let our GI's knock sense into their heads!" You horrify me. I don't want anyone to "knock sense" into anyone's head. To put the point sharply, I quote a great jurist: "Your freedom to move your fist ends at the point where my nose begins." I have a long nose.

As for the draft: I consider the present draft impractical, unnecessary and morally indefensible (it would take more than this page to explain why). The young have every right to speak, petition and argue against it (this has nothing to do with Vietnam)—peacefully.

"Why let these creeps wear stinking clothes and beards? Line them up, hold them down, bathe them, shave them, wash out their mouths with soap!!" I loathe your bullyboy views more than their childish flight into dirtiness. Kooky clothes break no laws (though courts have ruled on schoolboard regulations governing dress, hair, etc.). Young slobs pollute the nearby air—but the courts have not yet ruled on that.

The defiant cultivation of filth is, of course, a clinical sign of psychological disturbance. I feel sorry for the kids who cannot know the psychological price they will pay for regressing to the anal level. But your excessive response to the dirty is as distasteful to me as their sad glorification of discomfort disguised as "freedom."

You praise me for "speaking out for those students who are not newsworthy because they don't riot" and add: "Defend our wonderful Establishment!" Well, the only Establishment I defend is the one called Reason. I find violence abhorrent, fanaticism disgusting, and demagoguery unspeakable. The terrorist tactics of adolescents may parade as "idealism," but they shatter that consensus of civility that is the very heart of a civilization. Your blind veneration of the status quo cannot help us solve problems that must and can be solved—by intelligence, not force.

You ask, "What do students have to be so unhappy about in our colleges?" A great deal: gargantuan classes and bursting dormitories; professors who hate teaching because it interferes with their research; educator-bureaucrats who reward the publication of trivia much more than dedication to students and teaching; academic tenure, which encourages some pedants to "goof off" in lectures and subsidizes others to indulge their non-academic hobbies.

But this does not mean we should turn our colleges over to self-dramatizing militants whose most conspicuous talent is a capacity to over-simplify problems whose complexity they do not begin to comprehend. Rabble-rousers (Right or Left) are rabble-rousers, no matter what songs they sing, with what lumps in their throats, with whatever ambiguous dreams in their eyes. Nazi students also flaunted "rights" they held superior to the lawful processes of "hypocritical," "fake" democracy—and many of their professors, in Germany and Austria, cheered them on.

Rebels who think they should prevail because they dissent are deluded: Dissenters have no greater moral or political rights than non-dissenters.

You ask, "What has basically bugged these hippies, anyway?" First, their parents, I suspect, who confused political liberalism with indecisiveness; who felt so guilty about discipline that they appeased temper tantrums and rewarded rage with concessions (forgetting that infants want boundaries placed on their freedom); who never gave their progeny a clear model of responsible conduct. I think many militant students are unconsciously searching for adults who will act as adults—without apology or ambivalence or guilt; adults who will not be bamboozled by adolescent irrationality; adults who respond with swift rebuffs to those challenges to authority that are, at bottom, a testing by the young of the moral confidence of their elders. Professor David Riesman says we are witnessing the rebellion of the first generation in history "who were picked up whenever they cried."

You say, "Why not show the young how wonderful our educational system is?" It is remarkable in what it has done (the greatest, widest mass education in history) and in what it can achieve. But I hold a very gloomy view about schools that can produce students (and teachers) who are so strikingly ignorant about (1) how this society actually works; (2) what the economic bases of a democracy must be; (3) what the irreplaceable foundations of freedom, and the inviolable limits of civil liberties, must be; (4) how conflicts between minorities and majorities must be managed. (Suppose that Klu Klux Klanners in Alabama occupied classrooms, asserted the right to appoint faculty, threatened to burn down buildings, and demanded total amnesty in advance?)

Immature students are mesmerized by utopian slogans that rest on fantasies; and they are ill-educated enough to mouth the obsolete cliches of anarchism, the "revolutionary" nostrums even Lenin called "infantile leftism," the grandiose "demands" that demonstrate a plain lack of sense and a massive ignorance of history. ("Student power" has simply ruined South and Central American universities.)

You ask, "Why doesn't anyone brand these troublemakers as the Communists they are?!" That organizers plan and foment trouble, going from campus to campus, is becoming clearer each day. That they are professed Communists is neither clear nor likely. Student incantations about Ho Chi Minh, Che and Mao are not so much evidence of Communism as of naivete. The young enjoy baiting their elders with shocking symbols, and ignore what Che, Ho and Mao stand for —total despotism over the mind. Dictatorship is no less vicious because it claims to seek "superior" freedom.

Students who are not Communists are, alas, employing Communist/Fascist tactics: "confrontations" designed to force authorities to call in the police—and then to force the police to use force, which is decried (and televised) and used for propaganda purposes. They dare not reflect on what Mao has done to the Chinese "student cadres" he encouraged; or on what happens to students who criticize the Establishment in Moscow or Havana.

You say, "Professor Marcuse should not be allowed to teach at San Diego!" Dr. Marcuse has a right to say or write whatever he wants—however mushy, opaque, unsupported by data, insupportable in logic and ludicrous as economics it is. His competence and integrity as a teacher are for his colleagues—not you or me—to decide. And if San Diego has no professors who are able to punch holes in old Herbert's gaseous balloons, it should promptly hire some.

Incidentally, Marcuse, like you, wants to deny freedom of speech to "certain" people; you and he differ only on whom you want to confer the blessings of dictatorship: Marcuse has publicly said (at Rutgers, June, 1965) that since Negroes are "brainwashed," and presumably vote in a hypnotized manner, "I would prefer that they did not have the right to choose wrongly." Such thinking fills prisons and concentration camps.

Finally, to my angry old and young compatriots: If we cannot pursue knowledge with moderation and mutual respect in our colleges, then where on earth can we? "Society cannot exist," wrote Burke, "(without) a controlling power upon will . . . The less of it there is within, the more there must be without . . . Men of intemperate minds cannot be free. Their passions forge their fetters."

LEO ROSTEN

P.S. Once, after long and sober research, I estimated that 23.6% of the human race are mad. I was wrong. I am now convinced that 32.6% are.

QUESTIONS FOR DISCUSSION AND DIALOGUE

1. After comparing and contrasting both "letters" of Rosten, which do you think is the more valuable? Why?
2. Outline Rosten's criticisms of this kind of "Angry Old Man".
3. In this article Rosten speaks of a "consensus of civility that is the very heart of civilization". How do both the "Angry Young Man" and the "Angry Old Man" violate this consensus, in Rosten's view? Do you agree with his view?
4. Discuss the significance of Edmund Burke's statement: " . . . Men of intemperate minds can not be free. Their passions forge their fetters." Does this mean that commitment and activism are to be frowned upon at the expense of pursuing "knowledge with moderation and neutral respect in our colleges . . ."? When and how should the students be political activists?

'Alienation Is Being Taught by Professors'

S. I. Hayakawa

Reasons for campus protests and suggestions for coping with them are discussed by San Francisco State College President, S. I. Hayakawa. The title of the article is based on Hayakawa's statement to the President's Violence Commission. The reader might ask himself if Professors are capable of exerting this kind of influence on Students.

Following is the text of a statement on campus unrest given by Acting President S. I. Hayakawa of San Francisco State College to the task force studying the disorders on his campus for the National Commission on the Causes and Prevention of Violence.

Central to the problem of violence on campus is the existence of a large number of alienated young men and women who practically take pride in being outside the main stream of the culture, of being against the establishment, against authority, against the administration of the college, the administration of the State of California, the administration in Washington, whether it's a Republican or Democratic administration.

How did they get alienated? Well, besides the usual psychologically neurotic reasons for this alienation there is something else that's going on.

I think they are taught this alienation by professors—especially in the liberal arts departments—the humanities, English, philosophy, sometimes in social sciences.

There's a kind of cult of alienation among intellectuals, among intellectuals in literary fashion such as you find in the *New York Review of Books* or the *Partisan Review.* They sneer at the world the way it's run by politicians, businessmen, and generals. Knowing that they themselves are so much smarter than politicians, businessmen, or generals, they feel there's a dreadful world which they themselves ought to be running instead.

The first great enunciator of this theory was Plato, who believed that philosophers should be kings, and notice that he himself was a philosopher. The contemporary literary critics and philosophers feel the same way.

Influence over Students

Suppose you're an alienated intellectual. You're a professor of philosophy or something, you have no power, you have no influence in Sacramento or Washington. But you can influence your students. You use phrases like, well, a phrase I just picked up from a professor of English in San Diego the other day, 'the illegitimacy of contemporary authority.'

Now if contemporary authority, of the state government, the federal government, the San Francisco police, is illegitimate, then you are morally entitled to, in fact, it is your moral duty to oppose that force. It becomes moral duty to oppose that illegitimate authority.

The middle-aged professor passes this on to his young students. The young students are more likely to act upon this. The authority of the police is illegitimate, therefore it's proper and moral to throw bricks at them. It's proper and moral to resist the draft, to resist the authority of the government in any way.

And anyone who upholds civil authority or military authority is regarded as a tool of the interests, a tool of the military-industrial complex, etc., etc., and because the military-industrial complex is so powerful, so huge, it certainly looks huge if you lump everything together into one abstraction.

Outrageous Behavior of Young People

All means of bringing it down, fair or unfair, are justifiable. This is why you find among young people today, not simply violence, but completely outrageous forms of behavior.

You see, peaceful marchers protesting courageously racial injustice under the leadership of a Martin Luther King, never screamed obscenities. They held up for themselves very, very high and rigid moral standards. And by that they dignified their protest, they dignified their cause.

But our protests, especially from the white SDS, is full of obscenities, full of shocking behavior, full of absolute defiance of any values the civilized world insists upon.

This is what I find so terribly shocking, and I think it has its intellectual sources, in a kind of disaffection, among, shall I say, the frustrated intellectuals. To paraphrase a famous line, 'Hell hath no fury like the intellectuals scorned.'

Alienation Is Passed on

Now, professors tend, therefore, to give A's in their courses to students that are alienated. And as the students get A's, they get appointed graduate assistants. Then they soon become professors themselves. And then they pass on this alienation to another generation of students, and college generations of students come fast, after all. And before you know it, you have whole departments which are basically sources of resistance to the culture as a whole.

All this upsets me very, very much. The universities and the colleges should be centers for the dissemination of the values of our culture, and the passing on of those values. But dammit, with enough half-assed Platos in our university departments, they are trying to make of them centers of sedition and destruction.

QUESTIONS FOR DISCUSSION AND DIALOGUE

1. Discuss your reaction to what Hayakawa means by the term "half-assed Platos"?
2. Do you tend to agree that college professors can have this kind of influence over their students? Discuss.

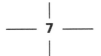

A Generation in Search of a Future

George Wald

> In this reprint of George Wald's speech is a dramatic and forceful version of why many youthful students, as well as some others, are so uneasy. Vietnam, the Military-Industrial (and Wald adds Labor Union) complex, the overhanging threat of nuclear war which will not allow youth to assume their future, and the population explosion are his main concerns. Instead of the "trivial thought that we're in competition with Russians or Chinese" . . . we need to concentrate on preserving and bettering life which we all share as one species, Wald states.

On Tuesday, March 4, (1969) in the Kresge Auditorium at the Massachusetts Institute of Technology, a group of scientists assembled, with students and others, to discuss the uses of scientific knowledge. There is nothing we might print in these columns that could be more urgent than the extemporaneous speech, made before that gathering by George Wald, professor of biology at Harvard and Nobel Prize winner, under the title "A Generation in Search of a Future." We therefore quote from it here in length:

"All of you know that in the last couple of years there has been student unrest, breaking at times into violence, in many parts of the world: in England, Germany, Italy, Spain, Mexico, Japan, and, needless to say, many parts of this country. There has been a great deal of discussion as to what it all means. Perfectly clearly, it means something different in Mexico from what it does in France, and something different in France from what it does in Tokyo, and something different in Tokyo from what it does in this country. Yet, unless we are to assume that students have gone crazy all over the world, or that they have just decided that it's the thing to do, it must have some meaning.

"I don't need to go so far afield to look for that meaning. I am a teacher, and at Harvard I have a class of about three hundred and fifty students—men and women—most of them freshmen and sophomores. Over these past few years, I have felt increasingly that something is terribly wrong—and this year ever so much more than last. Something has gone sour, in teaching and in learning. It's almost as though there were a widespread feeling that education has become irrelevant.

"A lecture is much more of a dialogue than many of you probably realize. As you lecture, you keep watching the faces, and information keeps coming back to you all the time. I began to feel, particularly this year, that I was missing much of what was coming back. I tried asking the students, but they didn't or couldn't help me very much.

"But I think I know what's the matter. I think that this whole generation of students is beset with a profound uneasiness, and I don't think that they have quite defined its source. I think I understand the reasons for their uneasiness even better than they do. What is more, I share their uneasiness.

"What's bothering those students? Some of them tell you it's the Vietnam war. I think the Vietnam war is the most shameful episode in the whole of American history. The concept of war crimes is an American invention. We've committed many war crimes in Vietnam—but I'll tell you something interesting about that. We were committing war crimes in World War II, before the Nuremberg trials were held and the principles of war crimes was stated. The saturation bombing of German cities was a war crime. Dropping those atomic bombs on Hiroshima and Nagasaki was a war crime. If we had lost the war, it might have been our leaders who had to answer for such actions. I've gone through all that history lately, and I find that there's a gimmick in it. It isn't written out, but I think we established it by precedent. That gimmick is that if one can allege that one is repelling or retaliating for an aggression, after that everything goes.

"And, you see, we are living in a world in which all wars are wars of defense. All War Departments are now Defense Departments. This is all part of the doubletalk of our time. The aggressor is always on the other side. I suppose this is why our ex-Secretary of State Dean Rusk went to such pains to insist, as he still insists, that in Vietnam we are repelling an aggression. And if that's what we are doing—so runs the doctrine—everything goes. If the concept of war crimes is ever to mean anything, they will have to be defined as categories of acts, regardless of alleged provocation. But that isn't so now.

"I think we've lost that war, as a lot of other people think, too. The Vietnamese have a secret weapon. It's their willingness to die beyond our willingness to kill. In effect, they've been saying, You can kill us, but you'll have to kill a lot of us; you may have to kill all of us. And, thank heaven, we are not yet ready to do that.

"Yet we have come a long way toward it—far enough to sicken many Americans, far enough to sicken even our fighting men. Far enough so that our national symbols have gone sour. How many of you can sing about 'the rockets' red glare, the bombs bursting in air' without thinking, Those are our bombs and our rockets, bursting over South Vietnamese villages? When those words were written, we were a people struggling for freedom against oppression. Now we are supporting open or thinly disguised military dictatorships all over the world, helping them to control and repress peoples struggling for their freedom.

"But that Vietnam war, shameful and terrible as it is, seems to me, only an immediate incident in a much larger and more stubborn situation.

"Part of my trouble with students is that almost all the students I teach were born after World War II. Just after World War II, a series of new and abnormal procedures came into American life. We regarded them at the time as temporary aberrations. We thought we would get back to normal American life someday.

"But those procedures have stayed with us now for more than twenty years, and those students of mine have never known anything else. They think those things are normal. They think that we've always had a Pentagon, that we have always had a big Army, and that we have always had a draft. But those are all new things in American life, and I think that they are incompatible with what America meant before.

"How many of you realize that just before World War II the entire American Army, including the Air Corps, numbered a hundred and thirty-nine thousand men? Then World War II started, but we weren't yet in it, and, seeing that there was great trouble in the world, we doubled this Army to two hundred and sixty-eight thousand men. Then, in World War II, it got to be eight million. And then World War II came to an end and we prepared to go back to a peacetime Army, somewhat as the American Army had always been before. And, indeed, in 1950—you think about 1950, our international commitments, the Cold War, the Truman Doctrine, and all the rest of it—in 1950, we got down to six hundred thousand men.

"Now we have three and a half million men under arms; about six hundred thousand in Vietnam, about three hundred thousand more in 'support areas' elsewhere in the Pacific, about two hundred and fifty thousand in Germany. And there are a lot at home. Some months ago, we were told that three hundred thousand National Guardsmen and two hundred thousand reservists—so half a million men—had been specially trained for riot duty in the cities.

"I say the Vietnam war is just an immediate incident because as long as we keep that big Army, it will always find things to do. If the Vietnam war stopped tomorrow, the chances are that with the big military establishment we would be in another such adventure, abroad or at home, before you knew it.

"The thing to do about the draft is not to reform it but to get rid of it.

"A peacetime draft is the most un-American thing I know. All the time I was growing up, I was told about oppressive Central European countries and Russia, where young men were forced into the Army, and I was told what they did about it. They chopped off a finger, or shot off a couple of toes, or, better still, if they could manage it, they came to this country. And we understood that, and sympathized, and were glad to welcome them.

"Now, by present estimates, from four to six thousand Americans of draft age have left this country for Canada, two or three thousand more have gone to Europe, and it looks as though many more were preparing to emigrate.

"A bill to stop the draft was recently introduced in the Senate (S. 503), sponsored by a group of senators that runs the gamut from McGovern and Hatfield to Barry Goldwater. I hope it goes through. But I think that when we get rid of the draft we must also drastically cut back the size of the armed forces.

"Yet there is something ever so much bigger and more important than the draft. That bigger thing, of course, is the militarization of our country. Ex-

President Eisenhower, in his farewell address, warned us of what he called the military-industrial complex. I am sad to say that we must begin to think of it now as the military-industrial-labor-union complex. What happened under the plea of the Cold War was not alone that we built up the first big peacetime Army in our history but that we institutionalized it. We built, I suppose, the biggest government building in our history to run it, and we institutionalized it.

"I don't think we can live with the present military establishment, and its eighty-billion-dollar-a-year budget, and keep America anything like the America we have known in the past. It is corrupting the life of the whole country. It is buying up everything in sight; industries, banks, investors, scientists—and lately it seems also to have bought up the labor unions.

"The Defense Department is always broke, but some of the things it does with that eighty billion dollars a year would make Buck Rogers envious. For example, the Rocky Mountain Arsenal, on the outskirts of Denver, was manufacturing a deadly nerve poison on such a scale that there was a problem of waste disposal. Nothing daunted, the people there dug a tunnel two miles deep under Denver, into which they have injected so much poisoned water that, beginning a couple of years ago, Denver has experienced a series of earth tremors of increasing severity. Now there is grave fear of a major earthquake. An interesting debate is in progress as to whether Denver will be safer if that lake of posioned water is removed or is left there in place.

"Perhaps you have read also of those six thousand sheep that suddenly died in Skull Valley, Utah, killed by another nerve poison—a strange and, I believe, still unexplained accident, since the nearest testing seems to have been thirty miles away.

"As for Vietnam, the expenditure of firepower there has been frightening. Some of you may still remember Khe Sanh, a hamlet just south of the Demilitarized Zone, where a force of United States Marines was beleaguered for a time. During that period, we dropped on the perimeter of Khe Sanh more explosives than fell on Japan throughout World War II, and more than fell on the whole of Europe during the years of 1942 and 1943.

"One of the officers there was quoted as having said afterward, 'It looks like the world caught smallpox and died.'

"The only point of government is to safeguard and foster life. Our government has become preoccupied with death, with the business of killing and being killed. So-called defense now absorbs sixty per cent of the national budget, and about twelve per cent of the Gross National Product.

"A lively debate is beginning again on whether or not we should deploy antiballistic missiles, the ABM. I don't have to talk about them—everyone else is doing that. But I should like to mention a curious circumstance. In September, 1967, or about a year and a half ago, we had a meeting of M.I.T. and Harvard people, including experts on these matters, to talk about whether anything could be done to block the Sentinel System—the deployment of ABM's. Everyone present thought them undesirable, but a few of the most knowledgeable persons took what seemed to be the practical view: 'Why fight about a dead issue? It has been decided, the funds have been appropriated. Let's go on from there.'

"Well, fortunately, it's not a dead issue."

"An ABM is a nuclear weapon. It takes a nuclear weapon to stop a nuclear weapon. And our concern must be with the whole issue of nuclear weapons.

"There is an entire semantics ready to deal with the sort of thing I am about to say. It involves such phrases as 'Those are the facts of life.' No—these are the facts of death. I don't accept them, and I advise you not to accept them. We are under repeated pressure to accept things that are presented to us as settled—decisions that have been made. Always there is the thought: Let's go on from there. But this time we don't see how to go on. We will have to stick with these issues.

"We are told that the United States and Russia, between them, by now have stockpiled nuclear weapons of approximately the explosive power of fifteen tons of TNT for every man, woman, and child on earth. And now it is suggested that we must make more. All very regrettable, of course, but 'those are the facts of life.' We really would like to disarm, but our new Secretary of Defense had made the ingenious proposal that now is the time to greatly increase our nuclear armaments, so that we can disarm from a position of strength.

"I think all of you know there is no adequate defense against massive nuclear attack. It is both easier and cheaper to circumvent any known nuclear-defense system than to provide it. It's all pretty crazy. At the very moment we talk of deploying ABM's, we are also building the MIRV, the weapon to circumvent ABM's.

"As far as I know, the most conservative estimates of the number of Americans who would be killed in a major nuclear attack, with everything working as well as can be hoped and all foreseeable precautions taken, run to about fifty million. We have become callous to gruesome statistics, and this seems at first to be only another gruesome statistic. You think, Bang!—and next morning, if you're still there, you read in the newspaper that fifty million people were killed.

"But that isn't the way it happens. When we killed close to two hundred thousand people with those first, little, old-fashioned uranium bombs that we dropped on Hiroshima and Nagasaki, about the same number of persons were maimed, blinded, burned, poisoned, and otherwise doomed. A lot of them took a long time to die.

"That's the way it would be. Not a bang and a certain number of corpses to bury but a nation filled with millions of helpless, maimed, tortured, and doomed persons, and the survivors huddled with their families in shelters, with guns ready to fight off their neighbors trying to get some uncontaminated food and water.

"A few months ago, Senator Richard Russell, of Georgia, ended a speech in the Senate with the words, 'If we have to start over again with another Adam and Eve, I want them to be Americans; and I want them on this continent and not in Europe.' That was a United States senator making a patriotic speech. Well, here is a Nobel laureate who thinks that those words are criminally insane.

"How real is the threat of full-scale nuclear war? I have my own very in-expert idea, but, realizing how little I know, and fearful that I may be a little paranoid on this subject, I take every opportunity to ask reputed experts. I asked that question of a distinguished professor of government at Harvard about a month ago. I asked him what sort of odds he would lay on the possibility of full-scale nuclear war within the foreseeable future. 'Oh,' he said comfortably, 'I think I can give you a pretty good answer to that question. I estimate the probability of full-scale nuclear war, provided that the situation remains about as it is now, at two per cent per year,' Anybody can do the simple calculation that shows the chance of having that full-scale nuclear war by 1970 is about one in three, and by 2000 it is about fifty-fifty.

"I think I know what is bothering the students. I think that what we are up against is a generation that is by no means sure that it has a future.

"I am growing old, and my future, so to speak, is already behind me. But there are those students of mine, who are in my mind always; and there are my children, the youngest of them now seven and nine, whose future is infinitely more precious to me than my own. So it isn't just their generation; it's mine, too. We're all in it together.

"Are we to have a chance to live? We don't ask for prosperity, or security. Only for a reasonable chance to live, to work out our destiny in peace and decency. Not to go down in history as the apocalyptic generation.

"And it isn't only nuclear war. Another overwhelming threat is in the population explosion. That has not yet even begun to come under control. There is every indication that the world population will double before the year 2000, and there is a widespread expectation of famine on an unprecedented scale in many parts of the world. The experts tend to differ only in their estimates of when those famines will begin. Some think by 1980; others think they can be staved off until 1990; very few expect that they will not occur by the year 2000.

"That is the problem. Unless we can be surer than we now are that this generation has a future, nothing else matters. It's not good enough to give it tender loving care, to supply it with breakfast food, to buy it expensive educations. Those things don't mean anything unless this generation has a future. And we're not sure that it does.

"I don't think that there are problems of youth, or student problems. All the real problems I know about are grown-up problems.

"Perhaps you will think me altogether absurd, or 'academic,' or hopelessly innocent—that is, until you think of the alternatives—if I say, as I do to you now: We have to get rid of those nuclear weapons. There is nothing worth having that can be obtained by nuclear war—nothing material or ideological—no tradition that it can defend. It is utterly self-defeating. Those atomic bombs represent an unstable weapon. The only use for an atomic bomb is to keep somebody else from using one. It can give us no protection—only the doubtful satisfaction of retaliation. Nuclear weapons offer us nothing but a balance of terror, and a balance of terror is still terror.

"We have to get rid of those atomic weapons, here and everywhere. We cannot live with them.

"I think we've reached a point of great decision, not just for our nation, not only for all humanity, but for life upon earth. I tell my students, with a feeling of pride that I hope they will share, that the carbon, nitrogen, and oxygen that make up ninety-nine per cent of our living substance were cooked in deep interiors of earlier generations of dying stars. Gathered up from the ends of the universe, over billions of years, eventually they came to form, in part, the substance of our sun, its planets, and ourselves. Three billion years ago, life arose upon the earth. It is the only life in the solar system.

"About two million years ago, man appeared. He has become the dominant species on the earth. All other living things, animals, and plants, live by his sufferance. He is the custodian of life on earth, and in the solar system. It's a big responsibility.

"The thought that we're in competition with Russians or with Chinese is all a mistake, and trivial. We are one species, with a world to win. There's life all over this universe, but the only life in the solar system is on earth, and in the whole universe we are the only men.

"Our business is with life, not death. Our challenge is to give what account we can of what becomes of life in the solar system, this corner of the universe that is our home; and, most of all, what becomes of men—all men, of all nations, colors, and creeds. This has become one world, a world for all men. It is only such a world that can now offer us life, and the chance to go on."

QUESTIONS FOR DISCUSSION AND DIALOGUE

1. Does Wald sound like the kind of intellectual Hayakawa is criticizing in the previous article? With whom do you tend to agree, Wald or Hayakawa? Why?
2. What does Wald mean when he says, "Our government has become preoccupied with death?" Do you agree? Why?
3. Do you agree with Wald's description of Senator Russell's statement quoted below as "criminally insane"? "If we have to start over again with another Adam and Eve, I want them to be Americans; and I want them on this continent and not in Europe." Discuss.
4. What is your response to Wald's statement that "the thought that we're in competition with Russians or with Chinese is all a mistake and trivial. We are one species, with a world to win ... "
5. Do you think Wald has put his finger on the most basic thing bothering the students when he says " ... what we are up against is a generation that is by no means sure that it has a future." Why? Can you offer examples of student behavior which demonstrate this feeling?

The Revolt against Democracy
Edgar A. Friedenberg

This article by Professor Friedenberg states the fundamental cause of student militancy is the feeling of the militants that mass democracy is illegitimate authority, and this illegitimacy can not be changed by due process and lawful means. He defends his contention with discussion of how, in his view, " . . . the American political process DOES respond to the will of the people; it is the mass of the people that does not respond to the moral imperatives of Vietnam and the slight of the poor and the black—or, rather, it responds with greater hostility as its own destructiveness mounts." Friedenberg's most bitter criticisms are reserved for the de-humanization which he claims is carried out against youth in high school.

There is a widespread conviction among dissenting youth today that they are oppressed by a fundamentally illegitimate authority. For the younger members of a gerontocracy like ours to regard the authority of the older generation as oppressive is a rational act; that such authority should be logically regarded as oppressive is implicit in the fact that it occasions revolt. But for authority to be regarded likewise as illegitimate is something new. It makes conflict far more disruptive. It is, in fact, the characteristic that most clearly distinguishes today's intergenerational conflict from that which commonly occurs between successive generations.

Legitimacy is the chief lubricant of the social mechanism; it prevents friction by inducing collaboration among its several parts even in situations in which conflict of interest is apparent. The extreme example is the quiet dignity with which the condemned so often cooperate with their executioners. In the ultimately terrifying situation, the victim takes what comfort he can from identifying himself as a member of the society which has officially certified him as so worthless that he must be publicly destroyed. By so doing he is not alone in his moment of mortal terror.

In a social system that has exhausted its legitimate authority, however, executions are regarded as publicly planned assassinations that invite resistance, escalation and, ultimately, role-confusion, as Danton and Robespierre discovered. Declining legitimacy leads to a rise in coercive violence, which is usually attributed to the disorderly provocation of those who have no respect for "authority" or "law and order." Analysis of the actual events more often discloses that the contrary is true: violence is launched and maintained by terrified officials who feel their authority threatened. As their legitimacy ebbs, they fall back on the resources for coercion which their official position affords, and modern technology has made these resources enormous. Whether this results in the re-establishment of legitimacy depends on whether a stable regime can be built on the wastelands of terror. In the past it has usually been possible, but it does take time —more than a generation.

Terror thus is not a very useful devise for restoring the faith of the younger generation in the legitimacy of the authority of their elders. Indeed, the authorities in this country have so structured their recent confrontations with the young as to reveal their own cognizance of the illegitimacy of their authority. This is the era of *plainclothes* police cracking the skulls of students, of *undercover* narcotics agents busting students for smoking pot. A uniform is an asset to the officer of a society whose legitimacy is accepted; the uniform, as with the soldier, legitimates even lethal hostility, if there is any legitimacy left. But out of uniform the adversary is a spy, and he himself becomes the legitimate object of condemnation. The widespread use of covert surveillance and coercion in a society indicates that the forces that bind it together have become even less legitimate than those that link hostile belligerents in the traditional context of war.

Authority, however, is no less dangerous because it lacks legitimacy; rather, because of its own anxieties, it is more dangerous. The more sensitive and intelligent young people I know today consider themselves to be living in some degree the lives of outlaws. They attempt to resign themselves to the prospects of being busted for smoking pot or dropping acid, imprisoned for draft evasion either directly or under a loose charge of conspiracy, or locked away in a concentration camp if resistance to the Vietnam war or revolt in the urban slums results in the declaration of a State of National Emergency or invocation of the Internal Security Act of 1950. All these are valid fears. There *is* real danger of becoming a political prisoner in the United States today through the normal operation of due process. Our military adventures and our treatment of poor and black people are political questions, and therefore offenses related to opposition to such policies are political offenses. It is less clear that classifying marijuana as a "dangerous drug"—in the absence of substantial evidence to that effect—and making its use a felony, and its distribution under some circumstances punishable by life imprisonment, are legal definitions designed to curb political offenses. But they are, and the very fact that the political character of such laws seem paradoxical makes the political function of the pot issue worth scrutinizing.

Smoking marijuana is essentially a ritual action by which young people assert a moral position. Careful research has shown that both the dangers and joys associated with its use have been grossly exaggerated. The satisfactions it affords are derived far less from its mildly stimulating effect on the central nervous system—which may be agreeable or disagreeable, depending on the circumstances—than from the sense of affirming a particular view of the world and of one's place in it. Potblowing is ideological; examination of the ideology it expresses reveals several characteristic components. The most important of these are:

1) People who are enjoying themselves without harming others have an inalienable right to privacy.

2) A drug whose effect is to turn its users inward upon their own experience, enriching their fantasy life at the expense of their sense of the need to achieve or

relate to others, is as moral as alcohol, which encourages a false gregariousness and increasingly pugnacious or competitive behavior.

3) Much of the solicitude of the older generation for the welfare of the young merely expresses a desire to dominate and control them for the sake of adult interests and the preservation of adult status and authority.

Pot is clearly less dangerous than pot-busts. It is also less dangerous to youth than the Selective Service System; parents who become hysterical and punitive about the dangers of drug abuse while being equally insistent that their sons go quietly to Vietnam when summoned are more concerned with the embarrassment of having children who are in trouble with the law than with their children's welfare. So we are back again to the issue of legitimacy, which is what the potblower's ideology basically questions. On their own terms, there can be no doubt that their position is valid: there are no demonstrable dangers to either the individual or society sufficient to justify or even explain the treatment accorded marijuana users. The effects of the drug are less obnoxious than those of alcohol; the solicitude of adults masks intense hostility and anxiety..

Institutionalized hostility toward marijuana users is intelligible, however, when the potblower's ideology is considered in relation to the class structure of American society. For that ideology expresses essentially an upper-middle to upper-class attitude toward life; indeed, for this century, it expresses one that is remarkably aristocratic. To value privacy and a rich inner life at the expense of achievement and the development of social skills in manipulating and competing with others—to value these is to reject the fundamental and official attitudes of American society, to fly in the face (and perhaps up the nose) of the school system, the Little League and the core virtues of the Land of Opportunity. The fact that marijuana is too mild a drug to do much for the fantasy-life does not affect the controversy. People get out of psychedelic drugs about what they expect and the use of marijuana has evolved in such a way that custom provides what the drug cannot—as it does for alcohol. Pot-parties have therefore become almost a photo-graphic negative of cocktail parties: communal experiences at which the joint is passed from mouth to mouth like a peace pipe or communion cup; the scene is tranquil rather than gregarious, with no one-upping permitted; there is not even much moving around.

Pot, then, both evokes and symbolizes a whole set of attitudes and behavior that are anathema to the lower-middle classes: laziness and fantastic ease, grooving with one's neighbor instead of competing with him, drifting into bed with the partner of your choice rather than conning her into it as proof of your none-too-evident manhood. Pot-busts have become primarily a form of interclass hostility, in which the working class attacks the sloth, depravity and decadence of gilded, long-haired youth.

Interclass hostility of this kind is ancient, of course. What is novel, and very dangerous, in the form of pot-bust is that the customary class roles have been fundamentally reversed. For here it is the lower of the adversary classes which, armed with legitimacy, attacks the upper in the name of law and order. And the upper defends itself, when it does so at all, by appealing to such values as civil liberty, the right to privacy, and freedom from arbitrary search and seizure which, although recognized in general terms in the Constitution or reflected in certain court decisions, have never been accepted by the American masses which see them as essentially a form of privilege.

And so they are; and this is the heart of the conflict. For what American society most apparently lacks today is a device by which social class differences may be legitimated. This, in fact, is what our institutions have evolved, since Jackson's time, to prevent. Privilege in America is illegitimate *per se.* Or in de Tocqueville's words, written in Jackson's day:

> The Americans hold, that, in every state, the supreme power ought to emanate from the people; but when once that power is constituted, they can conceive, as it were, no limits to it, and they are ready to admit that it has the right to do whatever it pleases. They have not the slightest notion of peculiar privileges granted to cities, families or persons: their minds appear never to have foreseen that it might be possible not to apply the same laws to every part of the state and to all its inhabitants.

This is not quite accurate. The Bill of Rights *does* conceive of limits to the supreme power of the people, and attempts to establish them—which is why the working class so often perceives the Supreme Court as opposed to law and order. The people certainly *do* have a notion of peculiar privileges granted to cities, families or persons—it is what they are most determined to prevent. They *do* foresee that it might be possible *not* to apply the same laws to every part of the state, and to all its inhabitants—which is why they enjoy lurid fantasies of the university as a privileged sanctuary for draft-dodgers, addicts and perverts. What they *don't* grant, even as a possibility, is that such privileges, and such a sanctuary, might have social value.

And for most of them, perhaps it would not. This is not an issue that need to be debated, for American society is as receptive to the claim of vested interest as it is hostile to that of privilege. There are social classes in America as elsewhere, and a society that recognizes and defers to the special interests and needs of oil-producers, speculative builders and labor unions can hardly justify rejection of the special interests of middle-class youth, which sorely needs a place to call its own. American society as a whole would surely be far better off if its most sensitive and articulate youth did not feel themselves to be outlaws. No more need be demanded on behalf of hippies or turned-on youth than is accorded Standard Oil or the friendly Chase Manhattan Bank: that their needs be recognized and reflected in the law of the land, and they they be allowed to go about their business unmolested without having to prove that what is good for them is good for the entire world.

But even this cannot be vouchsafed under our system. The answer adults give the beleaguered and fugitive young when finally forced to admit that the marijuana laws are Draconian and irrational, and the Selective Service Act capricious and inequitable, is to assert that for the sake of a stable and orderly society even unjust and unwise laws must be respected, and that procedures exist by which laws may be changed to make them wiser and more just. Unfortunately the idea that unwise and unjust laws—which reflect the hostilities and assuage the inferiority feelings and envy of the masses—can be effectively changed by due process and lawful means in a mass democracy is probably false. American law and public policy are almost always unresponsive to moral issues or minority needs, unless these find expression in terms of raw power. The fall of the Johnson administration, and subsequently of the Democratic party, under the impact of war protest may seem to belie this statement; so may the actual social progress the nation has made in the past fifty years. It is the blindness of the New Left to this record of past achievement, in fact, which most offends the surviving members of the Old Left. But neither case is a convincing indication that the American social or legal structure might be capable of a generous response to the demands of dissenting middle-class youth today. It seems very obvious that the Johnson administration would have been unaffected had the Vietnam war been prosecuted more successfully. Failure is punished by the electorate; but the war protest did not occasion the failure. Lyndon Johnson's defeat was not brought about by Benjamin Spock, Tom Hayden or Eugene McCarthy, but the Vietnamese themselves. And they did not do it by winning their case before the bar of American public opinion or through the channels of American legal process.

The accomplishments of the Old Left are more solid, and unquestionably theirs. It is quite true that virtually all the social legislation they fought for in the thirties—against opposition fully as repressive as anything the New Left faces today—has not only been enacted but is now taken wholly for granted. What is sad, as Norman Thomas observed a few years before his death, is that nobody seems to have much pleasure out of it. But the goals of the New Left have a different political, and a different moral, significance than those of the Old; their tasks are not really comparable and they cannot really be allies.

Broadly speaking, the reforms of the thirties were economic and addressed to the improvement of social justice and the abatement of the grossest economic insecurity. What was achieved was solid, and new to a country which still provides much less in the way of social services, especially to the ill and aged, than an Englishman or Scandinavian would expect as a matter of right. In any case, the radicals of the thirties emphasized economic need and the improvement of the political power of the working class far more than civil rights, civil liberty or personal freedom. This was not because they were oblivious of these issues, but because they saw economic threat and vulnerability to poverty and economic pressure as the most serious threats to freedom. Job security and a decent wage, and essential social services, were to serve as shields against coercion by bosses and the slings and arrows of outrageous fortune. The Wagner Act and the Federal Minimum Wage Law were thought of not only as guaranteeing certain important economic and political rights but also as part of the foundation on which human liberty would rest.

As such, they have not been particularly effective. They serve as necessary instruments of social justice in guaranteeing certain important economic rights to the organized working class, which is quite sufficient to justify them as legislation. But the working class has not proved to be devoted to liberty; it is more inclined to be devoted to George Wallace or Mayor Daley. It supports the war more zealously than the financial and industrial leadership of the country—a paradox in terms of the stereotypes of the thirties, which envisioned rough, honest, warmhearted labor as the undauntable defender of peace and international brotherhood against the rapacity of capitalist warmongers. The capitalist warmongers have proved rapacious enough. Nevertheless, I do not think the American economy as a whole is as committed to a policy of perpetual military and political malevolence as the mass of the American people; it is too easy to conceive of other and more pleasant ways of profiting by our not-altogether-free associations with our neighbors. Where generals and corporate executives support the Vietnam war out of economic and status interests, both labor leaders and the working-class people one meets from day to day actively hate the draft-dodgers, peaceniks and troublemakers who harass their country while their boy is risking his life to defend it against the savage and treacherous gook. *If he hadn't —if he had ever started to talk like those long-haired punks, they'd have had his ass themselves.* However the various factors add, support for the war is now strongest in the working class, at least among parents; their sons, chased by the draft, may be less enthusiastic. But resistance to the war remains primarily a middle-class value.

The reforms of the Old Left have thus added to the difficulties of the New by greatly strengthening the political power of what has proved to be the most repressive segment of the population—the real control-addicts, in William Burroughs' phrase: the supporters of law and order, so long as the law does not shackle their local police or protect fresh kids and hippies. The reforms of the Old Left have created also one final problem of legitimacy that the New Left is, I think, reluctant to face. For the Old Left reforms proved ultimately popular; they benefitted the masses at the expense of the classes, which not only gave the old radicals great satisfaction, it made their programs legitimate *per se.* They were on the side of democracy and they knew it; with the final triumph of FDR they could prove it. It is true that the forces of law were often arrayed against them, sometimes with a brutality equal—discounting the greater technological efficiency of the sixties—to anything the war-resisters encounter now. But when this happened in the thirties, just as when it happened later to civil-rights workers in the South, it was the law itself which had become illegitimate. This thought affords little protection to the body in confronting a group of murderous sheriff's deputies, but it does enhance the victim's self-esteem.

What seems to be the hardest today for young radicals to face, in their conviction that authority has become illegitimate, is the implication that the source of the illegitimacy is the American democratic process itself. It is one thing to assert that "the system" is corrupt, that the mass media conceal essential data and misrepresent what they do report, that political parties do not respond to the will of the electorate. It is another, and more difficult for a radical American, to grant that what is wrong with America may be characteristic of mass democracy itself.

Yet this seems to be the more valid conclusion. The mass media, for example, do not, I think, mislead people so much as they confirm them in the fantasies they wish to hold. When, as in the Chicago Convention coverage, they do not, all hell breaks loose as the public, in paroxysms of rage and self-pity, demands that its prejudices be confirmed. The public does not accept discordant interpretations of reality any more than a neurotic patient accepts an unwelcome interpretation; it was Walter Cronkite, not the public, who learned from the experience. And the American political process *does* respond to the will of the people; it is the mass of the people that does not respond to the moral imperatives of Vietnam and the plight of the poor and the black—or, rather, it responds with greater hostility as its own destructiveness mounts.

As the twentieth century, along perhaps with everything else, approaches its conclusion, it becomes apparent that democracy and fascism are not contrasting and opposing political systems, but different stages of evolution in the responsiveness of society to the fears, envies and resentments that pervade the lives of lower status groups. Democratic political structures are devised to legitimate the demands to which these feelings naturally give rise, and to increase the political power of the masses, and hence their capacity to command a better life. But in a society as open, invidious and competitive as ours, the kinds of people who succeed are usually incapable of responding to humand demands; and the political power of the masses is used merely to express the hatreds and the envy, and to destroy anything that looks like genuine human satisfaction, especially among the more vulnerable members of the higher social classes. Higher status youth— whose style of life infuriates the working class and whose status by no means compensates for their political helplessness as a disfranchised group with few established civil rights in law—have become the chief target of the working-class sense of outrage and defeat. It is difficult for white, middle-class parents to imagine—and most don't want to—the degree of harassment to which their adolescent children are subjected by hostile and vigilant school authorities, and by police who feel, and are, perfectly free to disperse groups of youngsters whose behavior is not at all threatening and who could not, if adults, be held to have given probable cause for suspicion on any offense.

Tyranny has taken many forms in history, but the graceless vulgarity and egregious, clumsy brutality of fascism are its most hideous form; and these grow best out of the democratic process itself. The masses came onto the stage of history too late to be credited with having invented tyranny—even the Russians have made no such claim—but they have made something new and more terrible of it by depriving it of style.

Those who complain of the failures of democracy are expected to provide a better political plan and, even more confidently, expected to recoil in fear of perplexity from the demand that they do so. Winston Churchill's much-quoted comment that democracy is the worst system of government in the world—except for all the others—is supposed to have settled the matter.

But, in fact, there is no reason to feel embarrassed by this demand. Our political system, like the rest of our society, has not become the way it is in response to free and conscious choice, and—unless we commit national suicide —it cannot be transformed by an act of will. It reflects, rather, the effects of years of use and abuse, insight and misunderstanding, discipline and indulgence—both often equally ill-considered—of its inherited structures. There is no question of choosing elitism or oligarchy or fascism or anything else instead of democracy.

There is only the question of how our present democratic system can respond to the demands placed on it by the needs of the people whose lives it affects, including those subject to its military and economic caprice who do not live within our borders. It is not possible to change or exchange political systems at will—even revolution does nothing like this; the new one grows back, often monstrously deformed, on the roots of the old.

The comprehensive public school, in its commendable attempt to give children of all social classes some experience of one another's lives, has become an institution in which lower- and upper-class children alike find themselves held hostage—if they do not escape—to the values and behavior patterns prized by the lower-middle class and imposed by it as a universal norm of conduct and moral judgment. Release with a satisfactory credential depends on the student's good conduct, and that of his parents, in not rejecting those norms or the values of the school system itself.

The pattern of anxieties thus established in the name of socialization has done much to cement our society together—as well as to make it more rigid when facing the need to devise alternative norms. But that need is now pressing, and the society is coming apart anyway. A major force in its disruption is the irritation that the upper and lower classes feel with each other; our society is splitting right down the middle-middle. And in a society that denies the legitimacy, if not the very existence, of class interests, and whose political leaders prattle of "law and order" as a remedy for "violence in the streets"—as if they had not seen a dozen times by now that the violence in the streets if often committed by the forces of law and order—nothing realistic can be done to recognize the serious nature of the conflict between those interests, or to resolve it.

It is almost certain that any effective measures to keep the American social system from bitter dissolution must indeed transcend present strucural limits and political arrangements. The crucial question is whether this is possible. The present political structure of America is precisely what is wrong, and there is no *a priori* reason to assume that it bears within itself the seeds of its own reform. But I am sure that if any radical improvement in the quality of our national life can be made—and our survival depends on this—the devices by which it can be done will seem outrageous, and will, indeed, cause widespread outrage. But as perhaps most surviving American Indians and Vietnamese might agree, there is no great risk in devising a system more outrageous than that which America already has, and has had for nearly two centuries.

QUESTIONS FOR DISCUSSION AND DIALOGUE

1. Why and how does Friedenberg view "pot" as a class symbol?
2. Do you agree with Friedenberg's pessimistic view that "the idea that unwise and unjust laws—which reflect the hostilities and assuage the inferiority feelings and envy of the masses—can be effectively changed by due process and lawful means in a mass democracy is probably false"? Discuss.
3. Many of you have recently been in high school. Is Friedenberg describing your high school when he talks about "hostile and vigilant school authorities", "an

institution in which lower- and upper-class children alike find themselves held hostage. . . to the values and behavior patterns prized by the lower-middle class and imposed by it as a universal norm of conduct and moral judgment"? Discuss.

The Professor's Had It

K. Ross Toole

A very different evaluation of the more militant students is presented here by Dr. K. Ross Toole who is a professor of western history at the University of Montana. This treatise, written as a letter to his brother, has gained national attention. It makes for an interesting contrast to the more favorable views of youthful militancy offered in the previous article by Friedenberg.

I am 49 years old. It took me many years and considerable anguish to get where I am—which isn't much of anyplace except exurbia. I was nurtured in depression; I lost four years to war; I am invested with sweat; I have had one coronary; I am a "liberal," a square and I am a professor. I am sick of the "younger generation," hippies, yippies, militants and nonsense.

I am a professor of history at the University of Montana, and I am supposed to have "liaison" with the young. Worse still, I am the father of seven children. They range in age from seven to 23—and I am fed up with nonsense. I am tired of being blamed, maimed and contrite; I am tired of tolerance and the reaching out (which is always my function) for understanding. I am sick of the total irrationality of the campus rebel, whose bearded visage, dirty hair, body odor and "tactics" are childish but brutal, naive but dangerous, and the essence of arrogant tyranny—the tyranny of spoiled brats.

I am terribly disturbed by the fact that I may be incubating more of the same as a father. Our household is permissive, our approach to discipline is an apology and a retreat from standards—usually accompanied by a gift in cash or kind.

It's time to call a halt; time to live in an adult world where we belong and time to put these people in their places. We have come by what we are through work, sweat, thought and time. We owe the younger generation what all older generations have owed younger generations—love, protection to a point, and respect when they deserve it. We do not owe them immunity from our mistakes, . . . or their own.

Affluent Country

Every generation makes mistakes, always has and always will. But my generation has made America the most affluent country on earth; it has tackled, head-on, a racial problem which no nation on earth in the history of mankind had dared to do. It has publicly declared war on poverty and it has gone to the moon; it has desegregated schools and abolished polio; it has presided over man's history. It has begun these things, not finished them. It has declared itself, and committed itself, and taxed itself, and darn near run itself into the ground in the cause of social justice and reform.

Its mistakes are fewer than my father's generation—or his father's, or his. Its greatest mistake is not Vietnam; it is the abdication of its first responsibility, its pusillanimous capitulation to its youth, and its sick preoccupation with the problems, the mind, the psyche, the raison d'etre of the young.

Since when have children ruled this country? By virtue of what right or what accomplishment should thousands of teen-agers, wet behind the ears and utterly without the benefit of having lived long enough to have either judgment or wisdom, become the sages of our time?

Well, say the psychologists, the educators and the preachers, the young are rebelling against our archaic mores and morals, our materialistic approach to life, our failures in diplomacy, our terrible ineptitude in racial matters, our narrowness as parents, our blindness to the root ills of society. Balderdash!

Society hangs together by the stitching of many threads. No 18-year-old is simply the product of his 18 years; he is the product of three thousand years of the development of mankind—and throughout those years, injustice has existed and been fought; rules have grown outmoded and been changed; doom has hung over the heads of men and been avoided; unjust wars have occurred; pain has been the cost of progress—and man has persevered.

Changes Direction

Society is obviously an imperfect production, but each generation changes its direction just a little—and most of the time it works.

As a professor and the father of seven, I have watched this new generation and concluded that most of them are fine. A minority are not—and the trouble is that the minority threatens to tyrannize the majority and take over. I dislike that minority; I am aghast that the majority takes it and allows itself to be used. And I address myself to both the minority and the majority thusly. I speak partly as a historian, partly as a father and partly as one fed-up, middle-aged and angry member of the so-called establishment—which, by the way, is nothing but a euphemism for society.

Common courtesy and a regard for the opinions of others is not merely a decoration on the pie crust of society, it is the heart of the pie. Too many youngsters are egocentric boors. They will not listen, they will only shout down. They will not discuss but, like four-year-olds, they throw rocks and shout.

Wisdom is not precocity; it is an amalgam of experience, reading, thought and the slow development of perception. While age is no guarantor of wisdom, whatever else the young are, they are not wise, precisely because they are young. Too many of them mistake glibness for wisdom and emotion for thought. My seven-year-old is emotional and glib but I will not loan him my loaded hand gun. Why then, do we place in the hands of boors and spoiled children the power to disrupt our machinery? Why do we listen seriously and attentively to the rantings of adolescents? Why, in effect, do we give the loaded hand gun to the seven-year-old?

Destructive

Arrogance is obnoxious; it is also destructive. Society has classically ostracized arrogance when it is without the backing of demonstrable accomplishment. Why, then, do we tolerate arrogant slobs who occupy our homes, our administration buildings, our streets and parks, urinating on our beliefs and defiling our premises? It is not the police we need, (our generation and theirs) it is an expression of our disgust and disdain. Yet we do more than permit it, we dignify it with introspective flagellation. Somehow it is our fault. Balderdash again!

Sensitivity is not the property of the young, nor was it invented in 1950. The young of any generation have felt the same impulse to grow, to reach out, to touch stars, to live freely and to let the mind loose along unexplored corridors. Young men and young women have always stood on the same hill and felt the same vague sense of restraint that separated them from the ultimate experience—the sudden and complete expansion of the mind, the final fulfillment. It is one of the oldest, sweetest and most bitter experiences of mankind.

Today's young people did not invent it; they do not own it. And what they seek to attain, all mankind has sought to attain throughout the ages. Shall we, therefore, approve the presumed attainment of it through heroin, speed, LSD and other drugs? And shall we, permissively, let them poison themselves simply because, as in most other respects, we feel vaguely guilty because we brought them into this world? Again it is not the police raids and tougher laws that we need; it is merely strength. The strength to explain, in our potty, middle-aged way, that what they seek we sought; that it is somewhere but not here and sure as heck not in drugs; that, in the meanwhile, they had better cease and desist the poison game. And this we must explain early and hard—and then police it ourselves.

Not Foreign

Society, the establishment, is not a foreign thing we seek to impose on the young. We know it is far from perfect. We did not make it; we have only sought to change it. The fact that we have only been minimally successful is the story of all generations—as it will be the story of the generation coming up. Yet we have worked a number of wonders with it. We have changed it. We are deeply concerned about our failures; we have not solved the racial problem but we have at least faced it; we are terribly worried about the degradation of our environment, about injustices, inequities, the military-industrial complex and bureacracy.

But we have attacked these things. We have, all our lives, taken arms against our sea of troubles—and fought effectively. But we also have fought with a rational knowledge of the strength of our adversary, and, above all, knowing that the war is one of attrition in which the unconditional surrender of the forces of evil is not about to occur. We win, if we win at all, slowly and painfully. That is the kind of war society has always fought—because man is what he is.

Knowing this, why do we listen subserviently to the violent tacticians of the new generation? Either they have total victory by Wednesday next or burn down our carefully built barricades in adolescent pique; either they win now or flee off to a commune and quit; either they solve all problems this week or join a wrecking crew of paranoids.

Always Idealists

Youth has always been characterized by impatient idealism. If it were not, there would be no change. But impatient idealism does not extend to guns, fire bombs, riots, vicious arrogance, and instant gratification. That is not idealism; it is childish tyranny. And the worst of it is that we (professors and faculties in particular) in a paroxysm of self-abnegation and apology, go along, abdicate, apologize as if we had personally created the ills of the world—and thus lend ourselves to chaos. We are the led, not the leaders. And we are fools.

As a professor I meet activists and revolutionaries of this new generation every day. They are not only boorish, they are inexcusably ignorant. If you want to make a revolution, do you not study the ways to do it? Of course not! Che Guevarra becomes their hero. He failed; he died in the jungles of Bolivia with an army of six. His every move was a miscalculation and a mistake.

Mao Tse-tung and Ho Chi Minh led revolutions based on a peasantry and an overwhelmingly ancient rural economy. They are the patternmakers for the SDS and the student militants. I have yet to talk to an activist who has read Crane Brinton's "The Anatomy of Revolution," of who is familiar with the works of Jefferson, Washington, Payne, Adams, or even Marx or Engels. And I have yet to talk to a student militant who has read about racism elsewhere and/or who understands, even primitively, the long and wonderous struggle of the NAACP and the genius of Martin Luther King—whose name they invariably take in vain.

An old and scarred member of the wars of organized labor in the U.S. in the 1930's recently remarked to me: "These 'radicals' couldn't organize well enough to produce a sensible platform, let alone revolt their way out of a paper bag." But they can, because we let them, destroy our universities, make our parks untenable, make a shambles of our streets and insult our flag.

Really a Liberal

I am not a conservative. I am a liberal. I am a concerned and fairly perceptive teacher and parent. I am neither blind to the ills of our society nor dedicated to the status quo.

I assert that we are in trouble with this younger generation not because we have failed our country, not because of affluence or stupidity, not because we are antediluvian, not because we are middle-class materialists—but simply because we have failed to keep that generation in its place and we have failed to put them back there when they got out of it. We have the power; we do not have will. We have the right, we have not exercised it.

To the extent that we now rely on the police, Mace, the national guard, tear gas, steel fences and a wringing of hands, we will fail. What we need is a reappraisal of our own middle-class selves, our worth and our hard-won progress. We need to use disdain, not mace; we need to reassess a weapon we came by the hard way, by travail and labor, firm authority as parents, teachers, businessmen, workers and politicians.

The vast majority of our children from one to 20 are fine kids. We need to back up this majority with authority and with the firm conviction that we owe it to them and to ourselves. Enough of apology, enough of analysis, enough of our abdication of our responsibility, enough of the denial of our own maturity and good sense.

The best place to start is at home. But, the most practical and effective place, right now, is our campuses. This does not mean a flood of angry edicts, a sudden clamp-down, a new policy. It simply means that faculties should stop playing chicken, that demonstrators should be met not with police but with expulsions. The power to expel (strangely unused) has been the legitimate recourse of universities since 1209.

More importantly it means that at freshman orientation, whatever form it takes, the administration should set forth the ground rules—not belligerently but forthrightly.

A university is the microcosm of society itself. It cannot function without rules for conduct. It cannot, as society cannot, legislate morals. It is dealing with young men and women 18 to 22. But it can, and must, promulgate rules. It cannot function without order—and, therefore, who disrupts order must leave. It cannot permit the students to determine when, what and where they shall be taught; it cannot permit the occupation of its premises, in violation both of the law and its regulation, by militants.

Not Violence

There is room within the university complex for basic student participation but there is no room for slobs, disruption and violence. Therefore, the first obligation of the administration is to lay down the rules, early in the game, clearly and positively, and to attach to this statement, the penalty for violation. It is profoundly simple—and the failure to state it—in advance—is the salient failure of university administrators in this age.

Expulsion is a dreaded verdict. The administration need not play Torquemada; it merely needs to make it clear, quite dispassionately, that expulsion is the inevitable consequence of the violation of the rules. And among the rules, even though it seems gratuitous, should be these:

1. Violence, armed or otherwise, the forceful occupation of buildings, the intimidation by covert or overt act of any student or faculty member of administrative personnel, the occupation of any university property, field, park, building, lot or other place, shall be cause for expulsion.

2. The disruption of any class, directly or indirectly, by voice or presence or the destruction of any university property, shall be cause for expulsion.

These two simple and clear-cut rules, with penalty attached, should be promulgated to every freshman as part of his general orientation and should be circulated by the means every university has, to all upper classmen.

This is neither new nor revolutionary. It is merely the reassertion of an old accepted and necessary right of the administration of any such institution. And the faculty should be informed, firmly, of this reassertion, before trouble starts. This does not constitute provocation. It is one of the oldest rights and necessities of the university community. The failure of university administrators to use it is one of the mysteries of our permissive age—and the blame must fall largely on faculties because they have consistently pressured administrators not to act.

And suppose the students refuse to recognize expulsion, suppose they march, riot, strike. The police? No. The matter by prearrangement, publicly stated, should then pass to the courts. If buildings are occupied, the court enjoins the participating students. It has the awful power to declare them in contempt. If violence ensues, it is in violation of the court's order. Courts are not subject to fears, not part of the action. And what militant will shout obscenities in court with contempt hanging over his head?

Too simple? Not at all. Merely an old process which we seem to have forgotten. It is too direct for those of us who seek to employ Freudian analysis, too positive for academic senates who long for philosophical debate and too prosaic for those who seek orgiastic self condemnation.

This is a country full of decent, worried people like myself. It is also a country full of people fed-up with nonsense. We need (those of us over 30, tax-ridden, harried, confused, weary and beat up) to reassert our hard won prerogatives. It is our country too. We have fought for it, bled for it, dreamed for it, and we love it. It is time to reclaim it.

QUESTIONS FOR DISCUSSION AND DIALOGUE

1. As Dr. Toole sees them, what are the accomplishments of his generation which the militant students refuse to sufficiently acknowledge?
2. If Toole is right, why are we "in trouble with this younger generation"? Do you agree? Discuss. Do you agree with the practical steps he would take to remedy this situation?
3. List, in outline form, some of the most important contrasting views of "Freidenberg vs. Toole" on student militancy.

Notes on Young Radicals

Kenneth Keniston

Kenneth Keniston states a position on students that amounts to something of a middle ground between Friedenberg and Toole. He says that "I consider the radicalism of a minority of today's college students a largely appropriate, reasonable and measured response to blatant injustices ... " Keniston uses empirical studies to back up his position, and he is very careful to distinguish between the advantages of viewing the students from psychological, sociological and other perspectives in terms of causes and effects.

In the summer of 1967, I studied a small group of anti-war radical student leaders. The study, clinical and exploratory, was published in May 1968. Even by that time, the radical scene had changed so drastically that many of my comments were already outdated. Now, two years later, still more needs to be said about the changes of the last two years, about how they alter earlier generalizations about the psycho-social origins of student radicalism, and about the lessons to be learned from recent studies of youthful activists.

I should state at the outset that I continue to see student activism as an essentially constructive force in American life. I am far more worried about police riots and American military violence than I am about "student violence," and I consider the radicalism of a minority of today's college students a largely appropriate, reasonable and measured response to blatant injustices in our foreign policies, our domestic policies and practices, and our university structure and policies. I do deplore (as a tendency) that special self-righteousness of a minority of today's student radicals, the nobility of whose purposes is not matched by an equal awareness of their own ambivalence or potential for corruption—a lack that sometimes allows them to treat their opponents as less-than-human—as pigs, for example. But in any case, the study of the psychology of radicals should never be equated with the study of the causes of radicalism, much less with its merits.

There was clearly something about the Civil Rights Movement—its style, its mood, the character of its members and its target—that won the sympathy of American liberals. (Many Southerners, of course, found the tactics and goals of the movement nihilistic, communistic, violent or, at the very least, provocative.) The tactic of militant nonviolence—whether adopted as a Gandhian first principle or as a useful tactic—seemed an altogether worthy and admirable principle. To be sure, the sit-in was essentially disruptive and confrontational. To the restaurant owner whose floor was covered by demonstrating civil rights workers, a sit-in seemed a violation of his property rights and an obstruction of his business. But to the greater part of the liberal American public, the disruptive and obstructive element in these tactics seemed justified, a relatively mild way of expressing opposition to unjust and discriminatory policies.

But as the student movement has journeyed from the South to the North, from the ghetto to the campus, new reactions have come to prevail. There is a new tendency to try to separate the "good guys" who remain nonviolent, constructive and idealistic from the "bad guys" who are nihilistic, violent, destructive and anarchistic. This distinction pervades political rhetoric and has found its way into scholarly publications as well. In several recent discussions, for example, I have been asked to contrast the "constructive and idealistic" young radicals I studied two years ago with the "nihilistic and violent" radicals who have purportedly replaced them today.

I believe there has been a change toward militancy, anger and dogmatism in the white student movement, but that it has been greatly exaggerated. At least part of the distance between sitting in at a Southern segregationist lunch counter (thereby preventing its owner from doing business) and occupying a Northern administration building (thereby "bringing the machine to a halt") is a difference in target, not tactics. In both cases, individuals use their bodies to obstruct, disrupt or prevent the orderly conduct of business as usual. To be sure, there are other differences, too; but the one central difference is in our attitude toward Southern segregationists and Northern college presidents. Part of the distance the student movement has traveled is the distance from Selma to Morningside Heights, from Bull Connor to Nathan Pusey.

Yet the mood, temper and rhetoric of the student movement *has* drastically changed. In place of a nonviolent willingness to endure the punishments decreed by law for violations of local ordinances, we instead see an often angry and militant demand for amnesty. (It should be recalled, of course, that in the early days of the Civil Rights Movement, a demand for amnesty would have been quixotic: civil rights workers had no choice but to accept the punishment that was inflicted upon them. Today, in contrast, *de facto* amnesty is often a real possibility, in practice if not in principle.)

More important, the often religiously Christian or Gandhian nonviolent mood of the Civil Rights Movement has been replaced by a more defiant, more angry, more politically revolutionary stance among today's student radicals. The influence of Mao Tse-tung, mediated through the Progressive Labor Party and Worker-Student Alliance, is only one of many new influences. The writings of Fanon, Debray and other apostles of armed revolution have had their effect; the model of revolutionary leaders like Castro, Guevara and Ho Chi Minh has become more important; and Marxist and neo-Marxist concepts increasingly dominate the political rhetoric of radicals. In addition, the rising militancy of portions of the black community has had its impact upon white students, now effectively excluded even from campus alliances with blacks. There often ensues something analogous to a game of "chicken": black militants and white radicals vie with each other to up the ante, each demonstrating to the other that they are more truly revolutionary.

How do we account for this shift in mood, tone and rhetoric in the student movement? Is the New Left recruiting new members who are more violent, more

uncontrolled, more nihilistic and destructive than the "gentle" civil rights workers of the past? Has there been an influx of what within the student movement
are called Crazies? Or is essentially the same group (in personality terms) reacting
differently because of a different political situation? Can we distinguish in any
useful way within the student movement between the "nihilistic" and "idealistic"
activists?

At this point, anyone who like myself is essentially a clinician must remind
himself of what we all know but frequently forget: the essential ambivalence of
human nature. Even the most cursory reading of the history of the Russian
revolutionary student movement shows that some of its most able and devoted
leaders began as populist idealists of the highest principle but moved on to become
members of the terrorist or "nihilist" movement, forever thereafter named after
them. It seems unlikely that their basic characters, ideals and personalities
changed in any fundamental way. Instead, we must posit "learning from experience," situational reactions to harassment, defeat and Czarist repression which
led to the surfacing of aspects of personality that were previously controlled,
suppressed or repressed. Introspection should further convince us that ambivalence is not confined to student activists, nor indeed to students; psychologists and
educators, among others, exhibit the same mixture of feelings. The point is
obvious: The same person, depending on circumstances, is invariably both an
idealist and a nihilist.

Some people, though, are more nihilistic or idealistic than others, and recent
research has pointed to the existence, within the student movement, of two
distinct personality types, which can be loosely associated with the nihilistic-
idealistic distinction. Robert Liebert, a New York psychoanalyst, after intensive
interviewing of a large group of white and black participants and nonparticipants
in the Columbia "liberation" of last year, found that students in the occupied
buildings fell along a continuum of idealistic and constructive to nihilistic and
destructive. He hypothesized different developmental patterns in each group, and
noted their different style and approach to political action. But he found that the
"great majority" of students in the buildings at Columbia were idealists, and
argued plausibly that most nihilists in his sense are never admitted to college (or
at least not to Columbia). So while the distinction between nihilists and idealists
can be made, the empirical conclusion nevertheless emphasizes the predominance
of idealists even among the purportedly obscene, destructive and nihilistic students involved in the Columbia disruption.

Similar conclusions emerge from far-reaching research conducted at the
University of California at Berkeley and San Francisco State College by Brewster
Smith, Jeanne Block and Norma Haan. Their research is especially conclusive in
its analysis of the relationship between moral development and participation in
student protest activities. Their study is built on the research into moral development by Lawrence Kohlberg, who, in essence, distinguishes three major stages
in moral reasoning: *pre-conventional* (the individual egocentrically defines right
and wrong in terms of what is good or pleasurable for him); *conventional* (the
individual identifies right and wrong either with being a "good boy" or a "good
girl," or with a more general concept of law and order—that is, with the existing

community standards); and *post-conventional* (a stage which most individuals never reach, in which right and wrong are identified with the long-range good of the community or with such abstract personal principles as the sanctity of life, the categorical imperative or the Golden Rule). In the post-conventional stage, the individual may, of course, find himself in sharp conflict with existing community standards; for example, with concepts of law and order.

Comparing large numbers of students who participated in protest activities at San Francisco State and Berkeley with students who had not, the Smith research group found massive differences. They found that 56 percent of the protesters were at the post-conventional stage of moral development as compared with 12 percent of the non-protesters, while 85 percent of the non-protesters were at the conventional stage as compared with 34 percent of the protesters. No other researcher, studying any other variable, has shown such massive differences between activists and non-activists. The Smith research thus supports what many commentators have also suggested—namely, that moral issues are at the heart of student revolt.

Smith and his colleagues, though, also found disproportionate numbers of "pre-conventionals" (egocentrics) among the protesters. In their sample, the pre-conventionals constituted 10 percent of the protest group, but only 3 percent of the non-protesters. The work of Smith and Kohlberg suggests that such young men and women are in a state of temporary moral regression, which often accompanies an individual's development from the conventional to the post-conventional stage. Kohlberg aptly terms this moral regression the "Raskolnikoff Syndrome." It might also be called the "Trobriand Island Syndrome," inasmuch as the moral reasoning that accompanies it is, "If they do it in the Trobriand Islands, why shouldn't I do it, too?"

Finally, Jeanne Block makes an important distinction between what she terms "parental continuity" and "parental discontinuity" groups among activists and protesters. The parental continuity group was extremely critical of American society, but its members evidenced strong continuity with their parents and their parents' values. The parental discontinuity group was critical of *both* American society *and* their parents. Contrasting these two groups, both active politically, Block found that they differed in a variety of respects: members of the discontinuity group (the "rebellion" group) adopted more of a hippie life-style, seemed more profoundly alienated from American society and were less conventionally "responsible" in their other activities. Members of the continuity group (the "chips-off-the-old-block") were less expressive, less irresponsible and less affected by personal conflicts.

These studies thus suggest the viability of a rough distinction between nihilistic and idealistic radical activism. Indeed, research on the relation between moral development and activism points to what may be a bipolar grouping within the activist camp. For Smith and his colleagues find that both extremes—the "post-conventionals" and the "pre-conventionals"—are overrepresented in the protesting group. But again there is the question of ambivalence. For even the pre-conventional (egocentric) student is, we know from other evidence, likely to be in a temporary and usually partial state of regression to earlier concepts of morality, all as a part of a long-range trajectory toward post-conventional ethical thinking. Which potential is activated in him—pre-conventional or post-conventional, egocentric or ethical—depends much upon the fate of his causes and the company he keeps. In short, if the distinction between nihilists and idealists among today's student radicals holds water, it is with the essential qualification that everyone is always a little of both.

Two years ago, in discussing the personality development of radicals, I contrasted two hypotheses. The first, the "Oedipal rebel" hypothesis, rests on the notion of strong Oedipally-based rebellion against the father "acted out" symbolically during late adolescence and youth in attacks on authority figures like college presidents, generals, the Establishment, and government policies and leaders. The second theory, the "red diaper baby" theory, posits that today's student radicals are the children of yesterday's radicals (raised in red diapers). Yet neither of these views adequately accounted for the feelings that male radicals reported about their fathers—a combination of genuine affection and determination to act more resolutely in the service of principle. This pattern contrasted sharply with the more truly rebellious pattern I had previously observed in a study of alienated students, none of whom were politically active and most of whom today would probably have been hippies rather than political radicals.

In the last two years, the Oedipal rebellion thesis has received widespread publicity. Lewis Feuer, in his brilliant but tendentious book, *The Conflict of Generations,* makes Oedipal rebellion the basis for his explanation of the psychodynamics of student radicalism. Bruno Bettelheim has offered Oedipal rebellion, among other explanations, as one of the causes of student revolt. Ben Rubenstein and Morton Levitt have analyzed the psychodynamics of the student movement in terms of "totem and taboo." And Stewart Alsop, in a recent article in *Newsweek,* lumped me together with Feuer and Bettelheim as one of those who "takes seriously" the Oedipal rebellion hypothesis.

I take it seriously enough to argue that it is incorrect. So, too, it should be noted, does virtually every other investigator who has done empirical research on the subject. Seymour Martin Lipset, the Harvard sociologist, hardly a hero of or apologist for today's student radicals, concludes a recent summary of research on student activism by noting that the central finding on politically active left-wing students, not only in America but elsewhere in the world, is that they come from liberal and politically active families. This is hardly evidence of Oedipal rebellion. Despite the great variety of personality types and motivations that enter into radicalism, empirical studies find continuity with parental values to be the rule and discontinuity the exception. Within any group of activist protesters, it is possible, as the new research shows, to distinguish two sub-groups, one of which consists of chips-off-the-old-block, the other of rebels. But even then the evidence suggests that the chips-off-the-old-block are more numerous and that unequivocal rebellion against the same-sex parent is more likely to lead to a withdrawn posture of dissent, to a hippie quietism.

Yet in considering relationships with parents, as with the whole question of generational continuity, one must again recall the central fact of ambivalence in human development. Even in working with students who present themselves as unqualifiedly hating their parents, we frequently find that beneath hatred, defiance and rebellion lie love and dependency, all the more intense because they have been so strongly repudiated. Similarly, *The Authoritarian Personality* and a series of later studies have shown that many individuals who portray their parents as virtually perfect turn out to possess at a less conscious level a contrasting and opposite view of harsh, tyrannical and hated parents. It would be contrary to everything we know about human development and generational relations were we not to find mixed feelings about parents in any group. What is impressive, then, in the studies of student radicals is the *relative* predominance of positive feelings, positive identification and basic value continuity.

Another thesis commonly advanced, especially in popular discussions of today's student radicalism, is that today's student activists behave as they do because of the Spockian permissiveness of their upbringing. "Permissiveness" is used as a bad word, and the explanation usually goes on to note that students have not learned self-restraint, have never experienced the force or coercion they desperately needed in order to develop inner controls, and have no respect for limits, older people, etc. This view has been advanced not only by such critics of the student movement as Bruno Bettelheim, but also, a number of years ago (in modified form), by Richard Flacks, a founder of SDS and now a distinguished researcher on student activism. Flacks found that the parents of activists, compared with those of non-activists, would be less distressed were their children to drop out of college or to live (unmarried) with a member of the opposite sex; he also found that activist students less often reported that their parents were strict. In his initial writings, he interpreted this as evidence of parental permissiveness, one factor in what he termed the "deviant socialization" of student radicals.

Three recent studies, however, discredit the permissiveness hypothesis. One, an unpublished PH.D. thesis by Lamar Thomas, a student of Flacks, compares the children of politically active parents of both the Right and the Left. It finds generally higher levels of political activity among the children of left-wing parents, but *no* relationship in either group between activism and permissiveness. A second study, by Norma Haan and Jeanne Block, concludes (on the basis of data on almost one thousand students) that permissiveness is not a determining variable of activism. And William Cowdry at Yale found no relationship between permissiveness and anti-war activism among college seniors.

But even if permissiveness is not the issue, recent studies suggest that methods of discipline and family values *are* important. In my study two years ago, my radical subjects emphasized the subtle yet pervasive power of parental principle in their upbringing. They had been brought up in families with a moral atmosphere that was largely implicit but nonetheless powerful. The methods of discipline used in these families generally avoided physical punishment, direct coercion, even ostracism. Instead, reasoning and the transmission of high expectations were the favored methods of inculcating family values. Parental expectations were communicated by the promotion of independence, by the assumption that the child would accept responsibility and control himself, and by the use of such indirect (but powerful) sanctions as the expression of disappointment in the child when he misbehaved.

Empirical research has in general confirmed these findings. Flacks' study, which involved intensive interviewing of the parents of activists and non-activists, found important distinctions in the value emphases of activist and non-activist families. In activist families, he found a greater emphasis on the importance of ideas (intellectualism), on the expression of feelings (romanticism), and on serving others (humanitarianism) and a lesser emphasis on strict control of impulse (low moralism). Approaching the same questions differently, the Smith research group found, in general, that the socialization experiences reported by protesters emphasized training for independence by parents who themselves had strong independent interests not involving their children. These studies are consistent with the hypothesis that the dominant socialization pattern for today's student activists involves not permissiveness but a highly principled family culture which is transmitted to children through the use of reasoning and persuasion, and the encouragement of independence in thought and action.

As for the critical question of social versus psychological determinants of political attitude and behavior, most researchers have found consistent demographic and socioeconomic correlates of political activism. In general, these point to a relationship between activism and high socioeconomic status, high parental education and high parental involvement in professional and, in particular, "helping" vocations. (Flacks finds that higher levels of education characterize even the grandparents of activists.)

But as Lipset points out, many socio-demographic characteristics have known psychological concomitants. The use of reasoning and persuasion in bringing up children, for example, is more common in upper-middle-class than in working-class families. Similarly, religion has been shown to be associated with activism: a disproportionate number of students from Jewish families are involved in radical protest activities. The theoretical problem these findings raise can be seen in an example. Suppose we find that the mothers of political activists show a distinctive concern for the nurture of their children. We still do not know how to interpret this finding. Does it indicate a causal relationship between maternal nurturance and filial activism? Or does it merely reflect the accidental fact that more radicals, being Jewish, have nurturant Jewish mothers? According to the second interpretation, radicalism might be "caused" by other factors directly connected with Jewishness (for example, familiarity with or enjoyment of the position of an òut-group member). Or it might be related to still other factors indirectly connected with Jewishness (for example, great stress on acting in the service of one's beliefs.) Without further studies that control for these factors, we do not know whether psychological or sociological variables are more important.

Several recent studies permit us to approach this question, however, at least in a preliminary way. Flacks' research controlled for type of college attended, area of residence and class in college. It thus provided at least an informal control on socioeconomic status, and the fact that Flacks found distinctive differences between the families of activists and non-activists is consistent with the view that "family culture" variables are critical in political activism. Haan and Block, moreover, have recently responded directly to Lipset's challenge by re-analyzing their data with religion controlled. Analyzing family socialization variables independently for two groups Jews and non-Jews, they found that within each of these groups the same socialization variables continued to be associated with political activism. And Cowdry, studying a highly homogeneous Yale College senior class, found many socialization variables, but no social, religious or demographic factors, associated with activism.

Still, the issue cannot be settled with only the evidence at hand. In all probability, several interacting factors are involved. On the one hand, it seems clear that *if* children are brought up in upper-middle-class professional families with humanitarian, expressive and intellectual values, and *if* the techniques of discipline emphasize independence and reasoning, and *if* the parents are themselves politically liberal and politically active, then the chances of the child's being an activist are greatly increased, regardless of factors like religion. But it is also clear that these conditions are fulfilled most often in Jewish families. And there may be still other factors associated with social class and religion that independently promote activism; for example, being in a Jewish minority group that has preserved its culture in the face of opposing community pressures for centuries may in some way prepare or permit the individual to take controversial positions as a student.

Another question left unanswered by most research on student activism is whether we have been studying the determinants of radical beliefs, of action in general, or of the interaction between a particular set of radical beliefs and a particular type of radical action. The typical study of student activists selects for intensive investigation a group defined by *behavioral* criteria: Were they or were they not arrested for disruption at Dartmouth in 1969? Did they or did they not take part in Mississippi Summer? Such "activists" then are typically compared with a "control group"—usually a random sample of the college population. The extremely consistent differences routinely found in such research provide the current portrait of the activist.

But how should the differences be interpreted? Do they reflect radical *beliefs?* If so, then occupying a building or participating in an anti-war protest presumably reflects the intensity of the beliefs: We suppose there is a direct connection between the strength of one's beliefs and the probability of acting on them. But it is equally possible that by contrasting activists defined by behavioral criteria with others in the college population, we are studying something besides beliefs —namely, a tendency to take action in the name of one's convictions. This factor of "consistency" between beliefs and behavior may, in fact, turn out to have determinants other than those of beliefs alone.

In his recent research on this issue, Cowdry, then a Yale College senior, studied a random sample of the Yale class of 1968. He was initially interested in examining how attitudes toward the war in Vietnam were related to plans concerning military service. But in the course of his study, a strongly-worded anti-war resolution was distributed, with wide publicity, to the entire senior class. Since two-thirds of the class said they opposed the war but only one-third signed the resolution, Cowdry was able to compare two groups with equally strong anti-war sentiments: the group which signed the resolution and the one which did not. His findings support the view that *with* anti-war attitudes held constant, the determinants of beliefs are different from the determinants of action (signing the resolution). Indeed, his study suggests that many of the characteristics of activists reported in previous studies may be related not as much to having radical beliefs as to behavior-belief "consistency." For the two groups that were "consistent" (the anti-war signers and the pro-war non-signers) were in many respects more like each other than either group was like the "inconsistent" group (the anti-war non-signers). One question raised by this finding is whether the observed characteristics of behaviorally-defined activists—especially the socialization variables associated with activism—have any necessary relation to left-wing (as opposed to right-wing) views, or whether they are concomitants of taking action consistent with one's beliefs—regardless of where these beliefs fall on the political spectrum.

One further finding of interest emerged from Cowdry's study. He found that anti-war beliefs were associated with a set of characteristic self-descriptions: The anti-war students described themselves as more expressive, more aesthetic, more idealistic than did the pro-war students. At the same time, Cowdry found that virtually these same characterizations were applied to their fathers by "consistent" students (anti-war signers), but *not* by "inconsistents" (anti-war non-signers). This suggests that the student most likely to hold radical beliefs *and* act on them is identified with a humanitarian, idealistic and expressive father. Conversely, the student most likely to hold radical beliefs but not act upon them is one who sees *himself* as humanitarian, idealistic and expressive, but has developed this self-characterization in rebellion against his father.

Several points, based on the voluminous body of research on student radicals, can be made:

—Student radicals are an elite group, and not the "rabble of rejects" they have been termed. There is an impressive uniformity in the finding of a great variety of studies conducted by different researchers using different methods with different populations: Free Speech Movement students at Berkeley, activists at San Francisco State, Mississippi Summer Volunteers, Columbia radicals, Michigan State and Penn State SDS members, Dartmouth College arrestees, and so on. These similarities can be summarized, perhaps oversimplified, in a sentence: The activist group is, compared to the student population from which it is drawn, an "elite" group in virtually every respect.

—Moral issues are central to student radicalism. The most impressive differences found between activists and non-activists have been in the area of moral development. There are many other statistically significant differences, but the moral differences observed are so overwhelming that they suggest that Smith and his co-workers are close to the heart of the matter. To be sure, the determinants of levels of moral development are themselves extremely complex, and not perfectly correlated with activism. Nevertheless, recent research strongly indicates that a central factor in radical political activism is level of moral development.

—There are several routes to radicalism. With regard to male radicals, for example, at least two pathways to radical beliefs can be distinguished. The first is the pathway of identification. Both father and son are described as expressive, humanitarian, and idealistic. The son identifies with his father, although the son is usually more radical. Such sons are very likely to be radicals in action as well as beliefs. They generally fall into the "idealistic radical" group. There is, however, clearly a second pathway to radical beliefs, though less often to radical actions: the pathway of rejection of identification. Such students describe themselves as expressive, idealistic, and humanitarian, but describe their fathers as distinctively *not* any of these things. They are rather less likely to be politically active, more likely to adopt an apolitical or "hippie" style of dissent, and, if they become involved in political action, more likely to fall within the "nihilist" group.

—A great many students with vehemently radical beliefs do not implement their beliefs in action. Most psychological research has so far emphasized the enduring states and characteristics of those who act. But for every activist, there are many others who share his beliefs but do not act. In our democratic society, it is commonly asserted that citizens with strong convictions should be willing to express them and work to implement them. If we assume that "consistency" between beliefs and action is desirable, we need to know better what produces it, regardless of political convictions. As yet, little is known about the psychological and social processes by which individuals are activated, by which a community is politicized, and by which potential activists find and activate each other. Nor do we know anything about short-term and long-term consequences to the individual of implementing—or not implementing—his beliefs.

—Psychological explanations alone are not adequate to understand today's student radicals. Student radicalism has developed within a social, cultural and, above all, a political context. High levels of moral development, for example, did not begin with the Civil Rights Movement; nor can we interpret the recent changes in mood, tone, rhetoric, ideology and style of the student movement primarily in terms of the changing personality composition of radical groups. More to the point, we must study the evolution and rationale of the student movement itself. For example, even such minimal goals of student activists as an end to the war in Vietnam, a major attack on racism and poverty, and a "restructuring" of the university have not been attained. Given this fact, it probably does not take complex psychological explanations to explain the rise in militancy, anger and dogmatism that we see.

—Most important, the study of student radicalism exposes the ideological bias and theoretical inadequacy of many of the concepts by which we have attemped to understand the relationship of men to politics and society. Until recently, the most widely-used concepts have focused largely upon processes that lead to stasis and stability in society and politics. The study of socialization has focused upon how children adapt their personalities to the social roles, norms and institutions of their society. The study of acculturation has emphasized how values and symbol systems are internalized so that they become part of the individual. And into many such analyses there has crept a covertly evaluative element: Viable societies are assumed to be those which "effectively socialize" the young into their available roles; valid cultures are those which inspire the greatest consensus and loyalty to their symbols and values. The evaluative weight of the concepts of "socialization" and "acculturation" becomes apparent when we reverse the terms: "de-socialization" connotes misanthropy, anomia and possibly psychiatric illness, while "dis-acculturation" connotes a collapse of values into barbarity or nihilism.

The study of student radicals indicates that these connotations are often incorrect, and that the study of socialization and acculturation must be complemented by the study of de-socialization and dis-acculturation as the psychological correlates and, to some extent, the causes of social and political change. Indeed, some purportedly "socializing" environments (like liberal arts colleges and universities) do anything but neatly "socialize" or "integrate" all their charges into available social roles, existing social institutions, traditional values and conventional symbol systems. On the contrary, we witness today, both in America and in other nations, a phenomenon that can be called *youthful de-socialization.* Traditional roles, institutions, values and symbols are critically scrutinized and often rejected, while new roles, institutions, values and symbols more adequate to the modern world are desperately sought.

Research on student activism points to the enormous complexity of youthful de-socialization. On the one hand, this research finds underlying value continuity between most activists and their families. But on the other hand, it also reveals discontinuity, innovation and change: rejection by the children of liberal parents of many liberal assumptions in favor of more radical political beliefs, the emergence of new political tactics, efforts to find new political procedures, roles, institutions and methods for change. Youthful de-socialization, then, is always *partial,* but it may still be far-reaching and politically decisive. The tumult, controversy and criticism that pervades higher education today, then, should remind us that if we are to understand change, innovation, reform and revolution, we cannot do so solely with concepts designed to explain stability and equilibrium. In addition, we must attempt to understand the forces that lead intelligent, talented and idealistic men and women (both young and old) to refuse, challenge or revitalize the conventional wisdom.

QUESTIONS FOR DISCUSSION AND DIALOGUE

1. It is obvious that Keniston is not "down on" student militants as is Toole. Would you call Keniston a "spokesman" for student militants? Why? Is there a difference between the words "radical" and "militant"?
2. Outline the way you think Keniston would go about arguing against this statement: "Parental permissiveness ("spocking" children instead of "spanking" them) is largely responsible for the irresponsibility of modern student radicals."
3. Now that you have read three different interpretations of student radicalism, which do you tend to agree with the most? Why?
4. As of 1969, there were 7.1 million students in U.S. colleges and universities. This number and the percentage of American youth in higher education is increasing. You have just finished a chapter devoted to considering them as one important group of Americans. Write a brief paragraph or develop a brief oral statement about the kind of politics you think will develop in the future when these students begin to exercise their influence more directly.

|
—————— CHAPTER THREE ——————
|

The Politicians and
their Parties

Now to the Politicians and Parties. The chapter opens with an article by Stephen K. Bailey, who considers some practical situations in which the Politician is asked to make political decisions in an ethical context. Next, Senator J. William Fulbright attempts an answer to the question, "Is Government by the people possible?" Daniel J. Boorstin shows a concern about the changing nature of American politics which he says is no longer "safe" and "predictable." Bill Moyers, an ex-Presidential advisor himself, reviews Theodore White's *The Making of the President, 1968* in such a way as to suggest that American politics has changed so deeply that White has not been able to comprehend the change. Stewart Alsop disagrees with this assessment by Moyers, criticizing it as representing "A fashionable political cult" which is "curiously snobbish and very powerful." *Time* magazine offers a pre-election study of the 1968 Presidential election victor, Richard Nixon. One of the surprise noncontenders in that election, Lyndon B. Johnson, is considered next in "before" and "after" terms by two *Newsweek* articles. Ev Dirksen is considered as a Politician and a man with some politically related economic interests, and as a contrast ex Barry Goldwater speech writer Karl Hess' "suddenly radicalized life style" is studied by a brief *Newsweek* article. A would-be Politician, John H. Knowles, who was "cut" at the last minute by the President reflects on his "tryout" and rejection.

Here then are some of the Politicians at work. Their interrelationships with the Americans as a whole and in their separate groups provide the most publicized and the most controversial aspects of the American political world.

Ethics and the Politician

Stephen K. Bailey

What motivates the Politicians beyond winning elections? An ex-Politi-cian—Stephen K. Bailey was Mayor of Middletown, Connecticut, a city of about 30,000 people—considers this question from theoretical and practical points of view. The reader is introduced here to the complexity of moral-practical and individual-social choices that all Politicians must face. Bailey concludes by considering "the ultimate ethical postulate in a democracy." It is well worth deep reflection by all concerned Americans.

Any attempt to construct what John Buchan once called "an essay in recol-lection" is fraught with ethical puzzles. When it is addressed to the moral dilem-mas of a political experience of some years ago, ethical issues are piled crazily one on top of the other. And they are nudged into further disarray by the tricks that rationalization and memory play upon all autobiographers. In view of the number of friends whose good names must be protected against my possibly accurate reporting of their (and my) occasional moral lapses; in view of the impossibility, six to eight years after events, of my recapturing the precise pattern of considerations which shaped the matrix within which decisions were made; and in view of the inscrutability of many of the ethical issues with which I, as mayor of a city of 30,000, had to deal, it is clear that this essay must be content with the perennially probable rather than the historically precise.

Insofar as I refer specifically to experiences in Middletown, Connecticut, during the years when I was mayor of that city, I hope that friends there will show me the same charity that Huckleberry Finn showed Mark Twain. Referring to *The Adventures of Tom Sawyer,* Huck commented, "That book was made by Mr. Mark Twain, and he told the truth, mainly. There was things which he stretched, but mainly he told the truth. That is nothing. I never seen anybody but lied one time or another, without it was Aunt Polly. . . . " And Huck Finn was perceptive in spotting the moral flaw in Aunt Polly and in her old maid sister, Miss Watson: a flaw of self-righteousness so hideous that when Huck learned that Miss Watson was living "so as to go to the good place," Huck could "see no advantage in going where she was going," so he made up his mind he wouldn't try for it.

I have worried far more about the ethical consequences of my decisions as mayor since leaving office than I ever did as an incumbent. And perhaps this is the first point to be made. Most elected executives find that there is an ethics of *action* which is normally far more compelling than the urge to balance with precision the ethical niceties of pressing public issues. There are times when the good of the community demands firmness and decision at the expense of marginal injustice. Those who would make justice the sole criterion of the good society are not only, in my judgment, myopic in their ethical vision, they establish an impossible operating norm for administrators. Justice, in the sense of "just deserts," presumes omnipotence and omniscience. An elected mayor in a "weak-mayor" form of government, alas, has neither. He may desire to be just, but occasions arise when justice is not the highest ethical priority. If a local hospital, which has run a countywide ambulance service for years, suddenly decides for budgetary reasons to disown this responsibility, it may be unjust to make the taxpayers of a single city in the county pick up the check for keeping the countywide ambulance service going on an emergency basis. But, here, what is necessary overrides what is just.

And emergency actions by an authorized executive have meaning and value quite apart from the justice or injustice of any decision taken by the executive under his emergency authority. The justification for the emergency powers of the public executive are, I believe, not only in the necessities of organization under stress; there is a most significant social therapy in the public's sense that "somebody is in charge." The sight of Winston Churchill making his way through the rubble of blitzed London and barking orders to subordinates had the effect of strengthening resolve and dissolving fear among the affected public. Even lowly political executives at times perform this valuable emergency role.

But even when an emergency does not exist, there are frequently statutory deadlines or political deadlines—budgets, elections, schedules of compliance established by a higher level of government—which precipitate executive decisions largely uncomplicated by labored ethical considerations. Deadlines are great strengtheners of the resolve to choose. Those who would build theories of decision-making removed from the context of the clock and the calendar know nothing of the inner life of a political executive. And, even then, no executive in public life is free from having his life arbitrarily and often whimsically scheduled by real or fancied immediacies which are superimposed upon the clock and calendar, no matter how carefully the latter have been anticipated.

In brief, although almost every issue with which an elected executive must deal is charged with ethical dilemmas, it is rare that the executive has either the time, the context, or the liver for constructing balanced ethical judgments. He does what he must. Ethically, elected executives tend, like successful fighter pilots, to "fly by the seat of their pants." Speed is the enemy of deliberation, and, in administration, speed—in the sense of dispatch—is often the condition of maintaining a tolerable if ineffable balance among those interests, obligations, and necessities which crowd the world of the elected executive.

All of this is not meant to suggest that ethical considerations are somehow peripheral to an elected executive's life. It is only to say that ethical issues are rarely trotted out for leisurely inspection and deliberate choice. This may be unfortunate, but my guess is that if ethical considerations were always carefully and honestly articulated in decision-making, the ensuing chaos—moral and administrative—would be impressive.

If we are talking about the real world, then, we are talking in large measure about the *inarticulate* moral premises of the office holder—the ethical signposts which a harried political executive catches out of the corner of his eye.

With this statement, of course, the essay could well end. Any attempt to list all of the precepts, proverbs, fables (and their rationalized versions) which conscience picks to guide or to justify actions would lead to an endless and formless recitation of the obvious and the inscrutable. And ultimately such a recitation would tell us nothing about conscience itself; that ego-tempered temperer of egos; that culture-bound transcender of culture; that ultimate sorter of ethical ambiguities. It gets us nowhere to suggest that all of the Philosophy 1-2 classroom stumpers are present in political life—as they are in all life. Should a cancer specialist be honest or kind? Ultimately, is it more honest to be kind or more kind to be honest? Is a half-truth a worse enemy of the truth than a falsehood? Should promises be kept if the situation changes (and when doesn't it change)? Should friends be reported if you know them to be mostly good and you know that they probably will not do it again? Should you subject someone to the consequences of wrongdoing if you are reasonably sure that the penalty is sufficiently harsh and inelastic as to be inequitable?

To pretend that there are clear religious, moral, or legal answers to such questions is to fly in the face of all sensitive moral inquiry.

How difficult the means-ends questions of living really are is known by every parent who ponders such matters. After a generation of permissiveness in raising children, we are finally returning to a belief that metes and bounds backed by sanctions are ultimately kinder to the growing child and the society than uninhibited license. But how many sanctions? How extensive the metes and bounds? Someone once commented that the Lord had left the two most difficult and important jobs in the world to amateurs: citizenship and parenthood. Elected political executives, at least most of them, are also amateurs, and their jobs may be no less difficult or important than the others mentioned. What is common to the life of all of these amateurs is that the value questions are extraordinarily complex, and the chances of adequate time for deliberation are slim.

But are there not peculiar ethical risks run by elected political executives? Surely, most people are not faced frequently with questions of bribery, spoils, corruption, favoritism. The difficulty is, neither are elected political executives, and even when venality raises its head it rarely looks to the responsible political executive as ugly as it appears in newspaper cartoons or Sunday sermons. Venality, like virtue, is rarely unambiguous. G. K. Chesterton wrote perceptively when he suggested that the error of Diogenes "lay in the fact that he omitted to notice that every man is both an honest and a dishonest man. Diogenes looked for his honest man inside every crypt and cavern. But he never thought of looking inside the thief. And that is where the Founder of Christianity found the honest man. He found him on a gibbet and promised him paradise."

When the nicest people have rationalized their selfishness with a tactical deference to the public interest, elected political executives are often grateful that they are too preoccupied to be ethically astute. Even where venality seems clearest, as in the rare case of an attempt at straight bribery ("Mayor, here's a thousand dollars in five-dollar bills if you get that easement through the council"—the political version of "payola"), the ethical issues may not be self-evident. Let us make some assumptions: suppose that the mayor knows that the easement will go through "on its merits" (begging what *that* slippery phrase means). Suppose further that the mayor knows that the party needs money not only to run the forthcoming election but to pay debts on a past election. Suppose the mayor knows further that the voting public has not responded favorably and positively to the appeal of the American Heritage Foundation for everyone to give to the party of his choice. Suppose finally that the mayor believes that a working two-party system is the nation's and the community's greatest safeguard of democracy and freedom. If it could be proved to the mayor's satisfaction that the lack of $1,000 at the moment could do irreparable damage to the two-party system in the area, would it be a higher principle in a naughty world for the mayor to accept the money on behalf of the party, or to refuse the money?

Stated this way, the issue is still not very complex for most people. "They've known what's right and wrong since they've been ten." You do not accept bribes, period; and you most certainly do not compound evil by cheating the briber. This is all very clear. But is it, really? There are ways of playing slight variations on this theme which would remove from the sternest Presbyterian moralist any burden of guilt. The briber has made a number of contributions to the party over the years. The latest thousand is simply another indication of his belief in the great principles of the party. On the easement question, every party member on the council, including the mayor, attempts to examine the issue on its merits. But a "will to believe" has set in—a subtle coloration of the problem. Good old Joe is a friend who provided all the favors for the party picnic. Isn't it fortunate that the merits of the easement case are on his side?

And bribery can take so many forms: money, favors, flattery, help in time of trouble, influence in building status. To pretend that bribery is a simple and easily spotted phenomenon is naive. To pretend it takes place only in politics is silly. I have seen the egos of older university professors successfully bribed by astute and ambitious instructors; I have seen great institutions bribe men into conformity with promises of promotions or demotions. I have seen them kill, spiritually, those who resisted. I have received threats that unless such-and-such happened, I'd be voted out of office at the next election. Is this not attempted bribery? Is money any more a thing of value than power or status or re-election? If there are clear moral distinctions here, they escape me, even though our cultural inheritance sanctions certain kinds of bribery and frowns on others.

I once asked a municipal judge in Middletown to tell me what pressures were most constant in trying to influence his impartial administration of justice. He thought a minute and then said, laughingly, "the university deans and the town clergy." But why should he have laughed? Certainly few would question the motives of deans and clergy in attempting to save the reputations of individuals known to them, and under their keep, who have been accused of wrongdoing. But what of the wrongdoer who has no "friend in court"? Anyone who has ever watched a municipal court in action over a period of time knows that "political influence" is frequently a corrective for the partial justice that results from the rich litigant's capacity to purchase superior legal talent. Middle-class justice is not always equitable to the poor. This is not to condone political influence in courts of law, it is to suggest that without political influence certain inequities might be greater than they are and that those inequities need as much attention as overt or covert political influence.

I was never asked to fix a traffic or parking ticket in Middletown; but I cannot swear that tickets were not occasionally fixed while I was mayor. And I am not sure that under certain circumstances (*e.g.,* a hectic woman delayed in buying her six children school clothes) I would not have paid the dollar fine myself rather than penalize her for something beyond her effective control. Nothing is more unjust than unexceptional law except law that is all exceptions. Surely, one of the most difficult ethical problems in all governance is the drawing of lines between rules and exceptions. That the lines, to be moral, must be drawn near the rules end of the spectrum I do not question. But that exceptions are never warranted seems to me the most callous of all moral judgments.

To the moralist, words like bribery, favoritism, spoils, patronage, graft, are as clear and as evil as though bottled and marked with skull and crossbones. To those with political responsibility, on the other hand, it occasionally seems clear that poison can be therapeutic. The fact that poison is labelled with a skull and crossbones and placed back on a high shelf of the medicine closet may not mean that it is never to be used; only that it is to be used with care and in small doses. It is possible that if an elected executive had infinite time he might be able to discern ways to achieve his goals without using morally uncomfortable means— although the question of where rationalizations begin and end with this sort of game plays hob with moral certainty. But if giving an unskilled job to a not-incompetent nationality-group representative might make the difference between winning or losing on an urban renewal referendum of vast benefit to the entire city for years to come, I know few elected executives who would boggle over making such an appointment even if the executive was convinced that someone else might do the unskilled job better.

George Bernard Shaw once wrote what many politicians must at times have felt. Shaw learned that a Labour candidate named Joseph Burgess had refused to compromise on some issue and had thereby lost his seat in Parliament. Shaw commented bitterly:

> When I think of my own unfortunate character, smirched with compromise, rotted with opportunism, mildewed by expediency—dragged through the mud of borough council and Battersea elections, stretched out of shape with wire-pulling, putrefied by permeation, worn out by twenty-five years pushing to gain an inch here, or straining to stem a backrush, I do think Joe might have put up with just a speck or two on those white robes of his for the sake of the millions of poor devils who cannot afford any character at all because they have no friend in Parliament. Oh, these moral dandies, these spiritual toffs, these superior persons. Who is Joe, anyhow, that he should not risk his soul occasionally like the rest of us?

I was once confronted with a possible kickback on a fire truck purchase. The party representative reminded me that it cost money to run elections; that generosity from fire truck manufacturers to those who had the insight to see the need for public safety in their communities was rather standard; and that no one would really suffer. The gift would come as a preordained slice of the salesman's commission, who would give of his own income because "he believed in the principles of the Democratic Party." I drew myself up to my maximum height, stared at my good friend, and said in what I am sure must have been the most patronizing of tones, "If the party needs four or five hundred dollars, I shall be happy to try to raise the money personally; but I shall not do it that way." I then went a step further. I called the poor fire truck salesman into the office and made him add about $400 worth of extra equipment to the fire truck at the bid price he had quoted. In a swift double blow I had proved my moral worth and defended the taxpayers' interests. I had proved that at least in one American community "public office is a public trust."

I had also proved that it is easy to be moral when the pressure is not really on. Suppose the party coffers *had* been empty? Suppose my confident bluff to raise "four or five hundred dollars" for the party had been called? Suppose the alternative to a Democratic re-election was the election of a rather disreputable Republican gang who would have practiced "boodle" with more frequency and with infinitely less flair than the Democrats? What then? And why should we refuse to accept money for the imperative cause of political party machinery, almost regardless of source, when the so-called "good" people of the community would not be caught dead giving to their political party—to the system of options which does far more than the Constitution to guarantee freedom and democracy?

I could not be a partner to a kickback, not because I had carefully weighed the moral issues but because my moral viscera told me it was wrong. Unfortunately, my moral viscera are not always right. If they were right in this particular case, they were right for reasons removed from the issue at hand. They were right because, without sufficient time and eloquence, I could not have explained any contrary action—if forced to by the local newspaper or an official inquiry—to the satisfaction of the adult public whose moral viscera are quite as dogmatic as mine. I thereby would have undercut the public's faith in my honesty and would have damaged that most priceless of all public executive resources: the public's confidence. There would then have been an unhappy and unproductive feedback into everything else I did or tried to do as an elected official. The moral dilemma remains, however: for I am confident that if I had had the insight to have taken the kickback and the time and eloquence to have explained to the public why I had done it—describing to them the impossible position they put politicians into by their not assuming disinterested responsibility for financing party campaigns —they would have seen the point and respected me for my action. They even might have taken the lesson to heart and decided to give to their party as frequently and as richly as they give to other causes they value—such as community chests and churches.

The only serious ethical struggle I had with party leaders in Middletown dealt with a request for a zoning exception. Here I was firm, morally aroused, and dogmatic, and would be to this day. A contractor, who had contributed liberally to both political parties locally, hired a leading Democratic lawyer to plead for a commercial spot zone in a strictly residential area. The people of the area were almost solidly opposed to the change. Even if they had not been, nothing can ruin the orderly and esthetic development of a growing city like politically inspired spot zoning in contravention of a general plan. The members of the zoning committee, to their credit, said to me, "Mayor, there's a lot we'll do for the party, but we won't do this." The final showdown on this case took place in the lawyer's office with all major party leaders present. I walked in swinging. I made it quite clear that if the plumbing broke down in city hall, I would hire a licensed Democratic plumber over a licensed Republican plumber any day of the week; that if the law did not force us to go to bid, I would buy insurance from a Democratic rather than a Republican insurance agent; but that when it came to what Edmund Burke once called "the permanent forces" in the community, I was ready to do battle. I suggested that although there was much in politics that one rendered to Caesar, almost without qualms, city planning was rendered only to God. A few party leaders were upset; but most of them were understanding; and the lawyer in question, who over the years has been one of the most brilliant as well as constructive forces in the community and state, had the grace to accept my position without rancor.

But I have already dwelt far too long on such matters. In my two years as mayor, these kinds of party issues would not have represented more than one-fiftieth of my working time.

Contrary to what many people seem to believe, the hard ethical issues of public life rarely concern party politics. Party decisions tend to roll according to pre-set patterns. Every elected executive works out a few obvious benchmarks for relationships with political leaders (for example, "consult party leaders on all appointments, but solicit their help in trading little appointments to the party for big appointments to you"). In any case, to suggest that most party officials are frequently ethical "problems" is to distort their normal role beyond recognition. For every occasion when a party leader asked me for a favor that disturbed my conscience, I can think of a dozen times when the same party leader helped me defend the public interest against the importunities of non-party pressure groups.

Upon reflection, it is my firm belief that insofar as party politics interferes with the pursuit of the public interest, it is largely a result of the necessities of campaign finance. Most venality in public life could be abolished or reduced to insignificance if the public would assume responsibility for broadly-based campaign financing and would insist upon the public auditing and disclosure of all campaign gifts and expenditures. This would not eliminate corruption entirely, for wherever power and money converge some venality will be found. But our present method of financing political campaigns is, in my estimation, the single most corrupting factor in our political life—local, national, and, especially, state.

If what have been discussed so far are not the major ethical issues of the elected executive, what are? To the man who is ethically sensitive, the hairturning issues are those which involve impossible choices among contending interpretations of the public interest. Again, the necessity of dispatch is psychologically therapeutic; but the drain on energy and conscience is substantial nonetheless. Take ten or a dozen problems which faced me as mayor, and which are typical of perhaps a hundred I faced in two years as an elected executive.

(1) A peacock farm on the edge of town kept neighbors awake for a month

or so a year during the peacock mating season. The city government was asked by the neighbors to see to it that the birds were quieted. Ethical question: is a temporary irritation—including loss of sleep—for ten families worth the destruction of a hobby and a partial livelihood for one person?

(2) A leading department store on Main Street said it had to have a rear access service garage on Broad Street or it would be forced to leave town. Broad Street was zoned residential. Ethical question: would the loss of the department store be a greater loss than a break in the city's zoning pattern?

(3) The best detective on the chronically underpaid police force is suspected of taking protection money from some local two-bit gamblers. The evidence is too vague and unsubstantial to stand in court. Ethical question: is the *possibility* of the evidence being correct important enough to warrant a substantial investigation, with a consequent probable loss in efficiency and morale in the police department during and long after the investigation, a certain loss in public confidence in the whole force, and the ever-present possibility that the rumor was planted by a crank? And out of the many pressing issues coming across the mayor's desk, how much time and effort does such an investigation warrant from the mayor himself?

(4) The whole scheme of volunteer fire departments is looked upon by the chief of the city's only paid department as wasteful, inefficient, and dangerous to the public safety. The volunteers claim that their fire-fighting record is topnotch, that they save the taxpayers money. Ethical question: if neither side can be proved incorrect, how does one weigh the values of volunteer community endeavors against marginal inefficiencies in operation of a vital service?

(5) Many years ago, one department store was farsighted enough to have bought up some land for off-street parking. This off-street parking gave the store quite a competitive advantage. The city, in a new municipal parking program, needed a portion of the private parking lot assembled by the department store years before. When established, the municipal lot might destroy the store's competitive advantage. Ethical question: at what point does the public interest demand that private farsightedness be penalized?

(6) Two mayors in four years happened to have lived on Wyllys Avenue. Wyllys Avenue desperately needed repaving. But so did some other streets in the city. Ethical question: should Wyllys Avenue be paved, granted a heavy presumption that many citizens would claim that the mayor had "taken care of himself"?

(7) A federal grant-in-aid cut in half the city's welfare load, making a sinecure out of one of the two city welfare positions. The holder of the sinecure was a Negro appointed by the opposition party. Ethical question: should work somehow be "made" for the Negro, or should he be dropped? (For anyone who knows the problems of status, morale, and upward mobility among Negroes in a largely white community, the political questions posed by this case are easy compared to the long-range ethical questions.)

(8) The virulent opposition of a local printer-publicist might be tamed on a few key issues with the proper placing of a few city printing contracts. Ethical question: obvious.

(9) Buying of tires in wholesale lots would save the taxpayers $300 a year

—about one cent per citizen per annum. A score of little Middletown tire merchants would lose ten dollars or more in income. Ethical question: how does one balance one cent each for 30,000 people *versus* ten dollars each for twenty merchants?

(10) Parents concerned with the safety of their children on the way to and from school are constantly demanding increased police protection and more sidewalks. A more legitimate demand would be hard to imagine. But there are limits. Ethical question: granted that *total* safety never can be assured, what grounds beyond obvious necessity and "the squeaky wheel gets the grease" can be found for awarding or denying protection?

(11) A health officer is technically qualified and conscientious, but egregiously officious. Ethical question: is the damage done to the city government's relations with its citizens by the meticulous and unfeeling enforcement of ordinances likely to be sufficiently serious to warrant the health officer's dismissal?

(12) There is a likelihood that one of the major industries in town will have to close down a sizable slice of its operations. This may mean 2,000 unemployed. A steel company is looking for a New England site for a steel mill. It finds an "ideal" location in Middletown. That "ideal" location is a stretch of the Connecticut River which is unspoiled and is deeply treasured by small-boat owners and by nature lovers. Ethical question: is the provision of employment for 2,000 people worth the destruction forever of natural beauty?

These are samples of the tough ones. And in most cases the ethical values are sufficiently balanced so that no matter which side the mayor takes, half the concerned citizens in the community will charge him—and with considerable justification in their own minds—with having sold out. This is one of the reasons for the low image of politicians in our society: the fact that the losing cause in public policy generally has substantial merit on its side, with the consequence that the loser can see nothing but venality or partiality in the elected official's decision. People get sore at politicians for the same reason they throw pop-bottles at umpires: the disagreements always come on the close ones. If only citizens could pause on occasion to realize that the issues really are complex; that most elected officials do the best they can to be fair; that the peaceful resolution of conflict is a vast service to humankind and a most difficult art; that Solomon himself was perplexed by some of the issues posed by communities of men!

If I should be asked today how I resolved, in my own mind, the ethical dilemmas posed in the previous paragraphs, I should not know how to answer. Most of the dilemmas were not mine to resolve alone. Other people shared official power with me, and many citizens without official power assumed substantial unofficial responsibility for community decisions. There is not the loneliness and, perhaps, terror in executive decision-making at the local level which I assume there must often be at higher executive levels in American government. Consequences of errors in judgment are far less apocalyptic.

But insofar as I had to make up my mind by myself, or felt that my judgment might be determining in the minds of others, I did repair to two or three very general propositions for ethical guidance. In practice, the propositions were never articulated, but in retrospect I know that they were there. All of them had been woven into my life by parental, religious, and academic influences—in most cases by all three. My father, although never a minister, was a Professor of Religion and a firm believer in the Social Gospel. My studies at Oxford had brought me close to Immanuel Kant and Jean Jacques Rousseau. Ideas like "the categorical imperative" and "the general will" were connected in my mind with such Biblical injunctions as "Let justice roll down as waters; and righteousness as a mighty stream." I had nothing in my system that told me what was right; but I did have something in my system that told me to search for what was right.

The most helpful single question I could ask myself seemed to be, "What do you want Middletown to be like ten years from now?" Against this, many things fell into place. I wanted more beauty, fewer slums, less bigotry, more recreation, more community spirit, a more sustained sense of public responsibility, a more dynamic and prosperous economy, better education, a stronger and more truly competitive two-party system, and a heightened sense of personal dignity for all. These were some of the benchmarks against which specific ethical issues were measured or rationalized. They were not my marks. They were the marks of the civilization of which I was a miniscule and clouded reflection. As Carl Becker once wrote:

To have faith in the dignity and worth of the individual man as an end in himself; to believe that it is better to be governed by persuasion than by coercion; to believe that fraternal goodwill is more worthy than a selfish and contentious spirit; to believe that in the long run all values are inseparable from the love of truth and the disinterested search for it; to believe that knowledge and the power it confers should be used to promote the welfare and happiness of all men rather than to serve the interests of those individuals and classes whom fortune and intelligence endow with temporary advantage—these are the values which are affirmed by the traditional democratic ideology. . . . They are the values which since the time of Buddha and Confucius, Solomon and Zoroaster, Plato and Aristotle, Socrates and Jesus, men have commonly employed to measure the advance or decline of civilization, the values they have celebrated in the saints and sages whom they have agreed to canonize. They are the values which readily lend themselves to rational justification, yet need no justification.

There are, perhaps, two other matters which ought to be touched upon in an essay of this nature. The first has to do with the effect of power upon personality. Acton is quite explicit that "All power corrupts and absolute power corrupts absolutely." This I cannot gainsay. I remember one evening when I was returning with political friends from a television performance. For a half hour they told me what a brilliant performance mine had been. By the end of the half hour I was aware only that a new political star had been born on the horizon: namely, myself, and that I could not long deny the people of the State of Connecticut the chance to vote for me either for Governor or at the very least for United States Senator. It was not until I got home that my wife—with that wonderful sixth sense of a level-headed and thoughtful woman—reminded me that my performance had, in fact, been a little on the mediocre side—but that she was sure I had just had an off night. The most devastating traps of public office are the ones set to catch the ego. It is so easy to forget that the tribute is to the office, not to the person. Even a mayor stands out a little: fathers bring up their daughters to "shake the mayor's hand"; the mayor sits at head tables; he officiates; he is often the central figure in ceremony. All this inflates the sense of personal worth and waters the thirsty garden of vanity. The consequences are often pathetic, often silly, sometimes dangerous.

But Acton was wrong in suggesting that the only flowers in the garden of vanity are the weeds of corruption. Power may corrupt, but it also can ennoble. The sense that you, and the office you hold, are widely valued often creates a heightened sense of responsibility, a desire to live close to the public expectation, a wish to become a kind of community example. Too few people appreciate the ennobling effect of public office. I have seen men utterly transformed by a judgeship. A politician—an old pro in western Connecticut—once confided to me that he hated all judges. "What are they but some hack lawyers who happened to know a politician?" And he went on, "After you've made 'em, what do they do? They turn around and kick you in the teeth! They draw their robes around them as though they were Solon or something! You can't touch them! Who the hell do they think they are?" The fact is that they think they *are* Solon; they suddenly realize that instead of petty politicians they are an essential part of the fabric of civilization—a fabric which can last only so long as there is a widespread public belief that judges in courts of law will try to be just. And what is true of judges is equally true of elected executives.

The ennobling effect of public office is one of its greatest psychic dividends. Those who believe that men seek to hold public office only because it gives them power and status do not appreciate the importance to many men of simply feeling that the job they hold makes them better members of the human race. The heightened capacity for doing good in the world is one of the key attractions of political power and, from my limited observations, is a far more fundamental factor in determining the direction of men's ambitions than the baubles and tinsel of temporary status and deference.

This brings me to my final point. All ethical questions ultimately revert to propositions about the nature of man. The underlying complexity of ethical questions stems from the fact that man is morally ambiguous and teleologically inscrutable. Perched precariously on a whirling planet, blind to his origins, blind to his reasons for being, beset by the terrors of nature and of his own creation, man wobbles drunkenly between a certainty that he is nothing and an occasional, blinding revelation that he has a transcendent dignity and perhaps destiny. When man feels alienated from his universe, he may huddle in fear with his fellow men; but he cannot reach them with that fullness of feeling, that intenseness of identity, which is suggested by the Christian concept of love, or by the civil concept of community. I am not a mystical person, but I sense strongly that my best moments as mayor came when I felt—in an almost religious way—that what we were attempting to do in Middletown had meaning beyond itself. I remember Fred Smith, the editor of the local paper, once writing me an intimate note when I was particularly discouraged about the public response to some issue. "Never," he wrote, "lose faith in your neighbors." And he went on to explain, not that they were perfect, but that he had known them for a long time, and that they would ultimately respond to the good if they could be shown the good.

Surely this is the ultimate ethical postulate in a democracy: not that man is good, but that he is capable of good; not that he is free from corruption, but that he is desperately sick of it; not that he has fashioned the good society, but that he has caught an unforgettable glimpse of it. Ultimately the ethical problems of the elected executive are what they are for all human beings: the struggle to discover ends and means which heighten man's sense of individual worth in an ever more extensive and inclusive community.

QUESTIONS FOR DISCUSSION AND DIALOGUE

1. After reading this article, would you guess Mayor Bailey was a "good politician"? Discuss.
2. What is your opinion of Bailey's view that our present method of financing politics is "the single most corrupting factor in our political life"? Discuss.
3. Does it seem to you that Bailey is in favor of limited bribery, favoritism, spoils, patronage, and graft? What is your opinion of this? Discuss.
4. Do you think people like "the university deans and the town clergy" are more qualified to make politically moral decisions than most of us? What does Bailey think? Discuss.
5. Do you think this article by Bailey demonstrates that ethics or morality doesn't "mix with" politics? Discuss.

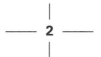

The Elite and the Electorate
Is Government by the People
Possible?

J. William Fulbright

J. William Fulbright, a Senator and a scholar, provides some deep reflection in answering the question above. Senator Fulbright addresses himself to this interrelationship of the Americans and the Politicians they elect by tracing some of our political heritage as well as by posing the most challenging dilemma of the politician in a democracy: "When should I follow the wishes of my constituents and when should I follow the dictates of my conscience?"

The question before us (posed by the title of this article) can be answered simply: government by the people is possible but highly improbable. The difficulties of self-government are manifest throughout the world.

The history of political thought in the last century and a half is largely one of qualification, modification, and outright repudiation of the heady democratic optimism of the eighteenth century. "The play is still on," writes Carl Becker, "and we are still betting on freedom of the mind, but the outcome seems now somewhat more dubious than it did in Jefferson's time, because a century and a half of experience makes it clear that men do not in fact always use their freedom of speech and of the press in quite the rational and disinterested way they are supposed to."

The major preoccupation of democratic thought in our time has been its continuing and troubled effort to reconcile the irrefutable evidences of human weakness and irrationality, which modern history has so abundantly provided, with a political philosophy whose very foundation is the assumption of human goodness and reason. The dilemma has troubled all of the free societies of the West, none more so than the United States, whose national experience until a generation ago seemed to represent the realization of classical democratic theory.

In addition to defects of concept and content, classical democratic thought is marked by a strikingly unhistoric spirit. It grandly and inexplicably conceived of democratic society as an organ created by a single act of human will and reason, ignoring the empirical lessons of the centuries of English history through which representative government had been tortuously evolving in the face of numberless obstacles and diversions. If Englishmen could fall prey to such delusions, it was far easier for Americans, whose revolution lent some credence to the abstractions of rationalist philosophy.

The revolutionaries of 1776 inherited a society that was already the freest in the world. Its freedom was built on solid foundations of English traditions and constitutional principles, which formed the bedrock of future stability. The revolution was not directed against a feudal *ancien regime* but against the most liberal and progressive monarchy of Europe, whose "oppression" of the colonists had consisted in recent and limited infringements on *long-established rights.* The great advantage of America, said Alexis de Tocqueville in a profound insight, lay in not having had "to endure a democratic revolution."

The American experience has thus had the appearance but not the reality of a society built by fiat to the specifications of rationalist philosophy. We have been permitted the romance of imagining ourselves revolutionaries when in fact our democracy is the product of long tradition and evolution. The mischief of our rationalist illusion is that it leads to erroneous inferences about our own free society and about the prospects of government by the people elsewhere in the world. Most notably, it blinds us to the powerful limitations on human action imposed by history, to the incalculable difficulties of building a free society, and to the basic incapacity of man to create viable institutions out of the abstractions of pure reason. Society, said Edmund Burke, is indeed a contract, but "as the ends of such a partnership cannot be obtained in many generations, it becomes a partnership not only between those who are living, but between those who are living, those who are dead, and those who are to be born."

The descent from democratic optimism in Western political thought has been more than borne out by events. As a result of the great conflicts of the twentieth century the world-wide dominance of the Western democracies has been lost.

These conflicts and upheavals have thrown the democracies on the defensive and generated powerful strains within the free Western societies themselves. There has developed, writes Walter Lippmann, "a functional derangement of the relationship between the mass of the people and the government." "The people," he writes, "have acquired power which they are incapable of exercising, and the governments they elect have lost powers which they must recover if they are to govern."

The impact of mass opinion on vital issues of war and peace, in Lippmann's analysis, is to impose a "massive negative" at critical junctures when new courses of policy are needed. Lagging disastrously behind the movement of events, Lippmann contends, public opinion forced a vindictive peace in 1919, then refused to act against a resurgent Germany in the inter-war years, and finally was aroused to paroxysms of hatred and unattainable hopes in a Second World War that need never have occurred. The impact of public opinion, says Lippmann, has been nothing less than a "compulsion to make mistakes."

For a politician who serves at the pleasure of his constituency, the course of prudence is to adhere to prevailing views. To be prematurely right is to court what, to the politician at least, is a premature retirement. We come at last to the ironic inversion of the classical democratic faith in the will of the people: not only does public opinion fail to hold the politician to the course of wisdom and responsibility but, on the contrary, to take the right course requires a singular act of courage on the part of the politician. A few might share the Wilsonian view that "There is nothing more honorable than to be driven from power because one was right." Far more prevalent is the outlook of Lloyd George, who on more than one occasion quite candidly rejected proposals whose merit he conceded on the grounds that he did not wish to be "crucified" at home. In the Lloyd George view, which is a prototype—and not without some merit in my opinion—there is little glory and still less constructive purpose in being defeated for failing to do the impossible.

Can we reconstruct the excessively optimistic democratic thought of the eighteenth century into a chastened but more realistic philosophy of government by the people? I believe we can, and this belief, I think, is prevalent among the wisest of statesmen and scholars.

The philosophers of the Age of Reason emphasized the hopes and possibilities of a free society, but the strength and viability of democracy rest not only on its aspirations but also on its accommodations to the limitations of human wisdom, to man's inability to perceive the infinite. Democracy, Winston Churchill once said, is the worst form of government men have ever devised—except for every other form. Or in Jefferson's words: "Sometimes it is said that man cannot be trusted with the government of himself. Can he, then, be trusted with the government of others? Or have we found angels in the form of kings to govern him?"

If men are often irrational in their political behavior, it does not follow that they are *always* irrational and, what is more important, it does not follow that they are *incapable* of reason. Whether in fact a people's capacity for self-government can be realized depends on the character and quality of education. It seems to me an astonishing distortion of priorities that the American people and their government gladly spend billions of dollars for space exploration while denying desperately needed funds to their public schools. I do not believe that a society that has shamefully starved and neglected its public education can claim to have exploited its fullest possibilities and found them wanting.

The case for government by elites is irrefutable insofar as it rests on the need for expert and specialized knowledge. The average citizen is no more qualified for the detailed administration of government than the average politician is qualified to practice medicine or to split an atom. But in the choice of basic goals, the fundamental moral judgments that shape the life of a society, the judgment of trained elites is no more valid than the judgment of an educated people. The knowledge of the navigator is essential to the conduct of a voyage, but his special skills have no relevance to the choice of whether to take the voyage and where we wish to go.

The distinction of course is between means and ends. The experience of modern times shows us that when the passengers take over the navigation of the ship it is likely to go on the rocks. This does not mean that their chosen destination is the wrong one or that an expert would have made a better choice, but only that they are unlikely to get there without the navigator's guidance.

The demonstrated superiority of democracy over dictatorship derives precisely from its refusal to let ruling elites make the basic moral decisions and value judgments of society. The core of classical democractic thought is the concept of free individuality as the ultimate moral value of human society. Stripped of its excessive optimism about human nature, the core of classical liberalism remains valid and intact. The value and strength of this concept are its promise of fulfillment for man's basic aspirations. The philosopher and the psychoanalyst agree that, whether it issues from reason or instinct, man's basic aspiration is to be a free individual.

A reconstructed philosophy of self-government, accepting the weaknesses as well as the strengths of human nature, must place heavy emphasis on the development of the human *capacity* for rational moral choice. The challenge to public education is nothing less than to prepare the individual for self-government, to cultivate his capacity for free inquiry and his more humane instincts, to teach him *how* rather than *what* to think, in short, to sustain democracy by what Ralph Barton Perry called "an express insistence upon quality and distinction."

A reconstructed philosophy of self-government must replace an ingenuous faith in human *nature* with a realistic faith in human *capacity,* recognizing that self-government, though the best form of political organization that men have devised, is also the most difficult. Democracy, in short, must come to terms with man's weaknesses and irrationalities while reaching for the best that is in him.

Such a revised approach to democracy has certain implications for the way in which we organize our government and conduct its affairs. As Americans with our deeply rooted and fundamentally healthy distrust of government power, we might start by at least reexamining certain long-held convictions based on this distrust of power. We might at least consider the proposition, as expressed by Lord Radcliffe, that "liberty looked upon as the right to find and to try to realize the best that is in oneself is not something to which power is necessarily hostile," that, indeed, "such liberty may even need the active intervention of authority to make it possible."

To return to my metaphor, we must guard against allowing the navigator to determine our destination, but we must allow him to steer the ship without amateur supervision of every turn of the wheel. A political leader is chosen because of his supposed qualifications for his job. If he is qualified, he should be allowed to carry it out according to his own best judgment. If his judgment is found defective by his electors, he can and should be removed. His constituents, however, must recognize that he has a duty to his office as well as to them and that their duty in turn is to fill the office but not to run it. We must distinguish between the functions of *representation* and of *government, requiring* our elected leaders to represent us while *allowing* them to govern.

It may well be questioned whether the enormously complex and slow-moving procedures of the American government are adequate to meet both the dangers and the opportunities of our foreign relations. Too often, decisions of principle are postponed or neglected and opportunities lost because of the obstacles to decision imposed by our policy processes. The source of this malady is the diffusion of authority between and within the executive and legislative branches and the accessibility of all of these centers of power to a wide variety of pressures and interests. The problem is compounded by the durable myth of Jacksonian democracy, the view that any literate citizen can do almost any job and that a democracy can do without a highly trained administrative elite.

"Foreign politics," wrote Tocqueville, "demand scarcely any of those qualities which a democracy possesses; and they require, on the contrary, the perfect use of almost all those faculties in which it is deficient . . . a democracy is unable to regulate the details of an important undertaking, to persevere in a design, and to work out its execution in the presence of serious obstacles. It cannot combine its measures with secrecy, and it will not await their consequences with patience. These are qualities which more especially belong to an individual, or to an aristocracy."

My question is not whether we might wish to alter our traditional foreign policy-making procedures but whether in fact we have any choice but to do so in a world that obstinately refuses to conduct its affairs under Anglo-Saxon rules of procedure.

The source of an effective foreign policy under our system is Presidential power. There are major areas of foreign policy—those relating more to long-term problems than to immediate crises—wherein Presidential authority is incommensurate with Presidential responsibility as a result of the diffusion of power between executive and legislative branches and within the latter. The foreign policy powers of Congress under the Constitution enable it to implement, modify, or thwart the President's proposals but not itself to initiate or shape policy. These powers, moreover, are widely dispersed within Congress among autonomous committees, each under a chairman who owes little if anything in the way of political obligation to the President.

The defects of Congress as an institution reflect the defects of classical

democratic thought. These pertain primarily to foreign policy. In domestic matters, it seems to me, the Congress is as well qualified to shape policy as the
executive, and in some respects more so because of the freedom of at least some
members from the particular electoral pressures that operate on the President.
The frequency of elections and the local orientation of party organizations, however, do not encourage serious and sustained study of international relations.
Congressmen are acutely susceptible to local and regional pressures and to the
waves of fear and emotion that sometimes sweep over public opinion. The legislator, in short, is under constant and intense pressure to adhere to the prevailing
tendencies of public opinion, however temporary and unstable.

Public opinion must be educated and led if it is to bolster a wise and effective
foreign policy. This is preeminently a task for Presidential leadership because the
Presidential office is the only one under our constitutional system that constitutes
a forum for moral and political leadership on a national scale. Accordingly, I
think that we must contemplate the further enhancement of Presidential authority in foreign affairs. The prospect is a disagreeable and perhaps a dangerous
one, but the alternative is immobility and the paralysis of national policy in a
revolutionary world, which can only lead to consequences immeasurably more
disagreeable and dangerous.

The preeminence of Presidential responsibility is in no way an implied license
for the legislator to evade national and international responsibility and to surrender to the pressures of local and parochial interest. I can find no better words to
define this responsibility than those of Edmund Burke in his classic statement to
his constituents at Bristol in 1774:

"Certainly, gentlemen, it ought to be the happiness and glory of a representative, to live
in the strictest union, the closest correspondence, and the most unreserved communication
with his constituents. Their wishes ought to have great weight with him; their opinion high
respect; their business unremitted attention. It is his duty to sacrifice his repose, his
pleasures, his satisfactions, to theirs; and, above all, ever, and in all cases, to prefer their
interest to his own. But, his unbiased opinion, his mature judgment, his enlightened
conscience, he ought not to sacrifice to you; to any man, or to any set of men living. These
he does not derive from your pleasure; no, nor from the law and the constitution. They
are a trust from Providence, for the abuse of which he is deeply answerable. Your representative owes you, not his industry only, but his judgment; and he betrays, instead of serving
you, if he sacrifices it to your opinion."

As a freshman Senator in 1946 I attempted in a speech at the University of
Chicago to define the proper role of the legislator in relation to his constituents,
to the nation, and to his own conscience. After seventeen years I see no reason
to alter the views I then expressed in these words:

"The average legislator early in his career discovers that there are certain interests, or
prejudices, of his constituents which are dangerous to trifle with. Some of these prejudices
may not be of fundamental importance to the welfare of the nation, in which case he is
justified in humoring them, even though he may disapprove. The difficult case is where
the prejudice concerns fundamental policy affecting the national welfare. A sound sense

of values, the ability to discriminate between that which is of fundamental importance and that which is only superficial, is an indispensable qualification of a good legislator. As an example of what I mean, let us take the poll-tax issue and isolationism. Regardless of how persuasive my colleagues or the national press may be about the evils of the poll tax, I do not see its fundamental importance, and I shall follow the views of the people of my state. Although it may be symbolic of conditions which many deplore, it is exceedingly doubtful that its abolition will cure any of our major problems. On the other hand, regardless of how strongly opposed my constituents may prove to be to the creation of, and participation in, an ever stronger United Nations Organization, I could not follow such a policy in that field unless it becomes clearly hopeless. . . . "

In conclusion, I should like to reiterate the theme of these remarks: government by the people, despite its failures and shortcomings, remains the one form of political organization that offers the promise of fulfillment for our highest aspirations. Although we have been compelled to qualify the unlimited optimism of classical democratic thought, we remain convinced that the core of that thought—the belief in the moral sanctity of the free mind and the free individual —remains the most valid of human philosophies. In Carl Becker's words: " . . . although we no longer have the unlimited and solvent backing of God or nature, we are still betting that freedom of the mind will never disprove the proposition that only through freedom of the mind can a reasonably just society ever be created. . . ."

QUESTIONS FOR DISCUSSION AND DIALOGUE

1. How does Fulbright develop the idea of the politician as a navigator steering the ship with its passengers? Do you agree with this comparison? Why? Discuss.
2. Do you agree with the way Fulbright has worked out the dilemma of following conscience or following constituents' wishes? (second last paragraph) Do you see possible problems here? Discuss.
3. Reread Edmund Burke's statement about how a politician betrays his constituents instead of serving them if he sacrifices his judgment to their opinions. (fourth last paragraph) Is this a "conservative" or a "liberal" view? Is it dated now? Do you agree with it? Why?
4. In recent years Senator Fulbright, Chairman of the Senate Foreign Relations Committee, has been one of the most bitter critics of presidential authority in developing foreign policy relating to U.S. involvement in Vietnam. Is this criticism contradictory to his views about the necessity for presidential as opposed to congressional leadership in foreign policy? Discuss.

———— **3** ————

The End of Our Two Party World
Daniel J. Boorstin

Daniel J. Boorstin is a noted American historian who has written among many other books, *The Genius of American Politics.* In it he argues that our avoidance of the revolutionary, issue-party-candidate polarization of European politics is part of our "Genius." Historical and economic consensus are at the heart of the American two party system, according to Boorstin. In this article, however, Boorstin traces "The End . . . " of this "Two Party World" which has been brought about by "voter science," and television's effect on the "myriad minorities" who were treated differently by the politicians and responded differently in the past. Disruption and violence is implied by Boorstin unless the American two party system is reformed to take these changes into account.

Seldom before in American history has so much "political" activity taken place outside of our political institutions. This is the age of the street demonstration, the sit-in, the teach-in, the shout-down. It is the age of political expression and political frustration. Some say our young people have become too political; others, that they are not political enough. We are confused not only about what our politics ought to be but even about what really is, or is not, political activity. Where does "politics" end, and where does agitation, insurrection or chaos begin?

Of course, many forces have helped to produce the current confusion. But among the most important is the revolution in our political consciousness. New ways of thinking have put our political world beyond the wildest imaginings of our grandfathers. Yet, while our ways of thinking and feeling and learning about politics have been transformed, our political system has remained virtually unchanged.

Can't we bring our traditional political institutions and our election system into harmony with our new ways of political thinking?

The widely heralded changes in our election system have not been as revolutionary as they seem. They have been only the latest steps along the familiar road of American political history. "Legislators represent people," Chief Justice Warren declared in 1964, "not trees or acres. Legislators are elected by voters, not farms or cities or economic interests." When the Supreme Court recently insisted that congressional districts be reapportioned on this principle, it was taking one late, long-overdue stride toward majority rule.

Much of the history of our political system since the founding of the nation has been the fulfillment of the principle of majority rule—a democracy of numbers—and its victory over competing principles. The Constitutional Convention of 1787 almost broke up because the small states feared that a democracy of regions—the principle of "One state, one vote," under the old Articles of Confederation—would be entirely displaced by a democracy of numbers in which representation would precisely correspond to population. Before the Civil War, John C. Calhoun and other Southern statesmen argued that the Founding Fathers had never intended to set up a democracy of numbers, but instead had aimed that legislators actually should represent "acres" or "economic interests." Fearing the numerical majority, they said that no action of the national government could be law unless every single economic interest agreed. The Civil War was the costly, but decisive, victory for the democracy of numbers.

Since then, we have aimed to make our government more and more a system of majority rule. We have tried to make the electorate an ever-larger proportion of the whole population and to give it more powers. By the time of the Civil War, property qualifications were no longer of much consequence, and the electorate included nearly all adult male white citizens. Six of our constitutional amendments—a greater number than has been devoted to any other single subject since the Bill of Rights, and about half of all those adopted since the Civil War—have concerned the right to vote. Each of these amendments has aimed to make the electorate more numerous.

The 14th and 15th amendments included Negroes; the 17th amendment took the election of senators from the state legislators and gave it to each state's whole electorate; the 19th amendment brought in women; the 23rd amendment gave the presidential franchise to residents of the District of Columbia, and the 24th amendment outlawed the restrictive poll tax. President Johnson, like President Eisenhower before him, has urged an amendment to include in the electorate all citizens above the age of 18. Meanwhile, many changes by individual states—for example, the reducing of residence requirements and the easing of absentee registration and absentee voting—have gone in the same direction. Since 1950, Alabama and South Carolina have reduced their residence requirements from two years to one; New York, to three months; Pennsylvania has reduced its requirements to 90 days; and New Jersey, to one of the lowest, 40 days. All this is impressive evidence of our historic determination to make ours truly a system of majority rule.

These are the changes that meet the eye, and that have made the headlines. They are not so much a revolution in American political life as a fulfillment of its promise. They are not beyond the imaginings of a Jefferson, a Jackson or a Lincoln.

But at the same time, there has taken place an unpredictable, unadvertised revolution in our political consciousness. It has been so deep, so widespread, and even so obvious, that it has gone almost unnoticed. It has been accomplished not by laws or constitutional amendments but by all the forces shaping American life —by our economy, our technology, our systems of education and our new modes of scientific thought. It had begun by the early years of this century, but reaches a clamorous climax in our time. It could not have been imagined by a Jefferson, a Jackson or a Lincoln. It has transformed the very meaning of political numbers, has given new content to the very notions of majority and minority. It has even undermined the very assumptions on which the system of majority rule traditionally had rested.

Majority rule rested on a democratic faith. This was a faith in the long-run prudence and wisdom of the greater number of voters. It translated into domestic politics Voltaire's assertion that "God is on the side of the big battalions." "In God we trust." Our political system, then, like others, has historically rested on belief that the right to govern derives from some higher power.

The higher mystery, in our representative government, has been embodied in the sacrament of the ballot box. There, the many become the one. On Election Day, the separate wills of millions of citizens become a single, clear "mandate." *"Vox populi, vox dei"*—the voice of the people is the voice of God—simply expresses "the divinity that doth hedge a majority."

The weaknesses and indecisions and selfishnesses of all the individual voters become purified and transformed. Behind this quasi-religious belief in the divine right of the majority, and giving it some reality in the commonsense world, was a simple fact. The majority really *was* a mystery. The single voice of the majority as it issued from thousands of ballot boxes could be heard loud and clear. But who could be sure of what it would say? Who could be sure of which particular voices had entered its resonance?

By a series of steps, now nearly forgotten, our voting system was changed to preserve, deepen, and keep sacred this mystery of the majority. Originally, most states actually did not have the secret ballot: Voters stood up before neighbors and announced their preference, which was then marked on a public scoreboard. Only gradually did the secrecy of each citizen's vote come to be protected. At first, each party printed its own "ticket" (commonly a different color from that of the other parties), but spectators could still see a voter's preference by the color of his voting paper.

The campaign for the secret (or so-called "Australian") ballot began in earnest in the 1880's. What was probably our first secret-ballot law was enacted by Kentucky on February 24, 1888. Other states followed. Reformers argued that there could be no true democracy without the secret ballot. For secrecy reduced incentives to bribery and intimidation, made it impossible for corrupt politicians to be sure they were getting the votes they were willing to pay for, and so purified the voice of the majority.

The democratic paradox, which itself became an article of faith, was that majority rule really worked only so long as it could not be known precisely who was in the majority. This was the Mystery of the Majority. Of course, the elections themselves produced some voting statistics—on wards, congressional districts, or states—from which shrewd politicians could draw their own conclusions. But these official statistics were always wholesale and geographic. The Mystery of the Majority remained a mystery, which an enlarging and mobile electorate and a secret ballot only made more impenetrable.

Then there came upon the American scene a potent new force. It did more than anyone had believed possible—within the ground rules of honest elections —to dissolve the Mystery of the Majority. It was destined to transform popular thinking about elections and about the makeup of majorities and minorities and voting blocs. It would become a new weapon in the arsenal of minorities. It quickly became so familiar that its novelty and its significance were not generally noted. I will call this new political force (for lack of a better name) Voter Science.

The roots of voter science went deep into the 19th century. Under the influence of such thinkers as Auguste Comte, Charles Darwin, Karl Marx, Herbert Spencer and others, the belief became widespread that human society itself could become the subject of science. More than that, they even argued that a new "social" science was essential to human progress. The new social scientists assigned themselves the task of describing and predicting human behavior. Their motto was "Nothing sacred!" After Darwin had penetrated the mysteries of the creation, after Marx had offered his "laws" of the origins of property and social classes, and then, in the early 20th century, after Freud had obtruded science into the private world of dreams and the intimacies of sex, it was inevitable that devotees of the new social sciences should make a science of the ballot box. The dimly lit salon where political "philosophers" conversed about the good society and the forms of government was displaced by the bright modern laboratory of the new political scientists. There—in the whole living, working, voting society —they counted, measured, interviewed and questionnaired in their effort to discover (in Harold Lasswell's phrase) "Who gets what, when, how."

The great development of voter science took place right here in the U.S.A. There was no one founder, for many currents of American thought flowed into this new stream. In his classic *Public Opinion* (1922) and *The Phantom Public* (1925), Walter Lippmann began to treat the mass of voters not as an unpredictable "mob" but as a real entity with laws of its own. Significantly, the needs of American advertisers gave birth to market researchers who were the first scientific opinion pollers. Their techniques were soon applied to politics. Elmo Roper's pioneering *Fortune* poll in 1935 replaced gentlemanly conjectures and crackerbarrel hunches by scientific sampling, facts, figures and statistics. George Gallup founded the American Institute of Public Opinion, followed by the National Opinion Research Center, and by the enterprises of Louis Harris and others. The polls became a potent new force for the self-fulfilling political prophecy—though not without some objections. In 1935, a bill was introduced into the 74th Congress to stop the "vicious practice" of opinion polling by prohibiting polls to use the mails. But the polls flourished. Within a decade, the pollsters became a well-organized profession, with a voluminous technical literature and annual receipts running into the millions. Despite occasional lapses—most notably in the presidential election of 1948—their margins of error generally tended to decrease. As they became more cautious, more aware of their public responsibilities, they gained the confidence of the voting public and of the candidates. Nowadays, when we talk of "the polls," we are less likely to mean the sacred ritual of the ballot box than the scientific predictions of the ubiquitous pollsters.

The techniques of statistical prediction of voting behavior were sharpened and broadened in still other ways. Enterprising voter scientists like Samuel Lubell spent months asking searching questions of individual voters, and developed new interviewing methods for depth studies of key towns and counties. Lubell's postmortem on the election of 1948, for example, did much to help pollsters discover where they had made their errors, and so helped them refine their instruments of prediction. Meanwhile, the unprecedented growth of all the social sciences, and especially of sociology, in prosperous American universities aided by newly rich foundations, provided new conceptual tools and vast new stores of facts and figures. In the United States—"A nation of immigrants"—sociology tended to become a science of minorities. Works like Znaniecki and Thomas' five volumes on the Polish immigrant (1918-21) and Louis Wirth's book on the Jewish ghetto (1928) set a pattern for many others, like Gunnar Myrdal's monumental study of the Negro in America (1944). This sociology of minorities, making each aware of its special traditions, problems, needs, powers and opportunities.

The majority soon discovered that it really consisted of myriad minorities. The lesson of it all was contained in the quip that nowadays 99.6 percent of the American people were members of minority groups. And these minorities were not all ethnic. The new popular sociology explained to more and more Americans that they were themselves members of statistically definable groups, some of which they had never imagined to exist. Categories like "white-collar workers," "junior executives," "senior citizens," "urbanites," "suburbanites" and "teen-agers" became familiar. More people began to think of themselves as "consum-ers." And our popular sociologists have done a great deal to give a regular minority status to "Poverty Americans."

The polls and the sociology of minorities were to domestic political strategy what intelligence was to battlefield strategy. Voter scientists, without even intend-ing it, became a kind of CIA for every American minority. To the Negroes, for example, who comprised only some 11 percent of the population, they heralded a new political power. Armed with newly detailed analyses of the past Negro vote, with scientifically sampled predictions of Negro voting behavior, social attitudes, aspirations and prejudices all over the country, Negro leaders (like other minority leaders) now had a new grasp of their voting power. Negroes now discovered that despite their disfranchisement in the South, they actually held the balance of voting power in crucial Northern cities in states with decisive blocs of electoral votes. It was such facts as these which understandably led the Washington director of the NAACP in 1951 to favor retention of the Electoral College and to oppose the direct election of the president. There was a good deal of informa-tion to support the claim that a few thousand strategically placed Negro votes actually gave John F. Kennedy his narrow victory in 1960.

While these developments have tended to fragment the voting public, still other new forces have drawn the voting public together. Television, for the first time in history, created a truly national political audience. The clue to TV's subtle transformation of our political consciousness is that the TV audience is *unselec-tive.*

The more revolutionary significance of the TV "Great Debates" between candidate Nixon and candidate Kennedy in 1960 was not that so many people now came face-to-face with their own candidate for president. The more potent novelty was that now for the first time, so many of the partisans of each candidate were forced to come face-to-face with the candidate they had *not* favored. By electronic magic, the political audiences of both parties were instantly combined. This was a new liberation, a new enlargement of life, that TV brought to the

American voter. This widened everybody's political world. It smuggled into everybody's consciousness the personalities and images and ideas of all the major candidates. It became virtually impossible for any citizen to confine his experience of a political campaign to seeing and hearing his own pre-chosen candidate.

This was the effect not only of the Great Debates but of the very nature of television, which accentuated the tendencies which came in with radio. Formerly, political information or propaganda had come to each voter in separate, small packages (for example, in a newspaper, a magazine, or a political pamphlet). The citizen, simply by choosing his newspaper or magazines, could imprison himself in his own point of view. He could confine his reading to a Republican paper, to a Democratic paper or even , if he chose, to the *Daily Worker.* "Other" points of view did not enter his mind uninvited; he purposely chose his news and propaganda packages because they left those out. He was unlikely to wander by accident into a rally for the party he disliked, much less to see the faces or hear the voices of extremists or revolutionaries. Television changed all that.

Now, political information and campaign propaganda come in constantly flowing streams through the networks' broadcasting channels. The same streams flow into at least 93 percent of American homes. Since it is impossible for the broadcaster to select his audience (repeated efforts to introduce pay TV have met little national success), the broadcaster must send out something for everybody. Now, therefore, almost everybody has to watch what anybody wants to watch. In one sense, of course, the programming is left to each TV viewer. But many words and pictures and ideas reach him before he can tune them out, and he is constantly being tempted to watch a little before deciding to change the channel.

The broadcasting flow brings all points of view into everybody's living room. People become tolerant of personalities and ideas that have some entertainment value, even if they hate the personalities and ideas and don't want to be persuaded. The whole spectrum of differing views now intrudes itself. Now, you actually have to turn the channel to send the unwanted spokesman away!

TV has had a revolutionary effect also on the conspicuousness and persuasive reach of political minorities. From their point of view, the old question of "equal time" begins to be obsolete. The very nature of TV offers a new national forum for spokesmen of unpopular views. New forms, like the vastly popular interview and conversation shows of David Susskind, Johnny Carson, Joey Bishop and others, give these new minorities a new voice, a vivid image and network time they could never afford to buy. The more violent their point of view or their personality, the more apt they are to be considered "newsworthy." Zany ideas, preferably expressed by zany people, have surefire appeal. They liven up the show, raise the Neilsen ratings—and make national celebrities out of political oddballs. No view is too marginal, no political slogan too outrageous to be denied its moment on the center of the stage. The network flow brings Democratic candidates into the homes of diehard Republicans and Republican candidates into the homes of diehard Democrats, but it also brings into everybody's home both George Wallace and Stokely Carmichael.

One obvious consequence of this nationalization of the voter audience, along with other forces, is a tendency (in Neal R. Peirce's phrase) toward the nationalization of our presidential politics. Not so long ago, presidential candidates did not even bother to campaign in the South: the Republican candidate found it useless, and the Democratic candidate found it unnecessary. Eight Southern states had never gone to a Republican candidate for president between 1876 and 1928; six other states had almost always gone Republican. But times have changed. And now, there are virtually no safe "one party" states. Since the first election of Franklin Roosevelt, only two states (Arkansas and North Carolina) have failed to vary their party allegiance. Even Vermont went Democratic in 1964; and even in North Carolina (with its Republican congressmen) and in Arkansas (with a Republican governor), we begin to see signs of the newly nationalized politics. It is significant, too, that the most populous states—New York, California, Pennsylvania, Illinois and Ohio—are among the most variable in their presidential voting allegiance and have tended to give the narrowest margins to the winners.

New forces, then, shape the consciousness of our voters. The components of the numerical majority are no longer shrouded in mystery. Voter science, reenforced by a new and newly popular sociology, has created newly self-conscious minorities, armed with new techniques and with a new sense of their voting power. Everywhere—minorities cover the country. For the first time, they know precisely who they are, precisely where they are, what they can demand and what they can deliver. The campaign audience, too, has been transformed—not only enlarged, but essentially changed. Campaigning, once it has moved into the flowing TV channels, tends more and more to preach to the unconverted. The eyes of the partisan citizen are opened, he is liberated from himself. And lest he be tempted to believe in a cozy two-party world, he is confronted willy-nilly by unsavory extremists who acquire a new national conspicuousness as they walk right into everybody's living room in the costumes of entertainers. The old, safe, two-party world, with its neat geographic blocs, is no longer with us. We may think we have a system of two-party politics, but American voters no longer live in the old two-party world.

Perhaps this discord between the new realities of our political thinking and feeling and learning and our time-honored election system helps explain why so much recent "political" activity has been extra-political. Is it surprising that Americans see a new unreality in our political and electoral system and come to find it less and less "representative"? The old cliches of majority rule will no longer serve. What we are getting is old answers to old questions. We hear new support for old movements to reform our election system. Direct election of the president by popular vote (in place of the old Electoral College), which was proposed in Congress as early as 1816, is more widely favored today than ever before. The next few years will probably see a constitutional amendment reducing the presidential voting age to 18. Residence requirements for presidential voting will be further reduced or abolished. We hear demands for a single national presidential primary to pick party candidates. We hear proposals to revise the procedures of the national party conventions and to change their time of meeting.

These and other reforms aim, quite properly, to make our presidential election a more accurate expression of the will of the majority. Many of them are desirable. Some, such as the direct election of the president, are urgent.

But new powers are abroad in the land—in the streets, in the factories, in the universities, on our television channels and even in our churches—nearly everywhere perhaps except in our national political system. Is it too much, in this presidential year of 1968, to expect our representative system to provide voters at the polls an opportunity to express their honest disagreement over the major questions of national policy? For example, will Americans be allowed to vote their opposition to the war in Vietnam or their criticisms of its conduct? Or will they be left to explode in myriad extra-political forms?

For the majority is no longer a mystery. The new minorities are plainer than ever to see and almost impossible to avoid hearing. Without ever having intended it, we have acquired a national politics and become a new democracy of minorities. The flexibility and adaptability of our system are being tested. Can it respond to a new world of voter science and electronic magic?

If our political life is to stay indoors—if more and more of our political life is not to move from the ballot box and the legislative hall into the street or onto the barricades—we must find new political voices for these new minorities, legitimate political voices, numerically registered and nationally audible.

QUESTIONS FOR DISCUSSION AND DIALOGUE

1. What are the changes that Boorstin sees for the Americans and their politicians because of "voter science" and television?
2. What is the significance of Boorstin's statement, "the majority WAS a mystery"? Why isn't it now? What political significance does this have?
3. Do you see "voter science" and television as evolutionary or revolutionary factors in American politics? Why? Discuss.
4. Sociologists and political scientists often use the term "selective perception" in discussing how people tend to choose only that information which they wish to consider before formulating opinions and conclusions. In this article Boorstin talks about the "unselective" nature of television's political audiences. What is the relationship of political party and candidate "selective perception" by the Americans before and after the advent of television?
5. What is your answer to the question posed in the second last paragraph: "Can our political system respond to a new world of voter science and electronic magic?" Discuss.

The Election in the Year of Decay
Bill Moyers

Bill Moyers takes the most well known American presidential campaign biographer Theodore H. White, to task in this critical review of *The Making of the President 1968*. Moyers accuses White of being so caught up in the establishment that he became lost in its rationalizations rather than grasping the significance of the confused, alienated, and outraged Americans during the 1968 election. Moyers offers many provocative observations in this article, not the least of which is that perhaps the evolving United States can no longer be understood by studying "what happened at the top." Or could it ever be understood in that manner?

If Theodore White did not exist, the Ford Foundation would have to award Harvard University a grant to create him. How else would the Establishment tell its story?

The Making of the President 1968 is essentially that: The authorized version, the view through the offical keyhole. For Teddy White, the most successful entrepreneur of political detail and perception in American journalism today, tells the story of 1968 as he did four and eight years ago, primarily through the momentum of a few stout and earnest persons. But things have changed. For the first time in my experience the lead actors in the theater of American politics were largely irrelevant, more acted upon than acting, scarcely permitted on center stage. The difference between what they believed to be happening and what in fact was happening is the real story of 1968.

In that sense it was not a reporter's year. Only a novelist, living the passions, could truly capture the phantasmagorical pageant of acrimony, pride, and violence that marched through our political world, leaving it upended. Character in decay, Mencken observed, is the theme of the great bulk of superior fiction. And 1968 was the Year of Decay. It was Norman Mailer's kind of year.

For one America, official America, *The Making of the President 1968* will nonetheless earn its place on the shelf next to Webster's and the Britannica. Unfortunately, we are no longer one America. We are two, three, many more. Richard Nixon has acknowledged that his most urgent task is to "bring us together again." Under such circumstances no single author, not even Teddy White, could chart the shifting boundaries of our political terrain.

That he has tried, against impossible odds, is a tribute to the man's intrepid will. Certainly his is the most coherent and the most eloquent account we are likely to get from any reporter's notes. And for the majority of Americans his interpretation will be illuminating and persuasive. White, after all, is the quintessential liberal middling American—an admirer of Adlai Stevenson, an early Kennedyphile, a devotee of the Great Society; and increasingly Fed-Up-to-Here with the excesses of the young and the black. To him Vietnam is "a cause of which no American need ever have been ashamed," LBJ a tragically misunderstood commander-in-chief, Nixon a healer. Black rioters, on the new morality of the young "aggressive infantilism."

Now Teddy White is usually the gentlest of men, the reach of his sensitivity putting most of us to shame. He has always—well, almost always—dipped his criticism of the central figures of American political life in the milk of human kindness, and not only because he may need to return again to his sources. White is by nature a kind man, the sweetest of Boswells, with little taste for the common-place meanness of the men he observes.

Yet he comes down hard on the outriders of society, indignant with hippies for fouling "the entryways of the beautiful old private homes that still line the northern rim of Beacon Street," led by a youth whose glands had outrun his learning." A sharp tongue from a gentle man! If he is only exercising the overdue obligation liberals have to restrain the excesses of their friends, fine. But there is a tone in it that we are not accustomed to hearing in Teddy White. If he is becoming preoccupied with the bad manners of this generation, if he hears only the obscenities and not the anger, what can we expect from lesser men?

In the light of that tone, it is not surprising to learn that he is hopeful for Richard Nixon in the White House. It is one of Teddy White's charms that he is forever beguiled by the good intentions of public men, and here he is assuring us that there is a New Nixon Mark III, that his subject has changed in eight years. "No more plastic President, none more open to suggestions and ideas, none more willing to admit mistakes or learn from error, has sat in the White House in recent times." Alas, I believe him. Richard Nixon is plastic and he is following a new script. What I wonder now is how much Theodore White may have changed.

As a reporter he remains the master. Illuminating details, such as the story of how Barry Goldwater's speechwriter became a welder because he could not get a political job after the debacle of 1964, are used to drive home a point (in this case, that the Republicans' plight was so miserable in 1964 as to make their comeback in 1966 and 1968 nothing less than miraculous.)

His descriptions of Nixon and Humphrey watching their own nominations, and receiving each others' congratulatory calls, do not surprise us; we have come to expect such color from White.

There are memorable sketches of Miami; of a harrassed and hounded Hubert Humphrey with no one to organize him (in that respect his campaign in 1968 resembled Nixon's in 1960); and of a meeting of the Student Mobilization Committee which White left in disgust.

His skill in drawing the line between the McCarthy-Lowenstein forces and the new left militants illustrates a discerning talent rare among political commentators. There endures, too, his command of the apt quote: Pat Lucey saying McCarthy's people hated each other more than any campaigners he had known, Stephen Smith's chilling remarks about McCarthy, and William Connell's statement that "Nothing would bring the real peaceniks back to our side unless Hubert urinated on a portrait of Lyndon Johnson in Times Square before television—and then they'd say to him, why didn't you do it before?"

White is constantly adding to our knowledge. He does us all a singular favor by filling in the real George Romney around the hills and valleys created by sophisticated journalists who never liked this square. In a revealing vignette he describes how Romney's "brainwashing" line was innocently dropped in the middle of a lengthy local television interview, where it remained until the opportunistic interviewer, seeking additional publicity, called it to the attention of *The New York Times* man in Detroit—three days after the interview.

The *Times* man reported the story to his desk, burying "brainwashing" down in his text. "The man on the desk caught the 'brainwashing' quote. On Tuesday, September 5th, the day after the telecast, on page 28 of *The New York Times,* a full five days after the blurt-out, the story came to national attention: "Romney Asserts He Underwent 'Brainwashing.' " If White is right, and we have reached the point where political campaigns resemble *Laugh-in* (didn't Billy Graham and Richard Nixon both appear?), we are in t-r-o-u-b-l-e.

These are the elements of superlative reporting which excite the admiration not only of intrigued readers but of professional colleagues who know how difficult the reconstruction of such events can be.

Professional competence is obviously not the problem with this book. So many of the "facts" are there; lengthy and generally perceptive passages are devoted to race, crime, Asia, and the media; the writing, as usual, flows gracefully and easily.

What, then, is the problem? Why does *The Making of the President 1968* leave us with a feeling of incompleteness that we did not have after reading its two predecessors?

It is because, in Samuel Johnson's words, "Seldom any splendid story is wholly true." This book is no exception. Most of what White reports is interesting; much of what he does not report is significant.

Something is missing because interpreting politics at the top so completely and so officially for eight years has finally caught up with Theodore White. The converging of complex social conflicts and new disparities of perceptions came upon our institutions with such force in 1968 as to render impossible any man's effort, no matter how gifted, to compile a political textbook widely credible within the country's factions. But White was already shut out of those factions as completely as he was included in official circles. He had become over the years so much a part of what the new furies were assaulting (I know of no one who has stronger links to the major organs of mass communications or closer ties to more exalted politicians) that he could not, in honest loyalty as well as by instinct, completely separate himself from the beseiged. He saw the struggle from across the moat, inside the battered fortress of the reigning powers, and while he was able to be fair toward those on the other side of the wall, he could never achieve total freedom from his prejudices.

Perhaps I can illustrate with his treatment of Vietnam. "The cause in Vietnam," he writes, " was the cause made clear to the world by the Democratic Party of the United States." Lyndon Johnson also believed that. But with all the influence of the Presidency behind him, he could not convince the country.

Neither can White, nor does he try; but the point is that he believes in the war, and it colors his sympathies.

He called upon Vice President Humphrey after the violence in Chicago and found him "stunned." Said the Vice President to the reporter, "The interesting thing about all this is that if anybody could qualify for the title of hawk, it would be Nixon, but he's never been picketed, only me." It is not recorded what the reporter said to the Vice President, but he might have said, "Well, Hubert, I can understand how you feel. But I am afraid your comment completely misses the point of how so many Democrats feel. They feel betrayed. After all, it wasn't Nixon who had escalated the war or who felt compelled officially to defend it. It was your party, the Democratic, not the Republican, which was in power when the fateful decisions were made; Nixon may be a hawk, but he didn't say four years ago that he was not going to send American boys to Asia, and he didn't then order them over. You had better snap out of this persecution complex and realize just why they are picketing you. Then maybe you can do something about it."

White, as everyone knows, is an old Asia hand who understands the historic mission of Asians to expel Westerners. He knows and details the thoughtless way in which we stumbled into the Vietnamese jungle. Like George Romney, Nelson Rockfeller, and Humphrey (like most of us, in fact, who have had to grapple with the strategical and moral contradictions of Vietnam), he battles within himself to reconcile the paradox of the war. His ties to power and the men who exercise it finally prevail.

When he writes that "In the highest possible sense, Vietnam was a matter of conscience for candidate Hubert Humphrey," there arises a serious problem of language. To millions of Americans who last year were concerned less with one man's moral agony than with the issue of war and death, this sentence must appear offensive, just as Hubert Humphrey appeared to his natural peace constituency. Again, White is right. Vietnam was a matter of conscience to the Vice President, and in the end his principles of loyalty, allegiance and propriety bound to a war he detested and to a man who regarded him with humiliating derogation. Right through to the end of the campaign. Conscientious, yes, but to vast numbers of people it was the lower scale of conscience, a distortion of moral priorities, conventional morality at its worst. The failure to perceive that it would be so regarded proved costly.

Yet White remains sympathetic: "He (HHH) had reason to be unsmiling. Pinioned in his official role of Vice President, he must suffer the denunciation of all his old friends for the war, as if his old record of twenty years service to the liberal cause had been sponged away by the rewriting of history." Here is the hint of an implication that men should judge a public official for his past, not present, conduct, as if previous virtues canceled present errors. But even this argument is not the essential issue. What it reveals is that Hubert Humphrey's problem is Teddy White's problem: They underestimated how strongly people felt about the war, how pervasively it had contaminated the moral climate of America, and how exclusively it had become the one issue that truly mattered to the very people White and Humphrey care about.

And so Humphrey would grieve because Nixon was ignored by the protesters and White would pass judgment on men and events he might otherwise see differently.

Witness: "Never before had a party gathering (the Democratic National Convention) attempted so violently to intrude itself in state policy while its party leaders were fighting a war" —as if a party has no stake in the issues of war and peace and no claim over the men who hold office by its investment. This was, frankly, what 1968 was all about.

Witness: "Men who had once sat around the table with JFK to outface the Russians in the Cuban missile crisis now, without credentials, darted about like lobbyists seeking a crevice of influence on decision. . . .—men who had never slept a night in an Asian village or learned a word of any Asian tongue, devoid of any learning in the realities of Asian power. . . ." —as if one should hold office or be a linguist in order to challenge a policy of his government.

Witness: White's reference to one of the two new movements in American politics—"a peace movement on the Left which believed that America had the capacity, all by itself, to sweet-talk the Communist world to peace." To whom is he referring? The "peace movement on the Left," if he means the radical movement, it cared not a whit for sweet-talking anyone; it only wanted out, period. And the peace movement within the Democratic Party, led by George McGovern and others, never rested its case on sweet-talking the Communists; it wanted action, specifically a halt to the bombing.

Witness: His reference to Paul O'Dwyer as "one of the more meager political figures in the Empire State." Now Paul O'Dwyer does not have power in the conventional sense, in the way, say, of a Nelson Rockfeller, for whom White had so much respect. But in 1968 terms, as a symbol of principled resistance to the war on the state and local level, he was anything but a "meager political figure." Meager, perhaps, as the political elite measures power, but the rules, remember, had changed by 1968. On the one burning issue of the year no one in the state of New York, including its governor, could inspire the trust of the disaffected as did Paul O'Dwyer, Al Lowenstein excepted. In 1968 the presumption of people *without credentials* to challenge "the cause of America for half a century became the true source of political power.

Which brings us to the young. With them White is now perceptive, now visceral. He skillfully describes the hypocrisies of the New Left, and he offers a new insight into the disaffection of the young that I had not heard before: the dwindling of opportunity for self-expression in independent careers ("Scores of thousands of students for example, study international affairs; yet the State Department absorbs only 150 new Foreign Service Officers a year, and American industry only a few thousand overseas.")

But, surprisingly, White makes very little effort to relate the frustrations of the young to the war itself. The war underlies the book (the first chapter is entitled "Tet! —The Shadow on the Walls"); however, that hardly diminishes the need to explain exactly what the war has done to the aspirations, values, dreams, and mores of the generation that was asked to sacrifice for it. People do not put their head within reach of a policeman's nightstick simply because they cannot join the

Foreign Service. As bizarre as some of their behavior has been, we have to look for the moral force behind it. Yet in his own major discussion of the students, White gives one paragraph to the draft (without mentioning Vietnam) and then, in the list of other grievances, inserts only this sentence: "Add again to this condition the menace of the Vietnam war never adequately explained to the young men who must fight." Even there is the implication that it is not the war itself that was the root of disaffection but the failure of people to understand it.

If the truth were known, I don't think Teddy White likes today's activist young. (Come to think of it, who really does?) He finds them arrogant, dirty, disruptive. And he tends to believe that their masses are manipulated at the mercy of calculating organizers. He has clearly crossed to the other side of the generation gap, or been pushed.

How did it happen? It happened because White stayed with the politicians long after the politicians ceased to matter. Thus, on the night of the main violence in Chicago, he watched from the window of his hotel, then walked "quite unimpeded and unchallenged by the swarming police" (the result, no doubt, of clean living!) across the street to join Hubert Humphrey in his suite. I recall seeing film clips of Humphrey viewing his own nomination on television—a few feet away stood Theodore White. They were there, but the action was somewhere else.

Let me not appear too unkind to a man whose work and integrity I admire, a man who has had more influence on modern political reporting than any of his contemporaries. I dwell on the failure of his book to transcend the divisions of America and to understand the full impact of the war on the young because it is the most immediate way to underline how so many of us have failed.

For Teddy White's dilemma is our dilemma, too. It is the dilemma of America in 1968 and now.

He is aghast at violence in the streets, but he supports the official use of violence in Vietman; he may try, as the government tried, to rationalize that position, but the young will not buy. The gap widens.

He is aghast at hippy defecation in the old brownstones on his home town of Boston; the young find their senses fouled infinitely more by the war than by occasional human feces.

He recoils before "barbaric" riots; when, pray tell, have the majority of us recoiled before the barbaric conditions that breed riots?

And where, in all of this, is the margin for reconciliation?

Theodore White did not do badly in 1968. Nixon gave him first-class treatment and Humphrey embraced him as the kindred spirit he is. Everybody at the top seemed eager to share their confidences with the official campaign historian, and even last year's President got a sympathetic nod in this year's book.

But there is an irony in all of it. The closer Teddy White got to our leaders, the futher away the country slipped from them. Johnson withdrew. Humphrey was defeated, and the people tried hard not to elect Nixon. And so White is left with this splendid story, not wholly true. For the story in 1968 was not in Nixon's campaign plane, Humphrey's hotel suite, or even Johnson's oval office. The story was among schemers in Lowenstein's apartment, blue-collar workers who listened to Wallace, and Oregon's new technocrats who gave a majority to

McCarthy. The story was on campuses, in New Hampshire's snow, Chicago's streets, and in the living rooms of Americans who watched the evening reports from Vietnam and silently shook their heads.

It is a shame, in a way, Theodore White told us what happened at the top, and he told it as no one else can. But the top was no longer that important. Teddy White is too honest and thoughtful not to sense this. Almost with regret he noted: "The fall of 1968 could, conceivably, be the last in which an election in America is best understood by trying to understand what the leaders sought to do and tell the people." He may have been one election too late.

QUESTIONS FOR DISCUSSION AND DIALOGUE

1. Why does Moyers think that it would take a novelist, not a reporter, to capture the spirit of the year 1968? Do you agree? Why?
2. Discuss Moyers' implied views on the Vietnam war as opposed to White's views as they are stated in this article.
3. Reread the second last paragraph. Refer back to the last article in Chapter One. Has Moyers accurately assessed where "the story was?" Or was "the story" of the 1968 election more told by the Americans discussed in the *Newsweek* article? Or do they overlap? Discuss.
4. Based on your personal experience as well as your reading, do you think the 1968 presidential election was drastically different from the 1960 and 1964 elections? Why? Discuss.

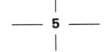

The New Snobbism

Stewart Alsop

"The New Snobbism" discussed here by Stewart Alsop was allegedly illustrated by the previous article in which Bill Moyers critically reviewed Theodore White's *The Making of the President 1968.* How the politicians and their activities get interpreted as well as who interprets them are obvious questions posed by both these articles. The confused student might receive some clarification by rereading the article in Chapter One, "Whose Facts Do You Read?" and by considering the press as one of the "Nonpolitical Influentials" discussed in Chapter Four.

Four words in a review in the Sunday New York Times recently impelled this reporter to write a letter to Theodore H. White, author of the brilliant "Making of the President" books. White wrote in reply about a phenomenon that has not been much noticed, and that White rightly calls "A political fact of enormous importance and real danger."

In the chapter on Lyndon Johnson in his current book, White wrote that it was only when Johnson renounced the Presidency "that any greatness first became faintly visible to his contemporaries." This notion infuriated the *Times* reviewer, political writer Patrick Anderson. The President withdrew, Anderson wrote, simply to avoid further humiliation at the hands of Eugene McCarthy and "the hated Robert Kennedy." This, wrote Anderson, is what "I believe and everyone I know believes. . . ."

Cult

"It seems to me," I wrote to Teddy White, "that something rather peculiar is happening to political writing in this country, and that the phrase tells a lot about what is happening. A man who exposes himself to only one point of view is not a journalist—he is a member of a fashionable political cult. Several reviewers of your book seem to be members of this curiously snobbish and very powerful cult. Perhaps you have some thought on the subject that I might plagiarize. . . . "

Back came several pages of thoughts, all well worth plagiarizing. "The root of the problem," White wrote, "is something, I call, vaguely, 'the new intolerance.' In the new intolerance, the United States Government is the master of all evil, the chief world agent of repression; the establishment is as corrupt as the Romanov dynasty; and the spokesmen of the new intolerance are infused with a morality so stark that any deviation from their morality is heresy, any difference of opinion villainy."

In his book, White expressed similar views—he wrote of a "new avant-garde" which now "dominates the heights of national communication," and which "has come to despise its own country and its traditions." The "heights of national communication" are of course in New York, and White's punishment was swift and merciless—his book, which received very enthusiastic reviews in other cities, was savagely attacked by almost every New York reviewer.

"The moral heights of New York," White wrote in his letter, are held by journals like *The Village Voice* and *The New York Review of Books.* They are so pure, and shriek with such passion that, in fashionable New York, they are the pulpit-voice of the Church of Good Liberals."

Tone

Jack Newfield, a leading "pulpit-voice in fashionable New York," reviewed White's book in *The Village Voice* ten days before publication, and set the tone. Newfield wrenched one sentence out of context ("I walked quite unimpeded and unchallenged by the swarming police across the street to the Blackstone") to prove that White was a cowardly rabbit of an "establishment" journalist.

Fashionable New York instantly fell into line. Two reviewers—Christopher Lehmann-Haupt in the daily Times and Bill Moyers (who used to defend Lyndon Johnson and the war with great eloquence) in *The Saturday Review*—unoriginally quoted the same sentence chosen by Newfield as a stick with which to beat

White. In various reviews, White, a passionate and lifelong liberal, was described as "anti-peace," "anti-intellectual," "against students," and "against blacks"—a choice collection of demonstrable untruths. Above all, White was an "establishment" journalist, and thus, by implication, a fink, a fake and a sellout.

If this sort of criticism were confined to a couple of New Left journals it would have no importance, White points out. But it is not. White believes that "the news-reporting in the news columns of *The New York Times* is still the best in the world," but that "the critical pages of the Times are suffused with the parochial, cultist, emotional standards of New York City."

White recalls in his letter his own experience as a journalist in France, where the American tradition of fair reporting is almost unknown, and journalism is dominated by "the other tradition—the reporter and his friends assume that they, and they alone, know the truth, and facts are relevant only as they demonstrate that truth." The Times, White points out, has more influence than any other paper in the world, and "if the Times turns its critical columns over exclusively to the journalists of commitment, *a la Francaise,* we have a unique and dangerous situation."

It may be said that Teddy White, whose ox has been rather brutally gored, exaggerates the importance of what he calls "the new intolerance." To this reporter, "the new snobbism" seems a better description of the phenomenon, and snobbism is always a bit difficult to take seriously.

In the new snobbism, for example, the word "establishment" is the equivalent of the word "vulgar" in the old snobbism—it is an essentially meaningless but very useful put-down word. To the new snobs, someone like Teddy White who does not believe that Lyndon Johnson is wholly a monster, or that our reasons for going into Vietnam were wholly immoral, is "establishment," just as to old snobs, someone who wore black silk socks in the daytime was "vulgar." In both cases, the offender is beyond the pale, rigidly excluded from the closed circle of "everyone I know."

Bore

The new snobbism is pretty well confined to "fashionable New York"—a Washington journalist whose sources are limited to "everyone I know" is likely in time to turn to some other trade. Moreover, because the new snobbism, like all snobbism, demands total conformity, it has become, again like all snobbisms, increasingly predictable and increasingly boring. So it is tempting to dismiss the whole phenomenon as interesting but not essentially important.

But it is important, and in the last paragraph of his letter, Teddy White suggests a main reason why it is important: "I regard the growing gap between the cult that dominates New York intellectual thought today and the reality perceived by thoughtful people elsewhere as a political fact of enormous importance and real danger." The danger is real, simply because New York is the American intellectual capital, and it is a capital that more and more has lost touch with America.

QUESTIONS FOR DISCUSSION AND DIALOGUE

1. What is the significance of the phrase "Everyone I know believes. . . ." as Alsop sees it? Do you agree? Discuss.
2. Are you tempted to agree more with Alsop's and White's assessment of the 1968 Presidential election or with Moyer's assessment? Why?
3. Can a student of politics find "objective" information on which he can base intelligent decisions? How?
4. Does this article and the previous Bill Moyers' article belong more in this chapter dealing with the "Politicians and their Parties" or in the next chapter on the "Nonpolitical Influentials"—the courts, policemen, press and academic community? Why? Discuss.

Now The Republic

Time

Time considers Richard Nixon in this article shortly after he won the 1968 Republican nomination. In November of 1968, he also won the presidency, a truly amazing accomplishment in light of the relatively recent political failures which Richard Nixon had suffered. Here the reader sees a controversial politician who excelled as a tactician and strategist. Whether he would excel in fulfilling the awsome responsibilities of the presidency would be for his constituents and the historians to assess.

At the end, he took the podium the way he had taken the convention—as if it belonged to him. He stretched out his arms to gather it all in. The fingers on both hands wigwagged victory Vs at the clapping, stamping, shouting, pulsing heart of the Republican Party. Four years ago, introducing Barry Goldwater at an identical moment, he had described himself as a "simple soldier" in the Republican ranks. Now the fortunes of political conflict had recommissioned him a five-star general. Richard Nixon was back for one more chance at Commander in Chief.

Which Richard Nixon? Friends, enemies and those between could not agree. They never could before. In a generally sympathetic biography nine years ago, Earl Mazo found in Nixon "a paradoxical combination of qualities that bring to mind Lincoln, Theodore Roosevelt, Harry Truman, and Joe McCarthy." The intervening years have polished Nixon and made him well-to-do, but they have not simplified him. He can still sound like the high-minded statesman and act like the cunning politico. He can talk eloquently of ideals and yet seem always preoccupied with tactics. He can plink out *Let Me Call You Sweetheart* for reporters on a piano or rib himself on television talk shows, but the grin never seems quite at home on his strong, heavy face. The almost mysterious quality about Richard Nixon is that he is a man of exceptional abilities and solid virtues, but somehow his many parts have always added up to less than a convincing whole. Today he seems closer than ever to overcoming this elusive handicap. He is certainly more confident, more self-assured—and with good reason. He has made an extraordinary political comeback. He worked harder than anyone else for the nomination, with total dedication to his goal and to the party. In that sense, he amply deserved his victory.

No Millennium. At any rate, the 29th G.O.P. Convention, looking up at its nominee, was not in a mood for character analysis. After a conclave made dull by the swift rout of Nixon's foes and enlivened only briefly by a spat over the vice-presidential nomination, it was time for exultation. One thing that his detractors have never understood about Nixon is his total identification with the Republican Party and his understanding of it. His acceptance speech was pure Nixon, telling it as the party would like it to be—1968 style.

He had worked for two weeks on the speech, writing it out himself on yellow legal pads. It contained major elements of the basic speech that he had delivered again and again during the primaries, and reporters who had followed him during those campaigns could finish many of the sentences as soon as they heard the first word or two. But the nation as a whole had not yet heard it. It was a mixture of carefully balanced political calculations and genuine personal warmth. It was, by any reasonable standard, corny, but it also was one of Nixon's most effective speeches in years. Gone was the excessive partisanship and professional anti-Communism of his early days. The nation wants a high-roader after Lyndon Johnson. The republic has survived subversion. The cold war is passe. Vietnam is something to be settled, not won. So Nixon told them what they wanted to hear. "Tonight I do not promise the millennium in the morning. I don't promise that we can eradicate proverty and end discrimination in the space of four or even eight years. But I do promise action. And a new policy for peace and progress and justice at home."

To the Communist world, he declared an end to the "era of confrontations," now that the "time has come for an era of negotiations." But the new Administration must "restore the strength of America so that we shall always negotiate from strength and never from weakness." He did not touch on arms control, a major point to be negotiated.

Greatest Engine. In parts, the speech followed the Nixon pattern of giving and taking away, of praising and then attacking. He paid his respects to the courts, but they have "gone too far in weakening the peace forces as against the criminal forces." And his Attorney General would be a real gangbuster. The black and the poor need rescue, but they "don't want to be a colony." Federal antipoverty efforts have not helped at all: "We have reaped from these programs an ugly harvest of frustrations, violence and failure." Therefore, urged Nixon, the Government must use its powers to "enlist in this battle the greatest engine of progress ever developed in the history of man: American private enterprise."

He was curiously touching in describing the son of the slums who "dreams the dreams of a child. And yet when he awakens, he awakens to a living nightmare." He was rather embrassing in the sketch of another child, himself, who hears a train go by and and dreams of far away places. "It seems like an impossible dream." But a self-sacrificing father, a "gentle Quaker mother," a dedicated teacher, a minister, a courageous wife, loyal offspring, devoted followers—plus a cast of millions of voters—combined to put that boy on the train that stopped last week in Miami Beach, possibly on the way to the White House.

The fact that Nixon spoke of himself as the hero of this American dream, even though his intent was plainly modest, seemed cloying to some. And the reference to a train whistle was an oddly old-fashioned note: trains do not symbolize escape and movement to today's young. Yet there could be little doubt that Nixon was sincere here, just as Lyndon Johnson is sincere when he talks about his years of poverty along the Pedernales. Certainly Nixon's audience in Miami knew what he was talking about and responded.

Good Avocation. His ability to evoke the good old days and look eagerly to the year 2000, and to make the mix sound coherent, points up his talent for accommodation, which is one explanation for Nixon's return from political limbo. The G.O.P.'s liberals can live with him. He picked up much support from the Goldwater wing (and won the blessing of Barry), not because he belonged to the party's right wing, but because he was acceptable to it. Many of the stauncher conservatives preferred Reagan, but they realized that the California governor was not a viable national candidate. Tom Stagg Jr., national committeeman from Louisiana, acknowledged: "We've had our shot at a candidate who totally met our qualifications, and that candidate got six states. We've had our druthers. Now shall we win one?"

Another factor is Nixon's capacity simply to endure. As a child, he survived serious illnesses and a buggy accident that gashed his skull; two of his four brothers died in childhood. As a politician, he lived through youthful success and middle-aged failure by dint of total industry and a fatalistic belief that in politics conditions create a right time for a man despite his actions. A Navy veteran in 1946, he won a House seat at the age of 33. He was elected Senator at 37 and Vice President at 39. Ten years later, defeated for the Presidency and the governorship of California, he certified himself politically kaput. Most of the press agreed, including *Time*. In 1966, sensing the vacuum in the party, Nixon campaigned tirelessly for G.O.P. candidates in 35 states and claimed a major share in that year's victory. Nixon is only 55, but he has been a national figure for nearly a generation. He has made survival an avocation.

In large measure, his current success flows from the ineptness or vulnerability of his opponents inside the party. George Romney, first in the ring, was the first to drop out. Ronald Reagan had possibilities, but was too new on the scene and too rigid in his views. Nelson Rockefeller, while a strong and attractive candidate in many ways, has never fully understood the difference between the politics of nomination and the politics of election. In three leap years, he approached the party as if it were a collection of voters on election eve instead of a coalition of interests about to hold a convention. It is a failing shared by the liberal Republican leadership, which apparently learned little from its rejection in 1964.

While Rockefeller fumbled with Romney's candidacy, supporting him with money (at least $250,000), staff help and increasingly hollow pronouncements of loyalty, Nixon continued to capitalize on the contacts and loyalties he had built up during 22 years in and around politics. Rocky staged his great revolving-door act over whether he would be an active candidate, in the process losing such important friends as Spiro Agnew. Nixon advanced cautiously, tying up delegate after delegate and winning primary after primary. The former Vice-President was able to campaign at a leisurely pace, usually accompanied by wife Pat—who looks more chic than in 1960—and their pretty daughters, Tricia, 22 and Julie, 20.

Fargo Friend. By the time Rockefeller clumped back into the race April 30, Nixon's momentum was almost impossible to stop. Rockefeller roared around the country, berating Nixon for refusing to stand up and fight. It was a weak argument coming from a man who had ducked the primaries. Rocky had style and good humor, and the crowds liked him. But he bet heavily on the public-opinion polls, only to have them backfire after the Harris and Gallup surveys clashed. When Rockefeller visited delegates, it was to get acquainted, "to show I don't have horns," as he himself acknowledged. When Nixon visited, it was old-home week. Nixon could drop in at Fargo, N. Dak., and say: "Hiya, George, remember that night when you were telling me about that time with Harry..."

Nixon took the Oregon primary on May 28 against the disembodied competition of Rockefeller and Reagan, and that 73% vote, he believed, assured him the nomination. Only some self-inflicted stab or an act of Providence could stop him. Privately he said: "Everyone is waiting for Nixon to blow his stack or confront Rockefeller directly. Well, it hasn't happened up to now, and I think it's too late to start."

In the final days before the convention, it was not Rockefeller who kept a whiff of competition alive but the increasingly obvious availability of Ronald Reagan and the threat that George Wallace would cut into Nixon's post-convention strength in the South. By this stage, Nixon's campaign organization was tooling along flawlessly. He assembled a talented crew of old and new aides from in and out of politics and from varying ideological backgrounds.

Logistical plans for the convention were already being made in November of 1967, three months before Nixon announced that he was running. Rooms in the Hilton Plaza were booked even before the hotel was finished. Finally, Nixon established a virtual colony in Miami Beach populated by 500 staffers and roughly 1,000 volunteers. An elaborate telephone and radio communications system was created. Besides command posts in Nixon's hotel and in a trailer outside Convention Hall, branch operations were maintained in 35 hotels housing delegates.

Nixon's game is poker, and in poker, he observed upon arriving in Miami Beach last among the candidates, "It's the fellow without the cards who does the strongest talking. I've got the cards." Nixon was so confident of his hand that he tarried on Long Island during the preconvention weekend. On Monday morning, he appeared at a naturalization proceeding in New York on behalf of his Cuban driver and cook, Manolo and Fina Sanchez. When he got to Miami Beach that evening, Rockefeller and Reagan were frantically and forlornly scampering after delegates. By this time, the hot Florida sun had finally hatched Reagan's offical candidacy.

Stirrings. Behind the convention scene of mixed turmoil and torpor (from her pinnacle of 84 years, Alice Roosevelt Longworth pronounced it "soporific"), there was a good deal of political jostling and even some drama. During the three days leading up to the Wednesday-night balloting, the main maneuvering centered on three elements: 1) a handful of uncommitted delegations, of which Maryland, Ohio, Michigan, New Jersey and Pennsylvania were the most important; 2) the South, which was largely in Nixon's camp already but vulnerable to Reagan; and 3) Nixon's choice of a running mate.

Michigan, under Governor George Romney, and Ohio, under Governor James Rhodes, were subject to raiding by Nixon. But the gains to be made there were not worth the cost of antagonizing their powerful leaders, who clung to their status as favorite sons. Romney was apparently prepared to hold out indefinitely. Rhodes, who had been generally regarded as eager to be in line with the winner, remained surprisingly stubborn. Not so secretly, he wanted a Rockefeller-Reagan ticket as the strongest draw in Ohio and, despite a well-earned reputation for sagacity, held out some hope for its success. "We've really stirred things up," he said at one point. "We've turned this into an open convention."

Most of the important stirring, however, was being done on Nixon's behalf. New Jersey was restless under its commitment to the favorite-son candidacy of Senator Clifford Case, and the Nixon forces decided to move in on it. On a golf course over the weekend, Nixon Aide Peter Glanigan told State G.O.P. Chairman Webster Todd: "Look, we need your delegation right now." Todd, whose wife was openly supporting Rockefeller, shot back: "Hell, no!" But pressure continued on individual delegates, who saw no purpose in holding out for a lost cause. By Tuesday night it was open knowledge that New Jersey would break, just as it had at the 1964 convention.

Conservative Trio. Pennsylvania Governor Raymond Shafer had dropped his favorite-son role in order to back Rockefeller. But neither Shafer's influence nor his choice to nominate Rockefeller could hold the entire delegation in line. Some of the Pennsylvanians had scant respect for their Governor, privately referring to him as "Dudley Do-Right," after the feckless cartoon character who usually ends up doing the wrong thing for the right reason. And Nixon had powerful supporters in the delegation, including George Bloom, chairman of the state public-utility commission, and Congressman James Fulton. When Rockefeller visited the Keystone Staters, District Attorney Robert Duggan of Allegheny County demanded: "And where in hell were you in 1964?" It became increasingly clear that Nixon would get some help from Pennsylvania.

Agnew's defection to Nixon was all but official before the convention started. Meanwhile, though, Nixon men were compelled to mount a defense operation among the Southern delegations. Reagan had been making inroads in Alabama, North Carolina and Texas particularly, and this trend could not be allowed to go on unchecked. Barry Goldwater, Senator John Tower of Texas and Senator Strom Thurmond of South Carolina—three of the most conservative men in the party—counter-attacked on Nixon's behalf. Goldwater chatted with Southerners in his hotel suite. Thurmond and Tower took some waverers for boat rides. Their message was basic and concise. The real contest was between Nixon and Rockefeller; every defection to Reagan would ultimately only benefit Rockefeller.

Rumors that Nixon was going to pick a liberal as a running mate were everywhere. When a Miami paper printed a front-page story that it would be Oregon Senator Mark Hatfield, Rockefeller's and Reagan's men distributed 3,000 copies on the convention floor to make sure that no one missed the point. Thurmond and company denied the report, but the most effective disclaimer came from Nixon in private meetings with Southerners. "I won't do anything that would hurt development of the two-party system in the South," Nixon told them. "I won't take anybody that I have to shove down the throats of any section of the country." Thus such Nixon loyalists as Party Chairman Harry Dent of South Carolina were able to tell skeptics on the floor: "I've got it written in blood."

Nixon was also artfully placating Southerners on certain sensitive issues. The Miami Herald managed to get a tape recorder into one of the private sessions. In the transcript it printed later, which Nixon's spokesmen did not knock down, he explained his public support of this year's open-housing civil rights bill as a matter of political tactics rather than conviction. "I felt then and I feel now," said the transcript, "that conditions are different in different parts of the country." But he wanted the issue "out of our sight" so as not to divide the party and risk a platform fight. The Southerners also remembered Nixon's criticism of Johnson's Supreme Court appointments. While Nixon did not quarrel with Abe Fortas' designation on personal grounds, the Southerners who did looked kindly on Nixon's position.

Collapsed Movement. Vote projections by the networks and the wire services bounced about a bit between Monday and Wednesday, while Rockefeller men insisted on talking about the "erosion" of Nixon's strength. The most accurate count, as it turned out, was by the Nixon organization, which earlier had talked about 700 and privately refined its calculations to 702. Needed to be nominated: 667. As the nominating speeches droned on, Nixon visited his command trailer outside the hall and got word that a first-ballot victory was assured.

As the roll call progressed, it was obvious that Nixon was faring exactly as he had expected. The candidate, watching television and keeping his own tally in his penthouse suite, could have noted in the first several states an extra vote here and there beyond his minimal requirements. Then Florida and Georgia came through with large majorities—evidence that the Reagan movement had collapsed. Maryland delivered 18 out of 26. Four Michiganders deserted Romney. Mississippi's unit rule held for the entire delegation of 20. The undermining of Case's position in New Jersey produced a welcome 18 out of 40. In Pennsylvania, Nixon picked up 22 more.

By the bottom fifth of the alphabetical listing, the fight was really over. After West Virginia, Nixon had 650, and Wisconsin's 30, won in that state's primary, broke through the magic number to make it 680. Wyoming added its twelve, for a first-ballot total of 692, compared with 277 for Rockefeller, 182 for Reagan and 182 sprinkled elsewhere. It was even less of a race than it seemed. Nixon had reserve votes in several favorite-son delegations that he could have called upon if necessary. Minnesota Congressman Ancher Nelsen, one of the nine whips working the floor for Nixon, had only one complaint: "We got rather hungry.

Getting a hot dog—that was the biggest crisis we had." Floor Manager Rogers Morton told reporters: "The only time I got worried was when my shirttail came out and I couldn't get it back in."

Coffee and Cokes. Nixon won with no help at all from California and Massachusetts and only token support from three of the other large states, New York, Ohio and Michigan. He owed his victory to Illinois, most of the smaller states in the West and Middle West, and particularly to the South and the Border States. Excluding Arkansas, which stayed with Governor Winthrop Rockefeller, 14 Southern and Border States delivered 298 votes, or 45% of the number needed to nominate. Thus Nixon's determination to keep the South happy.

It was after 2 a.m. Thursday when the voting ended. With scarcely time out for a round of congratulations, the candidate plunged into a round robin of meetings with advisers, aides and party leaders about the vice-presidential nomination. Ten days earlier, he had sent notes to a number of supporters, asking them to send suggestions to a post office box in New York, "anonymously, if you prefer." Whether he got any ideas from that source was not clear, but he did arrive in Miami with Agnew definitely on his mind.

As the meetings progressed through the early-morning hours, with a kaleidoscopic cast of participants sipping coffee and Cokes, a list containing scores of names was gradually shortened. New York Mayor John Lindsay, probably the most discussed possibility up to that point, was dismissed early as too unpopular among conservatives. John Gardner was briefly mentioned, soon dropped. Among others considered were Reagan and Tower, both of whom would have antagonized liberals. Hatfield, Romney and Keynoter Dan Evans were mentioned, then Tennessee Senator Howard Baker.

Overwhelmed. The shifting group of conferees contained its own roster of notables: Thomas Dewey, Herbert Brownell, Billy Graham, Everett Dirksen, Gerald Ford, Barry Goldwater, Karl Mundt, Party Chairman Ray Bliss. Finally, after a brief break for a nap and a breakfast of cold cereal, Nixon convened still another meeting. But this time, the possibilities had been reduced to five: Senator Charles Percy; Lieutenant Governor Robert Finch of Califronia, a longtime Nixon friend and associate; Congressman Rogers Morton of Maryland; Governor John Volpe of Massachusetts ("It might be nice," Nixon observed, "to have an Italian Catholic on the ticket"); and, of course, Agnew. Finch and Morton attended the meetings but left while they were being talked about.

It was past noon when Nixon ended the talks by observing: "Well, I think the meeting has accomplished about all that it can accomplish." Morton put in a call to Agnew. "Are you sitting down?" Morton inquired. Nixon got on the phone and broke the news. "I'm overwhelmed," said Agnew, whose stoic expression rarely admits of such a condition.

The Criteria. Overwhelmed also, but hardly in the same way, were many of the Republicans and much of the country when Nixon went on television 15 minutes later to announce his selection. Nixon laid out three criteria for the No. 2 man on the ticket: 1) he must be qualified to become President, 2) he must be an effective campaigner, and 3) he must be capable of assuming the new responsibilities for domestic affairs that Nixon says he will entrust to his Vice President.

Attaching Agnew's name to these requirements shocked many, because they knew virtually nothing about the man beyond the fact that he was a very new, moderately successful Governor with no national or international stature. Many Northern Republicans were rankled by the ready acceptance of the selection by Southerners and by conservatives generally. Although Agnew is a moderate by Maryland standards and a liberal by Deep South criteria, there was the suspicion that he was on the ticket to placate Thurmond and other segregationists. Not only liberals protested. Colorado Senator Peter Dominick howled: "There are 2,000,000 people in my state who have never heard of Agnew. It's a terrible choice."

Events during the rest of the day began to take care of Agnew's anonymity. Irate over the aura of a shabby deal that surrounded his selection and disturbed by some of his recent criticism of Negro activists, leaders in a number of delegations talked revolt. As usual, however, the liberals were disorganized. By the time the final night's session convened to name a vice-presidential candidate and hear both nominees' acceptance speeches, a coalition had been assembled to second Agnew's nomination: Lindsay, Percy, Tower and California's William Knowland. They covered all factions of the party.

The dissidents scrounged for a candidate willing to oppose Agnew, but were turned down by Lindsay. Rockefeller refused to cooperate with the revolt, even though some of his allies, notably Rhode Island Governor John Chafee, were leading it. Finally George Abbott of Nevada nominated Romney. The ensuing vote was a cruel slaughter: 1,128 for Agnew to 178 for Romney. The loser then followed tradition by moving to make the nomination unanimous.

Although the minirevolt against Agnew's selection may have satisfied bored delegates' desire for combat and excitement, it was not only futile but unwise as well. Both party tradition and U.S. history since Aaron Burr's day dictate that the President must have a No. 2 man whom he wants and trusts. And if by some fluke the convention had forced Romney or someone else on Nixon, and the ticket had gone on to win, the unwanted Veep could have looked forward to even more frustrations than the incumbent normally suffers.

Underrated. At the week's end, as Nixon and Agnew went to the L.B.J. ranch for a briefing on national-security affairs, it was uncertain how much permanent damage to the ticket's chances in November had been caused by the scuffle. Initially, Nixon was forced on the defensive, arguing that Agnew was an "underrated man." Agnew's own acceptance speech was short and almost humble in tone. Later Agnew complained that he was being unfairly tagged as an opponent of civil rights merely because he opposed civil disobedience.

Certainly the Marylander will be no asset to the ticket among Negro voters, although it is doubtful that Nixon will get much black support in any case. Agnew may be helpful, on the other hand, in the border regions and some Southern states, such as Virginia, Texas, Florida and North Carolina, in which Nixon has a fighting chance to best George Wallace. This is what Nixon men call a "peripheral strategy," more or less conceding the Deep South to Wallace. To capture the Presidency, however, the Republicans must sweep much of the West as well, while carrying some of the vote-heavy states, including Ohio, New Jersey and

Michigan. New York will probably be an insurmountable problem for Nixon. Illinois will be nearly as tough. California figures to be a tossup.

Humphrey's Problem. Nixon maintains that he will fight hard for all the crucial states, and says of the major industrial states: "I don't think we gave them adequate attention in 1960." He will avoid his 1960 mistake of barnstorming all 50 states. His mode of attack is best suited to opposing Hubert Humphrey. He sounded eager for it. "Two tough fighters like Hubert Humphrey and Dick Nixon," said Nixon after his nomination, "are going to slap each other around pretty hard on the issues. But I'm going to keep it on a high level—no personal attacks, just on the issues." In an interview with *Time* last month, he indicated his strategy: "Humphrey's problem," he said, "is that he carries the past on his back. He is the candidate of the past no matter how much he talks about his programs and the future." Nixon is hardly alone in his conclusion that "if there is one thing the American people don't want, it's what they've got."

Having won the Republicans, Nixon now has to win the Republic. Some of his friends and most of his foes are dubious that he can do it. At Rockefeller's headquarters before the Miami Beach convention, Gordon MacRae sang:

Richard Nixon's going far,
In his snappy Edsel car.
General Custer's coming in,
Gonna show Dick how to win.

Rockefeller's people have company in thinking that Nixon is a permanent loser, and Nixon knows it. Just after the Oregon primary, he described his feelings: "You know, politics is the cruelest sport of all. There are few loyalties, very few friends. But coming off the floor, that meant something to me. I kind of get a bang out of demonstrating that the old saws, the old myths about Nixon have no validity." He has yet to prove that, of course, but he is perhaps in better shape to do so now than ever before. In the weeks to come, the nation will observe a fascinating and peculiarly American human drama, the final testing of a man who almost had everything, almost lost everything and is now given a rare opportunity to try again.

QUESTIONS FOR DISCUSSION AND DIALOGUE

1. What does *Time's* description of the Rockefeller vs. Nixon pre-nomination struggle tell about the difference between issues and personality in contrast to power and influence?
2. Outline the characteristics of Richard Nixon that make you optimistic and and characteristics that make you pessimistic as they are described in the article. Would you add any to these? What information has led you to these other views about Richard Nixon?
3. Outline how Richard Nixon won the Republican nomination in 1968. Are there any lessons here for one who might wish to be a "successful politician"? Discuss.
4. Did you (or would you have favored) favor Richard Nixon for president in

1968? Why or why not? Is your response based on his stand on issues or other considerations? If you did not prefer Nixon, which 1968 presidential candidate did you prefer? Why?

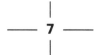

The Politics of Power: Portrait of a Master

Newsweek

> In this "Portrait of a Master" power politician, *Newsweek* describes President Lyndon Johnson at the peak of his influence. From August of 1965 to the 1970's is both such a short time and long time! In considering the article's emphasis on Johnson's handling of the press, his emphasis on secrecy, his coarseness, his mastery of the political arts, his comparative lack of foreign policy mastery, etc., the reader can see the previews of future problems. But as the tone of the article indicates, this is only with the benefit of historical hindsight. What went wrong? How much of what went wrong was LBJ's fault?

Were this an Age of Kings, what would he be called? Lyndon the Magnificent? Lyndon the Good? Lyndon the Just? Improbable. Nor would he quite be Lyndon the Terrible. Lyndon the Doer would be close; but on his record to date historians could best record the 36th President of the United States as Lyndon the Powerful.

At this moment, Lyndon Baines Johnson holds in his big, sunburned hands more raw power than any other peacetime President in the life of the Republic. By wielding it with remarkable skill, he has brought a new kind of political reign into the American experience. And his power radiates around the world. Never in the twenty months of his regime has he held greater sway at home nor been prepared to invoke such potentially fateful influence abroad as that implicit in the decisions he will make this week on the war in Vietnam.

At the White House, he rules over the royal household with a will of iron; he summons the dukes and barons of Congress to his chambers and they dutifully carry out his royal decrees; his every word and move is the constant and almost the only subject of discussion among all who attend his court, and he dominates Washington like a monarch of old.

'Do It My Way':

Writ large on his spiritual coat of arms is the idea of consensus; and the President all but acknowledges that consensus is more important to him than the system of constitutional checks and balances. Prideful of the nation's domestic unity, LBJ said recently: "There has never been less friction between the executive, lesiglative and judicial branches than there is today." To those who know him, "unity" is Johnson court rhetoric for "Let's do it my way."

How, in a democratic society, did Lyndon Johnson grow so powerful? The answer is that three forces converged to place him in this unique position.

First there is Mr. Johnson himself, a man with a vast appetite for power and an extraordinary skill in the politics of power. No President in history reached office so well trained to govern the United States. At the moment he took the oath of office, Mr. Johnson had 31 years of experience in manipulating the levers of the mammoth and intricate machinery of the Federal government—more than the pre-inaugural Federal experience of any other President.

High Popularity:

The second great force behind the President's unchallenged eminence is the sheer weight of his public support. His record-breaking victory last November has been followed by consistently high standings in national polls. The latest Harris Poll shows that 69 per cent of Americans approve of President Johnson's actions. His strong popularity with the public gives him even more leverage over a pliant and predominantly Democratic Congress. The result: the 89th Congress has already passed, or probably will pass, every major bill that President Johnson wants from this session; and thus far, it has passed no major bill that Johnson did not want. The President himself acutely appreciates his phenomenal success on Capitol Hill. "Come back in September and look at what we've done in legislation," he said recently. "Take any 50 years in our history and show me where more progress has been made."

And what of the third force that has led to LBJ's extraordinary power? It is, of course, the absence of serious political opposition. The Republicans, shattered by the Goldwater defeat, divided by internecine warfare and bereft of leadership, cannot even mount a respectable rear-guard action in or out of Congress. And since politics abhors a vacuum, the President has filled it with his weighty presence.

In the hands of any President, power unchecked can be and is dangerous. Thus far, to President Johnson's great credit, he has not misused that power. To him, power is not some sinister, corruptive evil, but an ultimate weapon for good. He hungers for power so that he can use it—by his own account, to right wrongs, correct injustices, educate children, feed the poor, house the homeless, bestow greater happiness on Americans and bring peace to the world. Utopian? He hungers for power because only power can fuel his rage for greatness.

The rage for greatness is the one thing about Lyndon Johnson that makes all other things understandable. He is obsessed, perhaps possessed, by ambition—ambition not merely to be a great President but to be the greatest President in history.

To less ambitious men, Mr. Johnson's goal may seem presumptuous or even outrageous; but the President is determined that in his mission to build The Great

Society, nothing shall daunt or defeat him. In his office one day recently, the President said with quiet determination: "For 35 years I have watched people read and write and talk about things that should be done; and in the limited time that I have, I'm going to do them."

Spares No Effort:

To get on with his impossible job, President Johnson spares no effort or person, wastes no time, tolerates no distractions. He is impatient, demanding, complex, cantankerous, vain, foresighted, shrewd, sensitive, unpredictable, tireless. He has the virtues and the failings of every successful man, and almost any criticism of him is valid.

Is Mr. Johnson domineering? Of course. The business of any President is to dominate the Executive Department. "They used to say the same thing about President Roosevelt," Vice President Hubert Humphrey said recently. "And John Kennedy was always in charge; I never felt like having an argument with him. Johnson is a strong man, a man of force and conviction."

Is President Johnson a slave driver? Certainly. He drives members of his staff twelve, fourteen, sixteen hours a day; but he drives himself harder. Says Defense Secretary Robert McNamara, a fourteen-hour-a-day man himself: "The President is absolutely tireless. He works nineteen hours a day, harder than anybody else in Washington, harder than any other executive I've ever known."

Is Mr. Johnson impatient? Absolutely. With all that he wants to accomplish, he cannot afford to waste time; he feels he must work fast while Congress and the country are so resoundingly behind him. Of her husband, Lady Bird Johnson once said: "Lyndon acts like there was never going to be a tomorrow."

Never Satisfied:

Up close, Mr. Johnson is compelling, forceful, at times overwhelming. He is a man of excesses and contradictions. He works too hard, gets too little sleep, attempts too much, is hurt too easily and is never satisfied.

He is hypersensitive to criticism, for two reasons. Personal criticism bruises the ego of any man in politics, and a Texas-size ego suffers Texas-size bruises.

More important, Mr. Johnson is convinced that public criticism cuts into his support with the public and Congress and that enough criticism could cut his support to the point where he could not act. "That is why he is so concerned about the criticism of our Vietnam policy by Walter Lippmann, Wayne Morse and the professors," says one member of the National Security Council.

Mr. Johnson is also piqued by critics of his personal style, and it particularly galls him to read the endless stories about John Kennedy's grace and elegance. Otherwise, he is becoming less sensitive about comparisons with JFK.

Since Dallas, LBJ has crossed two great political watersheds—his landslide re-election that gave him full title to the Presidency and his landslide legislative record, which, according to Lawrence F. O'Brien—who serves as Congressional liaison under LBJ as he did under JFK—already exceeds what Kennedy's could have been.

Freedom?

Apart from any comparison with Kennedy, there is an unpleasant side to Johnson. He can, for example, be vindictive. It is reported that he canceled the Presidential Medal of Freedom awards because he got mad at *Washington Post* cartoonist Herblock, one of the chosen recipients. Just before the President was to make the awards, Herblock published his slashingly critical "Happy Days on the Old Plantation" cartoon (Newsweek, July 12). The result, says one insider: President Johnson canceled all the awards.

Does the President abuse his staff? Frequently. One awed congressman re-counts that he was in the White House one night when the President rang for Jack Valenti, his special assistant. For three minutes Valenti failed to appear; and when he did show up, the President shouted, before a group from Congress:

"Where the hell you been?"

Valenti said he had gone for coffee.

"How many times have I got to tell you not to leave your office without telling me where you're going?"

(Valenti flatly denies the story.)

Quick to Abuse:

Yet the President really does admire Valenti—along with the rest of the staff he can be so quick to abuse. One day the President was fondly musing to a friend about some of them: "Now Bill Moyers. He's in on everything. He's a remarkable young man. I think he'll be dead at 40; he takes everything so hard. And Horace Busby, you know he's both objective and subjective. He can take a lot of legal language and make something out of it. And Jack Valenti, he's a genius, comes along and he takes a paragraph of Busby and makes a sentence out of it. It gets Busby mad, but it's even better. And Dick Goodwin, he's wonderful, that boy. He can cry a little. He cries a little with me whenever I need to cry over something. And Hubert, he's another who can cry pretty good over something. They get a lot of emotion into their work. . . . "

No official is exempt from the sharp side of the Presidential tongue. Once, the President tried to telephone former Budget Director Kermit Gordon at home one evening. Gordon had gone to a concert with his wife and was unreachable. The next morning the President said to Gordon: "Well, playboy, did you have a good time last night?"

President Johnson can be brutally blunt in giving orders. Once he told Under Secretary of State George Ball to get him a memorandum by 9 o'clock and be sure that it didn't appear in *The New York Times* first. During the Dominican crisis, the President was concerned one day about news reports that U.S. troops were openly aiding the right-wing junta. Mr. Johnson ordered Deputy Defense Secretary Cyrus Vance to find out from the U.S. military commander, Lt. Gen. Bruce Palmer, if the reports were true. The President told Vance: "Tell Palmer

I am going to bust him down to private, just another private, if he doesn't have the right answers." (Palmer had them.)

Earthy:

Is the President given to profanity? The private talk of many politicians is earthy—and Lyndon Johnson is second to none in this respect. Moreover, LBJ's imagery is always pertinent. One of his favorite derogatory expressions, which he often uses about his more inept political opponents is: "He couldn't find his ass with both hands."

He is the most secretive President of modern times, for he believes policy should be made in private, that is, without public discussion. At a meeting of task-force leaders for 1966 legislation, held in the White House on the night of July 8, the President said, "I want the best, boldest, most imaginative ideas you can supply. But you give them to *me*. Let *me* worry about how to implement them. I'm the politician. And it's been my observation over the past 35 years that ideas launched prematurely get nowhere."

He hates to be alone. He even will invite an aide, and sometimes a member of his Cabinet, along to the bathroom so that they can continue a conversation. Yet he has had no close friend since Speaker Sam Rayburn died, primarily because Mr. Johnson has not taken the time to make friends with anyone. "Lyndon Johnson doesn't need friends," says one of the most perceptive members of his Cabinet. "Friends wouldn't make the difference in what he wants to achieve as President."

The charge that Mr. Johnson surrounds himself with yes men is not strictly true. Actually, when the President is probing for a consensus, he searches tirelessly for ideas, information, new points of view. Indeed, he sees and telephones more people outside his official family—congressmen, businessmen, labor leaders, educators, governors, mayors, publishers, professional men—than any President before him. But once he has made up his mind the President expects total loyalty and no arguments.

The Broker:

Effective as he has been in dealing with the sprawling executive department, Mr. Johnson is even more effective in dealing with Congress. When he turns from his role as Chief Executive to confront his old colleagues on Capitol Hill, Mr. Johnson again becomes the inside operator, the cloak-room manipulator, the broker in power, the political middleman who calculates how much of a bill he can sell and who and how many will buy.

As the broker, Mr. Johnson begins with few firmly set ideas. He is loose and flexible, ready to shift ground. The secret of victory is to isolate the critical points of contention, find the sweeteners for both sides, apply pressure of the right sort in the right place, and come up not only with the solution but the power to enforce the solution. Thus, with Mr. Johnson, legislative means and ends merge and become inseparable. The medicare bill that can pass becomes the Administration's medicare bill that should pass. If the poll-tax ban demanded by liberals would jeopardize the voter-rights bill, throw it out. Says one Cabinet official: "The President will not listen to those who want him to do something for which there is no support."

In addition to his natural gift for the legislative art, the President is thoroughly familiar with every weapon in the White House arsenal, from the invitation to ride in the Presidential plane to the authorization of a campaign contribution from Democratic funds, from patronage to White House parties. Mr. Johnson can also bring outright pressure. But arm-twisting is not common. His favorite weapon is personal persuasion, face-to-face or on the telephone.

The President's own calls to congressmen are not routine or necessarily frequent; he calls when it counts. When the House was considering the rent-subsidy bill, a critical one in the President's view, Democratic Rep. Thomas (Tip) O'Neill Jr., a faithful Administration supporter and a powerful member of the House Rules Committee, decided to vote no and so informed Speaker John McCormack. "That night the President called," O'Neill said later. "He thanked me all over the place for the fine things I had said about him in a speech I had made in my home district, and for all the help I'd given him in the past. Then he got to the point. He said it would be damned embarrassing to lose this one, and didn't I know what problems he had without this thing falling flat?

'He'll Thank You':

"Well, hell, what do you say to the President of the United States? I told him I'd sleep on it. Then the next day I said to myself, I've always been a party man, and if he really needed me of course I'd go along even if the bill wasn't set up exactly the way I wanted it. Probably I took half a dozen guys with me. We won in the crunch by six votes. Now, I wouldn't have voted for it except for his telephone call. He made me feel a little guilty and cheap for letting him down, but he wasn't rough and he didn't twist my arm. He persuaded me to take a couple of steps back and put myself in his position. And the next time he sees me don't think he won't remember that vote. He damned well will. One thing I like about him: he'll ask you to do something but he'll thank you for it."

The President does not forget. Says Connecticut's Democratic Sen. Abraham Ribicoff: "The genius of Lyndon Johnson is that he not only calls you when he wants something, but he remembers to call you back and thank you for what you've done."

This is the Johnson way—tireless attention to people who count. And it works. Because of Mr. Johnson, this Congress is writing an unparalleled chapter in American social and economic change: a $1.3 billion bill providing Federal assistance to primary and secondary schools, a $1.1 billion bill to help the depressed Appalachian region, repeal of the nation's annual $4.7 billion in excise taxes; a voting-rights bill that will do more to enfranchise the Negro than any law or constitutional amendment ever passed; a medicare bill that gives 19 million elder citizens hospital and nursing care under social security; a new Cabinet post for housing and urban development; a bill to wipe out discrimination in immigration. Any one of the bills would have been a major Congressional achievement; under Mr. Johnson, all will probably pass.

One Ominous Fact:

It is a striking and ominous fact that what Lyndon Johnson has going for him on Capitol Hill—personal experience, confidence and men willing to go along with his plans—is exactly what he lacks in dealing with international affairs. Though he traveled over 125,000 miles abroad as Vice President, he developed no profound understanding of the world and its problems. His reaction to the Dominican Republic crisis was pure Johnson: his reading of the national mood told him that the American public did not want another Communist Cuba on its doorstep, so he promptly rushed in the U.S. Marines.

It is worthy of note that this President with a safecracker's touch for the sensibilities of the most junior congressman in Washington has scant feeling for the niceties of diplomacy:

The head of government of one of America's close allies telephoned the President one night to express his concern about the escalation of the war in Vietnam. The President listened briefly, told his caller to mind his own business and slammed down the phone.

When Prince Bernhard of the Netherlands visited the White House on April 13, he was only slightly amused when the President selected a dozen spectators at random and said, "Go on, have your picture taken with a real Prince."

The Spanish Foreign Minister, Fernando Maria de Castiella, paying a courtesy call on the President while in Washington, was taken aback when Mr. Johnson interrupted their social chitchat to demand why Spain continued to trade with Cuba. The President then turned to McGeorge Bundy and told him to tell the visitor what the Administration thought of such trade. The Foreign Minister left the White House sizzling.

Mr. Johnson is a constant critic of his press; no President—not even John Kennedy—has spent so much time worrying over his press notices as LBJ. He is forever privately complaining that one reporter or another has either recklessly repeated an unchecked rumor, or maliciously printed a lie. He is convinced that what he wants to do is right for the country and he believes that the press, like Congress and the people, should support him. He looks on newspapers, magazines and television as another powerful device to line up public support for the programs of his Great Society, or, as he puts it, "The press is one of the best servants I have."

Culprit:

When he looks bad in print the President's first instinct is to blame the press. In recent months, for example, he has held the press accountable for prematurely surfacing Antonio Guzman, the Administration's first choice to head a caretaker government in the Dominican Republic and for "blowing up" the meaning of his dis-invitation to India's Prime Minister Shastri.

Yet despite his battles with the press, Mr. Johnson invests more of his time in talking to reporters than any other President in history. The reporters' complaint is that for all the time they get, they learn very little about what the public most deserves to know—the possibility of immediate military mobilization, the widening of the war in Vietnam, disarmament talks with the Russians. Again, Mr. Johnson insists that government policy shall be made in private. Says columnist Joseph Alsop: "I don't believe we can have an active American Government without an open information policy. Secretiveness has gone further now under President Johnson than at any time in the past. You can't fight a major war in a stealthy manner."

For all these differences, no President has enjoyed a better press, and no President has made more news. For every printed word criticizing Mr. Johnson, there are a hundred that portray him as he likes—the man of action working to solve the problems of the nation and the world. The press support he has would be impressive for a Republican; for a Democratic President, it is unprecedented. As Mr. Johnson said at his last televised press conference, "There are very few Presidents in the history of this country that have had more support of more publishers and more magazines than the present President."

The reason is obvious. President Johnson enjoys the support of the press for the same reason that he has the support of Congress and official Washington and two out of every three Americans: he is turning out to be a strong, able, and enormously effective President.

The common criticisms of Mr. Johnson—that he is temperamental, difficult, vulgar—have little historical relevance. He is not the first President to lose his temper, drive his staff, or turn the air blue. In 1860 the Philadelphia Evening Journal looked down its nose at Abraham Lincoln and said: ". . . His coarse language, his illiterate style, and his vulgar and vituperative personalities in debate, contrast very strongly with the elegant and classical oratory of the eminent senator from New York (Seward)."

The Profound Test:

What does matter is that Mr. Johnson has used his power to accomplish major achievements. Further, in civil rights, the nation's most divisive domestic problem, he has been a leader in every sense of the word. He has retained many of the excellent men he inherited and on the whole made commendable appointments of his own. For all his knowledge of the art of politics, he is learning in his job and growing with his responsibilities. It is, however, history's ironic challenge to Mr. Johnson's consuming drive for greatness that the profound test of his Presidency will come in the world arena, where he has little experience and some handicaps of temperament.

How will he act to maintain the peace of the world? Will he deal with tomorrow's crises as directly as he dealt with the Dominican Republic? Specifically, and urgently, what will he do about Vietnam? Significantly, his 69 per cent popularity could be cut below 50 per cent by the wrong move in Vietnam, according to opinion analyst Louis Harris. How big will the Vietnamese war grow? When extreme provocation comes, as it will, how will President Johnson handle himself? Can he prevent the war in Asia from spreading? The answers to these questions will ultimately determine whether the 36th President gains what he passionately pursues: the historical encomium of Lyndon the Great.

QUESTIONS FOR DISCUSSION AND DIALOGUE

1. In outline form, describe the LBJ political style.
2. Do you find the Lyndon Johnson discussed in this article a good POLITI-CIAN? Why? Would you answer this question any differently if the word PRESIDENT was substituted for POLITICIAN? Why? Discuss.
3. Discuss the style of political behavior as described by the article in these words: "When (President Johnson) turns from his role as Chief Executive to confront his old colleagues on Capitol Hill, Mr. Johnson again becomes the inside operator, the cloakroom manipulator, the broker in power, the political middleman who calculates how much of a bill he can sell and who and how many will buy." In your opinion, is this the way politics should function? Why?
4. Although the tone of this article is generally favorable to Johnson, are there any hints about problems which will develop? Discuss.

The Johnson Years

Newsweek

Three and a half years later than when the previous article was written, a different assessment of Lyndon Johnson as President was given by this *Newsweek* article. The reasons for the change to a much more somber, modified, and much less optimistic view of Johnson's accomplishments are indicated by this article.

I do not want to be the President who built empires, or sought grandeur, or extended dominion. I want to be the President who educated young children to the wonders of their world. I want to be the President who helped to feed the hungry and to prepare them to be taxpayers instead of taxeaters. I want to be the President who helped the poor to find their own way and who protected the right of every citizen to vote in every election. I want to be the President who helped to end hatred among his fellow men and who prompted love among the people of all races and all regions and all parties. I want to be the President who ehlped to end war among the brothers of this earth.

—Lyndon B. Johnson, March 15, 1965

He had always been a prodigiously impatient man, daily driving self and staff toward fresh wonders of accomplishment for his Presidency. "I have so little time," he kept insisting—and now his time had run out. As Lyndon B. Johnson's White House days dwindled down to a precious few and his bags, belongings and 31 million pages of papers were packed for the trip back to Texas, 1600 Pennsylvania Avenue was left with a houseful of bittersweet memories of what had been —and might have been.

If Mr. Johnson was pained by his rites of passage, he gave no outward sign. Even in his final weeks, the dynamo of energy churned unchecked through what he boasted was "two days' work in the space of one"; his features betrayed nothing more than deeper lines, wavier hair, and modishly longer sideburns as the changes wrought by five years at the helm of state. But on the eve of his farewell, there was, undeniably, a difference: a certain wistful nostalgia as he trooped up to Capitol Hill to say good-by and a certain compulsion to trot some of his achievements onstage for a final curtain call, lest they be forgotten.

For Lyndon Johnson's exit had turned out not to be the triumphal march-past that once might have been envisioned. It had come, for one thing, four years earlier than expected, and it was accompanied not by wild cheers but by polite applause that barely muffled widespread sighs of relief. At the moment of its passing, the Johnson Administration's achievements were disfigured by its failures. He *had* been a President who helped educate young children, feed the hungry, lift up the poor, and protect the right to vote. But as he made ready to depart, he was also remembered as a President who had expanded rather than ended a bitter and perhaps futile war and, despite his dauntless quest for love, had sown distrust for himself and discord among his fellow men.

Questions:

He left behind him questions as massive and unfathomable as the man himself: what was responsible for his fall from grace—his own flaws or circumstances beyond his control? How would history judge him when the emotions of his contemporaries cooled and his enemies passed from the scene?

Even now, it took only the shortest of memories to recall a time when President Johnson was a towering figure of respect and apparent invincibility. After Dallas threw his countrymen into shock and Lyndon Johnson into an office he had never expected to inherit, he steered the nation through tragedy with strength and tactfulness. Soon he was working political miracles that had always been denied his more glamorous predecessor. At his coaxing, John F. Kennedy's tax-cut and civil-rights bills broke through the Congressional bottleneck. He rounded up a hostile pack of railroad owners and union men, sealed them in the Executive Office Building and cajoled them out of a nation-crippling strike. He won the most lopsided victory in the history of Presidential elections. He enlisted his Southern accent and legislative mastery in the cause of Negro justice, carrying the black man's refrain "We Shall Overcome" to a joint session of Congress and coming away with a landmark voting-rights bill.

That was just part of the bright garland of legislation he strung from the labors of the 89th Congress: medicare, aid to education, rent supplements for the poor, immigration reform, control of water pollution, the model-cities program, and the new Cabinet-level departments—Housing and Urban Development, and Transportation. "This isn't the Great Society—it's heaven," gasped Republican chieftain Everett Dirksen. Echoed a GOP colleague: "How are we going to fight creeping paradise?" For Americans long accustomed to knockdown battles between President and Congress, Lyndon Johnson was a phenomenon: the Chief Executive who seemed to be Chief Legislator as well.

Quirks:

Of course, everyone knew the 36th President had his quirks of personal style. From the very start his critics drew demeaning contrasts between his Texan earthiness and the Bostonian graces of John Kennedy, who would never have exposed the scar of a gall-bladder operation to the nation or tugged the ears of a pet beagle to make it yelp. Selections from Mr. Johnson's vivid vocabulary began sprouting from Washington's grapevine. "I've got earphones in Moscow and Manila, earphones in Rangoon and earphones in Hanoi," the President said of his peacemaking efforts in Asia, "and all I hear on them is, 'F--- you, Lyndon Johnson'."

Tokens of the Johnsonian vanity also became legendary: the LBJ brand that he affixed to wife, daughters, ranch, lake and state park (but not, curiously, his cattle, which are marked "JO"); the 250,000 photographs of himself in action produced by special White House photographer Yoichi R. Okamoto; the instant enshrinement of his Texas birthplace and boyhood home; his use of the royal "we"; the popularity polls that sprouted from his hip pocket until they ran into the ground.

'Thunderstorm':

The President could also be intimidating. Veterans of his years as Senate Majority Leader knew only too well the persuasive technique that George Smathers called "a great, overpowering thunderstorm." Lyndon Johnson would thrust his gigantic physical bulk (6 feet 4 inches, 212 pounds) just as close to his adversary as possible, violating that intimate shell of air space that ordinary mortals need for their composure while carrying on business conversations. Thus rattled, the subject would then be subjected to a wild Johnsonian monologue, sometimes of rage, sometimes of cajolery, often of both. George Wallace, for one, bent under this hurricane when he was incautious enough to seek a Presidential audience at the time of the Selma crises, and not even the most intimate members of the White House staff were immune from his browbeatings. One former aide has remarked that Mr. Johnson actually seemed to prefer shortish men—Jack Valenti, Marvin Watson, Bill Moyers, Horace Busby—as his subordinates.

Far worse for the President's public image was a growing sense that he was a devious man, to whom the truth, like his colleagues, was simply a tool to be bent for whatever task he had set himself. In fact, the credibility gap started to open almost as soon as he stepped into the White House. In late December 1963, in Texas, he told reporters he could not possibly keep his first budget under $100 billion; one week later he unveiled a budget of $97.9 billion—not only well under the $100 billion mark but below John Kennedy's last budget of $98.8 billion. The press assumed that Mr. Johnson had simply concocted the first story to magnify his achievement. On later occasions, the President seemed deliberately to mislead the nation in order to indulge his fanatical passion for secrecy over his plans and timing. Had the President given any thought to whom he might name to fill the vacancy on the Supreme Court, a reporter asked in July 1965. None at all, said Mr. Johnson. The following day, he nominated Abe Fortas.

In 1964 and 1965, however, none of these traits seriously threatened Lyndon Johnson's reputation for political wizardry. His personality, it was pointed out, had its bright side as well as its dark: boundless energy, an intuitive ability to judge a person's strengths and weaknesses with a cold, hard stare, genuine compassion for little people, sentimental devotion to the cause of education, and a fierce ambition to make his Administration the best since his hero Franklin Roosevelt's. Besides, his defenders argued, what if the President wasn't exactly lovable? He was probably the most brilliant manipulator of Washington's levers of power that the city had ever known. Things were going well, and it seemed petty to critcize.

Quagmire:

But things did not continue to go so well. In April 1965, Mr. Johnson sent 556 U.S. marines, then 30,000 more troops, storming into the revolt in the Dominican Republic, and his muddled explanations of what they were doing there (at first, protecting American lives; later, guarding against a possible Communist take-over) earned him his first hard knocks from liberals. Ten thousand miles to the west, American forces plunged deeper and deeper into the quagmire of Vietnam without moving appreciably closer to anything resembling victory. At home, Mr. Johnson's miracle fingers began to lose their touch in Congress, as war spending sapped funds from the appropriations-hungry programs of the Great Society and aborted others even before birth.

Once President Johnson began to lose the guardian angel of effectiveness, his critics swarmed in upon personal faults they had previously been willing to overlook. Vietnam brought disastrous new landslides of eroded confidence in Credibility Gap, with the doves charging that the President had deliberately oversimplified the issues, underestimated the cost and end-run the consent of public and Congress. As the criticism became more savage, Mr. Johnson turned instinctively to the counterattack with invective that occasionally made him sound like just the frenzied yahoo that his wilder assailants portrayed: at Cam Ranh Bay in South Vietnam, he exhorted the troops to "nail that coonskin to the wall"; at home, he ridiculed the war critics as "nervous Nellies." The gigantic majority of 1964 ebbed away; the national consensus that he had sought to forge split up into bitter, often battling factions; "All the way with LBJ" turned into "Hey, hey, LBJ, how many kids did you kill today?"

The End:

In the end, he himself was killed—and he knew it. "Jack Kennedy was assassinated and I am being assassinated," he told friends with unconscious unseemliness. "The only difference is that I am alive." The White House and the Texas ranch became his prison cells: whenever he ventured beyond their gates, angry demonstrations sprang up in the streets. He sat by, helpless, as first Eugene McCarthy, then his old foe Robert Kennedy sliced great chunks out of his political foundations. Then, proud and patriotic and a realistic judge of his own power even in decline, he quit.

Lyndon Johnson's rise and fall are already being treated by some historians as something of a tragic sequence. "The Tragedy of Lyndon Johnson" is, in fact, the title of a book his onetime adviser Eric Goldman will publish next month, and another former staffer (for two months after the Kennedy assassination), Arthur Schlesinger Jr., tends to view his Presidential career in the same light: "He began with wise and generous views on what had to be done inside the American national community. But his highly promising Great Society program became a casualty of his increasing obsession with the futile and ghastly war in Vietnam."

If the Johnson Presidency had a tragic fall, was Vietnam its major stumbling block? A strong case can be made for that view. However history may finally assess the wisdom of the U.S. policy in Vietnam over the past five years, it was certainly Vietnam that unlocked the furies among America's youth, intelligentsia, and ultimately its voters—and that drove Mr. Johnson from office. It was Vietnam that drained away the money so desperately needed by the fledgling domestic programs of the Great Society. Perhaps even more damaging, it was Vietnam that robbed the Great Society of the Presidential attention and care without which no newborn Federal venture can long keep its health.

Clinton Rossiter of Cornell, a longtime student of the Presidency, is among those who believe that Vietnam brought Lyndon Johnson down. "When you have a war you can't win and you can't lose, it saps your time, your energy, your prestige—and eventually it destroys you. Vietnam is not our biggest problem, but it is the one that destroyed this man." The irony for President Johnson, Schlesinger contends, is that "in the end he gave more time and attention to foreign affairs, which he did not particularly understand and in which his instincts were simplistic and rigid, than to domestic affairs, where his instincts, experience and knowledge could have done great things for the nation."

But was there, in addition to Vietnam, some tragic flaw in Lyndon Johnson himself that contributed to his collapse? A number of his countrymen thought so. Even the Vietnam agony, they sensed, might have been borne by the American public if only they had fully trusted the man who led them. Henry Graff of Columbia, who thinks Mr. Johnson was a "very good" President, believes that his efforts were "flawed by his inability to engage the affection or the sympathy of the people as a whole. Possibly he was a victim of the fact that public leadership, under the impact of television especially, is ceasing to have automatic mystique." Whatever the reason, Graff notes, "in a time when democracy has large need for magnetic champions, he was wanting in a number of the personal qualities that are required in addition to the managerial talents he had in such abundance."

In the end, public trust was something that Mr. Johnson never managed fully to win. "To understand Lyndon Johnson," says one former high official of his Administration, a generous-minded man who worked with him personally on a number of occasions, "you have to realize that he has never been completely honest with anyone about anything." Something of that harsh judgment ultimately made its way into the public consciousness.

Devious:

Too often his methods seemed devious, his forthrightness dubious, his pronouncements calculated for this or that effect. Undoubtedly these characteristics have been present to some degree in all Presidents. "There has not been a great leader in this century," Rossiter notes, "who wasn't devious at certain times when it was necessary to achieve his goals." But in Mr. Johnson, as with so many things about the man, the deviousness stood out a little more prominently.

The public suspicions thus aroused not only damaged the President's own repute; they undermined the programs that he sought to foster. The legislative achievements of the Great Society, for the most part, made their way onto the lawbooks unaccompanied by the spirit of national elan that greeted the Kennedy Administration's far more modest accomplishments. To many, Democrats as well as Republicans, LBJ's Great Society seemed to be laced with a generous dash of hokum.

Nor was there the migration of fresh talent to Washington that had marked the New Frontier. In fact, one of the minor hallmarks of the Johnson years was the outward-bound parade of superior public servants whose services and loyalties the President was unable to retain. Many of the brightest lights of the LBJ era—Bill Moyers, John W. Gardner, McGeorge Bundy, Robert McNamara—quit before President Johnson did.

The President was fully aware of his image problems, most of which he blamed upon the press, whose ways he found annoying and baffling. This was a problem that never haunted Lady Bird Johnson—or other members of his family. "Luci knows more about how to deal with the press than I do," Mr. Johnson once declared in exasperation. The comment was revealing, for Luci Johnson Nugent shares many of her father's extravagant characteristics. But whereas she behaved openly, incautiously and naturally in public, Lyndon Johnson often seemed calculating, suspicious and contrived.

Many observers have been tempted to conclude that much of Mr. Johnson's manner simply carried over from his Senate days, and that he was the victim of his own past success. For the wheeling-and-dealing politics of the Senate are very different from the politics of the Presidency, and Mr. Johnson's mastery of one made him vulnerable in the other. As the acknowledged King of the Senate, he ruled by an intimate, intuitive knowledge of each of his colleagues—their strengths, weaknesses, prejudices, and needs—that enabled him to judge just how far he could push them, which he then proceeded to do behind the scenes, with an absolute minimum of public debate.

Top and Bottom:

When he moved to the White House, he tried to carry with him the same method, and for a while it worked brilliantly. His days were filled with endless telephone calls—to business leaders, labor leaders, religious leaders, ethnic leaders, state-government leaders—and from them he fashioned his early "consensus." Mr. Johnson was an expert at dealing with powerful individuals, man to man. "In every town," he once said, "there's some guy on top of the hill in a big white house who can get things done. I want to get that man on my side." But after a while, it became clear that Lyndon Johnson had lost touch with the people at the bottom of the hill. His intuition—fantastically acute when it came to individuals—never worked very well with the public at large, and he never mastered the skills of mass communication, inspiration and education that are so vital a part of the American Presidency.

Perhaps there was an even deeper sense in which Mr. Johnson was a prisoner of the past, for it was his misfortune to apply solutions devised during the New Deal and the cold war at the very time when many people had come to wonder whether they were still applicable. "Lyndon Johnson," reflects Graff, "had the bad luck to be President when one historical epoch was drawing to a close and the next one only barely glimpsed, and he will pay the price in how he is remembered. The political ways and assumptions in which he was schooled and which he made his own proved effective but not ultimately persuasive in dealing with the nation's problems."

Thus the Great Society set up bigger Federal bureaucracies at the very moment when many social critics were calling for more decentralization. It provided money and models when many were looking for more personal signs of concern, and it seemed to embody the view that Federal action was the answer to social problems. The Vietnam war also was based on assumptions of an "international Communist conspiracy" that seemed less and less valid as time went on.

And so a shift in epochs, or Mr. Johnson's own shortcomings, or the tragedy of the Vietnam war may deprive his turbulent Presidency of history's seal of greatness. But history can hardly forget him. Hated or admired, he loomed a little larger than most Presidents, a fascinating, complex and awesome man. Of his paradoxical Presidency, one thing is certain, says White House scholar Richard Neustadt: "It will not be ignored. This is not because historians will like LBJ in the way they liked FDR or Kennedy, and thus will find his period fascinating to explore. Rather it is, I think, because historians will find his personality and operating style compelling and baffling, hence interesting—like them or not. He is most unlikely to suffer the fate of Mr. Truman, whom contemporary historians generally praise and ignore."

The Historians' Verdict

How will Lyndon B. Johnson go down in the history books? Only time will tell. For the present, here is how ten eminent Presidential scholars grade the 36th President as he leaves office. The ratings: "Great" (A), "Very Good" (B+), "Good" (B), "Fair" (C), and "Poor" (D).

	Domestic Affairs	Foreign Affairs	Over-all
Stephen K. Bailey Syracuse University	A	C	B+
James MacGregor Burns Williams College	A	B+	B+
Henry F. Graff Columbia University	B+	B	B+
Oscar Handlin Harvard University	B+	B+	B+
Louis W. Koenig New York University	B+	B	B+
Hans Morgenthau University of Chicago	B	D	C
Allan Nevins Ex-Columbia University	A	B+	A
Clinton Rossiter Cornell University	A	B	B+
Arthur Schlesinger Jr. City University of N.Y.	B+	D	*
C. Vann Woodward Yale University	B+	C	B

*Too early

Enigma:

One of the journalists who followed his Administration from its first minute in the grief-torn cabin of Air Force One, *Newsweek* Contributing Editor Charles Roberts, last week offered this synopsis of the intriguing American enigma that is Lyndon Johnson:

"He leaves office a man whose epitaph will someday defy the confines of even a Texas-size tombstone: the most militant civil-rights advocate ever to occupy the White House, reviled by Negro militants; a Southerner scorned by Southerners as a turncoat; a liberal depised by liberals despite the fact he achieved most of what they sought for 30 years; a friend of education—rejected by intellectuals; a compromiser who could not compromise a war 10,000 miles away; a consensus-seeker who in the clutch abandoned his consensus rather than his convictions; a power-hungry partisan politician who, in the end, shunned power and partisanship to achieve national unity."

Lyndon Johnson held power such as has been granted to few Presidents before him. To his credit, he never shied from using it in causes that he thought were just, even when it cost him the popularity he treasured. It is too early to attempt his political epitaph, but for the time being, this one, by Richard Neustadt, will do nicely: "He made large marks upon his time."

QUESTIONS FOR DISCUSSION AND DIALOGUE

1. (Refer back to previous article, Question 4.) Which of the Johnson characteristics mentioned in the previous article were most influential in leading to his political decline?
2. Outline the accomplishments of President Johnson mentioned in this article.
3. Reread the fifth last paragraph. What does this explain about terms such as "qualitative (instead of "quantitative") liberalism," the "New Politics," and the "New Left"?
4. Discuss the historical assessments made in this article about the Johnson years. Would you call them critical or favorable? Why?
5. Should a politician attempt to make ". . . large marks upon his time"? Discuss in the light of how Johnson attempted and definitely succeeded in doing this.

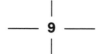

A. The Other Ev Dirksen
Charles Roberts

B. Ideologues: You Know He's Right
Newsweek

After considering presidents in the previous three articles, attention is now focussed on a congressional insider, Senator Ev Dirksen. In direct contrast is the ex-speechwriter for presidential candidate Barry Goldwater, Karl Hess. Dirksen's desire to remain unpublicized and exert behind the scenes influence is quite different from Hess' "suddenly radicalized life style." Politics includes both the Dirksen style, "broker" politicians and the Hess style, "ideological" politicians (in a looser definition of that word), although each seems to have a unique style, especially switch-hitter Hess!

A. The Other Ev Dirksen

Most newspaper readers and TV viewers see old Ev, at 73, in a kindly light —as the good chap who came to the aid of LBJ's party (to help pass three civil-rights bills and ratify the Nuclear Test-Ban Treaty); as an eloquent, if flowery, orator (the "Wizard of Ooze"); a fierce adversary in debate (many still recall his "You took us down the road to defeat" speech to Thomas E. Dewey at the 1952 Republican Convention); a considerable humorist and something of a gallant (he kisses ladies and champions the marigold as the national flower); and as an inspired reader of patriotic poetry (his "Gallant Men" album has sold some 400,000 copies). His fans chuckle when Dirksen says: "I am a man of principle and one of my first principles is flexibility"; and at another of his favorite one-liners: "The oil can is mightier than the sword."

But to many past and present government officials in Washington, Republican as well as Democrat, there is also the other Dirksen—and this one is a dark and even malevolent figure. Dirksen's critics—ex-Cabinet officers, White House staffers, members of regulatory agencies, and career bureaucrats who have dealt with him—see the glib, sonorous senator from Pekin, Ill., as neither a statesman nor a comic but as a tough, dollar-wise wheeler-dealer who works considerably harder for some constituents than for others.

"He is the most venal man in American politics today, and perhaps the most venal since Daniel Webster," swears one former top LBJ adviser who prefers to remain anonymous—like most Dirksen critics—because he still works in Washington. "He has a price for everything," says another, whose law practice would be jeopardized if his views were attributed to him.

Critics base their suspicion that Dirksen profited from his unique relationships with JFK and LBJ, politically and perhaps financially, on several counts:

His ties to the Peoria, Ill., law firm of Davis, Morgan & Witherell. The head of the firm, 72-year-old Arleigh Davis, rather reluctantly admits that Dirksen "brings us clients," but he refuses to name those clients or detail their financial agreements. So does Dirksen.

His extraordinary interest in legislation affecting certain industries—notably drugs, chemicals, gas pipelines, steel and lending institutions. Dirksen is an "advisory director" of Chicago's big First Federal Savings and Loan Association and his Illinois political agent, Harold E. Rainville, was until recently—on Dirksen's recommendation—a director of the Mercantile National Bank of Chicago. Dirksen acknowledges his directorship but denies he "represents" any industries.

His frequent contacts with members of Federal regulatory agencies. Virtually no such agency in Washington is without at least one "Dirksen man"—a member who was named or reappointed by Presidents Kennedy or Johnson at the senator's request.

His obvious personal affluence and his bitter opposition to legislation that would require public disclosure of income, or sources of income, by members of Congress. Dirksen maintains three homes—one in Illinois, one in Virginia, and one in Florida. He has spearheaded the fight against public disclosure ("This is an impertinence and an outrage") on the ground that "I don't want to become a Class B citizen."

These counts against Dirksen form only a web of circumstantial evidence. They do not prove that he has profited unduly as a lawmaker, or even that he has any conflict of interest. None of his detractors claims to have seen a canceled check with his name on it. But many have seen letters or received phone calls evidencing his interest in legislation and regulations affecting certain of his constituents—his accusers would say "clients"—and so an examination of the circumstantial evidence is in order. It may help determine which is the real Senator Dirksen—the warm, quotable, silver-tongued statesman, or the cynical opportunist serving special interests.

The Law Firm

Senator Dirksen joined the Peoria law firm now known as Davis, Morgan & Witherell in 1950, the year he was first elected to the Senate after serving sixteen years in the House.*

*Dirksen was admitted to the District of Columbia Bar in 1936, at the age of 40, when he was the ranking Republican member of the House District Committee. He had completed only three semesters of law study at the University of Minnesota before Army service in World War I, but was given what he calls a "special dispensation" to take the bar examination.

Until 1954, while serving in the Senate, he was listed in the Martindale-Hubbell Law Directory as a "member" of the firm, a title used by the firm's partners. Since then he has been listed as "of counsel," an arrangement (common among lawyer-legislators) that lends his prestige to the fifteen-man operation—and brings in law business—without requiring any onerous duties.

Clients of the firm listed in Martindale-Hubbell include many corporate giants that have operations in Illinois—International Harvester, International Paper, Archer-Daniels-Midland, and Panhandle Eastern Pipeline Co. But senior member Arleigh Davis says that the representative list of clients is by no means a complete guide to the firm's practice.

Court records in Peoria show that the firm has represented U.S. Steel. What about oil companies? "We represent some of the big oil companies occasionally—but not because of the senator," says Davis. Drug and finance companies? "We have clients in those areas," says Davis before adding: "I'm not going to talk about *all* our clients."

Dirksen is paid for his services under what Davis calls a "special arrangement . . . It's on special cases that he might have an interest in that he brings to us . . . He has friends who come to him and say they want a lawyer. He sends them to us."

The Dirksen arrangement was a secret one until 1965 when one of the partners, Harry Witherell, died. Then, in probating his estate, Witherell's executor filed a copy of a partnership agreement dated Oct. 1, 1962, which said: "The parties hereto agree that Everett M. Dirksen shall be associated with the partnership under the terms of a separate agreement negotiated on behalf of and executed in the name of the partnership by Harry E. Witherell." The agreement also provided that Dirksen should receive his remuneration from the firm "off the top" of its gross income. Davis says that the partnership agreement "hasn't materially changed" since 1962, but refuses to disclose a "supplemental agreement" referred to in the document, and insists that Dirksen's income from the firm is "very insignificant." Dirksen himself, when asked, refuses to discuss the arrangement or his income from it.

Last year, when Dirksen was running for re-election, his opponent, former Illinois Attorney General William G. Clark, charged that Dirksen's law firm connection raised "a question of ethics." Clark pointed out that the firm represented oil and steel companies while Dirksen, in Washington, was defending oil-depletion allowances and proposing steel-import quotas.

After this attack, last October, the frosted glass door bearing Dirksen's name was removed from its hinges in Peoria's First National Bank building and replaced with a wooden door bearing no names at all—not even the names of the senior members of the firm. Last week there were still no names on the door. "We ordered some brass nameplates and we're going to get them," senior partner Davis explained, "but there's been some labor trouble at the foundry or something and they haven't come."

Legislation

Senator Dirksen is a famed exponent of the "rider"—a gambit in which he attaches a legislative proposal of his own to a completely unrelated bill, authored by another member of Congress, which seems certain of passage.

The slyest Dirksen rider to date, according to his fans and foes alike, was a sleeper amendment he attached to a routine Oregon disaster-relief bill in 1965. The bill, sponsored by an Oregon congressman, had passed the House without any difficulty when it was suddenly amended by Dirksen and Louisiana's Sen. Russell Long, a Democrat, in the Senate.

When tax attorneys got a look at the Dirksen-Long amendment there, they emitted a long, low whistle. The rider, according to a report filed later by the Federal Power Commission, would have had utility customers paying "millions of dollars in excess of reasonable rates" for gas transported by pipeline companies. By permitting the big pipelines, such as the Tennessee Gas Transmission Co., to consolidate the tax losses and gains of their regulated and unregulated affiliates, it was charged, the rider would have made a tax windfall for the utilities with no savings going to consumers.

Agency Contacts

In July 1966, while the Federal Power Commission was deliberating an important gas pipeline case involving three Texas companies, a member of the commission, Carl E. Bagge, received a phone call from the office of Senator Dirksen. John R. Gomien, the senator's administrative assistant, invited Bagge to call on Dirksen the next day.

The call aroused misgivings in Bagge, a 42-year-old former Chicago lawyer who had been named to the FPC a year earlier as a "Dirksen man." Bagge, who had succeeded another "Dirksen man," the late Harold C. Woodward, on the commission, was aware that he had incurred Dirksen's wrath by signing the FPC report that scuttled the Dirksen-Long tax windfall for Tennessee Gas and other pipeline companies. He was also aware that the case then pending before the FPC involved the Gulf Pacific Pipeline Co.—like Tennessee Gas, a subsidiary of Tenneco, Inc., in Houston.

Suspecting that Dirksen wanted to discuss Gulf Pacific's bid for FPC approval of a pipeline into Los Angeles, Bagge decided to talk to FPC Chairman Lee White before accepting Dirksen's invitation. White, it turned out, shared Bagge's suspicion. So, instead of Bagge going to see Dirksen, the entire five-man Federal Power Commission went to call on Attorney General Nicholas Katzenbach.

The question put to Katzenbach was simple: should an FPC commissioner answer a senator's summons for a private meeting while an important case was pending? The Attorney General expressed the belief that ex parte contacts between members of quasi-judicial regulatory agencies and members of Congress had gone out of style when a couple of Southern Congressmen were convicted on conspiracy charges a couple of years earlier. His answer was "No."

Tenneco's Gulf Pacific bid failed before the FPC, and that phone call marked Dirksen's last effort to reach Bagge. (The Illinois senator said he was "disenchanted" with Bagge when LBJ reappointed him to the FPC two years later. "I had to choose between loyalty (to Dirksen) and integrity," said Bagge.) But this setback did not deter Dirksen from further contacts with FPC commissioners and members of other regulatory agencies.

There are "Dirksen men" on half a dozen other major regulatory boards.

At the Securities and Exchange Commission, it's Hamer H. Budge, a former congressman named by LBJ in 1964 and elevated to chairman by President Nixon this year. At the Federal Communications Commission, it's Robert E. Lee, an old friend of Dirksen's first appointed by President Eisenhower in 1953, renamed by President Johnson in 1967, and now hoping for elevation to the chairmanship by President Nixon.

At the Interstate Commerce Commission, the hard-working Illinois senator has two friends grateful for his sponsorship, Peoria-born Commissioner Dale W. Hardin and Commissioner Kenneth H. Tuggle. (President Johnson reappointed the 65-year-old Tuggle to the ICC at Dirksen's request last summer. The quid pro quo: Dirksen would not oppose LBJ's reappointment of Civil Aeronautics Board chairman John H. Crooker Jr., a Texas lawyer, for a new six-year term beginning just nineteen days before President Nixon's inauguration. Dirksen could have stalled the Crooker appointment and "saved" it for Mr. Nixon.)

At the Federal Trade Commission, Dirksen has a booster in Chairman Paul Rand Dixon, an ex-Kefauver committee counsel first appointed by JFK in 1961. When Dixon's first term on the FTC expired two years ago, some LBJ aides opposed his re-appointment, arguing he was not as "consumer-minded" as the Johnson Administration. Dirksen interceded in his behalf, and LBJ reappointed him. The Minority Leader even persuaded LBJ to find jobs for a couple of old "Dirksen men" who had outlived their usefulness at other agencies.

Former Labor Department officials have recollections of Dirksen cudgeling away for the Household Finance Corp., a Chicago-based small-loan firm, in a dispute over minimum wages last year. Clarence Lundquist, then Wage and Hour Administrator, ruled that HFC was not complying with the minimum wage law in Alabama. Dirksen disagreed and insisted that the company's pay plan met Federal standards.

"The senator called the Secretary (of Labor) half a dozen times on this one piddling case," says a former Labor Department official. "If he wasn't getting paid by Household, then Household was *really* violating the minimum wage law."

Was Dirksen or his Peoria law firm ever retained by Household? Dirksen addressed a conference of HFC executives at Ft. Lauderdale, Fla., in the spring of 1967 for an honorarium of $2,500. "Otherwise, we have never paid him or them a penny for anything," says Harold MacDonald, HFC's board chairman. "He is just a good friend who understands our problems."

Does Senator Dirksen know Nathaniel W. Barber, HFC's former "public relations" man in Washington, convicted in Massachusetts last year of trying to bribe the supervisor of the state's small loan agency? "I don't even think I know Barber," says Dirksen. "Whenever they (HFC) have come to me, they've come out of the Chicago office as constituents."

Does Barber know Senator Dirksen? "I just know him to say hello," says Barber. "The only times I ever met him were when I went into his office to see a couple of golfing friends of mine. I play golf with two guys who work in his office."

The Apparent Affluence

Perhaps the weakest link in the chain of circumstance adduced by those who accuse Senator Dirksen of venality is their argument that he appears to live beyond his $42,500-a-year salary as Senate Minority Leader. He has many sources of revenue outside his income from public service—from the Peoria law firm, from lecture fees, record-album royalties, his syndicated newspaper column, and from TV appearances. There is no way of estimating his total income, and this suits Ev Dirksen just fine.

"Just say it's between 50 cents and 5 million dollars," was his angry retort to a question about his earnings as a lawyer two years ago. "Now you're prying into my personal business."

Dirksen, who has asked Senate consideration of a law requiring Supreme Court justices to publish data on their outside income, was the most vocal opponent of the 1968 Senate resolution requiring limited financial disclosure by senators and their employees. As watered down (Dirksen himself offered five amendments), the Senate code of ethics requires public disclosure only of "contributions" and "honorariums" of over $300.

In his public report, covering the last six months of 1968, Dirksen reported lecture fees and honorariums totaling $18,158, which made him the Senate's No. 1 fee and honorarium earner. Because 1968 was an election year for Dirksen, he also reported on his campaign contributions and expenditures. To the astonishment of many seasoned politicians, for his third election in a row, he reported a campaign surplus. With contributions of $111,256 and disbursements of only $98,602, Dirksen wound up with $12,654 in unused funds, according to his report. His last time out, in 1962, he won with a $4,180 surplus, and in 1956 he had a $33,073 surplus.

Dinner a la Dodd:

Dirksen embarrassed his campaign managers last year by announcing that a $100-a-plate dinner for him in Chicago was going to be a "Dodd-style" testimonial. He said he saw "nothing whatsoever wrong" if the dinner tickets stated that the proceeds were for the personal—and not the political—use of the honored guest. "And that's what will be done here," he added.

A few days later his Chicago office manager, Harold Rainville, announced that this was all a mistake. "The senator tends to make offhand remarks that are subject to misinterpretation," Rainville said, adding that the $100 contributions would go to Dirksen's campaign fund. Dirksen, when asked about it later, said that he was just "putting on" reporters.

Given all his sources of income, Dirksen does not appear to live beyond his means. His No. 1 home, a twelve-year-old, eight-room stone and frame house near Leesburg in Loudoun County, Va., 32 miles up the Potomac River from the Capitol, had a market value of $82,000 when it was appraised six years ago. On 3.5 acres of good land sloping down to the river, with a profusion of marigolds and a swimming pool that has been added since its last appraisal, it would probably bring better than $100,000 today.

His No. 2 home, a palm-fringed winter retreat on an acre of land fronting a lily pond at De Bary, Fla., is assessed at $20,540. In the past Dirksen has commuted to it on Air Force planes provided by the White House. His No. 3 home, his voting address at 355 Buena Vista in Pekin, is a more modest dwelling —but even it is more comfortable than the house in Pekin's "Beantown," where old Ev started 73 years ago.

Style:

One thing Dirksen has never concealed is his firm conviction that a politician should live in style. He made that clear in 1965 when he flew to Chicago to testify for former Illinois Gov. William G. Stratton, accused of evading $46,676 in income taxes.

In his testimony, which helped win Stratton's acquittal, Dirksen took the position that the governor was justified in accepting "contributions that came to him from time to time." Dirksen then told the jury he had "clocked" his own expenses over a period of six months and found that they "ran at the rate of a hundred dollars a day"—a figure that required some "sustaining funds" beyond his salary.

"And from where are such funds obtained?" he was asked.

"Well," replied Dirksen, "there are helpful contributions from those who recognize the difficulty that public service interposes for you, and you undertake to use such funds, if you can, for that purpose."

B. Ideologues: You Know He's Right

Of the many things that distinguish a Black Panther rally from most other kinds of get-togethers, a major one is the distinct paucity of white folk in attendance. It was therefore a curiosity when a bearded, beefily handsome honkie strolled confidently to stage center at a recent Panther celebration in Washington and proceeded to perform as master of ceremonies for the whole show. Nor did the surprise stop there. For behind the honkie's ringing radical rhetoric is no one less than the right-wing ideologue who coined the phrase, "a choice and not an echo," the same who first contended that extremism in defense of liberty is no vice—yes indeed, behind those chin whiskers hides no other than Karl Hess, the nonpareil speechwriter and phrasemaker of Republican Sen. Barry Goldwater's 1964 Presidential campaign.

Hess's emergence at 46 as a Panther enthusiast is only one manifestation of a suddenly radicalized life style. Where once the right-wing paragrapher dwelt in high-rise apartments and shouldered high-priced suits, the New Leftish metaphysician creates metal sculptures with a blowtorch and lives in ascetic tatters aboard his girl friend's houseboat on the Anacostia River in Washington. "I splice lines, paint the deck and plot against the state," Hess says. "It was so good to throw all that other crap out. The books were hard to give up, but you suddenly realize the best things you can do with books is to have other people read them."

Hess's practical efforts as a revolutionary are in fact a bit marginal. When not playing Bert Parks at the Panthers' public outings, Hess chairs an occasional seminar at a New Left think tank in Washington, ghosts an occasional book and co-edits a bimonthly paper called *Libertarian Forum*. Mostly he lies on deck and reflects on what he perceives as the philosophical similarities between his New Leftism and his Old Goldwaterism. "The Black Panthers are saying things now that Republicans used to say," he argues. "They keep talking about returning power to the people. That slogan of Goldwater's, 'All power to the people,' is really SDS. It's tragic, very tragic, that Goldwater has now taken his stand on the side of established authority."

Speed Reader:

Hess's turn to the New Left is only the latest zag in a remarkably ziggy career. A Washington high school dropout at 15 ("I had read all the books"), he worked for several newspapers in and around Washington, getting fired from the *Daily News* in 1945 when he phoned in to his city desk that he didn't think FDR's death was "worth getting up for." In 1963 he joined Barry Goldwater's staff, contributing most of the ringing phrases that led to the debacle of 1964. Hess left Goldwater in 1967, but returned for the successful 1968 Senatorial campaign even though his blood was already ringing with the call of the left.

"I discussed with Goldwater during the campaign the fact that I felt the New Left was absolutely the place to be," Hess says. "He made a speech at one point saying that he had a lot of sympathy with the anarchist wing of the SDS." Not everyone is amused by these intellectual contortions; a Chicago activist calls Hess "a clown," and Goldwater won't talk about him at all. Hess thinks he understands his former boss's reluctance. "I wouldn't be surprised," he says thoughtfully, "if Barry thinks I'm crazy."

QUESTIONS FOR DISCUSSION AND DIALOGUE

1. Is it possible for an elected politician to remove himself from the kind of ethical suspicion raised by the Dirksen article? Discuss.
2. Outline the pro and con side of this debate proposition: "Resolved, public disclosure of all sources of income by U.S. Congressmen would make them class B citizens and discourage some of the best qualified persons in the U.S. from entering politics."
3. Discuss any two private-public relationships which involve Ev Dirksen in this article in the following context: In view of the U.S. political-economic structure, is this kind of relationship inevitable and relatively harmless?
4. The Dirksen and Hess styles of politics point up two extremes. Discuss the difference between practical politics as the "art of the possible" and ideological politics stressing rigid ideology and correctness.

—— **10** ——

The Man the A.M.A. Cut Down

John H. Knowles

A *Life* magazine article written by a potential politician who was "cut," John H. Knowles, leads the reader to some questions about the influence of special interest groups—the American Medical Association in this case—when they might be contrary to the interests of the general population.

When I shook hands with Bob Finch on January 15th and accepted his invitation to become Assistant Secretary for Health and Scientific Affairs in the Department of Health, Education and Welfare, there was no way for either of us to know what lay ahead, or how difficult the next five and a half irony-laden months would be. Within 24 hours we had a clue. I was told to "hold everything." A negative vote had been registered at the White House, reportedly by Dr. Edward A. Annis—past president of the American Medical Association and head of the national campaign of Physicians for Nixon and Agnew.

I was happy enough to wait. I was convinced that the right job had been offered to the right man at the right time.

The A.M.A. Board of Trustees, led by Dr. Annis, began to work on me through their Washington-based political arm, the American Medical Political Action Committee. The first A.M.P.A.C. balloons were easily shot down. It was put out that I was not a physician who understood patient care; that I was a captive of hospital interests; and that I was not broadly enough based to assume this high position effectively. But this was only the beginning. The struggle between Bob Finch and the A.M.A. would assume heroic proportions. While it went on, I ran the entire gamut of human emotion from indignation to anger to despair to elation. Necessarily I had to keep out of the fight—and I learned that being in limbo in an activist, achieving society is the worst form of Chinese torture.

I had from time to time been caustically critical of the A.M.A. Such passages were now carefully weeded out of my writings and congressional testimony and circulated by A.M.P.A.C. to their close friends in Congress. The A.M.A. is in fact the most conservative body in American medicine. Operating from a platform of negative vigilance they have steadily resisted many changes in American medicine. However, unlike some of my despairing colleagues who have given up hoping for constructive changes in the A.M.A., I have been a member of the association for many years and have served as a member of their long-range planning committee.

Perhaps the A.M.A. Board of Trustees and A.M.P.A.C. opposed me because of my deeply felt belief in the need for change in American medicine. I had indeed written and testified before Congress on the need for health insurance for all Americans, with at least minimal standards established for health insurance policies that would protect the consumer more effectively. I had made such heretical and far-out statements as "good health is the birthright of every American citizen." And I had also said quite emphatically that, with the rapidly mounting demand for medical services and the increasingly severe shortage of physicians, cost would rise prohibitively. Unless the medical profession exercised responsibility to the public interest, I had said, they were merely inviting more and more governmental controls—to which I was quite opposed. Many times I had preached that freedom from central control could only be guaranteed by increased public responsibility by the private sector of American medicine—that is, doctors, insurance companies, voluntary hospitals and medical schools. I had also said that while Medicare would be forever a monument to the failure of the private sector to solve an obvious problem in the public interest, Medicare, which takes care of older people, was in fact a good program while Medicaid, which is designed for the lowest income groups, left a great deal to be desired. I had long been an advocate of the expansion of medical schools and teaching hospitals to expand the output of trained physicians. I had urged regional planning to help avoid duplication of expensive health facilities. I had been dismayed by the overlapping of many health-related programs in the inner city. I had constantly pleaded for the development of preventive medicine and health education, and for the extension of services from the urban teaching hospitals to the inner city, where many were left without much-needed medical services.

The A.M.A. has steadfastly fought prepaid salaried group practices, although in many instances these have worked effectively in the public interest. It has tended to be fearful of institutional controls in hospitals—particularly teaching hospitals—while criticizing and hindering many long-range interests of medical schools and public health workers. The three major enemies to A.M.A. scripture are the teaching hospitals, the medical schools and the federal government. Perhaps the fact that I am a professor of medicine at the Harvard Medical School, the general director of Massachusetts General, a large urban teaching hospital, and was being considered for the number one health post in the U.S. made me look like the devil himself to the A.M.A. Board of Trustees. They knew that I knew the situation well, and that I knew what had to be done and was willing to speak out in order to do it.

And so, despite the fact that only a few months earlier I had worked hard for the election of President Nixon in a traditionally Democratic state, I was now depicted by the A.M.A. Board of Trustees and A.M.P.A.C. as a flaming liberal constantly pleading for so-called "socialized medicine." Nothing of course could be further from the truth. Nonetheless, in the political arena it is the perception of a man or an issue rather than the actual fact which frequently carries the day.

Would Knowles be voted in or out? Letters received by Secretary Finch, President Nixon and myself were about 20 to 1 in favor of the nomination. Virtually every major national organization in the field of health except the A.M.A. came out publicly for my nomination—for example, the Association of

American Medical Colleges, the American Hospital Association and the American Nurses Association.

When Senator Dirksen jumped in and said that I was not going to be appointed, I felt that I had been paid a left-handed compliment. I appeared to be in a fair way of becoming another scalp in Dirksen's campaign against moderates or liberals, which had already achieved the blocking of Dr. Franklin Long for the National Science Foundation, the deposing of Clifford Alexander of the Equal Employment Opportunities Commission and William Driver as head of the Veterans Administration.

Interestingly, all during this time, the good senator was also being subjected to pro-appointment pressure from concerned doctor friends and from several large contributors to the Republican party. His typical response to most of the letters written to him states that the wishes of "335,000 doctors" would not be entirely ignored. Perhaps Senator Dirksen didn't know that only 217,000 out of the 335,000 doctors in this country are actually members of the A.M.A., that no poll had been taken of them and that (as long as the situation had degenerated into a popularity contest) many A.M.A. members were very much in favor of my nomination.

The final crunch began the week of Monday, June 9. A count of the Senate showed 80 to 90 votes for the nomination and only 10 to 20 opposed. Bob Finch officially placed my name in nomination at the White House. The following week, on Thursday, June 19, President Nixon faced the nation on TV and said that it was Secretary Finch's responsibility to select his Assistant Secretaries and that he would support Finch's recommendation. I believed that man—so did my six children. I honestly thought this was the end of it.

Bob Finch returned from his vacation the following Monday and called me that day to say that the President would announce my nomination on Wednesday. I was to come to Washington on Thursday. On Tuesday, Finch saw Senator Dirksen, and I was called that night to say that apparently the last hurdle had been cleared, but that because of the impending tax surcharge vote the announcement would be delayed until Friday. I was now told to arrive in Washington Friday noon. On Wednesday evening I took my family to see *Hamlet*, making a note in the diary which I had kept since January: "Is this prophetic?" As I came out of the theater, I was besieged by newsmen asking me whether I had heard that Republican Representative Bob Wilson of California had said, "It's a whole new ball game," and that the appointment was once more in doubt.

"Well, here we go again," I said to my wife. "Unpack the bags!" For the umpty-umpth time I was in suspended animation. At about 7 o'clock Thursday evening the phone rang. It was Bob Finch telling me that the President would not make the appointment. I said I was sorry for all of us, and then I got a bit emotional with him. I said I thought *he* deserved better than this. At the end, Bob asked me what I thought of Roger Egeberg and if I wished to help recruit him for the job. I told him that I had the highest regard for Dr. Egeberg, whom I considered a good friend and a fellow worker for the improvement of the American health system. By 11 o'clock that night Egeberg called me from California and I urged him to accept the position or the situation would be an irreversible shambles. I also told him that Bob Finch was a good, thoughtful, reasonable man and that I had tremendous confidence in what he stands for. I still do.

I firmly believe that much good will come from this experience. First of all, the public is much more aware now of the importance of the post of Assistant Secretary for Health and Scientific Affairs. It should be clear to everyone—even to A.M.P.A.C. and the A.M.A.—that the post should be held by a fully qualified expert and that it should not become the object of political hassling. If a man accepts the post, he must of course agree implicitly to follow the prevailing ideology of the Administration in power.

Secondly, I think it should be clear to many congressmen—Dirksen, Wilson and John Tower of Texas, among others—that despite what they think, the A.M.A. should not have the power to name the Assistant Secretary. The man in this position should first and foremost serve the public interest. After that, he should represent the professional interests of *all* those who serve the American health system—not just the narrow interests of a particular segment of the professionals in the system.

It should also be made clear to our national legislators that by 1970 there will be nearly three million people working in the national health system and that the physician no longer stands alone in his care of the patient. The nurse, the technician, the public health worker, the maintenance worker, the medical administrator—representing almost 90% of the total—stand shoulder to shoulder with the physician in caring for the sick, preventing disease and rehabilitating those who need it. To let one small segment of such a large group control the Secretaryship is obviously inequitable. The A.M.A. trustees have once again strained their credibility as protectors of the public interest and, as a result, I think historians will look upon this whole episode as a watershed issue in the recent history of American medicine.

Bob Finch and Roger Egeberg will form a fine team. Currently, Dr. Egeberg and I have some similar values and ideals and have asked for certain changes in the American health system while constructively criticizing the A.M.A. This is the ultimate irony, which even the trustees of the A.M.A. must appreciate.

QUESTIONS FOR DISCUSSION AND DIALOGUE

1. What qualifications and lack of qualifications did Knowles possess as an almost "insider" in the Nixon administration?
2. Reread the last two paragraphs. Since Knowles seems to think Egeberg has "some similar values and ideals," and both "have asked for certain changes in the American Health system while constructively criticizing the A.M.A.," didn't this political episode have a "happy ending?" Discuss.
3. What does this article tell you about "public opinion" and "pressure groups?"

——— **CHAPTER FOUR** ———

The Nonpolitical Influentials

Those with a special kind of influence on the relationships of the Americans, their politicians, and parties are studied in Chapter Four. This authority is far from being completely impartial and completely uninfluenced by the other groups; but though imperfect, it is generally guided by different specific purposes. The nonpolitical influentials provide one more in a complex interrelationship of checks and balances among competing parties, governmental branches, various economic and other interest groups, and individual citizens with varied levels of motivation. To this is now added the courts and their judges, police, scholars in their "ivory towers" (as well as some scholars who want to escape!), the press and such nonpartisan organizations as the League of Women Voters. Each of these groups, in its own way, is essential to the functioning of the American political system.

Chapter Four begins with an assessment by a University of Michigan law professor of the Chief Justice who presided over the United States Supreme Court for fifteen years. Next the problem of the Court vs. the will of the majority is explored by a brief excerpt from a Herbert McCloskey article.

The new Chief Justice of the U.S. Supreme Court is studied by a *Time* article. The emphasis is then placed on the U.S. Supreme Court "vs." Law and Order debate which ex-Attorney General Nicholas de B. Katzenbach states is "nonsense" if its implication is that by "curbing the Court" crime will be curbed.

The police as nonpolitical influentials are considered next, first in articles by Richard Dougherty and Joseph D. Lohman which take different approaches to the problems of crime, how to stop it, and society's obligations. Yale Kamisar, the University of Michigan law school professor, who evaluated the work of ex-Chief Justice Earl Warren in an earlier article, considers the cost of effective crime fighting. A *Life* article contrasts the two very different approaches to policemanship of two very different policemen. A short *Los Angeles Times* article shares key statistical findings of a recent FBI crime report which offers little solace to any segment of the population.

The scholars—in this case the teachers in higher education—are examined next as they view the elements of politics from a different perspective. Robert MacIver's insights into the most basic questions of politics and society are studied in an essay book review by Seyom Brown. A review of the Hiyakawa, Wald, Friedenberg, Toole, and Keniston articles from Chapter Two would be helpful here.

The role of the press as a nonpolitical influential is studied by a book review of Joe McGinniss' *The Selling of the President 1968.* McGinniss demonstrates the difficulty almost all of the nonpolitical influentials experience in separating opinion from fact. Criticism, of course, is one of the most important functions of the press. Chris Welles' writing in *Esquire* discusses two of the most important newsweeklies—*Time* and *Newsweek,* both of which exercise their nonpolitical influential functions with certain lapses from impartial objectivity, but they also attempt to report the "facts" of the news as well. This debate about the objectivity of the press is studied next by a *Newsweek* article which reviews the complaints of Vice President Spiro Agnew against the "television press," many of whom, in Agnew's view, are guilty of "instant analysis and querulous criticism." The concerned student would do well to weigh the opinions of many more than one source in trying to interpret the complexities of politics!

One group that attempts to play a completely nonpartisan role as a citizenship service is the League of Women Voters. This chapter concludes with examples of the League's efforts to educate concerned Americans in an impartial and objective fashion. The thoughtful student of American politics will find groups like the League of Women Voters to shed light on his political views, and sources of information such as the newsweeklies, newspapers, and books to combine light and heat. Both the light and heat are essential for those who would become educated and concerned citizens.

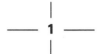

A. Assessment of Chief Justice Warren

Yale Kamisar

B. Implanting the Democratic Idea

Herbert McClosky

Kamisar studies ex-Chief Justice Warren as a man and a Chief Justice in the context of the three most significant areas of decisions of the "Warren Court": Reapportionment, desegregation and criminal procedure. The excerpts from the McClosky article elaborate one of the most difficult problems of a democracy: How to practice government by "consent of the governed" while restraining "the governed" from violating the basic principles of their government in their drive toward "immediate results and expediency".

A. Assessment of Chief Justice Warren

Many countries have provisions in their constitutions similar to our own. In only a few countries do these provisions find effect in the actual operation of the law. The failure of these constitutions is not in the concepts of their draftsmen but rather in the absence of an independent judiciary to uphold these rights or a professionally independent bar to assert and defend them.—Chief Justice Warren, Sept. 28, 1968.

The work of the Warren Court—and the inclination of Warren the Chief Justice—was aptly summed up several years ago by one of our great state judges, Walter Schaefer of the Illinois Supreme Court.

"What is happening," observed Judge Schaefer, is that the court is taking our ideals "down from the walls" where we have kept them inscribed "to be pointed at with pride on ceremonial occasions," and "putting flesh and blood" on them. "Coming face-to-face with our ideals and looking them in the teeth," he added, "is not always a comfortable process, nor is it always an easy one."

Three Principal Types

Judge Schaefer had three principal areas in mind: the cases compelling desegregation and wiping out the legal basis for discrimination in many other areas than public education; the cases requiring legislative reapportionment and thereby revitalizing local government—at a time when malapportionment had reached such disgraceful proportions that the integrity of representative government was endangered—and the cases "revolutionizing" criminal procedure or, I think more accurately, narrowing the gulf between the theory and reality of criminal procedure and removing much of the hypocrisy which so long had characterized our criminal process.

A year ago, shortly after the announcement that he would retire, Chief Justice Warren himself similarly assessed the work of the court during the past 15 years. He viewed *Baker v. Carr,* the 1962 reapportionment case, as the most significant decision during his tenure; *Brown v. Board of Education,* the 1954 school desegregation case, as the second most important; and ranked third the 1963 *Gideon* case, which assured indigent defendants the right to the assistance of counsel in criminal proceedings.

Opposition Created

In his very first term, of course, Chief Justice Warren wrote the unanimous opinion in the school desegregation case, triggering a violent and persistent attack on the court by the political leaders of a major section of the nation—and creating a large, vocal minority eager to discredit the court in every conceivable way.

Although he was not the author of *Baker v. Carr,* two years later he did write the far-reaching and bitterly criticized "one man, one vote" opinion in *Reynolds v. Sims,* rendering unconstitutional the then-composition of most state legislatures. Warren pointed out, in the exquisitely simple way that infuriates his critics but delights his admirers: "Legislators represent people, not trees or acres. Legislators are elected by voters, not farms or cities or economic interests. ... The equal protection clause requires that a state make an honest and good faith effort to construct districts in both houses of its legislature, as nearly of equal population as is practicable."

Although he was not the author of *Gideon* he did write the opinion for the court in a criminal procedure case of much more practical importance—the confession case of *Miranda v. Arizona*—which finally applied the privilege against self-incrimination and the right to counsel to the proceedings in the back rooms of the police stations as well as to those in the daylight of the courtroom.

That *Gideon* was fairly well received but *Miranda* widely and harshly criticized is due in no small measure, I think, to the fact that many people who are greatly troubled by any violation of the symbol of a public, ceremonial trial are completely unmoved by nonceremonial, invisible injustices.

Brown v. Board of Education, Miranda and *Reynolds* should suffice to support the recent observation of Assistant Solicitor General Francis X. Beytagh, one of Warren's former law clerks, that the chief justice "has chosen to take many of the most controversial opinions himself—obviously because he felt it was his obligation to do so. He has never shirked from the role of lightning rod for the court, which its opponents have forced him to play."

A consistent theme runs through most of the major decisions of the Warren Court: equal treatment by the law—for the white man and the black man; for the city voter, the suburbanite and the farmer; for the rich defendant and the defendant too poor to hire a lawyer or pay for the costs of a transcript; for the sophisticated defendant and the defendant too weak or ignorant to know his rights or to assert them without being told what his rights are.

As Dean A. Kenneth Pye of the Duke Law School has pointed out:

"The court's concern with criminal procedure can be understood only in the context of the struggle for civil rights ... It is hard to conceive of a court that would accept the challenge of guaranteeing the rights of Negroes and other disadvantaged groups to equality before the law and at the same time do nothing to ameliorate the invidious discrimination between rich and poor which existed in the criminal process. It would have been equally anomalous for such a court to ignore the clear evidence that members of disadvantaged groups generally bore the brunt of most unlawful police activity.

"If the court's espousal of equality before the law was to be credible, it required not only that the poor Negro be permitted to vote and to attend a school with whites, but also that he and other disadvantaged individuals be able to exercise, as well as possess, the same rights as the affluent white when suspected of crime. It required that the values expressed in the Bill of Rights have meaning to the vast majority of our citizens whose contact with the criminal process is limited to local police and local judges, and for whom protections in a federal criminal trial are only slightly more relevant than the criminal procedure of Afghanistan."

Another theme runs through the decisions of the Warren Court: they effectuate the rights of politically impotent minorities whose rights are frequently endangered by popular majorities and whose rights had been badly neglected by other agencies of government. Thus, as Jesse Choper, another former law clerk to Chief Justice Warren, and now a distinguished professor of constitutional law at the University of California, Berkeley, has written:

"The task of guarding these constitutionally prescribed liberties sensibly falls upon a body that is not politically responsible, that is not beholden to the grace of excited majoritarianism—the U.S. Supreme Court. Herein lies the great justification for the power of judicial review, the wisdom of *Marbury v. Madison* ... The Warren Court has admirably fulfilled this critical role. It has courageously spoken in behalf of individual rights and these decisions have produced the bulk of the attack against it."

That putting "flesh and blood" on our ideals not infrequently evokes much anger and bitterness should come as no surprise. Empirical studies of popular attitudes consistently reveal deep-rooted popular opposition to many provisions of the Bill of Rights, and ingrained hostility toward dissenters and advocates of change. Too many Americans fail to realize that the Constitution itself is antimajoritarian; that it and the enduring values it embodies are designed to withstand the inevitable strong pressure for immediate results and expediency.

Too many Americans are far more willing to accept constitutional principles "in principle" than to do what the Warren Court has done—carry them to the point where they really "bite." Too many Americans approach the Bill of Rights and the Fourteenth Amendment as they do the New Testament: in Samuel Butler's words they "would be equally horrified to hear it doubted or to see it practiced."

If the hostility generated by a court bent on giving substance and reality to the ideals we profess should come as no surprise, neither should the fact that such a court was presided over by Earl Warren.

His Personal Qualities

In an age of public cynicism and political sophistry, he was a man of simplicity, humanity and courage. He had an instinct for the rightness of things and an instinct for the jugular—qualities which many fine legal craftsmen lack and which, not infrequently, set the great apart from the good. The early years of his tenure coincided with the high tide of McCarthyism—a period of suspicion, fear, incipient isolationism and begrudging acceptance of constitutional freedoms, but his overriding commitment as a judge was to fairness, as evidenced by his frequent questioning of counsel who sought to rely on legalistic reasoning without regard to the equities—"but is it fair to do it that way?"

Whether Earl Warren was a great chief justice is hopelessly intertwined with one's concept of the role of the court in our society—with the extent to which one believes the court sits to do good when no other agency of government will do it and good is desperately needed—with whether one believes the office of chief justice calls primarily for statesmanship, a sense of history, an understanding of people or creative thinking or analytical brilliance.

I happen to think that Earl Warren will rank with Chief Justice John Marshall—now universally regarded as our preeminent chief justice, but in his own time the target of vicious attack.

Other Grim Attacks

In the case of Chief Justice Marshall, as elsewhere, the controversy and bitterness he generated has been obscured by a kind of historical amnesia. It may be instructive to recall that the demand for Marshall's impeachment came not from a handful of extremists (as has Warren's), but was a plank in the political program of the Jeffersonian Democrats, who held the presidency and controlled both houses of Congress.

As former Solicitor General Archibald Cox has recently reminded us, "the House of Representatives voted to impeach Marshall's colleague, Samuel Chase, and the Senate acquitted him only because a few senators ignored party discipline in order to preserve the independence of the judiciary. Had the vote been the reverse, Marshall's impeachment would surely have followed."

Only history will really know, of course, whether Warren and his court struck the balance right. In the meantime, I venture to say that the humane, moralistic, paternal, old-fashioned patriotic figure who steps down from the high court this month is our greatest living American. Certainly he is the most widely respected American outside this country. And at home or abroad he has long symbolized the hope and promise of America that our society would raise up the underprivileged and downtrodden without spilling blood in the streets.

B. Implanting the Democratic Idea

... It is pertinent to examine some findings about the status of democratic belief and the factors which influence our beliefs. We have been successful in getting people to express in general phrases, in large abstract phrases, their commitment to democracy. Ideas related to faith in freedom and other such broad values are well implanted. But we are far less successful in teaching people to support the specific forms of these freedoms.

Eighty-nine per cent of Americans readily accept this statement: "I believe in free speech for all, no matter what their views may be." Eighty-six per cent agree with the statement that "unless there is freedom for many points of view to be presented, there is little chance that the truth can ever be known."

Ninety-four per cent agree with the statement "no matter what a person's political belief, he is entitled to the same legal rights and protections as any one else."

On the other hand, only 48 per cent of the people say that people ought not to be allowed to vote if they can't do so intelligently. Fifty per cent say that a book that contains wrong political ideas cannot be a good book and does not deserve to be published. Over a third say that they do not think that people should be set free if they are convicted by illegal evidence. Over a third, 36 per cent, think that when the country is in danger we should force people to testify against themselves; 28 per cent believe that the majority has the right to abolish the minority if it wants to. Twenty-six per cent believe that at times it would be better for people to take the law into their own hands rather than wait for the machinery of government to act. Forty-seven per cent believe that most people don't have enough sense to pick their own leaders wisely. Forty-six per cent think that "when it comes to the things that count most, all races are certainly not equal." Fifty per cent believe that "certain races in the world just won't mix with Americans. ..."

QUESTIONS FOR DISCUSSION AND DIALOGUE

1. Briefly outline the significance of these three Supreme Court decisions:
   Brown vs. Board of Education
   Reynolds vs. Sims
   Miranda vs. Arizona
2. What is the relationship between the following quotation from the Kamisar article and the excerpt from the McClosky article?

"Too many Americans are far more willing to accept constitutional principles 'in principle' than to do what the Warren Court has done—carry them to the point where they really 'bite'. Too many Americans approach the Bill of Rights and the Fourteenth Amendment as they do the New Testament. In Samuel Butler's words, they would be equally horrified to hear it doubted or to see it practiced."

3. One of the United States' most distinguished jurists, Learned Hand, once observed that "Liberty lies in the hearts of men and women". He also said when liberty died in their hearts, constitution, law, or court could not save it. Recent studies have indicated a very sizable majority of Americans are

against major U.S. Supreme Court decisions in the areas of criminal procedure and public school prayer. How do you interpret this kind of public opinion in the light of Hand's observation?

4. Do you think ex Chief Justice Warren would be inclined to agree with this observation by Theodore Roosevelt?

"The majority in a democracy has no more right to tyrannize over a minority than, under a different system the latter would have to oppress the former . . . The saying that the voice of the people is the voice of God may be quite as untrue and do quite as much mischief as the old theory of the divine right of kings."

Do you agree with this observation? Why? Does the statement have any practical application to "the U.S. Supreme Court vs. Public Opinion" issue with reference to criminal procedure and public school prayer? Discuss.

5. Does anything Kamisar says about Warren lead you to believe he would have been a successful politician instead of a nonpolitical influential? Discuss. Do you tend to agree or disagree with Kamisar's statement that Warren "is our greatest living American"? Why?

—— 2 ——

A Professional for the High Court

TIME

New Chief Justice Warren Burger is the subject of this *Time* article. In contrast with the last article, this one must guess rather than assess, but informed guesses can be made based on Burger's past decisions and statements, which from 1956 on were related to his experience on the U.S. Court of Appeals for the District of Columbia Circuit. Time makes its own guesses about Burger as Chief Justice and offers the reader many others from highly credentialed students of the Court. Burger's position offers the potential for exercising the most powerful nonpolitical influence in the nation! The concerned student of the U.S. Supreme Court will also find this article valuable for its summary of recent Court history and review of certain key factors in how the Court functions.

In protocol, the Chief Justice of the United States stands behind the President, the Vice President and the Speaker of the House. But in his impact on the national life, he has the potential of surpassing even the Chief Executive. His tenure is measured in decades rather than years. His authority can influence the most important acts of the executive and legislative branches, as well as the fate of the individual citizen. Yet when President Nixon walked into the East Room of the White House last week to announce what he called the most important appointment of his Administration, reporters glanced at the very distinguished-looking man beside him and whispered to each other: "Who is he?"

Their confusion was understandable. Warren Earl Burger, Nixon's choice to replace Chief Justice Earl Warren, is in many ways a judge's judge—and an almost total unknown outside the legal community. In 13 years on the U.S. Court of Appeals for the District of Columbia Circuit, he has been intelligent but not brilliant, thorough but not imaginative, moderate but not innovative.

Strikingly similar to the President in temperament and background, Burger agrees firmly with Nixon that the Supreme Court has gone too far in areas such as protecting the rights of criminal defendants. Above all, he is the kind of man that Nixon feels the court needs in the wake of the Fortas scandal. Generally, centrist in politics and cautious in law, Burger, a Republican, is neither dogmatic on the bench nor strongly oriented ideologically. He is in every way a professional jurist and a man of unquestioned probity, with the Midwestern virtues that Nixon so much admires. If, as expected, Nixon appoints a man of similar convictions to replace Abe Fortas, the court will have a non-activist or moderate majority for the first time since the mid-1950s, giving Burger and his colleagues an opportunity to amend some of the court's most controversial decisions if they so choose.

The court that had seemed safely in the hands of activists—or judicial liberals —now seems destined for a somewhat less ambitious role that may last far longer than the Nixon administration. Though there is unlikely to be a sudden shift in direction, the differences could in time be profound. "We are under a Constitution," Charles Evans Hughes remarked before he himself became Chief Justice, "but the Constitution is what the judges say it is."

No. 1, No. 2, No. 3

Unlike the ill-fated Fortas, who immediately ran into trouble when President Johnson nominated him for the spot last year, Burger should have no difficulty winning Senate confirmation. He is not subject to the charge of cronyism, and Nixon is at the beginning rather than the end of his presidency. While Burger has known Nixon for 21 years, he has seen the President only three times in the past 13 years—the third time only three minutes before they walked into the East Room last week. While he is generally of the conservative school, he is moderate enough, particularly on racial issues, not to offend most liberals too greatly. Finally, as Nixon pointedly noted—his mind obviously on the financial dealings that forced Fortas to resign a fortnight ago—Burger has shown "unquestioned integrity throughout his private and public life."

Everett Dirksen, the Senate minority leader, ticked off some of the ingredients of prompt confirmation: "No. 1, he looks like a Chief Justice. No. 2, he acts like a Chief Justice. No. 3, he talks like a Chief Justice." Other Senate conservatives, particularly Southerners who lost no opportunity to attack the Warren Court, were extremely pleased and gratified at the prospect of a Burger Court. "I think it affords us the guarantee," said North Carolina's Sam Ervin, "that we will have a return to constitutional government in the United States as far as the Supreme Court is concerned."

Mixed Reception

Most Senate liberals offered either mild praise or silence for the man who a generation ago called himself a Harold Stassen progressive. Disagreement with the judge's views, acknowledged Edward Kennedy, would not be reason enough to withhold confirmation. Barring the unexpected, Warren Burger will be the 15th Chief Justice when the new term begins on the first Monday of October.

Away from the Capitol, reaction to Burger's appointment was less than unanimous. The University of Chicago's Philip Kurland, a conservative and a critic of the Warren Court who might have been expected to approve, was acerbic. "What you have here," he said, "is the opposite of the knee-jerk liberal—the knee-jerk conservative. In 13 years, he's been a hard-liner in criminal cases. That's the story of his life." On the bench itself, one liberal federal judge was extremely bitter. "He is basically a man who doesn't stand for anything except in the law-and-order area," he asserted. "It's just a shock to me that a person like him can gain the confidence of the President of the United States."

Not everyone was so intemperate. Said Princeton Historian Arthur Link: "Burger is neither a rightist nor a leftist, an authoritarian nor a libertarian. He's a middle-of-the-roader." In the same vein, the University of Pennsylvania's Anthony Amsterdam, a noted civil libertarian who has fought many cases for the N.A.A.C.P. and the American Civil Liberties Union, thought that Burger was "the best appointment that could have been expected from the Nixon Administration. He is a fine judge and a first-rate legal craftsman. He is a law-and-order man, but he is an enlightened law-and-order man."

Many experts found reason for enthusiasm. "He's got all the qualifications," said J. Edward Lumbard, a judge on the U.S. Court of Appeals, 2nd Circuit: "Moral courage, unquestioned integrity and a first-rate lawyer's knowledge and experience of the trial courts and the administration of criminal justice." Added F. William Andres, one of Boston's best-known lawyers: "The President went to the proper source for this appointment—to the judiciary itself and to a man who has been just a judge. This is terribly important to the country right now."

In large measure, Burger owed his nomination as much to Abe Fortas as to Richard Nixon, and the President said as much in an extraordinary 45-minute session with newsmen the day after the appointment. Speaking from notes he had written on his celebrated yellow legal pad, the President told not only why he had chosen Burger but why he had not chosen several others who had been prominently mentioned for the job. Other Presidents, including L.B.J., have held background sessions dealing with personalities or events. But never before has a President admitted the public so far into his thinking about an appointment. To some, it appeared to be a typical example of Nixonian psychology, a somewhat compulsive need to justify and explain himself. But the President's motives seemed straightforward enough. He wanted to use facts to stop press speculation that might prove embarrassing to his friends, and he wanted to contrast the candor of his Administration with the deviousness of his predecessor's. He succeeded in both goals, and he is expected now to repeat the briefing approach when fuller than usual background is again needed.

In Burger's favor, the President said, was his position on crime and the Constitution, his experience as a judge and his ability to lead. Going for him also was the fact that he was not close to the President, either personally or politically. As a result of the Fortas case, Nixon said, he had decided that the new Chief Justice—and any other Justices named later—should be neither a close friend nor a political associate.

Dewey Too Old

Thus two men, at least, were out: Charles Rhyne, former American Bar Association president, a Nixon classmate at Duke law school and a personal friend, and Attorney General John Mitchell, the 1968 campaign manager. A third, Herbert Brownell, Eisenhower's Attorney General—and Burger's boss for three years in the Justice Department in the early '50s—withdrew of his own accord because he thought his former job would raise opposition in the Senate. A fourth, Potter Stewart, an Eisenhower appointee to the court, took himself out because he thought that elevation of an Associate Justice would create friction and jealousy on the bench. Thomas Dewey, twice the Republican candidate for President, said simply that at 67 he was too old. A Chief Justice, said Dewey, should have at least ten years on the job. Burger, 61, at least has that prospect.

Nixon insisted that the timing of the appointment had nothing to do with Fortas. He wanted his nominee to have ample opportunity to confer with Warren, but he did not want the Senate hearings to begin until the court had ended its current session. Some time in May was thus indicated for the announcement. Still, the effect of the nomination last week, intended or not, was to draw attention from the Fortas affair and focus interest on the court's future rather than its troubled present.

Tremors of the Fortas affair, of course, were still being felt as Burger stood in front of the TV cameras. As the result of questions about the court's integrity, Justice William O. Douglas, a court veteran of 30 years, resigned from the presidency of the Parvin Foundation from which he has received about $12,000 annually for the past seven years. Though his relationship to Parvin was certainly less objectionable than Fortas' tie with the Wolfson Family Foundation—the contract was not for life, for one thing, and Douglas' duties were spelled out precisely—the connection was still questionable and invited the accusation of poor judgment at least. The foundation until recently had derived income from Las Vegas gambling operations. Even after Douglas quit the organization, the American Bar Association said it would ask its ethics committee to consider whether Douglas had violated A.B.A. canons.

At the same time, Chief Justice Warren, as one of his last official acts, requested senior federal judges to begin drafting a code of ethics for the federal judiciary. The prospective rules would not only bar judges from outside employment, excepting only lecturing, writing and teaching on legal subjects, but would also require disclosure within the Judicial branch of all income. In a sense, Warren was racing Congress, where three bills on judicial ethics have already been submitted. It is uncertain, however, how far Congress could go in clamping down on a supposedly coequal branch of government. Many Congressmen believe that the matter would best be resolved by the judges.

Ironically, Burger might also be affected by the proposed rules. He receives about $2,000 a year plus expenses for serving on the board of the Mayo Clinic in Minnesota (along with L.B.J., who was appointed in February). While this connection seems innocent enough, it too would probably be dissolved if Warren's proposed rules against outside activity went into effect.

Three-Legged Stool

Outside activity should be the very least of Burger's problems as Chief Justice. More important will be his ability to run the court and persuade his colleagues to accept his own traditional concept of the law, particularly in the controversial field of criminal justice. "A trial court," he likes to say to explain his point, "is like a three-legged stool: a judge, a prosecutor and a defense lawyer. Take anything away and the stool topples over." It is his feeling that the prosecutor has been so weakened by court decisions that the stool has in effect toppled over. As a result mainly of court decisions, he has stated, "We have today the most complicated system of criminal justice and the most difficult system to administer of any country in the world."

In a speech that particularly impressed Nixon, Burger said two years ago that "governments exist chiefly to foster the rights and interests of their citizens, to protect their homes and property, their persons and their lives. If a government fails in this basic duty, it is not redeemed by providing even the most perfect system for the protection of the rights of defendants in the criminal courts. It is a truism of political philosophy rooted in history that nations and societies often perish from an excess of their own basic principle."

To a great degree, he finds fault not with the spirit of the decisions but with the procedures they entail and the practical results they bring. Instead of deciding case by case, he says, the Supreme Court should have relied on a tool given it by Congress 30 years ago. Before it got too far into the criminal-law revolution, it could have set up an advisory committee of lawyers, judges and legal scholars to draw up detailed rules of procedure for federal courts and law-enforcement agencies. That way, Burger believes, much of the confusion and conflict that exist today, the inevitable results of piecemeal, sometimes contradictory decisions, could have been eliminated. The basic decisions—those that guarantee a lawyer to every person charged with a serious offense and those that protect him against coerced confession—Burger regards as so fundamental as to be beyond dispute. His opposition, generally, has been to rulings that affect mere procedural questions, such as how police should conduct line-ups, exactly when a lawyer should be present and what constitutes a legal search and seizure. These go into matters that Burger does not consider basic constitutional rights.

Beyond Dispute

That confusion exists cannot be denied. It is far from certain, however, that the court could or should have gone the route Burger recommends. Not only is his method slow, with acceptable results only theoretical in such a controversial area, but any rules adopted would provide no more than an example, to be accepted or rejected by the states. It is in state and local jurisdictions that the most serious abuses of police power have always occurred, and the top federal court has moved so far into criminal justice largely because state courts have been so shockingly negligent. Burger's position also implies the approval of Congress, which so far has been less than eager to examine criminal procedure with anything like dispassion or proper concern for the Bill of Rights.

One part of Burger's philosophy of law and order is beyond dispute. The U.S. has failed miserably in reforming people who have been sentenced. Though the system will devote great sums of money to giving a defendant a trial, with many chances of appeal, it will spend relatively little where resources would do the most good: making prisons over into institutions of correction rather than punishment. "In part, the terrible price we pay in crime," he says, "is because we have tended, once the drama of the trial is over, to regard all criminals as human rubbish."

In another, increasingly disputed area of criminal law—the place of the psychiatrist—Burger again has strong and somewhat unorthodox views. He believes firmly in psychiatry itself, sadly contrasting the number of psychiatrists serving the American penal system (as few as one for each 5,000 inmates in some states) with those in Denmark (one to 100). But he does not feel that the psychiatrist has a role in trial procedure, where the main question, in Burger's view, is what occurred, not why. He was, for example, opposed to acceptance by the District of Columbia of the famous Durham rule,* which greatly broadened the concept of criminal insanity. The winning lawyer on the other side: Abe Fortas.

Important as it now is, criminal justice is only one part, and not the largest at that, of the court's concerns. How will Burger view the others? If his statements and 13 years on a lower bench are indicative, he will fall into the school of the late Felix Frankfurter and John Marshall Harlan, Frankfurter's current disciple on the court. This tradition is not so much liberal or conservative in orthodox political terms—Frankfurter was considered an articulate advocate of civil liberties but was inclined against overruling other branches and levels of government unless there was a compelling reason. Burger has not expressed himself on many specific issues outside the field of criminal justice, but people familiar with his thinking expect him to be hard on disruptive campus dissent and to be unsympa-

*"An accused is not criminally responsible if his unlawful act was the product of mental disease or defect."

thetic to the court's new extensions of the one man, one vote doctrine, which carry the principle toward the city and county.

"We do well," Burger said in a decision last year, "to heed the admonition that judges confine themselves to the case at hand." That ruling knocked down Adam Clayton Powell's attempt to gain his seat in Congress by judicial decree. Though acknowledging his court's jurisdiction to act, Burger chose not to intervene. He was motivated by his respect for Congress' right to make its own rules and the practicality of the case—one of his constant concerns. Speculating about a confrontation with a recalcitrant Congress, Burger later asked rhetorically: "What if we had ordered the House to seat Powell and the House had refused? Could we have sent the Army up Capitol Hill to enforce it?"

No matter how firmly established their positions are, few officials are less predictable than newly appointed Supreme Court Justices. Wrapped in the black robes of one of the world's most august bodies, their jobs guaranteed for life, they often surprise and frequently offend the Presidents who appointed them. "I could carve a judge with more backbone out of a banana," Teddy Roosevelt supposedly growled after his appointee, Oliver Wendell Holmes, refused to vote the President's way on a trust case. Dwight Eisenhower was similarly shocked at Earl Warren's liberalism.

Precedents May Remain

By elevating a judge from a federal court, where the issues are like those that will go to the Supreme Court, Nixon knows better than most Presidents where his man stands, and has a better than average chance of finding comfort in his course. Indeed, the President was candid enough to hope publicly that his new appointee would begin to change the court's direction.

In this, if not in the man himself, Nixon may be disappointed. While Burger and the other yet-to-be-named Justice, together with the existing centrist faction of John Harlan, Potter Stewart and Byron White, may in fact reverse some of the controversial criminal decisions, it is just as likely that they will allow what has been done to remain done. Since the liberals in the past have been strongly criticized for violating the hallowed concept of *stare decisis*—let the precedent decide—the other side might feel uncomfortable in now jumping over precedents of the Warren era, new as some of the precedents may be. Thus Robert McKay, dean of the New York University Law School, thinks there may be "some trimming and tailoring" of the close decisions, but no radical backtracking.

Metaphysical Powers

Much depends on the man Nixon picks to replace Fortas—and on the man he has chosen to replace Earl Warren. If Burger is a strong Chief Justice, he may be able to move the court more than now looks likely; if he is weak or merely competent, whatever change comes about will probably be very gradual. First in prestige, first in rank, first in the public eye, the Chief Justice is still only one of nine when it comes to voting, and must depend on other, more subtle tools to make his presence any more powerful or persuasive than his colleagues'.

Set down on paper, his power appears scarcely more than metaphysical. He leads the judicial conferences, states the facts of the case under consideration, and, when he is in the majority, picks the man who will write the decision. On a closely fought issue, all three can be important. Some Chief Justices, like Warren, have been both forceful and tactful enough to use their tactical advantages to build up strong leadership. Others, like Fred Vinson, Warren's predecessor, have been all but overshadowed by more brilliant or more articulate Associate Justices.

With opinion so closely divided on everything else about him, it is not surprising that Burger is likened to both of the preceding Chief Justices. Like Warren, says former Attorney General Ramsey Clark, "he is quiet, modest and very warm. He meets people graciously and is interested and concerned with what they have to say. You can't be around him without thinking that here's a good, decent man." More decisive than title, power or personality, suggests Harvard Professor Ernest Brown, is the intellectual capability of a Justice. On that basis, guesses Brown, the liberal William Brennan might turn out to be the "key figure," and Warren's spiritual, if not titular successor.

New Issues

With all the talk of the Burger Court, one crucial fact is usually forgotten: even the Warren Court has been changing and becoming less activist. Brandeis Political Scientist George Kelly believes that that court reached its high-water mark several years ago with the one-man, one-vote decision. Since then, he says, it has moved more slowly and been less prone to embark on new courses. Leo Pfeffer, a political scientist at Long Island University, discerns the same deceleration—and the same reasons. First, the court has gone about as far as it can in many areas. Second, it, like any other human institution, is reacting to "the temper of the times and to the escalation of criticism."

If nothing else, Burger's appointment should act to quiet the more strident critics. Southerners like James Eastland, chairman of the Senate Judiciary Committee, will be less likely to claim, as he once did, that the court is "the greatest single threat to our Constitution." Even Eastland might find it hard to reverse his judgment of last week, which called Burger "an outstanding jurist and a very fine man."

In time, the main reason for Nixon's choice—Burger's stand on law and order—may seem far less important than it does today. New issues and new problems almost certainly will arise, and may very well overshadow the controversies of today. The question before the court of the '70s may not be criminal rights but citizen rights. Columbia Political Scientist Alan Westin, for instance, sees an impending collision between the old system of government, which depends upon political parties and established bureaucracy, and the new demands for participation by the poor and the powerless. There will be constant requests, predicts Westin, for the court to referee. If it refuses, he says, there will be "a decade unsurpassed in violence." Beyond that, there will be, without question, a paramount need to provide a legal framework to curb an overweening technology, which even today threatens to destroy both man and his works.

At first glance Judge Burger would seem an inappropriate Chief Justice for the possibly turbulent decade of the '70s. He is neither a simple nor an obvious man, however, and may very well confound both critics and friends. Significantly, perhaps, the decision he is most proud of affirmed those very citizen rights that Westin noted. When the Federal Communications Commission turned down a complaint by a group of blacks against a Mississippi radio station that they charged was racist, Burger, speaking for his court, affirmed the citizens' rights to challenge the FCC's renewal of a license. His decision, says an admiring lawyer, brought the public into an area that was until then the exclusive preserve of Government and industry.

The First Challenge

In the end, all prejudgments are suspect, in and out of court. In any event, the country has a way of educating its Justices—as well as its Presidents—and the Justices, in their turn, have a way of educating the country. A period of consolidation after a decade of hurried innovation may be, as Nixon believes, best for both court and country.

Still, it should not be forgotten how or why the period of intense activity came about. For the most part, it was caused by the default of other branches of Government, lower courts and society in general. When neither the executive nor the legislative branch cared enough about the Negro to guarantee his basic rights as a citizen, not to mention as a human being, the Warren Court outlawed school segregation, setting in motion the civil rights advances of the '50s and '60s. When no other body of Government seemed concerned that city dwellers were made second-class citizens by the grossest forms of malapportionment, the court said that one man was allowed one vote. When no one else took action against abuses of police power, the Justices launched their still controversial course of protecting the rights of those accused of crimes.

The court filled the vacuum, but at the same time it has paid the price of controversy. Its image as an Olympian arbiter above the political fray has usually been false. Still, its involvement in the most contentious issues of the last decade and its role of a *de facto* lawmaker were extraordinary—and raised questions about the court's function in American society that go far beyond the labels of liberal and conservative.

Now, in addition to fears about the court's widening power, the Fortas affair causes alarm about its integrity. There is no real evidence that the vast majority of the people have lost their awe and respect for the court, but there clearly has been some diminution of its prestige. That is hurtful, because public trust has been the court's main strength for 179 years. The 15th Chief Justice will now be challenged to reassert the court's moral authority.

QUESTIONS FOR DISCUSSION AND DIALOGUE

1. Briefly outline at least three "guestimates" which indicate how the new Chief Justice might perform in that office.

2. From the statements the article made about why President Nixon selected Burger as Chief Justice, do you think it would be fair to conclude that the President determines the role of the U.S. Supreme Court because of his appointment power? If this is true, isn't the Court really made up of politicians rather than nonpolitical influentials? Discuss.

3. Two key terms are usually used in discussing the role of the U.S. Supreme Court: Judicial activism and judicial restraint. From what you have just read, which do you think Burger would favor more? Discuss.

4. After rereading the last four paragraphs, what do you think is meant by the statement "the court filled the vacuum, but at the same time it has paid the price of controversy?" Do you think the U.S. Supreme Court should be a "de facto law maker?" Does this contradict basic American governmental-political principles of democracy and consent of the governed? (Restudy your responses to Questions 3 and 4 of the last article.)

Law and Order
Has the Supreme Court Gone too
Far?

Nicholas De B. Katzenbach

Former Attorney General of the United States, former chairman of the President's Commission on Law Enforcement and Administration of Justice, and recently Under Secretary of State.

Former Attorney General Katzenbach answers the question posed in the title with an emphatic "no," and puts the increase of crime in a social, economic and population increase framework. His comments about the U.S. Supreme Court's "job" as opposed to the "job" of the policemen make a very important theoretical distinction between two kinds of nonpolitical influentials. The other distinction that needs continued emphasis is between the allocation of resources—especially money—to do the job of coping with environmentally related problems, and the defense of constitutional rights. When these concerns are slighted by the proper respective Americans, politicians, and parties, the results of the Court's proper and necessary functions often take undeserved blame!

For politicians to charge that there is a substantial connection between the rising crime rate in our country and recent decisions of the U.S. Supreme Court is nonsense. The public should be concerned about crime, and the Court should not be immune from criticism. But "curbing the Court" is simply not going to curb crime.

That crime and the Court have become central issues in the current political campaign ['68] is hardly surprising. For some years now, the crime rate has been increasing rapidly, and during this same period, the Supreme Court, in a series of controversial decisions, has been extending constitutional protections to people accused of crime.

To many Americans, there seems an obvious connection. And a number of politicians—including those seeking high office—have not hesitated to suggest a relationship, though few have gone as far as the late Police Chief William Parker of Los Angeles. In his office hung a huge chart depicting the rise of crime; each jagged peak was topped with the title of a leading Supreme Court decision for that year.

The issue has been sharply drawn among the presidential candidates this year. The Republican candidate has accused the Supreme Court of giving the "green light" to the "criminal elements" in this country and has stated "our judges and courts must take a large measure of responsibility for the current lawlessness." In his acceptance speech last August, he said: ". . . let us also recognize that some of our courts in their decisions have gone too far in weakening the peace forces as against the criminal forces in this country. . . . And if we are to restore order and respect for law in this country, there's one place we're going to begin: We're going to have a new Attorney General of the United States of America." The Democratic candidate, in his acceptance address, voiced a directly contrary view: "The answer does not lie in an attack on our courts, our laws or our Attorney General." It is hardly necessary to add where former Governor Wallace stands; he has called the Supreme Court guilty of "handcuffing the police" and "sick."

The Court is an easy target for criticism because of the sense of frustration that results when a clearly guilty man is allowed to go free. What society loses by such judicial action seems quite clear. What it gains—the protection of all Americans against improper or undesirable police conduct—is much more subtle and intangible.

None of us should underestimate the strain placed on the public sense of security and on our system of justice when even a few persons guilty of serious crimes go free. But this strain has been greatly magnified by the exaggeration of critics. Visions of a helpless police force, of criminals quoting Supreme Court decisions on their way to the police station, of prosecutors rendered ineffective do not improve public confidence in our criminal system. This picture of an inept criminal system may well encourage crime. But the Court is not the culprit. Those who regularly and unreasonably attack it should bear the responsibility for their own exaggerations.

To understand the current attempts to blame the Court for crime, one must recognize two major trends in our country. The first is the movement toward both racial and economic justice. This is truly a national movement, in which the Court has sometimes led the other branches of Government. The Court has been centrally—and often controversially—involved through its decisions on school desegregation and the right of impoverished defendants to counsel in criminal trials. Its civil rights opinions have obviously earned it some passionate enemies.

The Court's civil rights decisions have not dealt with or created the kind of law-and-order problems that erupt from civil rights demonstrations and urban race riots. No Court decisions stimulated the disturbances in Cleveland and Detroit, and, unfortunately, no Court decisions moderated the activities of the police during the convention in Chicago. But there are those who are ready to make political capital out of the turbulence of our times by attempting to confuse a public disturbed by riots and civil disorder, puzzled by the rebellion of youth and anxious about crime.

Most of the charges that the Supreme Court hampers law and order arise from the second trend: the increase in crime. The President's Commission on Law Enforcement and Administration of Justice (the President's Crime Commission) found that the reasons for this increase lie in major social, economic and population changes. Our population is growing, and the number of young people (who commit most crimes) is growing even faster. Americans are today more mobile, more concentrated in cities and less subject to parental or other social controls. Prosperity frustrates those who don't share in it and at the same time increases the opportunities for crime: the more automobiles there are, the more there are to be stolen. The anonymity of big-city living makes identification and apprehension of criminals more difficult and gives rise to a sense of irresponsibility.

These complex reasons behind the nationwide increase in crime are well documented, but many people feel the need for a simpler explanation. They see only that sometimes a guilty man goes free.

When the Supreme Court reverses a criminal conviction, it may release an obviously guilty person on what seems "technical grounds": a confession was improperly obtained: a search, which in fact found heroin, was made without "probable cause"; a defendant was not informed of his right to be silent or to consult a lawyer. Why, they ask, should we permit such "technicalities" to shackle law and order?

Anyone who suggests that the Court bears a major responsibility for the rise in crime paints a deceptive picture. Such people depict the police as struggling against the growing menace of crime with "handcuffs" snapped on by the Court. They conclude that the Court should be handcuffed, not the police. They fail to recognize that the tension between the police and the judiciary has always been fundamental to our constitutional system. It is intentional and healthy and constitutes the real difference between a free society and a police state.

This tension results from the distinct roles of the courts and the police in a democratic society. Unquestionably, the Bill of Rights and Court decisions interpreting its provisions make the job of police and prosecution more difficult. Unquestionably, such decisions result in some guilty persons escaping the consequences of their crimes.

A policeman arrests and searches a suspected narcotics seller and finds heroin. Under the pressure of the moment, the officer may think he has sufficient basis—the constitutional phrase is "probable cause"—to make the arrest and search. And yet, when the Supreme Court reviews the case, it may look very different.

It is the policeman's job to make the arrest if he thinks he is reasonably entitled to do so. It is the Court's job to see whether the policeman acted consistently with the Bill of Rights. The policeman can take satisfaction when a hunch works. But the Court cannot be satisfied with hunches even if they sometimes pay off, because some police officers with less accurate hunches will be encouraged to engage in dragnet arrests and searches.

Conflict between police and courts is not confined to the control of police practices that are clearly improper. The Court also has a responsibility to ensure equal justice for rich and poor, white and black. The wealthy criminal can afford high-priced counsel, and the experienced syndicate mobster knows his constitutional rights. The syndicate itself will quickly provide a lawyer and bail to free its arrested member. But most people arrested have none of these advantages. They cannot afford a lawyer and probably do not even know one. If they cannot make bail, they must spend a long period in jail before trial—a period that makes their defense more difficult and inflicts hardships on their families as well as themselves.

The effort to give every man a full and equal measure of justice is revolutionary. The truth is that our system of justice has always favored the rich and prejudiced the poor. And the problem is further complicated because most policemen, prosecutors and judges are white, and many defendants black. A country torn by racial strife and with too long a tradition of prejudice in too many places must ensure that black defendants have, in fact as well as in theory, the same rights as whites.

The report of the National Advisory Commission on Civil Disorders suggests that efforts to equalize the rights of rich and poor, white and black, may actually reduce crime. High among the many grievances of the Negro communities in the inner city were found to be police practices and the sense that justice is administered in a discriminatory manner. Three times as many Negroes as whites think that the police "frisk or search people without good reason" and that "the police rough up people unnecessarily when they are arresting them or afterwards." In three-fourths of the 20 cities surveyed by the Commission, Negroes felt discriminated against by the courts. Compliance with law requires respect for the impartiality and fairness of the legal system.

Congress, on two recent occasions, has supported the Court's efforts to achieve equal justice. It endorsed the principle that every defendant, irrespective of his financial means, is entitled to competent counsel; and it provided money to help make this rule a reality in Federal courts. Congress also has reformed bail practices to ensure that the poor are not unduly prejudiced by the fact of poverty.

Ironically, these relatively noncontroversial reforms have created far more serious problems for our legal system than those that have stirred more controversy. Our system of prosecution and trial simply is not prepared to handle aggressive defense by everyone, rich and poor. These noncontroversial reforms have resulted in more non-guilty pleas, more trials, more acquittals, more burdens on prosecutors and more delays.

The Supreme Court decisions that have aroused the greatest storm of controversy are those dealing with police interrogation and the use of confessions. In *Miranda v. Arizona,* the Court barred the use of a confession obtained from a suspect in custody who had not been warned of his rights. These included his right to consult with a state-supplied lawyer before answering police questions. So strong were the feelings generated against the *Miranda* decision that the United States Senate added a provision (later eliminated in conference) in the Safe Streets and Crime Control Act to deprive the Court of jurisdiction over confessions in state trials.

Unquestionably, the *Miranda* decision creates problems for the police, but one can safely say that this decision, like other Court decisions, has little relevance to the amount of crime we face today, particularly to the sort of predatory "crime in the street" that is the cause of so much public fear and anger.

Miranda will result in letting some who are guilty go free. But probably it affects less than one percent of the serious crimes in the United States. This conclusion is based on findings by the President's Crime Commission.

Only a small portion of all crime gets reported to the police, and arrests are made in less than a quarter of the cases reported. One cannot blame *Miranda* for the crimes never reported and the arrests never made. Even when the police do make an arrest, the *Miranda* warning is crucial to the successful prosecution of relatively few cases. Many suspects did not confess before *Miranda,* and some now confess despite the warning. And even when there is a confession, other testimony and evidence are usually adequate to secure a conviction.

One further statistical point dramatizes the lack of impact on crime of Supreme Court decisions. According to the FBI, between 1960 and 1965, arrests of persons under 18 years of age for murder, rape, robbery, aggravated assault, burglary, larceny and auto theft rose 52 percent, while the increase for those over 18 was only 20 percent. Yet during that entire period, not one of the Court's decisions now under attack was applicable to persons under 18 years of age.

It is a cruel hoax to seek to persuade the American people that the Bill of Rights should be watered down in response to rising crime rates. Political debate about the Court diverts attention from the need to give our law-enforcement agencies far greater resources to do their job. The critics are actually making the crime problem worse.

We are paying a huge price for our historic neglect of the agencies of criminal justice. We should now support the measures—and the money—needed to strengthen police departments, speed up court processes and make prisons and correctional institutions something other than overcrowded, ineffectual warehouses.

Supreme Court critics too often call for bargain-basement solutions to crime. Members of Congress who express the gravest concern about the Court are too often unprepared to vote to give the agencies of justice the resources they need to make criminal administration effective. Crime control does cost money, while it seems to cost nothing in dollars to amend the Bill of Rights or curtail the Court.

The Court has a responsibility to review the conduct of law-enforcement agencies. It can do nothing to require that police, prosecutors, courts and correctional agencies be given adequate manpower. That responsibility lies with the other branches of Government. If recent Court decisions have imposed additional financial burdens on the law-enforcement agencies, the legislative branch must help them meet these costs. If a police force now needs two hundred men, a legislature is avoiding its responsibility if it simply complains that the police could have gotten along with 175 were it not for the Court's decisions. The nation's best police leaders—men like Howard Leary of New York City, Thomas Reddin of Los Angeles, Patrick Murphy of Washington, D.C., and Thomas Cahill of San Francisco—have concentrated their efforts on getting the money and manpower they need rather than on useless attacks on the Court.

Twenty months ago, President Johnson submitted to Congress the Safe Streets and Crime Control Act designed to support state and local law enforcement as recommended by the Crime Commission. After more than a year's delay —much of it devoted to debate about the Supreme Court—Congress passed the bill but sharply curtailed appropriations. Thus, the issue is posed: Are we prepared to turn to the task of strengthening criminal justice or will we continue to seek an easy solution where none exists?

In words that seem particularly apt in this political year, the Crime Commission said in concluding its report: "If America is to meet the challenge of crime it must do more, far more, than it is doing now. It must welcome new ideas and risk new actions. It must spend time and money. It must resist those who point to scapegoats, who use facile slogans about crime by habit or for selfish ends. It must recognize that the Government of a free society is obliged to act not only effectively but fairly."

We have to be prepared to live with high rates of crime in the years ahead as our young population grows. We can no longer afford to let politicians seek profit from this situation or to evade difficult problems by making a scapegoat of the Supreme Court. We must improve criminal administration and make law enforcement both effective and fair. And most of all, in order to make our nation safe, we must reverse the deplorable conditions of life that deprive many of our citizens of their stake in a lawful and orderly society and turn them to crime.

QUESTIONS FOR DISCUSSION AND DIALOGUE

1. Outline Katzenbach's distinction between the job of the policeman and the job of the Court. Why is it easy for someone who is uninformed to blame the Court for making the job of the policeman harder? Discuss.
2. Outline the reasons which the President's Crime Commission found for the

increase in crime. In the light of these "complex reasons" why do you think "many people feel the need for a simpler explanation?" Discuss.

3. (For future reference) After reading Article 7 in this chapter, "FBI Report Makes Our Insecurities Understandable," relate your response to the above question to as many of the statistical increases in crime from the FBI Report as possible. For example, what implication is there to the fact that "49% . . . of all persons charged with committing a major crime in 1968 were juveniles . . .?"

4. How do you think the U.S. will respond to the challenge of crime in the future? Do you think it will do what Katzenbach suggests in the last two paragraphs? Why?

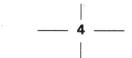

Crime, and Society's Obligations

Richard Dougherty
Joseph D. Lohman

Another group of nonpolitical influentials, the police, is the topic of these two articles. Two differing views are offered about crime, police, and society's problems and obligations. Perhaps "differing views" is not the best way to express how Dougherty and Lohman see the problems of crime prevention and how to cope with them. They seem to agree on what should be done, but not on the larger questions of "when, how, and by whom." These are questions of great long and short range significance to all Americans.

The report of the President's national crime commission is released today in the wake of Mr. Johnson's special message to Congress on the same topic. Clearly, crime at long last is the focal point of much serious and worried attention. In that context *Opinion* presents the views of two men who formerly served in official police capacities. Richard Dougherty, who returned to news reporting after two years as a deputy commissioner of police in New York City, is now chief of The Times Bureau there. Joseph D. Lohman was formerly sheriff of Cook County (Chicago), Ill., and has served as a consultant to both federal and state governments on matters of crime control. He is now dean of the School of Criminology, University of California, and his article is excerpted from a report made in that capacity.

Richard Dougherty

New York

With the possible exception of the American Indian, no underprivileged group in the country tends to get less attention than our boys in blue—or brown, or gray, depending on what city you happen to be in.

Now, it would appear, this injustice is in process of being corrected.

This very day, for example, is set for the unveiling of the report of the President's Commission on law enforcement and the administration of justice. That 340-page document is very much concerned with cops and their peculiar line of work.

So was the special message on crime which President Johnson sent to the Congress only a couple of weeks ago. So was a recent major address of Sen. Robert F. Kennedy which, among other things, suggested draft deferment for police volunteers.

Presently a lively hassle over police recruitment holds the spotlight here in the nation's biggest city. The New York cops are claiming recruitment is an extremely serious problem. Mayor John V. Lindsay is claiming it isn't.

Whatever their other complaints, our police can hardly contend that they are being ignored. At least for the moment.

Of course, whether all this attention from the White House and Capitol Hill and other quarters will lead to anything constructive in terms of improved police service is another matter.

We will hear a lot of high-sounding talk. We will be told that the answer to the crime problem in our cities lies within our grasp if we will only get rid of our slums and recruit our cops from Harvard. We will be told that crime has to be attacked "at its roots."

Meantime, those sounds we hear rising nightly from the streets of our cities —sounds of splintering glass, squealing tires, stifled screams and ugly thuds—will assure us that the burglar, the car thief and the mugger are still going about their appointed rounds with a minimum of inconvenience.

Difference in Approaches

Does this mean that I am opposed to attacking crime at its roots, or doing away with slums, or sending cops to Harvard?

It merely means that I regard this social-worker approach, so to speak, as having little if any immediate relevance to the problem of making the streets and parks of our cities safe for the ordinary law-abiding citizen.

There is, after all, more than one "root" cause in the committing of a criminal act. Let me offer an example.

If old Mr. Jones gets mugged by young Tommy Smith in the course of an evening stroll down Elm Street, to what should we attribute the crime? To Tommy's underprivileged childhood as recorded in a fat file at the juvenile aid bureau? Well, of course.

But is that all? What of the fact that nowhere down the length and breadth of Elm Street was there a sign of a cop—either on foot or in a radio patrol car? Doesn't the absence of this time-honored deterrent to crime bear a casual relationship to the attack on Mr. Jones? Surely it does.

If we are serious about law enforcement and the prevention of crime, we ought to be just as interested in old Mr. Jones' security as we are in Tommy Smith's emotional difficulties; we ought to be just as interested in what made Tommy think he could get away with the mugging as in what made him want to do it in the first place.

What we need, in other words, is to get our system of priorities straightened around. Attacking crime at its roots—through slum clearance, education, social justice and a better life for all—is going to take a long time.

Our problem is a clear and present one—to make life in New York, Los Angeles, Chicago, Detroit, all our cities, secure and free from lawlessness.

And how is this to be accomplished? Simple. By getting some cops on the street.

The classic function of the police is not so much to arrest people who have committed crimes. It is to prevent crimes from being committed at all.

The theory is that the uniformed cop, by his very presence, gives pause to the would-be robber, rapist or vandal and thus brings security and peace of mind to the law-abiding. There are several admirable things about this theory—its simplicity for one; but not the least is that it works.

I can cite two instances here in New York. One is an experiment carried out in 1954 by the New York Police Department, at a time when I was myself serving as the department's press and community relations officer. The other is still in operation.

Results in Harlem

The 1954 experiment, called Operation 25 because it was undertaken in the 25th precinct (in Manhattan's east Harlem) called for a doubling of police manpower. Special emphasis was given to the strengthening of uniformed patrols so that for the four months of the test you couldn't look down a street without seeing a cop.

The result: A drop of 55% in serious crime overall, and an even more drastic reduction in street crimes. Stickups and other types of robberies were cut 70%; so were auto thefts. Burglaries were down 68%. Muggings were almost completely erased.

At the same time the clearance rate for those crimes that were committed showed dramatic improvement, rising from 20% to 66% during the experiment. In effect, Operation 25 cut the incidence of crime by more than half in a very tough precinct, while it also brought two-thirds of still active felons to justice.

Another continuing example of the precincts to be won through proper police protection is demonstrated every night on the New York subway system. Between 8 p.m. and 4 a.m. there is a cop on every train and at every one of the 481 subway stations.

This service was introduced April 7, 1965, when public indignation about subway crimes prompted officialdom to do something. Since then subway crime has been cut by more than 60% and people are once more riding trains during the wee hours.

Given such evidence, which is hardly startling to knowledgeable police officers, it is not surprising that someone like the late Chief William H. Parker should have urged a doubling of the Los Angeles police force to more than 11,000 men. Nor is it surprising that New York's police commissioner Howard R. Leary should now be pressing for 1,000 more men for his 28,000-man department.

In truth no American city, whether its police officials admit it or not, is anywhere near being adequately policed. That's one of the reasons why I think of cops as a minority.

There are other reasons. We pay them wretchedly. We give them little in the way of respect: the liberals tend to regard them as fascist louts, the conservatives as something on the level of domestic servants whose main job is to keep "undesirables" at bay. Our courts, presumably brethren institutions in a nation governed by law, are defendant-oriented to an almost hostile degree. Our editorial writers are generally cut from the same cloth as the gentlemen on the bench.

Meyer Lansky and scores of other rackets bigwigs can live like kings in Miami and get written up by the *Saturday Evening Post.* Organized crime, already flourishing, will flourish all the more if wiretapping is eventually restricted to cases involving the national security only, as Mr. Johnson has recommended.

Meanwhile, look at the median salary of patrolmen in at least one of our "large cities," according to the President's crime commission. It's $5,300 a year. Maybe even "minority" isn't the word I'm looking for.

Joseph D. Lohman

Berkeley

Unhappily, and notwithstanding the earnestness of the effort, the accent in controlling crime has been on the old negative, punitive measures of arrest, detention, incarceration. The results are that the police are engulfed in inadequate and abortive routine and criminal justice and penal facilities are so dangerously over-taxed that they continue to generate the very conditions of behavior they were designed to repress.

It should be obvious that we must take an entirely new look at the phenomenon of crime, since lawlessness is only a surface symptom. For every delinquent or criminal who commits an overtly hostile and aggressive act there are the many disaffected whose latent hostilities result in their loss as a human productive resource.

Our society cannot afford to write off human resources on so vast a scale.

We continue to fail in our assumption, if not in our understanding, that crime is the lengthened shadow of the community. While the community is changing drastically, we are still strait-jacketed by its old shadow. We recognize statistical changes—over 3 million people added to the population since 1961 and more than 112 million now living in metropolitan areas. But we fail to see that metropolitan society is something more than new numbers and a new distribution of the population. There has been initiated a totally new set of social relations.

In the city, impersonality and detachment predominate. The individual works, plays, and worships at places remote from where he lives. Control by family, friends, and neighbors is atomized. The individual has become, more than ever before, a face in the crowd—bored, lonely, part of the great market for vice and crime.

Opportunities Expanded

The market for the kind of services toward which organized crime directs its predatory fingers has become enormously expanded by the increases in population and by the new concentration of that population beyond the ordinarily confining municipal boundaries.

Our answer to the increase in crime has been more traditional police work, more "crackdowns." We have tried this deterrence policy long enough. It does not work.

To begin with, the majority of criminals, including 61.5% of robbers and 70.5% of burglars, do not get caught. When a burglar does get nabbed, another burglar in the same city might not even know it. If Burglar No. 2 reads of the arrest in a newspaper, the event remains too remote to apply to him, for all about him is evidence that people get away with crime. He knows more unpunished than punished sinners, so the risk of arrest seems worth taking.

We, in turn, require policemen to waste energy on measures which they know will not pay off. Instead of working on the overall crime problem, they must be responsive to newspapers clamoring for circulation by gimmick "crusades" against this "outbreak" or that, politicians courting favor by offering voters a false security, fearful citizens who demand, "You've got to do something!"

Too many police departments are popularity-conscious. The new look is to *look good* with "business methods," public relations programs, shifting the blame for crime to the courts and their allegedly inadequate sentences, and pushing for more and more arrests.

The truth is that much police work is itself part of the crime-initiating process. Far too many police cases are not police problems at all. Much of the police officer's contact with the public should begin and end with referrals to education and welfare agencies, which we must strengthen so that they can handle minor offenses, especially first offenders.

There is too little concern with the stigmatizing and alienating effect of arrests on such violators. We equate them with bank robbers and murderers. Once a youngster has a police record, this fact, in the eyes of the law and of potential employers, is more real than the person himself.

We stop looking at a young man. We look at his record, his "sheet," as it is called. Over and over boys told me, "It isn't me; it's the sheet. They won't listen to me." We have pushed these boys on the other side of the law. They may well stay there.

If they do, the responsibility is shared by the machinery for alienation which we call our prison system.

First stop is the county jail, run by our friend, the sheriff. Like it or not, he is the nation's number one correctional officer. The Cook County jail, which I once administered, was no better than most. Built for 1300, its average occupancy was 2600. More than 17,000 prisoners a year spent time there. Largely unsegregated by age or seriousness of offense, they languished in bullpens, as many as 60 or 70 with nothing to do, sometimes for weeks and months while awaiting trial. These jails are an abomination. Even a short stay in one of them can corrupt a youngster forever.

Paradox in the Cities

It is a paradox of the new metropolitan development that we are constantly moving toward self-defeating extremes in our desperate and uninformed efforts to keep abreast of the changing community. The heartlands of our great metropolitan centers are becoming the provinces of the new minorities.

These groups are a potential threat that may express themselves in the traditional patterns of organized crime. They have come out of a segregated discriminatory experience, in search of freedom and opportunity, into a social environment which in many respects is as restrictive as the older pattern. It is not only crime that becomes the abortive fruit of our failure to understand this changing community.

The unwitting processes of the middle class "suburban drift" and the transformation of vast areas of the central city into an enormous racial slum have profound political implications. In many of our major cities it is affecting a change in the balance of political power.

We must recognize the coincidence of the development of these great racial blocs with the traditional organization and location of the urban political machines. The traditional alliances between crime and politics have focused on the immigrant community and the slum.

We may be ushering in a new era of unprecedented political conflict between the cities and their suburbs with aggravating overtones of race tension and conflict as an additional feature of organized crime. To ignore the social, economic, and cultural disabilities under which these populations labor and to try to contain their volcanic eruptions by the expedient of repressive and antiquated police measures can only have the effect of force-feeding the fires which are smoldering at the core of our metropolitan communities.

In short, many of the problems which confront us stem from the failure of the public to know and to understand the new dimensions and ramifications of community life. Our success in controlling the crime problem in general and organized crime in particular will depend upon our understanding of the complexities of the newly emerging communal life and the problems which it has engendered. An effective law enforcement function must be familiar with, and equal to, its target.

New Approach Necessary

The changing patterns of crime are a projection of the far-reaching changes in American community life. The police, the courts, the machinery of punishment and corrections are also projections of the community. It is not likely that we will be successful in controlling crime without seriously changing the organization and administration of criminal justice.

The ultimate answer is to see crime not alone as a problem in law enforcement but as a problem in education, family organization, employment opportunity, and housing. These are the structures inside of which deviance and hence crime and delinquency incubate.

It is a myth that man's behavior can be changed directly. It can be changed only by altering the conditions which underlie the behavior. We must learn to treat causes, not only effects, of crime.

We are at a critical juncture in the history of American community development. The resettlement of the American community and the emergence of the metropolitan community is not merely a change in the size of our population nor in its geographic location. It is something of far greater importance; namely, the modification and, indeed, creation of a whole new set of human relations.

QUESTIONS FOR DISCUSSION AND DIALOGUE

1. Do you think Joseph Lohman (and Nicholas de B. Katzenbach) would argue or agree with this statement by Richard Dougherty? ". . . I regard (the) social worker approach, so to speak, as having little if any immediate relevance to the problem of making the streets and parks of our cities safe for the ordinary law abiding citizen." Would you argue or agree with it? Discuss.
2. Do you think Richard Dougherty would argue or agree with this statement by Joseph Lohman? "It is a myth that man's behavior can be changed directly. It can be changed only by altering the conditions which underlie the behavior. We must learn to treat causes, not only effects, of crime." Would you argue or agree with it? Discuss.
3. Outline a list of police reforms which you think both of these writers could agree on.

Effective Crime Fighting Is Costly

Yale Kamisar

Yale Kamisar thinks many of the Americans, politicians, parties, and nonpolitical influentials are trying to find simple answers to the complex problems of "law and order." The simple answers being searched for are often the "cheapest" ones in financial terms, and the "cheapest" ones in terms of due process and minority rights as well.

Yale Kamisar is professor of law at the University of Michigan Law School. He is the co-author of, among other books, "Criminal Justice in Our Times" and "Modern Criminal Procedure: Cases and Commentaries."

Are the scales of justice evenly balanced? Over the years this question has often been asked in one form or another, and over the years the answer of almost all law enforcement officials and, I regret to say, most lawyers and lower court judges has been the same: the scales are heavily tilted—in favor of the defendant. Only the names of the cases seem to change.

Five years ago, for example, the topic of the American Bar Association's Criminal Law Section Roundtable was: "How Do We Live with Mallory, Mapp and Wong Sun?" Superintendent O. W. Wilson, then head of the Chicago Police Department, spoke for most prosecutors and police, I am sure, when he charged that "in the name of protecting individual liberties, we are permitting so many technicalities to creep into our system of criminal justice that . . . crime is overwhelming our society."

Long Standing Dispute

Twelve years ago the topic for the Criminal Law Section was: "Are the Courts Handcuffing the Police?" At that time neither Mallory nor Mapp, let alone Escobedo or Miranda, had yet been decided. The panelists concentrated their fire on People v. Cahan, a 1955 California case, which excluded illegally seized evidence from state prosecutions.

Chief Carl Hansson, past president of the International Association of Chiefs of Police and one of the roundtable panelists, pointed out that Cahan had aptly been called "the 'Magna Charta' for the criminals." And J. F. Coakley, widely known as the "dean of American prosecutors," reported that it "had broken the very backbone of narcotics enforcement."

One can go back much further than 1956 and cite many distinguished speakers to the same effect.

Thus in 1905 we find William Howard Taft, later to be President and then

Chief Justice of the United States, pummeling the courts for their "unduly tender" interpretations of the protection against unreasonable search and seizure and the privilege against self-incrimination.

A further look back, to 1883, reveals Professor Simeon E. Baldwin, one of the giants of the legal and teaching professions, pleading for an end to the "false humanitarianism" which had put the state at a disadvantage "in its judicial contests with those whom it charges with crime . . ."

It has well been said that the best defense is a good offense. The scales of justice were tilted in 1883—in favor of the prosecution. The administration of criminal justice was a disgrace in 1905—but not for the reasons cited by Mr. Taft. Rather, for such reasons as the widely prevalent "third degree" which the Wickersham Commission disclosed in the 1930's.

Surely we don't want to swing the pendulum back to 1883 or 1905. But do we even want to swing it back a few years—to a time, the very recent past, when many policemen were given no instruction whatever in the law of search and seizure and didn't give a hoot about the Fourth Amendment, because the illegally seized evidence would be received by the courts.

To a time when there was no constitutional limit whatever on electronic eavesdropping?

To a time when a suspect was not entitled to consult with a lawyer even though he specifically asked for one, and could afford one?

To a time when, in some states at least, an indigent defendant had to try his own felony case?

To a time when, in many states, an indigent could not obtain any appellate review of admissibility and sufficiency of evidence and other alleged trial errors because he could not afford to pay for the stenographic transcript of the trial proceedings?

I suggest that now, as in the past, much of this talk about "the scales being tilted heavily in favor of the defendant" hides present serious deficiencies in the criminal process from the defense viewpoint. Indeed, the defendant's purported procedural advantage over the government is one of the major arguments advanced to resist pretrial discovery, and thus prevent the defense from cutting down the great advantage the government's immense facilities and resources give it.

How can we take seriously cries of leading law enforcement spokesmen such as New York District Attorney Frank Hogan that the prosecution has been dealt a long series of crippling blows by the Warren Court when we learn, quite casually in a recent magazine piece:

"Once the New York D. A. decides you are guilty of a felony, you are. As of June 23, the office had prosecuted to a conclusion this year 2,182 people accused of a felony. Seven of them—one-third of 1%—had been acquitted. Seventy-two had been convicted by juries, and 2,103 had entered a plea of guilty to something (not necessarily the full original indictment)." (*New York Times Magazine,* July 23, 1967)

How can we believe that the pre-Miranda confession law worked well when as late as 1965, in New York City alone, six murder charges were dismissed against suspects who had given detailed "ironclad" confessions to the police? (One of the suspects, by unusual chance, had the perfect alibi of having been in jail when the murder occurred.) Indeed, how can we be content with Miranda when the New York Legal Aid Society, which represents 70% of all the defendants in Manhattan, reports that in the first six months after Miranda less than 20 "subjects" of police interrogation requested its aid?

The government possesses what Edward Bennett Williams has aptly called "the most superb engine for discovery ever invented by the legal mind—the grand jury." It enables the prosecutor to question anybody with any knowledge of the facts before trial and to do so in secrecy and with virtually no holds barred. For, of course, neither the accused nor his lawyer has any right to be present, or to object to procedures in the grand jury room.

There has been much complaint about recent developments which aid only the guilty, but it is obvious that the innocent defendant is the one who suffers most from the traditional, restrictive approach to criminal discovery. He may not even be aware of the identity of the witnesses against him. (If a false or misleading story is not revealed until trial, the defense lawyer is ill-prepared to break it down on cross-examination. He needs facts, not intuition. He needs time to turn up other witnesses or some tangible evidence which refutes the government's version.

The Supreme Court has not, as so many of its critics claim, downgraded or degraded law enforcement officials. If anything, the American public has—by viewing lawmen as little more than garbage collectors and by utilizing our criminal codes as society's garbage cans, thus further burdening an already overburdened group of police and prosecutors with a lot of stuff which ought not to be the criminal law's business.

As Professor Sanford Kadish of the University of California Berkeley Law School has aptly put it, excessive reliance upon the criminal law to declare or enforce public standards of private morality and to provide social services in default of other public agencies (for example, our public drunkenness, family-nonsupport and insufficient-fund bad check laws) has created a "crisis of over-criminalization," denigrating the entire criminal-justice system, inducing offensive and degrading police conduct (especially against the pathetic and impoverished) and diverting enormous police-prosecution resources away from really serious crimes.

Unfortunately, the legislative and popular zeal to pass criminal laws against this, that, and almost everything far outstrips any desire on the part of the public to pay more taxes in order to enable the appropriate agencies to really do the job. Thus, in those instances where the criminal law is an appropriate and useful tool of social control, those assigned the task are grossly understaffed, undertrained and underpaid.

The late Will Rogers used to say that the people of Kansas will vote dry as long as they can stagger to the polls. If he were around today, I suspect, he would note that the American people are prepared to do anything to win the war against crime—except pay for it. Not the least reason for coming out against "coddling criminals" and for stiffer sentences, stop-and-frisk laws, law enforcement wire tapping and eavesdropping, etc., is that proponents feel such measures won't require an increase in taxes.

Two years ago, New York City told a National League of Cities survey that it needed 6,000 more officers, an increase of almost 25%. The average need for increased manpower reported was 10%. Only one of four cities provide police with 200 hours of classroom instruction—considered a bare minimum by the International Association of Chiefs of Police. Less than one of three cities answering the National League of Cities survey had electronic data processing equipment, although most wanted it. In many cities, because there are no or not enough civilian clerks, detectives type out their own reports—with two fingers. In even our largest cities, underpaid police moonlight as cab drivers, bouncers, or "guns for hire."

In most counties in more than 40 of our states the job of district attorney is only a part-time occupation that supplements private practice. In many counties, the prosecutor can't afford to go to trial too often lest he lose too much private business.

Some years ago, when I taught at the University of Minnesota, I discovered there were several rural countries in that state where there hadn't been a criminal trial in 3 or 4 years—and if there was to be one, somebody from the state attorney general's office would have to handle it because the local prosecutor didn't deem himself competent.

Try to raise a police officer's salary to $10,000 a year; try to make the prosecutor's office a full-time job carrying a salary of $15,000 or $17,500 a year instead of the $5,000 or $7,500 the office pays now in so many rural counties. Then see how many people who are "for law enforcement" and "against crime" run for cover.

Roots Still Untouched

At a minimum, an efficiently run probation service requires one officer to every 50-75 probationers, but it is not uncommon for probation officers to be assigned 300 or 500 cases. No wonder that at a recent Department of Justice-sponsored Lawyers Conference on Crime Control I attended, Richard McGee, administrator of the California Youth and Adult Correction Agency, said that there is such a woeful shortage of personnel to supervise probationers and parolees that in general there just isn't any supervison—"the whole thing is a fraud on the American public which thinks there is supervision."

I haven't even mentioned the "roots" of crime—just the obvious need to strengthen the various services which "combat crime." We simply do not come to grips with the "crime problem" because most politicians and most citizens talk big, but think small, about this whole subject. Attacking the Supreme Court doesn't "cost anything," but it doesn't accomplish anything either—other than fulfill an irrational demand on the part of a frightened and disturbed public for simplistic solutions to enormously complex problems.

A Glossary of Court Decisions

Wong Sun (1963)—The United States Supreme Court held that statements made by a suspect during an illegal search and seizure are not admissible as evidence.

Mapp (1961)—The United States Supreme Court ruled that courts would have to exclude evidence obtained by search or seizure in violation of the Fourth Amendment.

Mallory (1957)—The United States Supreme Court held that an arrested person in a case coming under federal jurisdiction must be arraigned without unnecessary delay.

Escobedo (1964)—The United States Supreme Court extended a suspect's right to counsel to that point in police work "when the process shifts from investigatory to accusatory—when the focus is on the accused and its purpose is to elicit a confession."

Miranda (1966)—The United States Supreme Court ruled that a person in custody must be advised of his right to remain silent or to have counsel present during interrogation.

Cahan (1955)—The California Supreme Court held that evidence obtained illegally is not admissible in court.

QUESTIONS FOR DISCUSSION AND DIALOGUE

1. Why do you think there seems to be a tendency of "most lawyers and lower court judges" to claim that the scales of justice are heavily tilted in favor of the defendant?
2. Why does Kamisar think this view (above question) is wrong? Do you agree with "most lawyers and lower court judges" or with Kamisar? Why? Discuss.
3. Do you agree with Kamisar's statements about how the American public has viewed lawmen as "little more than garbage collectors"? Discuss.
4. Outline two or three of the reforms Kamisar thinks are necessary to cope with police and crime problems. With which do you agree and disagree? Why?
5. What does the author mean by the phrase "crisis of overcriminalization"? Does this relate to anything you have read in the last two articles?

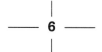

A Hard Cop and His Patient Partner on a Menacing Beat

L. H. Whittemore

Mr. Whittemore looks at two policemen with very different ideas about policing the Haight-Ashbury area of San Francisco. Professional policemanship in the face of deliberate provocation is a very difficult task, but as Officer Cummings seems to demonstrate in this article, not impossible. On the other hand, some might argue that Officer Barker's approach is closer to that of the truly professional policeman. Which model of the ideal policeman is chosen by the Americans will be a crucial decision for the future of the United States.

For more than a month the author followed the two policemen described in this excerpt from his book COP! A Closeup of Violence and Tragedy, *which will be published by Holt, Rinehart and Winston in July. Both men, whose names have been changed here, are still with the San Francisco police force. . . .*

Patrolman Colin Barker waded in. To the tune of Here Comes the Bride, someone in the crowd of disheveled young people began to sing: "Here comes the pig, here comes the pig . . ."

"Hey, he looks even younger than me."

"Gestapo!"

"I could be his mother."

"Then you should have had an abortion."

Colin Barker, who wore a crew cut beneath his police hat, indeed looked much younger than his 23 years. His uniform appeared a bit stiff, especially with the walkie-talkie resting awkwardly on his chest. Out of self-consciousness he adjusted it from time to time.

To several young men lounging on the hood of a convertible, the cop yelled, "Is this your car?"

"No."

"Then get off it!"

His suddenly asserted authority, plus the chorus of hisses that followed, brought fresh color to Colin's face.

"Hi, officer," said a pretty young girl. "Want to buy a necklace?"

"No . . . no thanks."

"There's a pig in our midst!"

The patrolman paused before a doorway, where three unkempt young men sprawled.

"This isn't your doorway, is it?"

"Nope."

"Then get on your feet."

As they picked themselves up, a wine bottle sheathed in a paper bag rolled off the top step and bounced to the pavement. Colin picked it up and poured the wine between two parked cars, to a chorus of boos and hisses.

On the sidewalk ahead, several boys and girls were kneeling over a lovely design in multicolored chalk. A huge set of flowers had been drawn in pink, purple, blue and white; and a message was printed below the flowers: "I, YOU, WE ARE GOD."

"All right," said Colin. "Get some water and scrub this off."

"We worked hard on this. Is it really against the law?"

"You're blocking the entrance to this man's establishment," said Colin, looking in the window of the Laundromat. The middle-aged storekeeper shrugged from behind the glass. A crowd gathered and watched as the youngsters, supplied with buckets of water and brushes from the Laundromat, scrubbed off the chalk design.

Colin continued his stroll. A girl with bare feet jumped in front of him, held a flower to his face and danced backward. "Have a flower, officer."

"No thanks, but thanks."

The girl stared defiantly and shouted, "TAKE THE FLOWER!" Suddenly the patrolman's hand shot out and batted the flower away. The sound of his hand smacking hers seemed too loud. Red-faced, he turned and began walking back. "That wasn't very nice," the girl called after him.

Colin heard someone following him, whistling. The faces he passed were smiling, expectant. The whistling grew louder at the back of his head. Colin stopped. The whistler continued on one long high note; then silence. Colin heard the person breathing behind him, but refused to turn around. "ATTENTION!"

The sound hurt Colin's ears. Turning abruptly, he faced a tall young man with flowing blond hair, dirty face and frazzled clothing. Colin whispered: "What did you say?"

"I said, F--- you, cop! That's what I said."

Colin threw the young man against the wall and flayed at him with his fists. The young man screamed and kicked. Colin tried to grab his shirt, but the young man reached up and tore off the patrolman's badge. The crowd cheered and Colin smashed his nightstick down—once, twice, a third time. The mob surged in, but Colin already was on his walkie-talkie calling for help. The young man on the sidewalk shouted, "Revolution, now! Kill him!" Colin folded his arms.

"I hope," screamed the young man, "that somebody jumps on you some day."

"Cool off, fella."

"Next time, brother, you'll be in front of my gunsight. You pig!"

At last the paddy wagon rolled up and two patrolmen helped Colin drag the screaming young man into the back.

"What's the trouble, Colin?"

"I think he's on LSD or something. He's out of his head."

Behind the paddy wagon, in an unmarked car, sat four members of the San Francisco tactical patrol. One of them jumped from the car and stood, legs apart, challenging anyone to provoke him. The crowd seemed to fear him, because the heckling stopped abruptly. Colin hopped into the cab of the paddy wagon as it rolled down the foggy street to the station house in Golden Gate Park.

Colin Barker had arrived at Park Station, his first and only police post, in early 1967. Already there was resentment among working people, Negro and white, toward Haight-Ashbury hippies, who had caused an increase in rents and a decline in property values as a result of the publicity they generated.

Colin said, "If the whole thing hadn't been publicized, the original hippies and the store owners probably could have gotten along. They weren't really happy about each other, but I think they would have made it all right. Before, when we had a robbery suspect, it was never a hippie. But the scene is all changed now. We're getting a lot of shootings, some stabbings—two people killed last week— robbery, assault.

"There are only a few Flower Children left. Now you've got the juveniles, maybe 16 through 19. They're pitiful, really pitiful. And then there are the political activists who want to overthrow the government, the older guys who sell dope and chase some of the young girls, and the mentally ill. I would say at least 15% of the people I've arrested for one thing or another have either been in a mental institution or were out-patients from some psychiatric clinic. And some of these nuts are on drugs!

"Then the Negro kids from the Fillmore bring phony drugs onto the street. For every piece of legitimate narcotics sold up here, there's four or five times as much phony stuff. If you buy from a stranger, you're either gonna get done in —beat up or your money taken or both—or you'll wind up with phony stuff.

"The hippies just wanted to be left alone. Now it's fashionable to grow a beard and wear weird clothes and say you're a hippie. They're dirty people, that's all."

Unlike his brother, a poet who teaches literature at Harvard, Colin Barker studied economics at a California junior college. "Believe it or not, I asked to work on Haight Street, maybe because I'm dealing with my own generation. I wanted to see what it was like to walk the beat. I've even made friends with guys I've busted for felony charges. Guys say, 'Hey, Colin, what's going on?' and 'Don't bust me again this week, not again—that kind of thing."

But Colin quickly became more defensive and even hostile on the job. One night he and a 22-year-old patrolman named Fred Rennie were walking through the park shortly after 11 p.m. when they heard footsteps in the darkness beyond some foliage. Colin started to his left and Fred to his right, so that they would approach the person from two sides. Suddenly there was a shotgun blast. Shining his flashlight, Colin saw Fred Rennie lying dead on his back. The blast had caught him directly in the face. Ten minutes later the tactical squad picked up two Negro teen-agers as suspects. They also found the shotgun nearby.

Colin's hardening attitude was influenced by his association with Gary Cummings, who was assigned to share his beat. Together they walked the 4 p.m.-to-midnight and midnight-to-8 a.m. shifts in and around Haight Street, occasionally covering a wider area in a prowl car. One night they had an argument in the locker room at Park Station. Gary Cummings, reading a newspaper story about the two youths charged with killing Fred Rennie, remarked, "The two boys are pleading self-defense."

"Self-defense?" Colin cried. "It was outright murder!"

"You know," Gary Cummings said, "there's always the possibility that self-defense might be a valid claim."

"It's plain and simple: Fred was killed by two colored punks, both of whom were known to peddle narcotics in The Haight."

"But there is the possibility," Gary insisted, "that the cop who gets shot by some Negro maybe had threatened the black guy. You don't know if Fred had stopped those same Negro guys two or three times before that night and told them, 'Niggers, if I ever stop you again, I'm gonna blow your heads off.'"

"Look, Gary, what are you trying to say? That Fred Rennie should have been shot? What the hell kind of kick are you on?"

"You know as well as I do!" Gary said, "Fred was famous for planting phony stuff on his prisoners. And you know that when he got shot in the park they looked through his clothing and found about a dozen needles in his pocket. Now, he wasn't using them on himself. And the chances are very good that those two Negro guys knew this about him, and they maybe figured he was going to plant stuff on them illegally."

"Well, why don't you go to court and testify in their behalf?" Colin shouted. "Sounds to me like you're on the opposite side."

Gary Cummings, 26, had been on the force two years before being transferred to Park Station. In appearance and outlook he differed from most of the policemen around him. He wore his black curly hair longer than the other officers and sprinkled his speech with "hip" lingo.

"I became a cop almost on a dare," he said. "I knew a guy from Boston, a very bright guy, and yet he had this sadistic personality. And the cat wanted to be a policeman!

"I was working at a part-time job in San Francisco, and when that got to be too much I quit and went on unemployment. And then that friend of mine from Boston was trying the police department there. He sent me letters about himself, and I thought about it. I didn't really think I could make it. I thought I was too thin. I took the test anyhow, and before I knew it I was in the Police Academy. Next thing I knew I was out in the car, scared to death. I remember the guy I was with trying to tell me, 'Hey, relax, it's not that bad.'

"And it really isn't that bad. Obviously, insurance clerks don't get killed proportionately to policemen, but I'm a little fatalistic about it now."

Before being transferred to Park Station, Gary Cummings was in a San Francisco police station when three white patrolmen from the tactical squad brought in a Negro prisoner. The black man kept saying, "Get your hands off me, you white bastards." The officers said nothing to him, but among themselves, and to Gary, they expressed a desire to "kick his ass."

The prisoner asked to make a call and was allowed to use a public telephone in a corner of the room.

After about five minutes, the sergeant said, "Hey, that guy's been on the phone a long time."

"Then," Gary said, "I saw the cops putting on their lead gloves and they stood there like vultures." As Gary recalled it, one officer went to the booth and said, "Let's go. Hey, Hey! Let's go—get off that phone!"

Startled, the Negro said, "Hey, hold it. Wait a minute, I'm almost through."

Gary said, "As soon as he said, 'Wait a minute,' that was enough." They dragged him out of the phone booth and, according to Gary, five policemen jumped on the prisoner, punching and kicking until he could no longer move.

"I just stood there," Gary remembered, "and at first I was so shocked that I couldn't say anything. Then I found myself shouting at the sergeant. He just looked at me like I was a traitor or something and walked away."

When he was transferred to Park Station, says Gary, "The word was already here. Some sort of reputation had preceded me."

Gary's transfer put him with Colin Barker on foot patrol. Colin explained to his new partner that a foot patrolman in Haight-Ashbury can almost regulate the amount of "business" he generates. "For me," Colin said, "it's an exception to walk through The Haight and not send at least one guy back to the station. The old-timers avoid trouble. A lot of them see something and look the other way."

"Why don't you look the other way?" Gary asked. "You like putting people in jail?"

"No, but it's a matter of selectivity. Sometimes, like I've told guys to move off the steps or out of the street and they've gotten angry. And if they get mean, I have to grab 'em. It's a personal matter, sometimes. With each partner I tend to act differently, because each guy has a special kick, you know?"

"I'll let you know when I find my kick."

"Like one guy I walked with used to be a bus driver, so he always gave out tickets to cars parked in bus zones. When I wasn't with him, I'd never bother with any of that stuff."

The two patrolmen emerged from the winding path of Golden Gate Park and entered the cool sunshine of an uphill lawn, where four Navajo Indians were sprawled on the grass. A young Negro man and a girl with long blonde hair were with the Indians. Some in the group were sleeping, others were eating French fries that had been dumped on a blanket.

Colin and Gary walked up to the group, but no one moved or spoke. Colin pulled back a blanket, revealing a fifth Indian who was embracing a gallon jug of wine. Colin emptied the jug on the grass. "Get up," he said to the Indian. "I want to see you walk." The Indian adjusted his orange headband, stood up and walked a few steps, then stumbled. One by one, Colin made the Indians rise and then take seats on a park bench, where they slumped against each other.

"Look at them," said Colin. "I've locked two of them up before."

Gary said, "Why arrest them? They're not bothering anybody."

"They've helped ruin this park, for one thing," Colin said. "I hope you noticed back there, the way they've left their crud right on the pathways. And look at all that food. No wonder there are rats in the park now."

About 30 yards down the pathway a young man began shouting, "Pig, pig, pig!" His long, sandy hair curled at the shoulders and he wore an unkempt beard. Another young man, dressed in a gray windbreaker and blue jeans, was holding him by the shirt. "Get your hands offa me, goddam narko pig!" The plainclothes narcotics agent slapped him. He fell down and the cop picked him up again. "Nark! Pig!" Colin rushed over and helped bring the screaming young man back to the bench.

The blonde girl gave a dollar bill to each Indian. Strolling away with her Negro companion, she remarked to no one in particular, "My daddy doesn't know it but he just gave his first donation to the American Indian."

The wagon rolled up. One of the Indians, wrapped in a faded pink blanket, began wandering aimlessly away. "Hey!" shouted Colin, grabbing him and steering him back to the wagon. "Get in there, Sam Running Drunk."

"What did this cat do?" Gary asked the narcotics agent, who was pushing his prisoner into the back of the wagon with the Indians.

"He offered to sell me LSD."

Colin and Gary took another pathway near a small pond. Walking toward them was a young Negro who stopped as if he were waiting for the cops to pass. Colin said, "What are you doing in here?"

"Walking, man."

"Put your hands out."

"Oh, no, man . . ." He put his arms straight out. "What was I doing just now 'cept standing, huh?" The black man's voice betrayed a feeling of helplessness. "I ain't done nothing, so I stopped and did absolutely nothing. And still you stop me."

Concluding his frisk, Colin said, "Now, get out of here!"

"I'm going. But I don't know what I'm gonna do with you."

As they walked on, Gary said, "You just made that guy hate your guts, you know that?"

"So what? That's the same type of guy who killed Fred. I've stopped many guys and found guns on 'em. As I've said, the love generation is dead around here."

"Well, exactly how long could you say 'I love you' when you're getting beat by the cops?"

Colin glared. "Sounds like you'll be out there with them next time, throwing the rocks at us."

The evening had been extremely quiet and Colin and Gary were assigned to investigate a complaint that a "noisy party" was going on in the Fillmore, an all-black area.

"Man," Gary exclaimed, "What kind of police call is that?"

"A noisy party could be just about anything," Colin said. "It could be anything from a family fight to a riot."

The patrolmen parked outside a two-story wooden building containing only two apartments. Dozens of young black men, in their late teens and early twenties, were milling about the lawn and sitting on the small wooden porch, drinking wine and beer.

"You know what I really think about this deal?" Colin asked.

"No. What?"

"I think we shouldn't even get out of the car."

"Keep cool, man," Gary urged. "Did you ever think of something like this as an opportunity?"

"An opportunity for what? To get killed?"

"Calm down. I mean an opportunity to give these cats a feeling that all cops really aren't so bad, you know? Just act friendly to them."

"For how long? Listen, we're just gonna walk into trouble. Nothing but black militants out there."

"Come on," Gary said. "We've got to talk to the complainant."

The two cops got out of their car while the black youngsters watched stoically. "Don't walk on the grass," Gary commanded Colin in a near whisper. "You wouldn't do that in a white neighborhood."

They entered a dark hallway with a flight of stairs at the far end, leading to the apartment where the party was taking place. A "soul" record reverberated through the building. Gary knocked on the downstairs apartment door and an elderly Negro woman opened it as far as the chain would allow.

"Police, ma'am. May we come inside?"

"Yes, just a second." She undid the door chain and the cops entered her small living room. "My husband is in the other room," the woman said, "and he can't sleep for the noise up there. He has to be up at four o'clock in the morning for his job. They been having these parties up there every week, it seems to me. Me and my husband are too old, and. . . ."

"Look," Gary interrupted. "I'll go up there and talk to whoever is giving the party, and I'll ask him if he'll turn down the noise a little bit. Do you know the name of the guy who lives up there?"

"His name is Robert Ellis."

"Bobby Ellis?" Colin asked.

"Yeah, I know, cause I seen his mail."

Colin turned to Gary and said, "Bobby Ellis is head of that black student union. He's militant as hell." Gary said nothing.

Starting for the stairs in the hall, Gary said, "Come on, will you?"

When they reached a landing, Gary paused to look out the side window. Down in the darkness he saw two young black men leaning against the patrol car.

"Oh, man," Gary said. "I left the doors unlocked. I just hope to hell they haven't taken the shotgun out of the car."

"Boy, you are an idiot, you know that?" Colin felt his gun. "If I see one of these guys with that shotgun . . ."

"What will you do? Start a shoot-out like the Wild West? Come on, we'll just go down to the car and check it."

Some 25 young men were outside, watching. Gary looked in the back seat; the shotgun was there.

"Okay," he said. "I'll lock the doors and then we'll go back."

"Forget it," said Colin. "I'm not going up there again. If something breaks out we wouldn't have a chance."

"Okay, buddy, I'll tell you what. Put in a call and ask for one more car to back us up while we go upstairs."

Colin hesitated, then slipped into the driver's seat and reached for the microphone under the dashboard. "They've cut it out of the car! They've cut the goddam microphone! It's gone! We can't even call for help!"

"Colin, buddy, we don't need any help—not yet, anyway, so relax a minute, will you?"

"Let's get out of here."

"So they cut out the microphone, what's the big deal? It was done in a Halloween spirit."

"You must be kidding," Colin said from inside the car.

"Hey, hey! Before I was a policeman, when I was a kid? And when I saw an empty police car? Listen, I had to resist like hell so as not to take the car for a ride or something. It's the same with these guys."

Colin got out of the car and looked at the Negro youngsters, who seemed unconcerned. Almost to himself, Gary said, "Goddam, now when we go back to the station tonight I'll have to make a report explaining why that microphone got cut out of the car."

"Well, let's just get out of here," Colin urged.

Gary handed Colin a dime and said, "Go across the street to that bar and call Communications. Ask for another car."

"All right," Colin muttered, taking the dime and running across to the tavern. In minutes the car radio crackled and Gary heard the dispatcher saying, "Attention all units, all units, we got a 904 Code Two, all units . . ." Gary stood in shock as he heard his location cited as a major trouble spot.

As Colin emerged from the tavern, sirens could already be heard. Then came the whirling red lights as five cars pulled into the block.

"What the hell's going on?" Gary screamed to Colin. A sixth car and a seventh rolled up. "What the hell did you tell them?"

"I just said we needed help right away."

"Well, damn! Those guys are coming from everywhere!" Almost crying with embarrassment, Gary said, "All these cars—and nothing has happened!" Then from the house came Bobby Ellis, a slightly-built, clear-eyed young man in a yellow windbreaker. Gary walked up and began to apologize, but Ellis, his black beret tipped forward proudly, shook his head.

"Nobody talks to nobody," Ellis said, "not with all this pig out here. What is all this?"

Gary swallowed: "Uh, you got a noisy party up there."

"Well, God damn," Bobby Ellis said, "you didn't have to call out the whole police force, did you?" The other black youngsters began yelling, "Honkies! Pigs!"

Almost whispering, Gary said, "Listen, man, this was a mistake. I apologize."

The heckling grew more angry in tone, but Ellis seemed in complete control. "What do you want?" he asked.

"Nothing," said Gary. "Just a little less noise. This ain't a bust or anything."

"Okay. I'll quiet the party down if you can get all these cops out of here. Can you do that?"

After a moment, Gary said, "Yeah, I'll get 'em out of here." He walked back to the car where Colin was talking to the Sergeant. "God damn it, sergeant," Gary yelled. "Get those policemen out of here!"

"You sure everything's okay?"

"It won't be okay if these guys stay here much longer."

The sergeant returned to his car, went on the air and told all the units to return to wherever they had come from. The patrolmen, almost reluctantly, walked back to their cars, a chorus of jeers at their backs.

The next day, Gary placed a phone call to Bobby Ellis. "Ellis told me," Gary said, "that there were still a couple of those patrol cars riding around that area for hours, harassing every goddam kid who left that party."

There was at least one thing about which Gary and Colin had similar feelings: next to members of the Tactical Patrol Force, both men felt like sensitive social workers. Unlike the two young patrolmen, both weighing under 160 pounds, the tactical police are mostly above average in height and weight. They wear impressive black leather jackets, white crash helmets and big gun belts with equipment that jangles as they stride. They cruise in unmarked cars, two men in front and two in back; in the station house they stay together, enjoying their status as an elite group.

Early one evening Gary and Colin were in a corner of the station house watching three tactical cops getting ready to charge outside for the beginning of a shift. They were waiting impatiently for a fourth to come down from the locker room. One was clapping his hands together and rocking up and down on his feet. A partner suddenly threw him a black leather glove and barked, "Think fast!" The cop caught the glove, shouted "Hey!" and tossed it back.

"They have so much damn energy," Colin said. "I went to a house call with that guy," he said, pointing to the cop who was smacking his hands together. "He doesn't walk upstairs; he runs."

The fourth member of the squadron nimbly descended the stairs and shouted, "Ready?"

"Right!"

They put on their white helmets and strode outside.

"They act like they're constantly on riot duty," Gary said.

"They're great for riots, though," said Colin. "If you want a display of force, if you need that display, they're it. But I have to agree—they're kind of like animals."

"Well," Gary admitted, "they probably do serve a need. Obviously, in certain tough situations you don't need a bunch of policemen who are as disorganized as the rioters. My only complaint is that they don't have enough emphasis on restraint."

"Well, whenever I'm in trouble I'm glad to see them around," said Colin.

A tactical patrol returned. A young Negro, arms handcuffed behind his back, sailed headfirst into the room landing on the floor. His friend, also handcuffed, was shoved down on the bench so hard that his head snapped against the wall.

His dark glasses fell from one ear and dangled on his face. A huge tactical cop took one step and kicked the man on the floor.

"Take these cuffs offa me!" he screamed. "I'll fight!"

Three members of the patrol smiled as their prisoner managed to stand. "Why don't you shoot me!" he pleaded. "If I had a gun I'd shoot you." He was thrown toward the window and held there while another cop felt through his clothing.

"How old are you?" asked the sergeant from behind the window.

"I'm 18! White man! Knocking me down, for nothing! Never in my life . . .! If you're gonna kill me, why don't you just kill me!"

He was thrown toward the bench. He fell, still shouting, alongside his friend. He stood up, struggling with the handcuffs behind him, and charged at the tactical police. Again he was hurled against the bench.

"YOU'RE A PRISONER, CLOWN! YOU DO WHAT YOU'RE TOLD!"

Gary walked over to the tac police. "What's going on, fellas?"

"What's it to you?"

"Hey, man, I'm a policeman like you. I just thought I'd find out why you're kicking this guy's ass." Gary added, "I just want to find out what side I'm on."

"Listen, Cummings," said the sergeant, "there's only one side of the story —our side."

The middle-aged restaurant proprietress seemed glad to see Gary and Colin. She had been held up a few nights before "by three Mexican-Indian types."

"How much did they get?" asked Gary.

"About $90. If you boys had come in here, they would have killed you. You wouldn't have had a chance."

"Did all three have guns?"

"Two of 'em did for sure."

The two patrolmen ate a large, inexpensive dinner of chicken and rice. As they left the restaurant, a girl came up and informed the patrolmen that a man in a parked car was exposing himself. She led them to a small red car on Haight Street. Colin rapped at the window and motioned for the well-dressed man to step out. "He's the kind who makes speeches about young people being sick," said the girl. "And look at him! He's perverted!" Colin politely asked the man what he was doing in Hippieville. The man shrugged. "Arrest him!" the girl demanded.

Colin said, "The girl says you were exposing yourself."

"No, I didn't do that."

"Liar!" the girl yelled.

"I think you'd better leave this area," Colin said as the man jumped back into his car.

"We could have arrested that guy," Gary said.

"I checked his driver's license," Colin said. "Lots of credit cards. He might be a big shot. A perverted big shot. He'd be out on bail and we'd be in hot water."

The cops heard a call, "Officer! Officer!" From a side street ran a squat, middle-aged woman.

"Take your time," Gary said.

She caught her breath: "I heard a girl yelling. Just a block down."

"On the street, was she?"

"No, no. Up in the house. Something about a man holding a gun on her."

"Okay, okay," said Colin. "We'll follow you." The woman nodded, still breathing heavily as she led the way. She pointed to the second floor of a Victorian home and said, "Up there."

The cops went to the second floor. They heard a girl's voice: "I see my mother. Hello, Mom! Don't let the bad men take me away. La, la, la." Colin knocked on the door and the girl screamed, "They're coming!"

Colin tried to push open the door, but it was locked. "Open up! Police!"

A bearded, shirtless man with a medallion around his neck greeted them. The girl screamed again.

"What's going on?" Gary asked.

"She's high, man. Real high. She's not harming anyone." The girl screamed again. White and naked, she was dancing about and apparently having drug-induced hallucinations. "Don't go near her," the man pleaded.

"Shut up," Colin ordered. "Hey," he called to the girl. "Are you all right?"

The girl stopped dancing—there was no music—and stared at Colin. She turned away, looked back at Colin's uniform and rushed straight into a window, splashing glass. Instantly Colin was behind her, pulling her by the legs back over the broken glass. Gary covered her with a shirt and helped her to stand. Colin called for a patrol car and an ambulance.

"You shouldn't have gone in there," said the bearded man. "You had no right. She wasn't harming anybody."

"Not much," Colin snapped.

"You had no . . ."

"Shut your fat head."

Somehow the girl managed to wriggle into a sacklike dress. Blood dripped down her legs. The man demanded to be taken with the girl in the ambulance.

"You're going to the station," Colin told him.

"What for? You won't find any acid on me, man!"

"Then get the hell out of here!" Colin said. "No, stay here!"

The two patrolmen searched the apartment but found no drugs.

Back on the street Colin angrily kicked the sidewalk. "These kids," he said. "Sometimes they don't even know what they've put inside themselves. I asked a kid once and he said, "No, I don't know what I shot up with. If it kills me, so what? Dying might be a good trip."

Four young men were sitting on stairs, almost hidden by shadow. Colin splashed his flashlight beam across their faces. "How're you doing, fellas?" There was no answer, so he added, "I'd like to see your IDs." Three of the young men immediately reached for their wallets, while the fourth, wearing a bright-gold blouse and shoulder-length hair, seemed upset. Gary checked the identification cards of the other three and the nervous boy walked to the sidewalk, fishing a crumpled pink paper from his pocket.

Colin trained his flashlight on the pink sheet and the boy said, "You can't arrest me."

Colin had no intention of arresting him, but he asked, "Why can't I?"

"Because I'm a juvenile."

Without warning the boy sprinted across the street. Instantly Colin was on his heels. Gary ordered the others to get off the steps and stand facing the wall as he watched Colin's pursuit. The fleeing boy reached a small grass embankment, tripped and fell. He wheeled and Colin drew his gun. The boy, luckily for himself, froze.

After Colin had called for the wagon, he asked the handcuffed boy some questions.

"Where do you live?"

"Anywhere."

"What's your name?"

"Jingle Bells."

"Occupation?"

"I'm a tourist attraction."

"Are you a student?" Colin shouted the question.

"No! I'm a juvenile!"

Colin pushed his hand against the back of the boy's head, smashing his face into a garage door.

"And on the side," the boy said defiantly, "I keep a lookout for police brutality."

"I should have shot your face off over there," Colin told him.

Later Colin said, "We had had two murders in the week and, for all I knew, this was the kid that did it. He could have had a gun. How would I know?"

Next evening, Colin and Gary returned to the same cafe to order the same meal of chicken and rice. Right down the street, a plainclothes narcotics agent was "buying" some acid from two black dealers from Oakland. As soon as the transaction was made, he said, "You're under arrest." The agent moved quickly, handcuffing the men together and using a box nearby to call for a patrol car.

The dealers broke loose and ran around the corner, ducking into a saloon. The black owner told them to leave. Then the radio car pulled up and two officers, plus the undercover man, attempted to drag the prisoners out of the bar.

In 30 seconds most of the Haight knew something big was on. Colin and Gary heard the sirens and dashed toward the crowd, leaving their half-eaten dinner behind.

Colin went to a rooftop to prevent people from throwing things and Gary mingled with the people on the street, trying to calm things down. "I'm up there watching the action," Colin said later, "and as soon as the cops left, the crowd started throwing more bottles, bricks, sticks—every kind of thing—at cars . . . they hit a couple of buses real good. The most frustrating thing is to be in a position where you can see people doing things that are absolutely wrong, and being totally helpless.

"Many people were just spectators. So one group started smashing windows in the store directly underneath me! What was I gonna do? Shoot 10 people standing down below because they're burglarizing a store?"

The riot ended with a "sweep" by tactical cops. Afterwards Gary brought the following allegation, printed in an underground paper, to Colin's attention:

"The cops who had arrested us took us into the interrogation room, closed the door and proceeded to methodically, carefully and skillfully beat us up. . . . The cops concentrated on my kidneys, chest and groin."

"The other side to that story," Colin said, "is that the kids wanted the police to beat them up. Many of them tried their best to make the police break the law."

To Gary it had been "a bad scene." He said, "These kids have made police brutality a part of their lives. I think it helps them to identify with black people.

"And here we get into the personality of the cop, which is something that's not supposed to matter. But some guys, they don't care if it's a Negro or not. Some guys just like to whip a guy's head.

"They have to put caliber people in these kinds of areas who are willing to take whatever crap is flying and try to apply some imagination to it and turn it around. A cat you send to any area that is explodable should be your most talented person, not your most off-balance.

"Meanwhile," Gary sighed, "it's as if Haight-Ashbury was an arena, with the kids on one side and the cops on the other, while the rest of society just sits back and chooses sides."

QUESTIONS FOR DISCUSSION AND DIALOGUE

1. What does Officer Barker's handling of the "perverted big shot" situation say about the "law and order" issue in an area like Haight-Ashbury?
2. Reread the "noisy party" situation. What does it tell you about police-community relationships in areas like Haight-Ashbury? Discuss.
3. Reread the "four Navajo Indians" situation. Officer Barker wanted to arrest them. Officer Cummings evidently did not. Who was right? Why? Discuss.
4. Outline the pros and cons of the following debate proposition: "Resolved, Officer Colin Barker demonstrates professional police behavior more than Officer Gary Cummings."

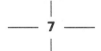

FBI Report Makes Our Insecurities Understandable

James E. Clayton

This consideration of the police as nonpolitical influentials concludes with a short review of the FBI's 1968 report on crime in the United States. The dramatic statistical increases in all categories of the "crime index" which includes "murder, rape, robbery, aggravated assault, burglary, larceny of more than $50.00 and auto theft" are not accounted for by some of the most commonly heard simplistic explanations. In spite of the observation that "there are lies, damned lies, and statistics", these statistics, especially about juvenile crime, fit into a confused picture of Americans living through one of the most complicated revolutionary periods in American history.

The FBI's annual report on crime in the United States, published a few weeks ago, is a dreadful document—dreadful because of what it reveals about everyday life in this country.

Anyone who wades through the pages of statistics has to recognize that there is nothing phony about the sense of insecurity that leads to department store displays of window and door locking devices and newspaper advertisements of trained watchdogs.

Simply put, the report says that in the 57 cities with populations of more than 250,000 one major crime was committed last year for every 22 residents. Elsewhere in the country, there was one major crime for every 62 residents.

This count is based on what the FBI calls the crime index. It includes murder, rape, robbery, aggravated assault, burglary, larceny of more than $50 and auto theft. Since larceny and auto theft hardly strike the same note of terror as the others, what might be called the fear index is not uniformly quite so high. But it is high enough.

Even after eliminating those two categories, one of the remaining crimes was committed for every 41 residents in the big cities and for every 114 residents elsewhere.

If those raw numbers aren't sufficiently disturbing, what underlies them must be. You learn by studying the report that almost half—49%—of all persons charged with committing a major crime in 1968 were juveniles, that a quarter of those arrested for major thefts were not yet 15 years old, that the number of juveniles arrested for all offenses (except traffic) has doubled since 1960 while the number of adults arrested has increased by only 4%, and that there was one arrest of a teen-ager last year for every 16 in the nation.

Probe deeper and you learn something about the conditions that led to all this crime. You discover, for instance, that robbery is a crime occurring primarily in big cities, that murder and assault are Southern crimes, that theft is the most popular crime where population is rapidly growing or where tourist traffic is heavy and that the arrests of juveniles are increasing in the suburbs at a slightly faster clip than they are in the cities.

The report also points up the great variations between cities of the same size and between similar metropolitan areas, some of which have logical explanations and some of which do not. Philadelphia, Boston and Cleveland have lower crime rates, for example, than New York, the District of Columbia and Los Angeles. But the metropolitan areas of Washington, Chicago and St. Louis have lower crime rates than those of San Francisco, Baltimore and Detroit.

There are, of course, some problems with reading the FBI's data too literally. Not all jurisdictions categorize crimes the same way nor do all police forces report accurately. For that matter, many crimes are never reported to the police in the first place.

There is, most likely, an annual upward bias in the FBI's figures if for no reasons other than better reporting techniques, and the discovery by police chiefs that they can report increases in crime without being fired. But even that doesn't really change the trend. The FBI was told of 2 million major crimes in 1960 and of 4.4 million in 1968; even an error of 25% on the high side (far too large an error to assume) wouldn't change the terrifying aspects of those two numbers. It would still mean that the number of crimes per capita has increased by 50% in eight years.

This increase has not been uniform in different kinds of crimes. Those involving money, particularly robbery and major larceny, have increased much more rapidly than those involving personal injury. In 1960, there were four robberies for each murder or rape; last year there were six, yet the frequency of murder or rape had increased from one per 7,000 residents to one per 4,400 residents.

Underlying all this is the story of the juveniles. The number of them charged with crimes of violence—murder, rape, robbery and assault—was up 125% since 1960. More juveniles than adults were arrested last year on larceny, burglary or auto theft. Almost a fourth of all persons arrested for any major crime were under 15. The median age of those arrested for burglary was 17, for larceny 17, for auto theft 17, for robbery 20, for rape 22.

This surge in juvenile crime is not coming just in the slums and adjoining parts of big cities. Crime rates went up as much in the suburbs as they did in the cities last year and the percentage of juveniles among those charged with serious crimes is somewhat higher in the suburbs than in the cities.

Most of the juvenile crime, naturally, involves boys, 75% of it. But last year the number of girls arrested for major crimes increased at precisely the same rate as the number of boys. Interestingly enough, twice as many white juveniles as black were arrested for major thefts and almost twice as many blacks as whites for crimes of violence. White juveniles were arrested for major crimes not only more frequently in the suburbs (6 out of 7) but also in the cities (3 out of 5).

Add to these statistics the greater difficulty the police say they now have in solving crime and the picture becomes even bleaker. Last year, the FBI reports, less than two out of every 10 thefts was solved, less than three out of every 10 robberies, and less than six out of 10 rapes. Seven years ago, the clearance rate was three out of 10 thefts, four out of 10 robberies, and seven out of 10 rapes.

The FBI offers no solutions to this crime problem in its report. Its only hopeful comment is that the rate of increase in the number of policemen surpassed the rate of population growth last year for the first time since 1960. That is something—but not much.

QUESTIONS FOR DISCUSSION AND DIALOGUE

1. Select any two statistical increases in crime from this summary of the 1968 FBI crime report and explain why these increases occurred. (The last few articles will be helpful here.)
2. What do these statistics indicate about the exaggeration and over-simplification of some politicians who use such terms as "soft on crime" and "coddling criminals"? Discuss.

3. What conclusion does the "story of the juveniles" in this article lead you to? What are the implications for the institutions of society other than the police and courts from the "story of the juveniles"? Discuss.

— 8 —

The Unbalance of Our Times

Seyom Brown

The "Unbalance" that Brown discusses in his essay-review of Robert MacIver's works is between "arid social science" and "mushy polemics". This article advocates social scientists who are a combination of scientist and philospher, and who come to grips with "the central philosophical questions: the essential nature of man and his good."

Seyom Brown is Senior Fellow at The Brookings Institution and author of "The Faces of Power."

The most basic questions of politics and society are being raised by the young and inadequately answered by their immediate elders. The middle generation of political scientists and sociologists—now in control of the prestigious university departments and academic journals—reacted in its youth against the big-picture approach of the social philosophers who then held sway. Having won its battle, this middle generation has instituted a social *science* concerned primarily with how the various institutions of society work, not whether they are worth preserving; the measurement of popular beliefs and election results, not the larger social consequences of the victory of various social philosophies; the "inputs" to decision-making, not the evaluation of alternative policies.

In this climate, with arid social science issuing from the halls of academia, and mushy polemics issuing from those who are storming the halls, how heartening it is to encounter the latest volume of essays by eighty-seven-year-old Robert M. MacIver. And yet how sad.

Edited by David Spitz, *Politics and Society* (Atherton Press, 571 pp., $11.50), a retrospective of MacIver's best shorter pieces, some of them previously unpublished, shows this renowned teacher at his most politically pertinent but, with respect to prevailing social science fashions, most academically irrelevant. It is refreshing to realize that the timely subject of the competing claims of social order and individual conscience can be analyzed with precision and profundity; and it is exciting to find that MacIver's essays on this theme that were written between 1905 and 1912 grasp the jugular of today's controversies. But it is sad to realize that similar pieces probably would be rejected for publication today by the *American Sociological Review* or the *American Political Science Review*—not because the essays lack contemporary social significance, but because they are methodologically old hat. This is doubly sad when one recalls that Robert MacIver was a leader in the efforts of the 1920s and 1930s to make the study of society more scientific.

He stimulated his students and colleagues to make better use of tangible behavioral data. But he also sensed the dangers in their trying too hard for scientific purity—the fascination with technique over substance, with formal neat mathematical statement over social pertinence, with the narrowly framed research question (where the evidence was something that could be counted) over the wide-ranging issue on which speculative discourse was still in order. MacIver warned that the tendency to falsely equate science with the techniques developed in the natural sciences would dehumanize the social sciences. His 1938 essay "The Social Sciences," reprinted now in *Politics and Society,* is one of the most eloquent statements in the literature on the consequences of such distorted scientism.

Although the trend went against him, MacIver continued to write and teach in the tradition of pertinent social inquiry, aiming to illuminate, rather than to categorize and measure as definitive, the essential but ever-changing relationships of human society. He would continue to search for the "more inclusive and meaningful" facts where knowledge "is always relative and never fully attained." The simple fact of Caesar having crossed the Rubicon, says MacIver, was a "mere act of locomotion." The social scientist should be interested in Caesar's imperial ambition and the tangle of conditions that gave it play, and its impact on the further course of human life. "These things are not in the public record. You cannot photograph Caesar's ambition on a sensitive plate. You cannot see it or interpret it except in the light of your own discernment."

The light of the discernment of men with the scope and depth of MacIver is precisely what one misses so much now when the social fabric appears to be pulling apart at the seams. Who today has the discerning light—and intellectual courage—to set down in writing a comprehensive analysis of the social fabric and its relationships to government, as MacIver did twenty-two years ago in *The Web of Government?*

David Spitz, MacIver's dedicated disciple and editor, did well to make the theme of *The Web of Government*—which will likely be the author's most lasting work—the leitmotif of the essays in *Politics and Society.* The rights and obligations of the individual in relation to the many individuals and groups he affects and is affected by, and (especially as transmitted through the instruments of government) the rights and obligations of the many with respect to the individual are in urgent need of clarification.

How does MacIver discern these rights and obligations?

Unabashedly more the philosopher than the social scientist, he comes to grips with the central philosophical questions: the essential nature of man, and his good. These questions are not the sort that should be taken for granted by him who would advance a particular social or political philosophy. MacIver thought about them intensively before spinning his theories on the web of government, and then continued to relate his social science inquiries to them.

Both questions—the nature of man, and his good—find MacIver humble before the variety of answers mankind has offered, not humble because he thinks that any of them are better than those he has worked out for himself, but rather because he understands that we still know only a fragment of what we need to comprehend before we can answer these questions with justifiable confidence. Yet we live in social and political systems that imply a lot about the nature of man, and what is good for him; we fashion laws and debate the merits of reforms and revolutions as if we were totally aware. It is this very paradox, that we know so little and yet must choose between competing ways of life as if omniscient, that lies at the base of MacIver's analyses of the limits of one individual's claim upon another, and the claims of the larger society upon the individual.

The paradox of our ignorance, coupled with our need to decide, drives MacIver back to the "Golden Rule" as the ethical basis for his social philosophy. *Do to others as you would have them do to you,* claims MacIver, "is the only rule that stands by itself in the light of its own reason, the only rule that can stand by itself in the naked, warring universe, in the face of the contending values of men and groups." Thus the ethical philosopher is led, through his humility, to rely on a rule of procedure—which is the realm of politics—but procedure leavened by empathy.

Social and political systems cannot enforce such a rule throughout their jurisdictions, but they can by their design either facilitate its widest application or negate the rule by rewarding those who consistently violate its spirit.

The central virtue of the democratic political process, MacIver shows, is that it asks each individual to require of himself no more but no less than he expects of others. It asks that he adhere to the outcome of the procedure whereby a choice between conflicting courses of action is made on the basis of popular preference. The democratic political process does not demand that he change his views on what is the best decision, or abandon his efforts to get a decision reversed, only that he accept the outcome of the basic procedure, and rely on the same basic procedure to gain a different outcome.

The political institutions of a democracy must respect the limitations on their authority—that is, they must not attempt to compel belief; but the individual citizen is expected to respect the laws freely arrived at through the essential democratic procedures. Without such mutual restraint the whole system would crumble.

The attempt by a majority to control the beliefs of the whole society would undermine the democratic system, which assumes an opportunity to hear, debate, and freely deliberate alternative courses of action. Minorities cannot be expected to tolerate majority suppression of these conditions of democratic choice (even if approved by a majority), since it is only through attempting to change the beliefs of the majority that a discontented minority can hope to get a better break within the system. "Since human beings are always variant," writes MacIver, "the common is likely to be more securely established if its guardians do not demand the complete conformity that contradicts or suppresses such differences as are not irreconcilable with the basic unity."

Minorities without hope of peaceful change within the system will eventually grasp at opportunities to subvert the system itself. Thus the Bill of Rights, restricting the authority of the majority to limit freedom of expression and assembly, is a practical bulwark of the peaceful society.

However, MacIver will not please those looking for philosophical rationalizations for "doing their own thing" whenever and wherever they please. To equate freedom with an absence of restraint, he shows, is to be guilty of the frequent error of posing a simple antithesis between the realm of liberty and the realm of law.

MacIver demonstrates this argument to be patently fallacious. It is true, he says, that "every law restrains *some* liberty for *some.* But in so doing it may well establish some other liberty for some others—or indeed for all. The law that forbids an employer to dismiss a worker because he joins a trade union gives the worker a liberty that, as a worker, he lacked before. The law that forbids another to trespass on my property assures me the liberty to enjoy my property."

Every law restrains some liberty, but this does not mean that the fewer laws a society has, the greater its liberty. Rather, the exercise of liberty unrestrained by a legal system would lead to an increase in relationships based on brute force; since certain liberties are incompatible with one another, without an agreed-upon basis for settling conflicts among interests those individuals and groups who were most adept at coercing others would get their way.

MacIver is not content just to point out these basic relationships, but moves on to the complicated yet essential question: "What combination of liberties and restraints is most serviceable for the existence of what men seek when they place a high value on liberty?"

It is on this question that MacIver dwelled for the most productive portion of his mature years, developing his concept of "The Multigroup Society." Society, he points out, is more than the state. "Society exists wherever and insofar as human beings recognize any sort of community with one another and in any way organize themselves for the sake of common life or the furtherance of common ends. . . . The greater our individuality, the more societies does it demand for its satisfaction." Society has a "multitudinous spontaneous activity which is largely undetermined by the political order."

Thus, the state is one among other societies—"fundamental, necessary, and the most authoritative, but neither alone fundamental nor alone necessary." The survival of the political order is often an essential condition for the ability of man to realize his nature as a social animal, and for men to pursue their frequently conflicting interests without doing violence to one another's personality. But the ever dynamic web of social relationships can outgrow the particular state; the geographic scope and legal system identified with a particular state may be inadequate to comprehend the real community relationships that have come into being.

In such cases other values may have to supersede those of preservation of the state. This is often the fate of the state whose legal/political order is structured for the purpose of intervening in and controlling those aspects of life subject to great variation. Too many individual wills are offended, too many groups feel put upon by the state's command, and ultimately a major segment of the citizenry becomes alienated from those institutions from which the commands issue. (Public school officials who foolishly attempt to enforce standards of dress and hair styles in the face of fluctuating tastes should read their MacIver.)

In large measure the reason for the resilience of the American democratic system has been its adaptability to the multigroup nature of modern society. Indeed, the philosophical basis of the American democracy was, from the outset, that of limited government: separation of church and state; restrictions on legislation that would compel belief, interfere with freedom of association, or suppress the interplay of ideas. Then why the crisis of American democracy that we are experiencing today? Why has the government, even "the system" *per se,* become so unpopular? Why are the young taking to the streets, and to physical coercion, to effect change?

It is not enough to point to the sluggishness of government in responding to the new awareness of the disadvantaged. The American democracy *is* sluggish to respond, and those deprived have a right to mobilize pressure for change, but disparities have existed in the past, demands for their rectification have been shrill before, and the system has ultimately been adapted with ameliorants for the socio-economic ills, and with greater political power for upwardly mobile groups. There is no reason to assume that it cannot again change, to accommodate the new social forces produced by pockets of poverty amid plenty.

Nor is it a sufficient explanation to point to the widespread souring on bigness and vast centralized institutions. The "post-industrial" American society *is* experiencing widespread alienation of individuals from the mammoth bureaucracies of government. But the traditions of federalism, localism, and decentralization are highly compatible with a healthy, however belated, experimental adaptation of the political system to the craving for more direct impact by citizens on the institutional policies that affect their daily lives—call it "participatory democracy" or what you will. Here too there are grounds for impatience with the slowness of the American political system, which nevertheless should be able to respond to the new social forces without discarding its Constitutional framework.

MacIver digs deeper to seek the sources of the "the unbalance of our times," as he calls it. He traces the shrillness of discontent, and the resort to philosophies and tactics that seem to violate the fundamental respect for persons, to the shock of awareness that millions can be blotted out in a holocaust that makes "no distinction of age or sex, of valor or cowardice, of good or evil." And for what purpose the annihilation? For the settling of conflicts over interests surely of lesser value than the survival of mankind itself. Yet we are prepared to go to the brink of this holocaust, and justify our and our adversaries' preparations to do so, because of the lack of a system for handling conflicts among nations analogous to the system we demand within the nation.

Reading MacIver's essays, one becomes intensely aware of the irony of our present situation. A multigroup community is rapidly forming on an international scale at a very time that the paranoid fears of military inferiority on the part of most nations drive political leaders to glorify the nation in arms and to condemn internationalist pacifism as antithetical to the security of that which we value.

MacIver insists that the security of what we value—the opportunity to implement the Golden Rule in interpersonal relationships, coupled with the opportunity for individual persons to develop their own potentials—is increasingly more realizable in associations that transcend the nation-state than in those identified with it.

Social forces have today outpassed the boundaries of states, claims MacIver. "Society gaining freedom within the territorial state of the modern world passes also beyond its borders. For society has no frontiers, no limitation. . . . The greatest social phenomenon of the present age is the expansion of society beyond the limits of any one state . . ., but as yet we have failed to bring our political thought in accord with this development."

Nations are becoming intersocialized. "Each country is becoming more and more bound up with the welfare of each." And the lines of social grouping and stratification tend less and less to conform to established political boundaries. These basic social forces, driven powerfully by the advances in science, especially those resulting in new communications and transportation linkages among peoples, are producing a new civilization. To those who comprehend this civilization —this multigroup global society—war between nation-states has become unintelligible. (It is only understandable as "civil war.")

The spread of this new civilization, the perception of its reality and the identification of millions with it "will someday make war impossible." But, recognizes MacIver, "the unintelligible often has a long life, in politics at any rate. Meanwhile the burden of an inferior civilization retards the steps of its successor."

If those currently tearing at "the system" were fully conscious of the meaning of their own acts, they might sense and constructively ride the progressive undercurrent of the times that MacIver illuminates, instead of getting seduced by those who preach a return to pre-technological forms of social organization.

QUESTIONS FOR DISCUSSION AND DIALOGUE

1. Why does Brown claim the *American Sociological Review* or the *American Political Science Review* would probably reject some of the best articles written by Robert MacIver? Do you think social science should concentrate more on measuring and categorizing or interpreting and philosophizing? Why? Discuss.
2. In discussing the middle path of exerting authority yet not going to the extreme "of intervening in and controlling those aspects of life subject to great variation", Brown offers this comment:

"Public school officials who foolishly attempt to enforce standards of dress and hair styles in the face of fluctuating tastes should read their MacIver."

What does he mean? Do you agree? Why?

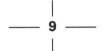

The Selling of the President 1968, Joe McGinniss

Book Review by Herbert J. Teison

First, the court, then the police and academic nonpolitical influentials were considered in this chapter. This and the next article sample two different kinds of press influentials. Joe McGinniss, whose book *The Selling of the President 1968* is reviewed by Herbert J. Teison here, is certainly not a "value-free" observer. For that matter, neither is his reviewer, Herbert Teison! But in their evaluations both McGinniss and Teison illustrate how the press exercises its influences on politics. The reader again might find a review of William H. Stringer's "Whose Facts Do You Read?" (Chapter One) helpful here.

In the Spring of 1968, Joe McGinniss, a twenty-six-year-old former sports writer and columnist for the *Philadelphia Inquirer,* learned through an account-executive friend that the Doyle Dane Bernbach advertising agency intended "to turn Hubert H. Humphrey into Abraham Lincoln" by election time. McGinniss thought he would like to document this ambitious feat in a book. But apparently DDB had other thoughts; it would't let McGinness get close.

Undaunted, the author put a dime into a pay-station phone and called Harry Treleaven, previously a vice president at J. Walter Thompson and at the time of the call in charge of advertising for the Nixon campaign. Certainly, they would be willing to talk to him about covering the Nixon side of the campaign. Could he come over? The result is *The Selling of the President 1968.*

From it the reader gathers that the Nixon campaign managers not only accepted Mr. McGinniss's presence; they enthusiastically expressed to him their innermost thoughts and apparently showered him with confidential memos. Although they must have tacitly assumed that Mr. McGinniss's book would offer a sympathetic view and that their self-compromising remarks would be omitted, they were wrong on both counts. Mr. McGinniss quotes paragraph after paragraph of obviously embarrassing statements, and includes the confidential memos *in toto.*

What must be equally unsettling to those who were involved in Mr. Nixon's bid for the Presidency is the book's detailed reportage of the theatrical machinery that led to victory. With wit, insight and a low-key sense of irony, McGinniss takes the reader backstage at a Nixon TV "special" in Chicago on the first day of the campaign. The press had been excluded because a top strategist of the Nixon campaign, Frank Shakespeare, formerly of CBS and now director of the U.S. Information Agency, wanted them kept out.

"It's a television show," McGinniss quotes Shakespeare as saying. "Our television show. And the press has no business on the set. And goddammit. . . . the problem is that this is an electronic election. The first there's ever been. TV has the power now. Some of the guys get arrogant and rub the reporters' faces in it and then the reporters get pissed and go out of their way to rap anything they consider staged for TV. . . . You let them in with the regular audience and they see the warmup. They see Jack Rourke (a production assistant) out there telling the audience to applaud and to mob Nixon at the end, and that's all they'd write about. . . ."

McGinniss, who was, of course, accepted as part of the scene, describes in great detail and with a fresh and compelling style what the newspapermen were not allowed even to see.

The Chicago "special" was actually the first of ten one-hour panel shows that would be produced individually and go on the air live around the country. A small panel would put questions to the candidate, and a studio audience would, according to McGinniss, be invited in "to cheer Nixon's answers and make it seem to home viewers that enthusiasm for his candidacy was all but uncontrollable."

The strategy behind the series, he says, was that each show would only be seen by the people who lived in a particular area. "This meant it made no difference if Nixon's statements—for they were not really answers—were exactly the same, phrase for phrase, gesture for gesture from state to state. Only the press would be bored, and the press had been written off already. So Nixon could get through the campaign with a dozen or so carefully worded responses that would cover all the problems of America in 1968."

The person responsible for the panel series and virtually all the rest of Richard Nixon's commercial TV appearances was Roger Ailes, who had been executive producer of *The Mike Douglas Show*. McGinniss shows Ailes—at that time twenty-eight—as an irreverent highly competent technician whose primary interest was to produce shows that would not only make the candidate look good but would keep the TV audience awake. Ailes's biggest problem, McGinniss says, was with the panel. Shakespeare, Treleaven and Leonard Garment, who was a partner in Nixon's law firm and is now Special Assistant to the President, had felt it essential to have a "balanced" group. "First, this meant a Negro. One Negro. Not two. Two would be offensive to whites, perhaps to Negroes as well. Two would be trying too hard. . . . Texas would be tricky, though. Do you have a Negro *and* a Mexican-American. . . .?

"Besides the Negro, the panel for the first show included a Jewish attorney, the president of a Polish-Hungarian group, a suburban housewife, a businessman, a representative of the white lower middle class, and, for authenticity, two newsmen. . . .

But then someone had called from New York and insisted that he add a farmer. A farmer for Christ's sake. Roger Ailes had been born in Ohio, but even so he knew you did not want a farmer on a television show. All they did was ask complicated questions about things like parities, which nobody else understood or cared about. Including Richard Nixon. . . ."

The Selling of the President 1968 shows the master strategists, the cool-eyed businessmen, laying out the parameters of the candidate's image, and the creative people—TV producers and directors along with writers and set designers—shaping the image and projecting it to the electorate. And then there were the pollsters measuring the temperature of public opinion to find out how well the image had registered.

Most significantly, the book displays the candidate himself being directed through it all—half unaware that he, too, is being manipulated. An example of this occurs when Nixon, standing in front of the camera at the end of a taping session, spontaneously decided to do one more commercial on his own. He makes an extemporaneous, hard-line law-and-order statement about the New York City teachers' strike then in progress. But the message is sharply out of keeping with the soft, friendly Nixon image, and Garment in the control room is upset. Treleaven, however, reassures him. "That's all right, Len," he says, "it'll never get on the air."

More than an expose, *The Selling of the President 1968* is an indication of where it's at in American politics at the end of the Sixties. McGinniss is quite aware of this as indicated by his many asides on the philosophy of image-making and projection. He concludes that the goal of the politician today is to become a TV celebrity, to achieve a status jump that will allow him to be "measured not against his predecessors—not against a standard of performance established by two centuries of democracy—but against Mike Douglas. . . . Style becomes substance. The medium is the massage and the masseur gets the votes."

Actually, Joe McGinniss is not quite accurate in suggesting that American candidates over the past 200 years ran and were elected on the basis of how they measured up to their predecessors' "standards of performance." Race, religion, marital status or lack of same, hair style, and smile are only the more obvious among the extraneous factors that have gotten American candidates into political offices.

There is even the story that George Washington failed to make it into the House of Burgesses the first time around because his opponent awarded every "aye" voter a tot of rum for his support. At the next election the future father of our country had a whole hogshead of rum stationed at a polling place, and all comers had as much as they wished before going into the voting booth.

As the country grew older and more sophisticated, out-and-out bribery was replaced by somewhat subtler means of currying favor. Baby kissing, torch light parades, party-sponsored picnics, candidates driving locomotives and wearing Indian bonnets were among them.

With the advent of radio and television they were able for the first time to expose their personalities to citizens all over the country simultaneously and yet on a one-to-one basis. Even better, because of the flexibility of the electronic media, the personality they displayed could be more pleasing than the one they actually had. The two didn't even have to have too much in common.

FDR was among the first to realize this. His fireside chats were not just a series of speeches but, rather because of the versatility—or as McLuhan might put it, "coolness"—of radio and Roosevelt's use of it they became visits with a warm, friendly neighbor in the intimacy of his home. Their effectiveness is probably best attested to by the fact that though in all there were only three or four actual Hyde Park "chats," anyone who was around at the time will swear they heard many more.

The BBDO advertising agency did some experimentation with image manipulation during the Eisenhower campaign. Flight after flight of spot TV commercials projected a "take charge" image for the General who was going to "clean up the mess in Washington." In another set of commercials, during a campaign against an opponent whose divorce was a major political liability, Eisenhower talked about "my wife Mamie." Almost pathetically in retrospect, Stevenson countered this "happy home" image with a film showing him with Adlai, Jr., and his daughter-in-law in their "happy home." But these were only the feeble beginnings.

The effectiveness of electronic image projection was never more dramatically demonstrated than by the Nixon-Kennedy debates of 1960. Virtually no one will deny that JFK "won" though few, then or now, could tell you the questions debated. What people are really saying is that Kennedy's image—young, vibrant, self-assured—triumphed over that of Nixon, which seemed gray, tense and tired. There was no debate in the classic sense, only an electronic contest of images.

The lessons of these encounters were not lost on Nixon. In a post-graduate course of eight years Richard Nixon and his team learned that it is not what the candidate is but what he can be made to appear to be that will pay off at the polls. Obviously, it was a course worth taking, and McGinniss daringly documents the final exam.

But what of the future? Will candidates be sold more and more like packaged goods? Will campaigns end up entirely in the hands of the personal image manipulators? And will the public be casting ballots in proportion to the talent of one or the other group of image makers or the financial ability of the partisans to buy air time? Probably.

At a two-day conference of the American Association of Campaign Consultants late in September, at which, incidentally, Joe McGinniss was key-note speaker, much talk was devoted to the morality of image manipulation. Some felt that TV commercials were okay only if the candidate appeared in them, others that image development was all right provided the image resembled the "real" candidate. But in the end the participants—campaign managers, candidates and advertising men—were all there for one purpose: to learn the newest and most effective techniques to insure victory. And the products of these techniques are what we, as voters, can look to in the future.

If there are any counterbalances to this movement they will come through legislation and education.

Legislation guaranteeing equitable distribution of air time regardless of budgets would give each candidate similar access to the electorate. (The present "equal-time" provision of the broadcast law affords equal time only to the extent that the candidate can afford to pay for it.) A bill currently in Congress would assure Congressional candidates a basic block of air time at a 70 per cent discount. It is essentially a weak bill, but because Congress is made up of potentially incumbent candidates who are reluctant to make access to broadcast time easy for challengers, only a weak bill stands a chance of passage.

On the other side of the TV screen is voter education. Every secondary school in the United States has history courses that teach how democracy in America came about. Civics courses describe how democracy works. But few, if any, courses explain how to participate in a democracy. The single, solitary reason for political image-making is that the public can be seduced. Indeed, it often invites seduction as an alternative to hard decision-making. If children can be taught to reach voting conclusions on the basis of fact rather than emotion, a long step will have been taken in keeping the hidden persuaders from running off with politics.

QUESTIONS FOR DISCUSSION AND DIALOGUE

1. What does the ability of McGinniss to be accepted by Nixon's campaign managers and yet write a book which was very critical of Richard Nixon's campaign say about the role of the Press in American Politics?
2. Outline some of the pros and cons of this debate topic:

"Resolved, that since the goal of major national politicians today is to become television celebrities instead of debate and take stands on issues, politics has been cheapened and the possibility of citizens understanding major issues by listening to the politicians is decidedly much less than it was in the past."

3. How would Teison use education and legislation to counterbalance the dangers of television image manipulation? Do you agree with him? Why?

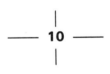

Newsweek (a Fact) Is the New Hot Book (an Opinion)

Chris Welles

Two of the most important newsweeklies in the United States, *Time* and *Newsweek,* are discussed by Chris Welles in this article. Six million four hundred thousand copies a week of both magazines are sold. Their influence and their difficulties in always distinguishing between fact and opinion are key considerations to the American who wonders whose "facts" he should read. Welles discusses what goes into news reporting and editorializing and he uses *Newsweek—Time* case studies which indicate relative accuracy and reliability—youth, racial, and Vietnam coverage for example. After considering this article, the reader might be inclined to wonder if the question "Whose Facts Do You Read?" is the best way to ask this kind of question about the press!

The February 27, 1933, *Time* magazine carried a brief, thirty-seven-line item in its Press section about the first issue, dated February 17, of a new newsmagazine called *News-Week*. *News-Week,* it said, had been organized by Thomas J. C. Martyn, "a spirited little Britisher" (and, it neglected to mention, a former foreign-news editor of *Time*) whose "backing is derived partly from the Cheney Silk family, into which he married three years ago." *News-Week* said in advertisements it was written "for men and women who want a sharply etched perspective of the ceaseless spectacle of news."

On February 15, 1937, the *Time* Press section carried another item which read, in part:

"Four years ago this week, the U.S. reading public was told that, since it had approved and for ten years supported its first weekly newsmagazine, *Time,* now it should have another, an improvement on the original. 'We believe there is a field unplowed,' said the editors, 'and we are sharpening another plow. . . . *News-Week's* ample treasury is the sum total of more than 120 individual investments, made by men and women who believe that thousands of Americans *want and need* the particular kind of newsmagazine that *News-Week* is.'

"Last week, *News-Week's* investors found their ample original treasury, plus subsequent investments to a grand sum of $2,250,000, completely wiped out."

Time pointed out that Time Inc.'s original capital had been $86,000.

Newsweek of course was rescued (and its hyphen dropped), but the kind of attention paid to it by *Time* continued to be somewhere between haughty aloofness and total neglect. Traditionally, *Time* editors rarely, if ever, even glanced at the magazine. When and if they thought about it, they regarded it—with justification—as an amateur effort, a feeble copy of Henry Luce's great journalistic inspiration, clumsily endeavoring to capture a few rays of *Time's* august incandescence.

Time today continues to have more readers, more revenue from advertising, and doubtless more influence on public opinion. Employees in the *Newsweek* morgue continue to clip diligently for their files stories from copies of *Time,* while the *Time* morgue file clerks would not dream of clipping anything from *Newsweek*. *Newsweek* people still refer to *Time* as "Brand X" and "the Opposition" (though not with the same reverent awe of past years) and issues of *Time* abound in the *Newsweek* editorial offices at the start of every week. *Time* people do not refer to *Newsweek* at all. About its only imposition into their editorial lives is the tower of the *Newsweek* building, which is clearly visible from the elegant forty-seventh-floor private dining rooms of the Time & Life Building two blocks westward and whose electric time and temperature sign is occasionally glanced at toward the end of long lunches. *Time* Managing Editor Henry Anatole Grunwald wants the record clear that despite an allegation in a recent magazine story, "I look *Newsweek* over when I can but I don't really *read* it as the story said I did. I just don't have the time. There are so many other things to read."

Nevertheless, *Newsweek* has become, in the parlance of advertising executives and other members of New York's communications complex, the "hot book." The term is vague, meaning roughly a magazine which they are talking about, which is creating excitement, which has an aura of with-it-ness and success. "There is a real flair about *Newsweek,*" says Paul Zuckerman of Jack Tinker

& Partners. "There is a whole atmosphere of involvement, a sense of riding with what is happening in society. It talks to you in people terms. It's a much more contemporary package." "*Newsweek* reflects what society, not just the Establishment is talking about," says Robert Engelke, Media Director of Wells, Rich, Greene. *Time,* says Clifford Botway, one of Tinker's partners, "has a touch of being archaic. It does a fine job. It's sort of a classic. But it hasn't changed very much. It's edited from things, from facts. *Newsweek* is edited from the gut, from feelings, which is more in keeping with the times."

One statistical gauge of hotness is advertising. While decisions of which magazine to advertise in are based to large degree on "the numbers"—demographic surveys of readers' average income, age, education, etc.—impressions of hotness can play an important role in the choice between two media with similar numbers like *Time* and *Newsweek*. "When you buy TV, you look strictly for audience," says Clifford Botway. "When you buy magazines, you look for editorial values, for the contribution of the medium to the ad message. If the book has vitality, if it's with the times, then it reflects that on our advertising." Last year for the first time (except for a fluke in 1958), *Newsweek* ran more domestic ad pages than *Time,* 3008 to 2913. While *Time's* ad pages have been declining for four straight years, *Newsweek's* have been climbing sharply, and this year, *Newsweek* will beat *Time* by more than three hundred pages. *Time's* ad revenues are still much higher, because its greater circulation—4,000,000 to 2,400,000, domestic—yields a higher ad-rate per page. But in the first six months of this year, *Newseek's* dollar revenue gain was not only more than *Time's* but greater than that of any other major magazine. In addition, there are a lot of people with at least some credentials for making judgments about media who are now saying that underdog, also-ran, Avis-like *Newsweek* has become a *better* magazine than famous, powerful, influential *Time.* Can this be true? Does hotness imply editorial superiority? If so, then it is truly an event, to which we should all pay close attention.

There is no question at least that *Time* and *Newsweek* have very different ideas on how to present last week's news. As has been noted in several recent magazine stories, many of *Time's* ideas are of recent vintage, the result of the replacement as Managing Editor of Otto Fuerbringer with Henry Grunwald in May of last year. While Fuerbringer tended to reflect the stern, conservative, strong-willed didacticism of his Germanic-Lutheran-Midwest background, the forty-seven-year-old Grunwald, a squat, barrel-shaped man with askew, curly grey hair that juts from his head like small springs, is more sophisticated and urbane. Though born in Vienna, he is a product of New York City. He received his Phi Beta Kappa key in philosophy from New York University, then in 1945 joined *Time* as a copyboy, where he has been ever since. While Fuerbringer (who contrary to persistent reports was *never* called "the Iron Chancellor" by his staff) tended to be concerned with tangibles—people, events, swatches of colorful detail and anecdotes (he was a regular New York *Daily News* reader)—Grunwald is more interested in intangibles—issues, ideas, clashing concepts and dialectics. (Grunwald was always known, says a former *Time* writer, "for his psychological manipulation of the cover conference. This is a high art, because the number of covers a guy gets is the kind of proof of his potency. . . . Well, it was marvelous to watch the way Henry could marshal his arguments, expose inconsistencies in other people's reasons for their covers and bring the group around to his own suggestion. Henry was the champion.")

The most noticeable change is in style. The famous, oft-parodied sarcastic asides, the strained puns and etymological oddities have nearly all been expunged, though many of these aberrations were on the way out before Grunwald took over. People in *Time,* for instance, seldom snort, huff, wail, mutter and snarl, depending on how *Time* feels about them. People now say, note, suggest, contend and maintain. While *Time* language rarely rises to eloquence (an exception was a recent cover story on Vladimir Nabokov), it is almost always clean and smooth. This, plus a decline in *Time's* feistiness, however, often gives the language a certain remote, monotonous flatness. Few can get mad at *Time* anymore.

More important are changes in substance. Grunwald, who originated *Time's* Essay section, has expanded the idea of the essay, in its classical sense, throughout the magazine. Stories are longer, less pithy, more comprehensive. Complex foreign-policy problems and broad social trends are confronted with a precise weighing of a plethora of options, opinions, judgments and recommendations based on interviews with scores of experts and libraries-full of research. The magazine is filled with conjunctions—however, nevertheless, even so, yet, still, hence, thus— to signal shifts in the march of argument. *Time's* judgment is no longer a sweeping, lusty blow to the solar plexus but a finely honed communique to the cerebrum. While *Time* continues to strive for a certain broad philosophical consistency, its tenacious doctrinairism has been largely replaced by aggressive judiciousness and formerly steadfast positions are allowed to appear less certain, and to evolve gradually. There is an apparently deep fear of overstatement. Conclusions are studied with hedges and qualifiers: perhaps, to a certain degree, somewhat, it would appear.

Typical of *Time's* analysis was a story on the debate over Hamburger Hill in Vietnam. After examining the military argument that the attack by U. S. forces was justified, *Time* concluded: "As so often before in the baffling, complicated war (the military case) was easy to fault, but difficult to refute, possessing an interior logic of its own, but lacking in reference points to reality on which reasonable men might agree." The sentence does not exactly rattle the reader in his seat. A *Time* Essay on U. S. policy toward Communist China assessed so many subtly graduated possibilities for new approaches (noticeably absent were Lucean romantic notions of Chiang Kai-shek, whom *Time* now calls a "living anachronism") that it resembled a State Department position paper. The conclusion: "Any overtures toward China at this point may turn out to be a mistake because they might be based on a misreading of Chinese psychology and the country's political mechanisms. But on balance the risks involved seem relatively slight and the case for a change in U. S. policy is powerful."

Newsweek, in contrast, tends to be a melange of widely varying writing styles, points of view, methods of argument. Often there are wide variances of interpretations of a subject from one issue to the next. At its best, *Newsweek* prose has an excitement, a fresh liveliness, a strong sense of being close to events.

There is a willingness to experiment in ideas in format, such as in Movie Critic Joseph Morgenstern's evocative, impressionalistic set of personal musings last summer on Apollo 11. His misgivings and uncertainties about the event—expressed in part through interviews with Indians, blind people and children—tended to make the more awestruck posture of commentators like Walter Cronkite and even *Time* seem a bit naive and frivolous. But often *Newsweek* is bumpy and rickety, crammed with stark cliches and leaden phrases that would embarrass the copy editor of a small-town newspaper. In a recent cover story on a meeting of world Communist parties in Moscow, *Newsweek* discussed the conflict between Russia and China thusly:

"Unquestionably, the vitriolic challenge posed by this Asiatic giant has touched raw racial nerves in the Soviet Union. For stripped of its rhetoric, the Sino-Soviet dispute is not a hairsplitting debate over Communist ideology, but a gut confrontation between two intensely nationalistic states—one of which considers itself to be the wave of the Maoist future and the other that sees itself as the Dutch boy with a finger in the dike of white, European civilization."

A kind of Armageddon-like quality pervades much of the prose: there is a surfeit of burning issues, crying needs, pent-up desires, heated debates, dim views, solid footholds, glimmers of hope. Guns are stuck to, needs are underscored, ties are buttressed, battle lines are drawn, influence is knuckled under to, sympathetic chords are struck. Sometimes images are confusingly mixed.

Newsweek is much more anxious to make broad pronouncements about the significance of a week's events, to practice the art of the "hype," by which the routine is blown up into the incredible and the sensational. It is filled with "crises," "turning points" and "watersheds," especially in the "Violin," *Newsweek* slang for the lead story in the magazine. (The term originated in the late 1940's when a *Nation* editor, wrestling with the lead story, was advised by the Editorial Director to "paint your picture with sweeping and impressive strokes. Or if you prefer a different metaphor, wind up your arm and play your violin.") Here is the way *Time* began a story not long ago about Teddy Kennedy (before the Martha's Vineyard accident) : "In the best tradition of his brother Robert, Edward Kennedy last week was being heard and seen on diverse issues." *Newsweek* grandly announced that "For better or worse, the last surviving Kennedy brother was finally ready to claim his legacy as a political warrior."

Sometimes these pronouncements have a way of going awry. A story on the influence of The New York *Times* editorial page said that before "thousands of citizens" cast their ballots in the following week's primary election, they would examine, among other things, "the endorsements of The New York *Times* that they have carefully clipped." Unfortunately every single one of The *Times'* major endorsements lost.

Time, of course, also can get its conclusions mixed. When Richard Nixon last May announced a detailed peace proposal for Vietnam, *Time* said that "In a sense, Johnson's war had now formally become Nixon's war." Two issues later, though, half the war apparently was mysteriously handed back to Lyndon Johnson. After Nixon had flown to Midway Island to meet with South Vietnamese President Nguyen Van Thieu, *Time* proclaimed that Nixon "was in mid-passage between a war he had inherited and a war that would soon become his own liability." *Newsweek,* after the President's peace proposals, agreed with *Time* that "From now on, in the eyes of all his countrymen, Vietnam would be, at least in part, 'Mr. Nixon's war.'" After Nixon had gone "winging westward" to Midway Island, *Newsweek,* perhaps mixing up the status of its various decrees and proclamations, said that "Clearly, starting from Midway, the sorrily blotted copybook of the past was turned finally to a new page: from now on, for better or for worse, it is Mr. Nixon's war."

For better or for worse, some of *Newsweek's* most impassioned writing occurs in its reviews of the arts. A story on the blues and Janis Joplin, who became a "volatile vial of nitroglycerin" after the music of Otis Redding had "etched in Janis' mind the belief in music as a kind of truth in itself," was replete with sibilant phrases like "great towers of sinuous sound," "searing soliloquies," "the circular hell of the saloon circuit." Part of the story talked about Fillmore East, one of the "pop palaces" which "serve as secular churches where the truth is unleashed in 100-decibel thunder." Here, the music suddenly "explodes, searing the ears into a pleasant numbness, drilling its way into the heads of the audience. Behind the blasting band, a psychedelic light show, like the pulsations of volcanic lava, dazzles the eyes. The audience, some swaying, others sitting quietly, are *sic* gradually recharged like Frankenstein's monster." In another review a theatre critic, who perhaps had misplaced his thesaurus, gushed forth with such descriptive terms as "terrific," "amazing," "splendid," "marvelous," "beautiful," "excellent" and "brilliant."

The distinction between the two magazines is especially evident in their cover stories, which for both are often formal occasions for the awarding of superlatives (Nabokov in *Time* is "the greatest living American novelist," Beverly Sills in *Newsweek* is "the greatest singing actress in the world"). However *Time* almost always overwhelms Newsweek with the sheet force of research and a comprehensive description of meanings and implications. One gets a feeling in *Time* of mass, bulk, depth. This is especially evident when both do covers on the same subject, such as, in recent issues, the Moscow Communist Party meeting and the sex "explosion" (as *Time* called it) in the arts. *Newsweek's* stories appeared almost to have been pieced together from New York *Times* clips. The sex cover was, in fact, assembled—including research, writing, checking, editing—in only four days.

Newsweek editors freely admit their magazine can be uneven, inconsistent and a little shabby. "I'm all for sloppiness," maintains Managing Editor Kermit Lansner. "I would rather have rough spots, along with bursts of real feeling, than try to cultivate a beautifully polished texture where the point is lost. *Time* smells of research, of the library. You never get a sense of the real texture of today's complicated, hectic events, of effort going into their writing, of the quirks and hazards of trying to tell what's going on. I don't consider *Newsweek* in the course of a year a coherent set of themes like a book. This magazine isn't engraved in gold."

Time editors are rather reluctant to be drawn into a debate of the merits of their magazine against *Newsweek.* "We don't compete with *Newsweek* anyway,"

Henry Grunwald points out. "We compete with the world, with men's minds." But he apparently glances through *Newsweek* often enough to state when pressed that "it just reads like a not very carefully edited magazine. I'm not saying you can't change over a period of time, but I think *Time* should have a consistent policy on important questions. It makes no sense to be terribly for something one week, and terribly against it the next. Look, I have a great respect for them—many of them once worked over here—but sometimes they do a very poor, very superficial job. Look at their recent issue on the moon (a report on Apollo 10 and a preview of Apollo 11). It was a great big nothing, an endless rehash. What did it prove? Not only was it carelessly done, but it wasn't very interesting."

Time people see no validity in *Newsweek's* claims of the superiority of its writing. *Newsweek* often "is really a failure of intelligent writing and editing, a cop out," says Foreign Editor Jason McManus. "If they really believe their goal is to be ragged, untidy, with the stitching showing, then that says something extraordinarily demeaning about how they view their readers. Their writing is just cheap liveliness. You can be just as lively with better writing and better editing. Elegance is not necessarily effete, nor is excellence necessarily dull."

Much of *Newsweek's* hotness, it appears, is the result of skillful packaging and promotion. *Newsweek's* main advertising slogan, the brainstorm of a copywriter at N. W. Ayer, *Newsweek's* ad agency, asserts it is "the newsweekly that separates fact from opinion." This is an obvious attempt to play on criticisms of *Time* for slanting the news. (*Time,* of course, has never intended to provide a straight, factual account. In his original prospectus for *Time,* Luce wrote that "*Time* gives both sides, but clearly indicates which side it believes to have the stronger position.") Opinion is supposed to be limited to *Newsweek's* signed columns and art reviews. Everything else is supposed to be fact.

This claim, as is obvious to any intelligent *Newsweek* reader, is nonsense. The unsigned parts of the magazine are filled with as much opinion as *Time.* (A *Columbia Journalism Review* article last year on *Newsweek* cited numerous loaded words like "unhappily," "understandably," "tragically," "clearly." It concluded that *Newsweek* should "separate fact from fantasy in their advertising.") "If the facts warrant it, if they justify it, then we draw a conclusion," says Executive Editor Lester Bernstein. "And of course this has to be opinion." He adds that the slogan has been very effective." Further questioning reveals a diversity of rationalizations:

Harry C. Thompson, *Newsweek's* Publisher: "Is there really opinion in the news column? (He smiles broadly.) Well, of course you know that is a very subjective thing. I guess you might characterize the slogan as our aspiration editorially. Obviously, separating fact from opinion is a very difficult thing for a human being to fulfill. But we are trying."

William Scherman, Director of Promotion: "Sure, maybe the slogan's a little unfair. But it's legitimate advertisingese. I mean, if we separated fact from opinion one hundred percent, *Newsweek* would be a complete blah. Right? What we're really saying is that we separate fact from opinion more than *Time* does."

Katharine Graham, president of the Washington Post Company, which owns *Newsweek:* "Sure, if you pick it apart, maybe it isn't really true. But I think in a quick phrase, it sums up what we're trying to do. I mean we're really striving for fairness, which is not necessarily objectivity. I don't want to say we're not objective, because we are, but when most people talk about objectivity and fact, they are usually talking about fairness. The main thing is to report without bias or prejudice."

A couple of years ago, several of the editors, led by Lester Bernstein, a former writer for *Time* and The New York *Times,* asked that the slogan be dropped. After some skirmishing, the ad people surrendered, and for about six months it lay dead. But then Osborn Elliott, *Newsweek's* Editor, whose brother is chairman of Ogilvy & Mather, a large ad agency, allowed them to revive it. "What the hell?" says Elliott. "If they want to use it, let them use it. I don't take ad slogans all that seriously."

Newsweek's other slogan is that it is "the most quoted news-weekly." the implication being that it is more on top of the news. *Newsweek* does in fact possess an extremely energetic and enterprising bureau system, especially in Washington, which directs much of its effort to rooting out scoops and "news-breaks." It has consistently beaten *Time* to lively snatches of exclusive detail. Most recently, *Newsweek* uncovered information of President Nixon's dispatch of Attorney General Mitchell to Chief Justice Earl Warren to get Abe Fortas to resign, and spelled out details before anyone else did of Nixon's plans for the Strategic Arms Limitation Talks.

"I tell our guys three things," says Washington Bureau Chief Mel Elfin. "'Be right, be fair and be first.' We're geared to The Periscope (a section on the front of the magazine of rumors and inside stories) formula, and our guys are always going after Periscope items." Elfin acknowledges dedication to such a policy has its anxieties. "Every Sunday (the day after *Time* and *Newsweek* close their issues) I pick up The *Times* or listen to the radio on Sunday night in fear that we've missed something big. Remember when Bobby Kennedy went to Lyndon Johnson and offered to withdraw from the Presidential race? Well, a friend of mine called me with the news before it had gotten out. I managed to confirm it and we closed it in the magazine. Then on Monday (when the new issues are first available on newsstands) I found that *Time* had the item too, and I thought, my God! Suppose my friend hadn't called? I mean, it's a little like losing an astronaut. Pretty soon, we're going to blow a big one, and it's really going to be rough."

Once the editorial staff has dug up hot news, an extensive promotional apparatus moves into action to assist the quotation process. Members of the "News Bureau" read and reread every word of final copy on Saturday and Sunday to spot anything that might get a mention. Late Sunday, six hundred early copies of the magazine and releases summarizing "Editorial Exclusives & Highlights" are air-expressed throughout the country and, if the news is really hot, sent by messenger to the most important media outlets. Mention on the Huntley-Brinkley show Sunday night and the Monday New York *Times* are considered the prime coups.

To substantiate the most-quoted claim, *Newsweek* compiles voluminous statistics from clippings and radio and TV monitoring services on how many times the magazine is mentioned. According to "News Bureau" head Hank

Wexler's figures, *Newsweek* typically outscores *Time* and *U. S. News & World Report* more than two to one. "It's a pain in the ass to count all those papers," he says, "but if somebody asks us to put our money on the table, we can do it. Believe me, I love to compete against *Time.* I've got a killer instinct."

Time men are generally disdainful of *Newsweek's* approach. "I think you can get too involved in a little intramural game of who's got what, of little scoops and minutiae and advantages," says *Time* Washington Bureau Chief Hugh Sidey. "You end up playing with each other while the world goes to hell. Our idea is the concept story, where you expand on the news and analyze it."

Much of *Newsweek's* reporting, especially from Washington, is, however, way above the level of mere fragments, and *Newsweek* is usually better informed about major, fast-breaking stories out of Washington than *Time.* Unfortunately, to capitalize on this advantage, the magazine at times not only rushes through stories without taking the time for comprehensive treatment, but has a tendency to try to cover next week's events instead of this week's. *Newsweek* will often try to have an issue on the stands, frequently with a cover about the event, the week an important event is due to occur. The impression generated over a period of time hopefully will be that *Time* is somewhat behind the news. Unfortunately, it is not easy to write a long story about something that hasn't happened yet. "I think the coin of our cover has been pretty badly devalued," says one *Newsweek* editor. *"Newsweek* is edited for Madison Avenue," claims another. "We'll do anything if it will make the guys at J. Walter Thompson (the country's largest ad agency) talk about it in the john."

So is it mostly ballyhoo, puffery and frilly-ribboned gimmickery that's behind the talk in J. Walter Thompson's john? Fortunately for *Newsweek,* there is more. Over the past few years, *Newsweek* has often been superior to *Time* in assessing the meaning, significance and implication of the news—one of the principal *raison d'etres* of the newsmagazine—and in recognizing many of the major trends of the 1960's, such as the awakening of black aspirations, changes in the mood of the younger generation, the decline of the validity of and belief in the Cold War dialectic of anti-communism and containment. *Time,* of course, covered these trends, often with considerable insight. But because of its rather conservative ideological stance, it often seemed more interested in discrediting the developments or downgrading their importance than reporting what was going on. *Newsweek* uncommitted to any formal ideological position, was more receptive to deviations from traditional thinking and as a result usually covered these events with more perception and accuracy.

In its stories on the campus and young people, for instance, *Newsweek* has tried to find out what young people were thinking and why, and to explain why so many are rebelling against many of the philosophies of the older generation. *Newsweek* has quickly detected new moods and feelings, and was the first national magazine to run a story on the hippies of Haight-Ashbury and the first to report Haight-Ashbury's decline seven months later. (It could be argued, of course, that the latter was the result of the former.)

Time, on the other hand, has tended to display a rather smug adult superiority, rarely missing an opportunity to scold young people for their childish shenanigans, long hair, weird clothes, juvenile emotionalism and illogical criticisms of their parents. The magazine's approach has mollified recently, but even their coverage of the "People's Park" incident in Berkeley last spring is illustrative. To *Newsweek* and most of the other media, the episode went as follows: a group of students and local hippies decided to beautify a dingy, unused piece of university-owned property near the campus with sod, shrubs and children's swings; the university decided to assert forcefully its right to the property; the confrontation escalated into a bloody battle involving tear gas and the National Guard. *Time,* however, put the entire blame for causing the incident on local "radicals" who were "irritated" because Berkeley, once "the cradle of the U. S. student rebellion" had become "Dullsville," and thus they were "spoiling for a fight." Spotting the new park, they declared squatter's rights" on the land and "dared the university to throw them off." *Time* was critical of the university's "hard line" approach which had "backfired" but it implied that the "radicals" had more or less received what they deserved. Property rights are, after all, property rights. *Newsweek's* San Francisco correspondent, in a by-lined side-bar, saw the significance in a different way: "When youthful citizens can be wantonly gassed and beaten, all because of a small, unauthorized park, what has happened to America? What has happened to our sense of perspective, our tradition of tolerance, our view of the armed force as a last—never a first—resort?"

Newsweek also has reflected before *Time* national concern with such social issues as poverty, urban blight and the birth-control pill, though *Time* eventually did comprehensive reports. *Newsweek* recognized the importance in 1962 and 1963 of the early Negro demonstrations. While *Time* was covering the events briefly and offhandedly, *Newsweek* in 1963 published a special issue detailing, for the first time by a major national magazine, the depth and intensity of black feelings. And rather than rely on *Time's* traditional device of "most Americans feel that. . . " *Newsweek* hired pollster Louis Harris to find out what people really thought. (*Time* recently adopted polling methods by luring Harris away from *Newsweek,* neglecting to mention in the Publisher's Letter heralding the coup that Harris had ever worked for *Newsweek. Newsweek* has retaliated by hiring George Gallup and Richard Scammon.) In the coverage of urban riots and black-power movements, *Time* spent most of its time condemning them as threats to the social order while *Newsweek* attempted to find what caused them. On November 20, 1967, in its first "excursion into advocacy," *Newsweek* published another special issue on the Negro, recommending "What Must Be Done," which won *Newsweek* the National Magazine Award. (*Time,* in what some of its writers called "our *Newsweek* issue," took up similar technique with a special twenty-page section last January on "The Task Before the President.")

One can argue that sometimes *Newsweek's* eagerness to embrace the new and different can go to as much excess as *Time's* defense to the status quo. When Andy Warhol's movie *The Chelsea Girls* was released, *Newsweek* went into ecstasy. Calling Warhol "that smiling, alfalfa-haired, infant-eyes, no-aged Peter Pan of pop art," the review said the movie was "a fascinating and significant movie event," which "touches more nerves than a multifariously perverse world will ever admit." *Time* called Warhol "the Cecil B. De Sade of underground cinema, the depth of whose movies ranged from below the belt to beneath discussion." *The Chelsea Girls,* it said, was "a very dirty and very dull peep show. . . . The characters are all homosexuals and junkies, and they spend most of their screen time lying around and trying to think of something to say or do. When they do think of something, it is pretty sure to be something infantile. . . . There is a place for this sort of thing, and it is definitely underground. Like in a sewer." Last year, *Newsweek* greeted the ascendancy of Tiny Tim by calling him "one of the last true innocents" who had "remained inviolate to time. . . . He is the Douanier Rousseau of pop music, a primitive-sophisticate whose singing is a perilously but perfectly balanced blend of poignant nostalgia and the razor-edged put-on." To *Time,* he was "the most bizarre entertainer this side of Barnum & Bailey's sideshow," who looked like "Bea Lillie in drag." After noting that he brushed his teeth with papaya powder, *Time* concluded that he was part of "a cultish tradition that goes back through Shakespeare's clowns all the way to the Roman Circus—that of holy fool. But holy papaya powder, who is fooling whom?" Nevertheless, both *Chelsea Girls* and Tiny Tim were immensely popular, and the *Newsweek* reader does obtain a sense of why, while the *Time* reader comes away shaking his head, hopelessly baffled on how the public can be so idiotic.

No subject, though, illuminates the differences between the two magazines more than Vietnam. Until last year, *Time's* and to a large degree Time Inc.'s support of the American position was resolute and unswerving, and its prognosis consistently optimistic. After a trip to Vietnam, Hedley Donovan, Henry Luce's chosen successor as Time Inc.'s Editor-in-Chief, wrote in an article called "Vietnam: The War Is Worth Winning" in the February 25, 1966, issue of *Life* that "There is a reasonably good chance the present phase of the war can be successfully wound up in 1967, or even late 1966." *Newsweek's* coverage, though, had long since begun to reflect doubts. In January, 1965, a year before Donovan's piece, *Newsweek* wrote: "For three years the U. S. has been pouring men and money into the Vietnamese war with ever greater profusion. . . . The Administration cannot much longer avoid making a clear-cut decision as to exactly what the U. S. is doing in Vietnam and what it hopes to achieve there."

Donovan returned to Vietnam in 1967. In a *Life* article in the June 2 issue called "Vietnam: Slow, Tough, But Coming Along," he admitted he had been "overoptimistic" in his previous appraisal, but he now felt that "there are in fact some grounds—a mixture perhaps of hunch, faith, impression, information—for thinking our Vietnam policy nine or ten months hence could be looking like a success." Foreign Editor Jason McManus was quoted in a July *Wall Street Journal* story that Vietnam is "the right war in the right place at the right time." *Newsweek* Managing Editor Kermit Lansner, on the same tour as Donovan, wrote in *Newsweek* that he was impressed by the power and depth of the U. S. forces and their "calm professionalism." But he said that "I was surprised at how unsure a hold on the country the Saigon government and its U. S. allies have." He concluded that "I left Vietnam more pessimistic than when I arrived." These stories appeared seven months before the famous cathartic 1968 Tet Offensive. . . . Not only do horrendous abortions seep through into *Newsweek* but so also do innovative means of expression, fresh opinions, new ideas and information that may not square with the beliefs of the people in charge. *Newsweek's* recognition of the black revolution was the result of the insistence of its Southern correspondents that what was happening in the South was important and deserved space. The early tinges of dovishness and pessimism in *Newsweek's* Vietnam coverage were the result of files from Saigon. Elliott admits he himself was quite hawkish until after the Tet Offensive, yet he allowed his magazine to reflect a contrary view.

Time's misjudgment on Vietnam, would appear to raise serious questions about the way in which the magazine is organized. As is now well-known, Otto Fuerbringer steadfastly ignored the assessments of his Saigon correspondents in favor of his own ideas. After he ran a story in *Time's* Press section rebuking the Saigon press crops, and by implication his own men, for pessimism and negativism, Southeast Asia Bureau Chief Charles Mohr and an associate, Merton Perry, heatedly and publicly resigned. Less well-known are the similar troubles of Frank McCullock, Mohr's successor, formerly of The Los Angeles *Times*. The files of his men were also questioned and contradicted by New York. "One time they asked us to file for a cover story on the American buildup," recalls Art Zich, a *Time* correspondent in Saigon from 1965-7 and now an editor with *Newsweek.* "When the story came out, it had a cover slash *a diagonal headline across the top* of something like 'Turning Point in Vietnam' and it read like, you know, Yippie! the Yanks are coming and we're going to show those little fellows how to do it! There was no suggestion of that whatsoever in our files. We just said the buildup was the beginning of a long, long fight.'" McCullock, according to Zich, "felt a deep personal anguish. He felt the magazine was leading the public in the wrong direction and he tried to keep the bureau from falling apart." A contributing problem for McCullock was the intense personal feud between Fuerbringer and Richard Clurman, then head of the Time-Life News Service, which further separated Fuerbringer from the correspondents. Eventually, McCullock was called back to New York, whereupon he quit to become *Life's* Washington Bureau Chief and recently returned to *Time.*

Despite such dark allegations that Vietnam was Fuerbringer's "holy war," a view which implies he was deliberately trying to mislead his readers, it is far more likely that *Time* was wrong because Donovan and Fuerbringer believed that they were right and the correspondents were wrong. It is true that Time Inc. executives feel *Time's* viewpoint carries much weight in Washington and that it would be a serious act for Time Inc. to turn against the U. S. government in time of war. Still, if Donovan and Fuerbringer had become convinced that such action was necessary, it is highly likely they would have taken it. "The President would call Otto down to the ranch and show him a lot of information about how well the war was going, and Otto simply couldn't believe the government was lying to him," says a former *Time* editor. Donovan and other top editors visited Vietnam to be sure they were correct. However Osborn Elliott attests to the effectiveness of these quick, whirlwind V.I.P. visits. "When I went in 1965, I won't say like Romney that I was brainwashed, but I was snowed. I admit it. And when I went back in 1966, I came away just as bullish. You couldn't help but be impressed by the sheer massiveness of the American presence. But look, when you have people in the field, you either trust them or fire them."

(After the trauma of the Tet Offensive, *Time's* stance on the war shifted to the point where it now no longer demands a military victory and favors gradual de-escalation and a"dwindling" of U. S. involvement. Yet some of the flavor of earlier Vietnam coverage remains. *Time* may come to regret a cover story last March on President Thieu. While it said "every assessment of the war is self-contradictory," it went on to make some presumably non-self-contradictory assessments such as "things are perhaps going somewhat better for the allied cause than ever before—or than most outsiders realize" (one notices Grunwald's pencil at work), and that the Thieu government is "reasonably secure and stable." *Newsweek* remains skeptical both of the Thieu government's stability and the outlook for the allied cause.)

One cannot help feeling, in view, if nothing else, of *Time's* troubles covering Vietnam, that the duty of the *Time* managing editor to serve as the all-knowing ultimate arbiter of the truth on the basis, perhaps, of nothing but his hunches and faith, may be questionable. Furthermore, Luce and his messianism are now gone, and he has been replaced by men who are apparently anxious to be judicious and fair. Why then should *Time* remain organized to serve as an efficient propagator of the view from the top? Clearly, a relaxation of central control need not degenerate into total abdication of authority at the top or the kind of stylistic miscarriage that slip into *Newsweek*. *(Life* has had great editorial success—its reporting of youth and the black revolution for instance—with a *Newsweek*-like system.)

If Henry Grunwald is bothered by any of these questions, he does not show it. "Sitting here in New York," he maintains, "you have an overview of the situation that the man on the scene, who can become too emotionally close to it, just does not have." Nevertheless, a reader gets a growing sense, if not from *Time's* still rather Gospel-like style, at least from its hedged and carefully drawn conclusions, of the complexity and even the enigma of today's events. It is startling, though not necessarily commendable, that after reading a long, heavily researched cover story on the A.B.M., one is not really sure whether *Time* is for it or against it. Only gradually, in successive issues, do *Time's* doubts become more clearly defined. "I think there are times when you shouldn't make up your mind," Grunwald contends. "If you are puzzled and baffled, you should watch the situation a while and think it out. There is a great danger in oversimplifying things, and you just can't breezily jump to conclusions. We need to have a sense of fallibility to get away from the impression we are bringing tablets down from the mountain." In a recent *Fortune* article, Hedley Donovan wrote: "The real world is fantastically diverse, and getting more so. We should rejoice in that and stop trying to fit it all into a few old and outdated boxes." It would seem that sooner or later these ideas would have to reflect themselves in the way *Time* is organized.

Newsweek, meanwhile, now the "hot book" (practically every member of the staff can quote the ad-page score) has perhaps become too sure of itself. It used to be *Newsweek* which desperately stopped presses over the weekend to insert fast-breaking news. But when the French voters rejected General de Gaulle last spring on a Sunday, it was *Time* which rushed six columns of analysis into their magazine, while *Newsweek* calmly did nothing. "Other magazines either couldn't cover the event—or chose not to," *Time* said in a big New York *Times* ad. "It was the result of complacency and bad judgment," concedes a *Newsweek* editor. "I'm promising you it won't happen again for a long time." (After Apollo 11 landed *Newsweek* hurriedly put on its cover a striking photo of the TV screen of Neil Armstrong on the moon. *Time* ran a ghastly Norman Rockwellesque painting drawn before the event.)

Newsweek's judgments and conclusions now are becoming broad, sweeping and unequivocal, and *Newsweek* editors scoff at Grunwald's cautious and circumspect prose. "In the old days, *Time* had a viewpoint and no information," says Kermit Lansner. "Now it has information but no viewpoint." The careful reader of *Newsweek* now perceives tinges of ideology, of fixed positions, of dogma. *Newsweek,* whose hierarchy came to power during the initial euphoria of the New Frontier, has become a key spokesman for the liberal middle class, and it may be getting caught up in the phenomenon of rising doctrinairism among liberals, especially radicals, and decreasing doctrinairism among conservatives. There is a developing atmosphere at *Newsweek* of missions, of crusades, of *engagé.* Ed Diamond says, "I know a guy from *Time*. He is a very grey man. He never appears anywhere else in the press. He is never heard from in the community. You don't see him anywhere. I mean I'm not running for Senator but.. . . "

It is possible, in fact, to make a good case that *Newsweek's* enthusiastic support of the black revolution is now based on as many strong preconceptions as *Time's* support of U. S. Vietnam policy. Fortunately, the black revolution has a lot more going for it than Vietnam policy. Fortunately, *Newsweek's* feelings are the result of a solid staff consensus, which can be an insurance against fixed positions. And fortunately, a great deal of permeability still exists. But *Newsweek* may be moving in the wrong direction. In its 1967 advocacy issue on the Negro, Osborn Elliott wrote that *Newsweek* editors "could not fulfill their journalistic responsibility or their responsibility as citizens by simply reporting what X thinks of Y, and why Z disagrees." The country's newsstands, however, are filled with journals of advocacy and polemics. A recent article on *Time* in *Harper's* was critical of *Time* for not sufficiently scrutinizing the "corrupt powers" of our society. But is it the function of a newsmagazine to decide that certain powers are corrupt and then go out and campaign that the corrupters be brought to task? It is certainly a proper role, even a duty, for a newsmagazine to make judgments, but it should also reflect the complexity of the news, the opposing ideas, and it should describe what is going on. What would *Newsweek* do if the black revolution were to take an extremely destructive and dangerous direction? Would *Newsweek's* reporting continue to be "fair"? "I am really beginning to get afraid we are much too sure where the Truth lies," says one of the older senior editors. "Perhaps we are being tempted by our success to start playing God, which of course is the same syndrome *Time* suffered from." But *Newsweek* editors seem wary in making any basic changes. As one writer puts it, "When your restaurant is packing them in, you don't change the menu. But that's when you have to watch out. That's the danger time."

Senior Editor Edwin Diamond characterizes the differences between *Time* and *Newsweek* this way: "I feel most of us here are becoming, rather than being." It would be one of journalism's more fascinating ironies if the roles were to become reversed.

QUESTIONS FOR DISCUSSION AND DIALOGUE

1. Outline the desirable and undesirable characteristics of *Time* and *Newsweek*. In your opinion (and perhaps from your own reading of both) which is the better newsweekly? Why?
2. Assuming there must be a choice, should a news magazine attempt to be "a finely honed communique to the cerebrum" (*Time*), or a "contemporary package" that "talks to you in people terms" (*Newsweek*)? Which would you prefer? Why? Do you see a danger to one of these approaches or both? Discuss.
3. Working in your views about the United States in the 1970's, explain why you think *Newsweek* will or will not decrease the 4-2.4 million weekly sales lead *Time* has over it. Does the answer to this question have bearing on which of the two magazines is better? Discuss.

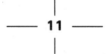

Agnew's Complaint: The Trouble with TV

Newsweek

One of the top politicians, Vice President Spiro Agnew, took issue with the three national television networks at a Fall, 1969 meeting of the Midwest Republican Committee in Des Moines, Iowa. Here is an example of political concern about supposed nonpolitical impartiality which has many implications. The differing responses to the Vice President's criticisms of "the men who select, encapsulate and analyze TV news" offer an important lesson about the inter-relationships of Americans, their politicians and parties, and the nonpolitical influentials.

To the millions of U. S. television viewers who tuned in their favorite evening news wrap-up last Thursday, the handsome, avuncular face that glowed from the screen seemed familiar enough—but not because it belonged to Walter, Chet, David or Frank. There behind the lectern at a regional meeting of the Midwest Republican Committee in Des Moines stood Vice President Spiro T. Agnew, his somber countenance glistening under the brilliant lights of all three networks—

and if the viewers were momentarily surprised to find the regular anchormen absent, they quickly realized they were witnesses to a rare, prime-time event.

For what followed from the Vice President was a bitter, slashing attack not just on the absent stars but also on the whole news operation of the three television networks. As the immediate targets of his attack, Agnew centered on what he termed the "tiny and closed fraternity of privileged men" who package, present and interpret the nation's TV network news. But by the time the Veep was finished there seemed little doubt that the onslaught had been long in planning, carefully orchestrated and patently designed to force U. S. television news programs into a mold more clearly to the liking of the Administration of President Richard M. Nixon.

Marshaling his characteristically pungent idiom, Agnew quickly got down to the major source of his wrath—what he termed the "instant analysis and querulous criticism" offered by network commentators immediately following President Nixon's Vietnam address on Nov. 3. "It was obvious that their minds were made up in advance," charged Agnew. "One commentator (CBS's Marvin Kalb) twice contradicted the President's statement about the exchange of correspondence with Ho Chi Minh. Another (ABC's Bill Lawrence) challenged the President's abilities as a politician. A third (ABC's Bill Downs) asserted that the President was now following the Pentagon line. Others, by the expressions on their faces, the tone of questions and the sarcasm of their responses made clear their sharp disapproval."

For all their "urbane and assured presence," said Agnew, the men who select, encapsulate and analyze TV news are philosophically out of step with most of their audience. "To a man," he claimed, "*they* live and work in the geographical and intellectual confines of Washington, D.C., or New York City. . . . Both communities bask in their own provincialism, their own parochialism. We can deduce that these men read the same newspapers. They draw their political and social views from the same sources. Worse, they talk constantly to one another, thereby providing artificial reinforcement to their shared viewpoints."

Agnew was at considerable pains to deny he was proposing some form of censorship. Instead, he wondered "whether a form of censorship already exists when the news that 40 million Americans receive each night is. . . . filtered through a handful of commentators who admit to their own set of biases." A moment later the Vice President sounded an ominous note, indeed. He questioned whether the wide press freedoms guaranteed to print media by the First Amendment should also apply to television.

Until now the speech had generated a fair amount of applause, but as Agnew uncorked a flurry of finishing-off punches the audience warmed enthusiastically:

"Gresham's Law seems to be operating in the network news. Bad news drives out good news. . . . One minute of Eldridge Cleaver is worth ten minutes of Roy Wilkins."

"How many marches and demonstrations would we have if the marchers did not know that the ever-faithful TV cameras would be there to record their antics?"

"It's time we questioned (such power) in the hands of a small and unelected elite. The great networks have dominated America's air waves for decades. The people are entitled to a full accounting of their stewardship."

The Vice President studiously chose not to define what such an accounting might entail. Thus, his only specific call was for critical self-examination by "the media men" and for viewers to register their own complaints through letters and phone calls to the networks. "This is one case," he said, "where the people must defend themselves."

Response: Within a few hours it was quite clear that Agnew's speech had struck an especially sensitive nerve through the Middle-America that was his audience. Calls to network outlets numbered in the thousands, and Agnew clearly was the winner in the post-speech numbers game. In five cities, NBC received 9,312 pro-Agnew calls and 6,627 endorsing its news policies; CBS reported the same 9 to 7 breakdown, while at ABC the ratio was about 6 to 4. At the Vice President's office, however, the ratio was 35 to 1 in favor of the speech, and White House sources said the favorable response received there was much larger than that accorded President Nixon's plea for similar expressions of support this month for his Vietnam policy. For invective, at least, the tone of the comments matched the Vice President's. "Either shape up or shut down," snapped one caller to CBS.

For their part, the networks contented themselves at the outset with brief statements from their chiefs. NBC president Julian Goodman termed Agnew's address "an appeal to prejudice. Evidently," said Goodman, "he would prefer a different kind of. . . . reporting—one that would be subservient to whatever political group was in authority at the time." To CBS president Frank Stanton, the speech was "an unprecedented attempt by the Vice President. . . . to intimidate a news medium." The mildest response came from ABC head Leonard H. Goldenson, who expressed confidence in "the ultimate judgment of the American public."

Privately, however, the mood among the men who run U. S. television was a bitter blend of anger and apprehension. "It's just another case of the messenger being blamed for the message," said NBC news president Reuven Frank. "If we hurt them with our coverage, they say we say too much. If we hurt them by not covering, they say we say too little." Richard Salant, Frank's counterpart at CBS, called the speech "terribly disheartening" and then voiced the widespread industry conviction that it represented the opening shot in a major Administration offensive.

NBC's Chet Huntley felt the same way. "I hesitate to get into the gutter with this guy," he said of the Vice President, "but this speech is obviously not off the top of Spiro Agnew's head. We've known that the White House has been very unhappy about the remarks after Nixon's speech. This is a concerted drive on the part of the Administration. It could get very vicious and very bloody."

On this point, the agreement in the TV news community was almost unanimous. "That was one of the most significant and one of the most sinister speeches I have ever heard made by a public figure," said ABC's Edward P. Morgan, who holds six awards for broadcasting excellence. "It is significant because it is a perfect gauge of what this Administration is doing. They've been trying to manage the news ever since the campaign." Morgan and others voiced particular despair over what they saw as the Nixon Administration's apparent incapacity to comprehend the real role of the press in general. "These Nixon people," said Morgan, "don't understand and don't want to understand that the function of the press is to stimulate controversy. The fascinating thing is that Mr. Agnew said he wasn't for government censorship. But then he clearly seemed to imply that unless we shape up, we'd better look out. That's the approach of the whole Administration."

By all accounts, the Administration first began gathering basic research material for what was to become Agnew's Des Moines speech the morning after the President's Nov. 3 plea for public support on Vietnam.

Assembled in the Oval Office in the White House West Wing were Presidential aides John Ehrlichman, H. R. (Bob) Haldeman, press secretary Ron Ziegler, Director of Communications Herbert Klein and the President himself. Mr. Nixon had read a number of the telegrams of support pouring in, and someone asked him what he thought of them.

Pleased: The President was pleased with what he had read. He observed rather in passing that he thought the TV commentators had jumped in too fast after the speech and went on to express pleasure at how well the public in general had responded to his plea. A fair number of the telegrams apparently reflected the President's reaction to the TV commentaries, and Herb Klein last week admitted that Agnew's speech "came as a result of a lot of discussion after the letters about Nov. 3 came in."

But the fact is that there was a great deal more going on at the White House than discussion. For one thing, the President's aides had for some time been compiling a dossier of sorts on a least one TV commentator, ABC's Frank Reynolds, who is regarded at the White House with special venom because Nixon staffers feel he was biased and unfair during the campaign.

On Nov. 5, some unusual phone calls were made by Dean Burch, the Administration's newly appointed chairman of the Federal Communications Commission, which has the authority to grant, withhold or refuse to renew broadcasting licenses. Burch last week admitted he took the extraordinary step of personally calling the heads of all three networks following the President's Vietnam address to request transcripts of the commentaries that followed the Vietnam speech. Burch, who as GOP national chairman once sued the FCC in the cause of Sen. Barry Goldwater, said he based his request on complaints he had received.

Opinion: When the storm over Agnew's attack broke, press secretary Ziegler insisted doggedly that Nixon had not discussed the speech with Agnew. But later, deputy counsel Clark Mollenhoff told reporters: "The speech was developed in the White House. It represents White House concern about getting through to the public." The actual composition of the speech fell first to Patrick Buchanan, a member of the President's speech-writing team. Later Buchanan's draft was worked over by Agnew writer Cynthia Rosenthal, by other aides and by the Veep himself.

Presidential assistant Bob Haldeman would only confirm that Mr. Nixon watched Agnew's speech with Mrs. Nixon and Tricia but he was at some pains to elaborate on the view the White House takes of television news programs. "TV news critics are not identified as critics," said Haldeman. "They're identified as newsmen." Is the President overly disturbed by the problem? "The President knows what the situation is," Haldeman replied, "and he knows it's been there a long time."

According to another White House aide, the Presidential appraisal of the different television commentators varies considerably from network to network. Thus ABC's Howard K. Smith is considered fairer than he used to be. Walter Cronkite is generally admired ("The President is personally very fond of Walter") and so are the rest of the CBS team. David Brinkley? "A cynic," snaps the aide. "NBC is the worst." He added: "I could take most of the networks' sloppiness if it weren't for their institutionalized self-righteousness."

As the reaction to Agnew's speech continued to pour in throughout the week, the networks themselves seemed to react ever more defensively. From CBS, a directive went out ordering correspondents and commentators to clam up about the issue on the air or when questioned by reporters, and at ABC the gloom was everywhere. "The big test is the attitude of the networks," said one top ABC staffer. "They have to make up their minds whether they'll stand up to Agnew or lie down—and thus encourage further attacks from him and others." Like others who invoked the shade of Joseph McCarthy, a veteran CBS Washington commentator admitted deep alarm. "My feeling," he said, "is that the White House is out to get all of us, all the liberals in all the media. They've taken on television first because we are the most easily intimidated and because the right wing hates us most. We're in for some dangerous times."

Other industry officials, particularly at the corporate level, were considerably less shrill. "I don't see any dire plot here to muzzle freedom of speech," said Edwin James, executive editor of Broadcast Magazine, television's influential trade publication. "That speech is the fruit of a long-simmering resentment against the networks by the current Administration. But any time a Vice President of the United States gets up and gives this kind of talk, you've got to assume that there are dangers involved. The long-term ramifications are worrying. The Vice President's rather pointed reference to the Supreme Court decision giving broadcasting much less protection under the Constitution than the press, for example. What Agnew was saying fundamentally is that the First Amendment is no damn good (as protection for broadcasters). This deterioration of regard for the First Amendment can't lead to anything good."

At the FCC itself, chairman Burch issued a noncommittal statement summing up Agnew's comments as thoughtful, provocative—not at all censorial—and deserving of careful consideration by the industry and public. Other staffers, however, feared that the commission's traditional policy of scrupulous non-interference with TV news programs may now be substantially altered, and with direct approval from the White House itself.

Former FCC chairman William Henry summed up this apprehension in these words: "When the government licenses a facility the government should be very cautious in even appearing to exert force or pressure on the content, particularly on a shotgun basis like this. Agnew threatened that the government is watching. I would hope that this does not foreshadow a trend. If it does, I think everything possible should be done to stop it."

For all the outcry against the Administration's attack on television, there were also a number of responsible voices raised to protest any suggestion that the media in general and television in particular are above criticism.

"I don't share Agnew's paranoia," said Brandeis University political science professor John Roche, who as one of Lyndon Johnson's foreign-policy advisers had ample chance to assess television's shortcomings. "I don't share his notions of what he sees as objective truth. But I think anything that contributes to competitiveness in the news media is all for the good. I can't count the number of times I've turned off the television set in the last four years because of one-sided coverage of Vietnam or seriously loaded coverage of riots and the demands of black militants."

Roche scoffs at Agnew's view of a conspiracy at the top. "They're only interested in making a buck," he says. "They couldn't let their political views interfere with corporate profits."

The Cutting Edge: What Roche and others profess to see is danger from a much lower level in the television industry. "At the junior producer level," he says, "there are a lot of very bright, college-educated guys still in their twenties who decide which film clips to run. They are the industry's operational cutting edge. They decide which shots will be used in covering a civil-rights march. The vigor of the tapes they produce determines how much time is given to a single subject.

"I've been in television studios while working for President Johnson. Just before going on the air, staffers would ask me how anyone can support an immoral war. On one news program I felt like a nun in a whorehouse. The producer was using a picture of Johnson for a dartboard. The whole atmosphere was of contempt for me and the views I accept."

Later in the week, another former LBJ aide summed up his reaction to Agnew's performance in Des Moines. "It's a shame that Agnew had to make that speech," said Bill Moyers, now publisher of Long Island's *Newsday,* "because there was a meanness in the speech that I think the discussion should avoid. But I think it's a legitimate debate, don't you?"

It was clear that many Americans were prepared to join that debate. On the one hand, there was no doubt that the Vice President's attack had struck a sympathetic chord among those who question the credibility of what they see on their TV screens. On the other, it was certain that TV journalism would attract defenders against the prospect of improper governmental pressure. And in a broader context, Agnew had raised ugly suspicions about the news media in general—suspicions that threaten to divide the nation for some time to come.

QUESTIONS FOR DISCUSSION AND DIALOGUE

1. Reread ABC's Edward P. Morgan's views, John Roche's views, and Vice President Agnew's views on national television news. Write a brief summary of these differing views. With which do you agree the most? Why?

2. Should television "news" be considered the same as traditional newspaper "news"? Why? Should first amendment protections of free press apply to television also? Equally? Why?
3. (Refer back to Stewart Alsop's "The New Snobbism"—Chapter Three.) From Alsop's article and from the excerpts of Agnew's speech reprinted in this article, do you think Alsop and Agnew are speaking about the same thing? Discuss.

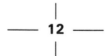

It's Your Party

League of Women Voters of California

On the back of the pamphlet "It's Your Party" is the following statement: "Membership in the League of Women Voters is open to all women of voting age. Experts qualified to judge accuracy and balanced presentation have reviewed this publication before printing." The League describes itself as "a non-partisan organization whose purpose is to promote political responsibility; it does not support, oppose, or evaluate political parties or candidates, nor do candidates pay for space in League election publications." This chapter concluding example of a publication by this distinguished nonpartisan organization demonstrates how the nonpolitical influential function is exercised with less of the need for qualifying and limiting the prefix "non" than with courts, police, scholars, and press. In the excerpts taken from "It's Your Party," the League describes California political party membership and activity. The American who wishes objective information about politics finds a guide that certainly has a different ring to it than television commercials and campaign brochures! The League of Women Voters has the same kind of information available about candidates, as well as information regarding many other citizenship concerns. This particular information is about the status of California law concerning political parties, but it offers some general idea of the legal status of political parties as well as how the League of Women Voters informs citizens about politics.

"Political parties are voluntary organizations of citizens or groups of citizens advocating certain principles and policies for the general conduct of government."

The legal basis for political parties is found in the laws of the states. National political party organizations influence but do not have absolute control over the state groupings of political parties. The most obvious function of political parties is that they present for nomination and election candidates for public office. Having achieved election, the former candidate now has the responsibility to make an honest attempt to apply in office the principles of the party which has nominated, worked for and elected him. However, there are many other functions of political parties besides selecting candidates for office.

I. Political Party Membership

Are you an "idiote?" The ancient Greeks called the qualified non-voter "idiote," describing how the community felt about those who were qualified, and did not vote. Most people believe that a responsible adult citizen should be registered, vote in primary as well as general elections, be aware of party platforms, issues, and background and beliefs of candidates, and VOTE!

Many people ask, "What good will one vote do?" Historically one vote has accomplished many things:

One vote brought California into the Union.

One vote paved the way for American independence.

One vote elected three Presidents—Thomas Jefferson, John Quincy Adams, Rutherford B. Hayes.

One vote resulted in adoption of Prohibition.

One vote passed the Draft Act in World War II.

The first step to full citizenship is to be registered. The second step is to exercise your voting privilege. Your vote is more effective if you are a member of a political party. Political organizations lack strength and influence unless their members are qualified electors, registered in the party affiliation of the organization.

II. Political Party Structure

Individuals usually enter political activity through local units of volunteer organizations or as non-voting members of regular committees of their County Central Committee, in their own Assembly or Congressional District. With time, work, and experience, they may be appointed members or associate members of their State Central Committee. Or they may decide to run for election to the County Central Committee, or be appointed alternate members of that unit within their Assembly District as a reward for party work.

Basically, political party structure may be broken down to three parts:

(1) party officials and official party organizations

(2) volunteer organizations

(3) auxiliary groups

The *party organization* may be defined as the working official organization of the party. Some officials are elected, some appointed, depending on the post. Officials may be elected by the entire party, or may be elected by members of the particular committee only, depending again upon the post. *Volunteer organizations* do the great bulk of the work for the official party. The third type, *auxiliary groups,* are those unofficial clubs or unaffiliated groups which sometimes join with both the volunteer organizations and the official party organization in support of a candidate or cause, or slate of candidates.

No clear cut authority-responsibility line exists between levels (county, state, national) and coordination really occurs through the application of custom and common sense; *e.g.* County Central Committee chairmen serve on their State Central Committee. Nominees and elected state officials serve on both the County Central Committee and the State Central Committee. The party's National Committeemen and Committeewomen, among others, serve on the State Central Committee Executive Committee. The heads of several volunteer organizations serve on the Executive Committees of the County, State, and National Committees of each "official" party. ...

Functions of County Central Committees

1. *County Central Committee:* the body established by California law to assume the responsibility for political party affairs in the county under California Elections Code, section 8442, "County Central Committees shall perform. . . duties and services for their respective political parties as seem to be for the benefit of each party." Members are elected by the voters every two years at the Primary Election. They also include the party's candidates for Assembly at the last General Election as ex-officio members. The term of office is two years.

2. Basic countywide programs of the parties are usually carried out by the County Central Committees:
   a) Precinct organization
   b) Candidate search and development
   c) Candidate campaign plans and strategy
   d) Information and communications
   e) Coordinating the various groups which carry out the above program
   f) Chartering clubs of volunteer organizations

3. Relationship of the County Central Committees to volunteer organizations:
   a) Responsibility for developing overall plans belongs to the County Central Committees which recruit hundreds of additional volunteer workers to carry out the objectives of each party.
   b) Organization charts of county, state and national party structure and lists of local organizations are usually available at party headquarters.

Functions of the State Central Committee

1. *State Central Committee:* the body established by California law to assume the responsibility for political party affairs in the state, under California Elections Code, section 231, "Each State Central Committee shall conduct party campaigns for the party to which it belongs and in behalf of candidates of its party ... and perfect whatever campaign organizations it deems suitable or desirable for the best interest of the party."

2. Composition of the State Central Committee:
   a) All delegates to the state convention of each major political party
   b) The chairmen of County Central Committees of each party
   c) Members appointed by nominees for statewide Congressional and State Senate and Assembly offices of each party, selected at the Primary Election every two years
   d) The National Committeeman and National Committeewoman of the party

e) Term of office; two years

3. Relationship of the County Central Committees to volunteer or—State Central Committee of the party in close cooperation with the County Central Committee:

   a) Precinct organization
   b) Candidate search and development
   c) Candidate campaign plans and strategy, particularly for state-wide offices every four years (as Governor, Lieutenant Governor, Secretary of State, Controller, Treasurer, Attorney General)
   d) Information and communication statewide
   e) Financing of the party's state activities
   f) Coordinating the various statewide groups which carry out the above program

4. Relationship of the State Central Committee to each party, and their volunteer groups:

   a) Responsibility for developing overall plans belongs to the State Central Committees working in close cooperation with the County Central Committees.
   b) Organization charts of structure are available at party offices.

Party Executive Committees

The various County Central Committees, the State Central Committee, and the National Committee all have executive committees. The reason for these smaller executive committees is obvious; the central Committees are very large and it is more practical to have a smaller, housekeeping force to "run the shop." The executive committees do this.

1. The County Executive Committee handles day-to-day affairs. It consists of the Congressional District Chairman within the county, several County Vice-Chairmen, and the Officers elected by the full County Central Committees. The Presidents of the various volunteer organizations (the county president(s) only) are usually members of the Executive Committee, and additional members are elected to assure representation from all Assembly Districts. The Executive Committee develops and supervises programs, and attempts to coordinate precinct work, finance, public relations and candidate development. The county committee level presents one area where there is some contact between official and volunteer activities.

2. The State Executive Committee is selected by and from the membership of the State Central Committee and attempts coordination of the State Central Committee, the State Senate Campaign Committee, the State Assembly Campaign Committee, the County Central Committees, statewide volunteer organizations, and the National Committee. Its members consist of State Central Committee officers, California U.S. Senators, certain County Central Committee Chairmen, California National Committeeman and Committeewoman, representatives of the most important volunteer organizations, and certain Assemblymen

and State Senators. In addition, all county chairmen and party members of the California Legislature are ex-officio members of the Executive Committee.

3. The National Executive Committee carries on the administrative functions of the national party. Members include the National Chairman, Vice-chairman, Secretary, Treasurer, General Counsel, and members elected from among National Committee members-at-large. Sometimes included are national presidents of the most important volunteer organizations.

Convention Structure: State and National

1. *The State Convention* is recognized by statute. It meets every two years between the June primary and the November Election. It is composed in part of the party nominees or most recent nominee, if the office is not up for re-election that year for partisan office. Thus it would be composed of Assembly nominees, State Senators or nominees, and State Constitutional Officers or nominees—Governor, Lieutenant Governor, Attorney General, Secretary of State, Controller, Treasurer, 4-member Board of Equalization, U.S. Representative nominees, U.S. Senators or nominees. Chief activity of the State Convention is adoption of a California Party Platform. In Presidential election years the State Convention nominates the members of the Electoral College.

2. *National Convention:* delegates are elected as a slate by the voters at the Primary Election. The actual number of allotted delegates is set every four years by the National Committee and is based on a number of factors including state-wide results in the most recent Presidential and Gubernatorial elections. Republicans and Democrats use different formulae to determine the size of various state delegations to national conventions and thus the size of these two parties' California delegations differ. Delegates for both national party conventions are elected as a state favoring, but not necessarily pledged to, a given candidate. Delegation size may vary in rough proportion to the number of Congressmen a state has. Convention delegates are of varying political importance—and may include anyone from presidential possibilities down to a precinct captain. They may be pledged to a specific candidate, may be "uninstructed," or may be pledged for the first ballot only. Delegates usually vote as instructed by party leaders, with occasional "bolting."

National Committee

The National Committee is delegated authority by the party convention for conduct of national party affairs between conventions. It consists of one committeeman and one committeewoman from each state, territory and territorial possession. Other members include State Chairmen whose state achieved a certain measure of political strength (depends on party specification). The National Executive Committee acts as "Board of Directors" of the National Committee. There is no law establishing the National Convention or National Committee. These groups have evolved by custom and have established their own rules.

National Congressional and Senatorial Campaign Committees

These are composed of members from the House of Representatives and Senate selected biennially in each new Congress at conferences of party membership. These committees direct their activities and funds to assist party nominees for the House and Senate of the nation in their campaigns, and survey the field to see where assistance is particularly needed, or where it may count most.

Professional Full-time Staffs

These persons perform jobs at various levels which range from secretary-receptionist for one of the volunteer organizations to the salaried public relations director for the County Central Committee. These paid staffs do much of the routine work and day-to-day chores but take little part in nominating candidates.

III. Parties under California Law

In order to qualify as a political party California law requires:

1. If at the last preceding November election at which a Governor was elected there was polled for any one of the party's candidates for statewide office at least 2% of the entire vote of the State; or

2. If at the last preceding election of a Governor there was polled for any one of its candidates who was the joint candidate with any other party for statewide office 6% of the entire vote of the State; or

3. If on or before the 135th day preceding any primary election the record shows that registered voters equal to at least 1% of the entire vote of the State at the last preceding election of a Governor have declared their intention to affiliate with such political party or organization; or

4. If on or before the 135th day preceding any primary election, a petition is filed with the Secretary of State signed by registered qualified voters equal to 10% of all the votes cast in the last preceding November election of a Governor, declaring that they represent a political party or organization; provided that the name of the proposed political party is not so similar to that of an existing party of organization as to mislead the voters. The petition is handled in substantially the same manner as an initiative petition;

5. Except that whenever the registration of any party which qualified in the previous direct primary election falls below one fifteenth of one percent of the total state registration, that party shall not be qualified to participate in the primary election, but shall be deemed to have been abandoned by the voters.

No party which either directly or indirectly carries on, advocates, teaches, justifies, aids, or abets the overthrow by any unlawful means of the government of the United States or this State shall be recognized or qualified to participate in any primary election. Within 125 days before a primary election, the Secretary of State, with the advice and consent of the Attorney General, determines which parties are disqualified to participate. Notice of disqualification must be given: If the party desires a hearing it must, within ten days after notice has been served, file an affidavit in the Supreme Court of California.

The election laws of the State of California provide for the duties and responsibilities of political parties beginning with Section 8000 and extending through Section 8474 of the Election Code.

IV. Citizen Participation

There are a great many political organizations. Participation may vary from bazaar craft projects, to solicitations, to door-knocking precinct work, to participation in issue discussion and candidate selection.

Precinct Work: The precinct is the smallest political unit, a small area of a few blocks. If you do not know your precinct number, you may obtain it from the office of the Registrar of Voters. The precinct contains between 250-300 registered voters and is identified by a number, and the city or county in which it is located. A number of precincts make up the larger geographical groupings of Assembly Districts, Congressional Districts, and County and State groupings.

As the precinct is the basic political voting unit, citizen participation is readily possible in precinct work during elections. Precinct work, besides the ease with which it is open to newcomers, gives the citizens a feeling of direct participation in the democratic voting processes. In addition, as political parties have a difficult time finding enough people to man every precinct, precinct workers are especially welcome to both parties.

Precinct work involves registering unregistered voters, helping voters to the polls, and such jobs as distributing campaign literature.

If your precinct is well organized, there is a block worker in your block who knows every family and maintains a card file on each, showing the number of eligible voters, their party affiliations, and a notation as to how often each has voted in the past. The block worker makes certain that each member of this party is registered, and that he votes. He also distributes party literature in his block and keeps people informed of meetings and party functions. Precinct voters hold the key to party power, not only in the precinct, but in the ward, which is composed of several precincts, and the county, which has as few as 30 or as many as 12,000 precincts.

Block workers report to the precinct captain, whose job it is to maintain an efficient organization in order to guarantee the largest possible vote on election day. A good precinct leader (or "captain") will lend what aid he can to families within his precinct, often in matters far removed from politics.

The bulk of the efforts of the precinct captain and his block workers is performed in three stages twice each election year; once during the primaries and once during the general election. These stages are:

1.　Thirty days before the close of registration, the block worker makes certain all members of the party are registered, and brings the card file up to date.

2.　Four to six weeks before the election he calls on members of his party and answers any questions.

3.　On election day, he keeps a close tab on the voters he is responsible for and maintains close contact with his captain and district precinct chairman.

Volunteer Organizations and Clubs: These. . . They offer a number of advantages which include:

1. They operate year-round, allowing members to observe, to take part in all aspects of political activity, and to learn the ground rules.

2. Anyone can join at any time.

3. The structure of clubs is much less formal, and individuals can readily enter and find a place to learn political skills. Members learn by doing, making the transition to active party workers much easier because of knowledge gained. For these and several other reasons, party clubs may be worthy of your consideration. Their needs, if they are to remain effective, require that they have active members whose talents and skills cover a wide range.

QUESTIONS FOR DISCUSSION AND DIALOGUE

1. Outline some activities a citizen could perform in support of his political party. By definition, one who registers "Independent" is not a party member. Do you think this limits the contributions he might make as a citizen? If your answer is "no," discuss why. If your answer is "yes," are there any balancing factors to this limitation?

2. How would you answer this question about the League of Women Voters: What's in it for them? Is this a different answer than you would expect from the other groups that have been studied—the Americans, the Students, the Politicians and their Parties, the other Nonpolitical Influentials? Discuss.

3. If you do not live in California, are the laws of your state about political parties similar to those of California? Is the opportunity for "Citizen Participation" the same? Discuss.

———— CHAPTER FIVE ————

The Stakes

The idealistic motivations of politics, the changes in political-social-economic America of the 1970's, and suggestions about how concerned Americans can influence the course of their nation are considered by this chapter.

A sad and memorable speech about human and political responsibility opens Chapter Five, followed by the late President John F. Kennedy's words on the "moral crisis" the United States faces in righting the wrongs of discrimination against Negroes. The problems of what to do about racial discrimination are considered in the following article from another point of view by Whitney Young, who thinks that colleges and universities must " 'reeducate' the type of white people who voted for George C. Wallace." The real culprits of organized crime —ourselves—get indicted by Wilfrid Laurier Husband in his book review of *Theft of a Nation,* and Herbert Gans discusses what he terms the "Equality Revolution of the 60's" in the *New York Times Student Weekly.* Eric Sevareid, in a *Look* article, claims the American dream is neither dead nor dying. Next an excerpt from Stewart Udall's book *1976 Agenda for Tomorrow* explains the effort of the will needed by Americans to meet the qualitative, ecological problems of the 1970's. The chapter concludes with former Secretary of Health, Education, and Welfare John Gardner suggesting how we can renew our institutions generally and by specific advice "For a Revolutionary Generation."

Text of a Brother's Funeral Eulogy

Edward Kennedy

Edward Kennedy's Eulogy of his assassinated brother sums up the idealism and courage of Robert Kennedy. It is an eloquent expression of what is at stake politically in our nation as well as throughout the world.

On behalf of Mrs. Robert Kennedy, her children and the parents and sisters of Robert Kennedy, I want to express what we feel to those who mourn with us today in this cathedral and around the world. We loved him as a brother, as a father and as a son. From his parents, and from his older brothers and sisters—Joe, Kathleen and Jack—he received inspiration which he passed on to all of us. He gave us strength in time of trouble, wisdom in time of uncertainty, and sharing in time of happiness. He was always by our side.

Love is not an easy feeling to put into words. Nor is loyalty, or trust, or joy. But he was all of these. He loved life completely and lived it intensely.

A few years back, Robert Kennedy wrote some words about his own father and they expressed the way we in the family feel about him. He said of what his father meant to him: "What it really all adds up to is love—not love as it is described with such futility in popular magazines, but the kind of love that is affection and respect, order, encouragement and support.

"Our awareness of this was an incalculable source of strength, and because real love is something unselfish and involves sacrifice and giving, we could not help but profit from it.

"Beneath it all, he has tried to engender a social conscience. There were wrongs which needed attention. There were people who were poor and needed help. And we have a responsibility to them and to this country. Through no virtues and accomplishments of our own, we have been fortunate enough to be born in the United States under the most comfortable conditions. We, therefore, have a responsibility to others who are less well off."

This is what Robert Kennedy was given. What he leaves us is what he said, what he did and what he stood for. A speech he made to the young people of South Africa on their day of affirmation in 1966 sums it up the best, and I would read it now:

"There is a discrimination in this world and slavery and slaughter and starvation. Governments repress their people; and millions are trapped in poverty while the nation grows rich; and wealth is lavished on armaments everywhere.

"These are differing evils, but they are the common works of man. They reflect the imperfection of human justice, the inadequacy of human compassion, our lack of sensibility toward the sufferings of our fellows.

"But we can perhaps remember—even if only for a time—that those who live with us are our brothers, that they share with us the same short moment of life; that they seek—as we do—nothing but the chance to live out their lives in purposes and happiness, winning what satisfaction and fulfillment they can.

"Surely this bond of common faith, this bond of common goal, can begin to teach us something. Surely we can learn, at least, to look at those around us as fellow men. And surely we can begin to work a little harder to bind up the wounds among us and to become in our own hearts brothers and countrymen once again.

"Our answer is to rely on youth—not a time of life but a state of mind—a temper of the will, a quality of imagination, a predominance of courage over timidity, of the appetite for adventure over the love of ease. The cruelties and obstacles of this swiftly changing planet will not yield to obsolete dogmas and outworn slogans. They cannot be moved by those who cling to a present that is already dying, who prefer the illusion of security to the excitement and danger that come with even the most peaceful progress.

"It is a revolutionary world we live in; and this generation at home and around the world has had thrust upon it a greater burden of responsibility than any generation that has ever lived.

"Some believe there is nothing one man or one woman can do against the enormous array of the world's ills. Yet many of the world's great movements, of thought and action, have flowed from the work of a single man. A young monk began the Protestant Reformation, a young general extended an empire from Macedonia to the borders of the earth, and a young woman reclaimed the territory of France. It was a young Italian explorer who discovered the New World, and the 32-year-old Thomas Jefferson who proclaimed that all men are created equal.

"These men moved the world, and so can we all. Few will have the greatness to bend history itself, but each of us can work to change a small portion of events and in the total of all those acts will be written the history of this generation. It is from numberless diverse acts of courage and belief that human history is shaped. Each time a man stands up for an ideal, or acts to improve the lot of others, or strikes out against injustice, he sends forth a tiny ripple of hope, and crossing each other from a million different centers of energy and daring, those ripples build a current that can sweep down the mightiest walls of oppression and resistance.

"Few are willing to brave the disapproval of their fellows, the censure of their colleagues, the wrath of their society. Moral courage is a rarer commodity than bravery in battle or great intelligence. Yet it is the one essential, vital quality for those who seek to change a world that yields most painfully to change. And I believe that in this generation those with the courage to enter the moral conflict will find themselves with companions in every corner of the globe.

"For the fortunate among us, there is the temptation to follow the easy and familiar paths of personal ambition and financial success so grandly spread before those who enjoy the privilege of education. But that is not the road history has marked out for us. Like it or not, we live in times of danger and uncertainty, but they are also more open to the creative energy of men than any other time in history. All of us will ultimately be judged and as the years pass we will surely judge ourselves, on the effort we have contributed to building a new world society and the extent to which our ideals and goals have shaped that effort.

"The future does not belong to those who are content with today, apathetic toward common problems and their fellow man alike, timid and fearful in the face of new ideas and bold projects. Rather it will belong to those who can blend vision, reason and courage in a personal commitment to the ideals and great enterprises of American society.

"Our future may lie beyond our vision, but it is not completely beyond our control. It is the shaping impulse of America, neither fate nor the irresistible tides of history, but the work of our own hands, matched to reason and principle, that will determine our destiny. There is pride in that, even elegance, but there is also experience and truth. In any event, it is the only way we can live."

This is the way he lived. My brother need not be idealized or enlarged in death beyond what he was in life, to be remembered simply as a good and decent man, who saw wrong and tried to right it, saw suffering and tried to heal it, saw war and tried to stop it.

Those of us who loved him and who take him to his rest today, pray that what he was to us, and what he wished for others will some day come to pass for all the world.

As he said many times, in many parts of this nation, to those he touched and who sought to touch him:

"Some men see things as they are and say why.

"I dream things that never were and say why not."

QUESTIONS FOR DISCUSSION AND DIALOGUE

1. How did Robert Kennedy respond to this kind of statement? "There is nothing one man or one woman can do against the enormous array of the world's ills." Do you agree with his response? Why?
2. Reread the seventh last paragraph. Do you agree with Kennedy's observations about who the future belongs to? Based on what you see in the United States of the 1970's, do you think the U.S. "can blend vision, reason, and courage in a personal commitment to the ideals and great enterprises of American society?" Discuss.
3. What are the implications of these lines for the Americans? "Some men see things as they are and say why?" "I dream things that never were and say why not?" Discuss.

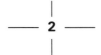

A. "We Face... A Moral Crisis... As a People"
John F. Kennedy

B. Re-educate 'Affluent Peasants,' Young Tells Colleges
Philip Semas

Though delivered in a June 1963 speech, these words of President Kennedy touch home today as well. The moral problem of blatant racial discrimination which denied Negroes admission to the University of Alabama was far easier for most Americans in the North to condemn than housing discrimination and ghetto schools which did not provide education. President Kennedy discusses these problems in terms of simple human justice, and recognizes that "law alone cannot make man see right." Whitney Young addresses himself to the same kind of problem— discrimination—but he recommends re-educating "the type of white people who voted for George C. Wallace" in order to help resolve it.

A. "We Face... A Moral Crisis... As a People"

Excerpts from the President's TV-radio talk to the nation on Civil Rights:

I hope that every American, regardless of where he lives, will stop and examine his conscience about the (Tuscaloosa case) and other related incidents.

This is not a sectional issue. Difficulties over segregation and discrimination exist in every city, in every state of the Union. . . . Nor is this a partisan issue. This is not even a legal . . . issue alone. It is better to settle these matters in the courts than on the streets, and new laws are needed at every level. But law alone cannot make man see right.

We are confronted primarily with a moral issue. It is as old as the Scriptures and is as clear as the American Constitution. The heart of the question is whether all Americans are to be afforded equal rights and equal opportunities; whether we. . . treat our fellow Americans as we want to be treated.

If an American, because his skin is dark, cannot eat lunch in a restaurant open to the public; if he cannot send his children to the best public school available; if he cannot vote for the public officials who represent him; if, in short, he cannot enjoy the full and free life which all of us want, then who among us would be content to have the color of his skin changed and stand in his place?

Who among us would then be content with the counsels of patience and delay? One hundred years of delay have passed since President Lincoln freed the slaves, yet their heirs, their grandsons, are not fully free. They are not yet freed from the bonds of injustice; they are not yet freed from social and economic oppression.

And this nation, for all its hopes and all its boasts, will not be fully free until all its citizens are free.

WE MEAN IT: We preach freedom around the world, and we mean it. And we cherish our freedom here at home. But are we to say to the world—and much more importantly to each other—that this is the land of the free, except for the Negroes; that we have no second-class citizens, except Negroes; that we have no class or caste system, no ghettos, no master race, except with respect to Negroes?

Now the time has come for this nation to fulfill its promise. The events in Birmingham and elsewhere have so increased the cries for equality that no city or state or legislative body can prudently choose to ignore them.

The fires of frustration and discord are burning in every city, North and South. Where legal remedies are not at hand, redress is sought in the streets in demonstrations, parades, and protests, which create tensions and threaten violence—and threaten lives.

We face, therefore, a moral crisis as a country and a people. It cannot be met by repressive police action. It cannot be left to increased demonstrations in the streets. It cannot be quieted by token moves or talk. It is a time to act in the Congress, in your state and local legislative body, and, above all, in all of our daily lives.

It is not enought to pin the blame on others, to say this is a problem of one section of the country or another, or deplore the facts that we face. A great change is at hand, and our task, our obligation is to make that revolution, that change peaceful and constructive for all.

Those who do nothing are inviting shame as well as violence. Those who act boldly are recognizing right as well as reality. . . .

It seems to me that these are matters which concern us all. . . every citizen of the United States.

B. Re-Educate 'Affluent Peasants,' Young Tells Colleges

Colleges and universities not only must provide better education for Negroes but must work to "re-educate" the type of white people who voted for George C. Wallace, says one of the nation's top Negro leaders.

Whitney Young, executive director of the Urban League, told the Association of University Evening Colleges that they must teach what he called the "affluent peasants" that "it is no longer cosmopolitan or sophisticated for them to surround themselves with people who look just like them."

Militant Negroes are saying that "white people will never give up their advantage, privilege, and wealth unless we destroy the system," Mr. Young said, while moderates are trying to convince Negroes that the system is still workable. "It's up to you to decide who's going to be the prophet," he told the 300 deans and extension division directors attending the meeting.

He said educators could convince whites to give up power to Negroes "if you identify an enlightened self-interest and show how the alternatives are worse."

Mr. Young said he supports students when they demand courses in Negro history, admission of more non-white students, and "relevance to the problems of the community."

He said university night schools must stop "adjusting programs to the status quo and serving the establishment." He said too many night schools are aimed at "helping junior executives reach the executive level and providing a little culture for those little old ladies in tennis shoes."

Pointing out that Negroes may soon be a majority in 10 of the nation's 11 largest cities, Mr. Young said urban colleges, especially night schools, must train Negroes to be leaders in these communities. "The question is, Do you want Rap Brown or Eddie Brooks to be the mayor?" he said, referring to the Negro militant and the Massachusetts Senator.

QUESTIONS FOR DISCUSSION AND DIALOGUE

1. Why does John Kennedy discuss racial discrimination as a "moral issue?" Do you agree? Why?
2. Many whites suggest blacks should be patient and delay their drive for civil rights. How does Kennedy answer this kind of advice? How would you answer? How did Eldridge Cleaver and Martin Luther King respond to this kind of advice? (Chapter One)
3. Reread the last four paragraphs of President Kennedy's speech. Outline the suggestions contained for meeting the "moral crisis" of discrimination. Which points do you think are the most important?
4. What do you think about his statement in the Whitney Young article?. . . "Educators could convince whites to give up power to Negroes 'if you identify an enlightened self-interest and show how the alternatives are worse.' " Discuss.

—— 3 ——

Theft of the Nation: The Structure and Operations of Organized Crime in America, Donald R. Cressey

Reviewed by Wilfrid Laurier Husband

The actual roots of organized crime are discussed in this book review. We are the roots. As Americans we often expect the politicians and nonpolitical influentials to deal with crime. "It's their job, isn't it?" Husband's book review of *Theft of the Nation* indicates otherwise. In the words of the book: "We are concerned because millions of Americans are, in hundreds of minor ways, already paying ransom to organized criminals." As with other major problems of American society and politics, future reform must involve an interaction of groups; but in the long run the general American citizenry will make the most important decisions.

United States Attorney Robert Morgenthau was quoted by the *New York Times* for February 16 as saying: "The death of Vito Genovese presents a 'great opportunity' to strike a crippling blow at his Mafia gang before it can regroup under new leadership."

This statement appears unrealistic in light of the information presented by the California criminologist Donald Cressey in his book *Theft of the Nation,* which was completed shortly before Genovese died. Mr. Cressey writes: "For each vacant Cosa Nostra membership position, there are at least a hundred applicants. Incarceration of members disrupts the organization only for the time needed to obtain replacements. Thus, for example, imprisonment of one New York 'Family' boss, Vito Genovese, has had no discernible effect on the amount of crime committed by his Family."

Cressey's book clearly shows that crime in the United States is highly organized and far-reaching. In it he analyzes and expands the facts contained in his earlier report to the President's Commission on Law Enforcement.

A nationwide alliance of at least twenty-four tightly knit Families of criminals exists in this country. Those on the Eastern seaboard call the system "Cosa Nostra" (otherwise known as the Mafia, the syndicate, the underworld). The names, criminal records, and activities of about five thousand members are well known to law-enforcement officials. As one example, the book charts the hierarchy of the Greater New York Family. Among other things it shows three men ruling in the absence of Genovese: Tom Eboli, Jerry Catena, Mike Miranda. Key positions in each Family are boss, underboss, lieutenant, counselor. Low-ranking members are "soldiers" or "button men." Other positions include "money mover," "enforcer," and "executioner."

Families are linked to each other and to non-Cosa Nostra syndicates by "treaties" and by mutual deference to a "Commission" made up of leaders of the most powerful Families, which control almost all illegal gambling. They are also the principal loan sharks and the big importers as well as wholesalers of narcotics. They have infiltrated numerous labor unions where, through "sweetheart contracts" and other devices, they extort money from employers and at the same time cheat union members. A common trick is their use of the role of "labor consultant" to sell influence over certain unions to employers who seek unfair advantages over legitimate competitors. Alfred Scotti, head of the Rackets Bureau in New York District Attorney Frank Hogan's office, believes this abuse could be eliminated by requiring labor consultants to be licensed.

Moreover, "syndicate members," Cressey points out, "also have a virtual monopoly on an increasing number of legitimate enterprises: Cigarette vending machines and juke boxes and. . . retail firms, restaurants and bars, hotels, trucking, food companies, linen-supply houses, garbage collection, and factories. Until recently, they owned a large part of Las Vegas. They owned several state legislators and federal Congressmen and other officials in the legislative, executive and judicial branch of the government—at local, state and federal levels. Some government officials (including judges) are considered, and consider themselves, members.

In brief, what we must face is that Americans—you and I—have let the cancer of organized crime proliferate in American life. Even those who know this conveniently blame "criminals." We are blind to the fact that by apathy, acquiescence, timidity, or downright collusion we are largely to blame for giving the underworld its sinister power. Cressey hammers this home: "Organized crime exists to provide the illicit goods and services demanded by legitimate society." In that sense, the "respectable" world is poisoning itself.

A star crime reporter who prefers anonymity cites an example: "J. Edgar Hoover is now over seventy-five, yet top political and business leaders are still in awe of him and shudder politely at those who think Hoover should retire. This reverence goes beyond respect for the FBI. Can it be that the FBI head knows of certain relations between business and political bigwigs, on the one hand, and the underworld, on the other? If Hoover pressed too hard against the Mafia, its bosses might retaliate by implicating VIPs in government and business. Final disposition of the Bobby Baker case, among others, has yet to be made."

The book's major value is its revelation of the unholy marriage between organized crime and "respectable" society. But, mercifully, Cressey limits his moral preachments; perhaps he feels there is not enough moral concern to which he can appeal. His thesis is all the more persuasive because it is addressed primarily to our practical self-interest. He makes us see the wisdom of having no truck with the activities from which the Mafia amasses its riches and thereby the power to destroy our integrity and our democracy. Cut off from sustenance which, up to now, we have shamefully given, organized crime would wither.

Another problem touched on in *Theft of the Nation* is the rapid increase of unorganized criminal "loners." They steal cars, burglarize, mug, rape, embezzle, murder, etc. Many are from ghettos and other poverty areas. This development is serious because such loners are steadily recruited into the ranks of organized crime. What excuse is there for the richest nation to permit such poverty, which costs us so dearly?

Cressey is understandably absorbed in the quest to improve law enforcement techniques and to augment trained personnel. But he weakens his effect by devoting so much effort to seeking a perfect definition of "organized crime"; and when he advocates appeasement of kingpins in the underworld, he is unconvincing.

Most law enforcement officials agree with Cressey that "electronic surveillance" (wiretaps, bugging) is an indispensable tool in combating organized crime. Like New York District Attorney Hogan, however, Cressey insists that electronic eavesdropping must be done under court supervision and with proper safeguards.

But important as these and other related problems are, they are secondary to educating the public to the absolute necessity of refusing to buy the Mafia's illicit goods and services. *Theft of the Nation* admirably contributes to that end. For your own self-preservation, get this book and read it.

Tribute to the Mob (Quotation from the book)

We are concerned because millions of Americans are, in hundreds of minor ways, already paying ransom to organized criminals. We do not mean the man who bets a dollar at 1 to 500 or 1 to 600 odds when the "honest" odds are 1 to 1,000. We mean the housewife who must pay a few cents extra each day to have her trash hauled by a company controlled by criminals. We mean the teen-ager who pays a few cents more for a hamburger and a glass of milk because the vendor must buy his supplies from companies controlled by criminals. We mean the college student and the lawyer who must pay a few cents more for their books because they have at some stage been hauled by a truck operator who must, in order to maintain labor peace, buy his tires from a company controlled by criminals. We mean all the other citizens who are required to spend a quarter here and a dollar there because someone, somewhere in the chain from raw material to finished product, must pay a tribute to criminals. We also mean the taxpayer, the poor taxpayer, who must in the long run finance kickbacks to organized criminals and who must pay both his own taxes and a large proportion of the syndicate member's share of taxes. "If organized criminals paid income tax on every cent of the vast earnings, everybody's tax bill would go down, but no one knows how much." In the four-year period 1961-1965 the Internal Revenue Service assessed organized criminals almost a quarter of a billion dollars in taxes and penalties beyond the amounts paid by the criminals when they filed their income-tax forms. In 1965 the City and State of New York lost over $50 million in cigarette-tax revenues to cigarette smuggling by organized criminals. Further, since the smugglers paid no tax on the income derived from the sale of about $138 million worth of cigarettes, another tax source also dried up.

QUESTIONS FOR DISCUSSION AND DIALOGUE

1. Outline some of the major ways the Americans pay ransom to organized criminals.
2. How does this book review demonstrate the oversimplifications of crime and criminal problems inherent in such slogans as "Support your local police" and "law and order?"

Equality Revolution of the 60's

Herbert J. Gans

Students of politics before and after John Locke and Jean Jacques Rousseau have argued about the difference between liberty and equality. The implications of the difference between the two terms are in large part what distinguishes philosophical conservatives and liberals. Herbert Gans looks at modern America as he sees it reinterpreting the liberty-equality equation toward more equality and less liberty, as those terms have been defined traditionally in the post 1930's United States. Must there be a contradiction between liberty and equality? Gans' conclusion is optimistic, but he admits his conclusion is that of a citizen rather than a sociologist. Hopefully for all of us, the sociologists' data will not contradict and negate the citizens' hopes!

Mr. Gans is a sociologist-planner on the staff of the Center for Urban Education and a member of the faculty of Teachers College, Columbia University.

Someday, when historians write about the nineteen-sixties they may describe them as the years in which America rediscovered the poverty still in its midst and in which social protest, ranging from demonstrations to violent uprisings, reappeared on the American scene. But the historians may also note a curious fact, that the social protest of the sixties has very little to do with poverty. Most of the demonstrators and marchers who followed Martin Luther King were not poor; the college students who have been protesting and sitting-in on campus are well-to-do, and even the participants in the ghetto uprisings of the last few years —although hardly affluent—were not drawn from the poorest sectors of the ghetto.

The social protest of the nineteen-sixties has to do with *inequality,* with the pervasive inequities remaining in American life. So far the demand for greater equality has come largely from the young and the black, but I wish to suggest that in the years to come, America will face a demand for more equality in various aspects of life from many other types of citizens—a demand so pervasive that it might well be described as the "equality revolution."

This demand will take many forms. Some will ask for *equality,* pure and simple; others will press for more *democracy,* for greater participation in and responsiveness by their places of work and their governments; yet others will ask for more *autonomy,* for the freedom to be what they want to be and to choose how they will live. All these demands add up to a desire for greater control over one's life, requiring the reduction of the many inequities—economic, political and social—that now prevent people from determining how they will spend their short time on this earth.

Ever since the Declaration of Independence decreed that all men are created equal, Americans have generally believed that they were or could be equal. Of course, the Constitution argued by omission that slaves were unequal, and we all know that many other inequities exist in America. Undoubtedly, the most serious of these is economic.

About a fifth of the country lives on incomes below the so-called Federal "poverty line" of $3,300 for an urban family of four, and the proportion is higher if the population not counted by the last census (14 per cent of all Negro males, for example) is included. An additional 7 per cent of households, earning between $3,300 and $4,300 a year, are considered "near poor" by the Social Security Administration. Altogether, then, probably about a third of the country is living at or below the barest subsistence level—and about two-thirds of this population is white.

Moreover, despite the conventional description of America as an affluent society, few of its citizens actually enjoy affluence. The Bureau of Labor Statistics estimates that an urban family of four needs $9,376 a year (and more than $10,000 in New York City) for a "modest but adequate standard of living"; but in 1966, 69 per cent of American families with two children were earning less than $10,000. (Their median income was $7,945, although a recent City University study showed the median income of New York families in 1966 to be only $6,684 —and those of Negroes and Puerto Ricans to be $4,754 and $3,949 respectively.)

Even $9,400 is hardly a comfortable income, and it is fair to say that today the affluent society includes only the 9 per cent of Americans who earn more than $15,000 a year. Everyone else still worries about how to make ends meet, particularly since the standards of the good life have shot up tremendously in the last two decades.

Of course, income levels have also risen in the last 20 years, and an income of $9,400 would classify anyone as rich in most countries. Even the earnings of America's poor would constitute affluence in a country like India. But comparisons with the past and with other countries are irrelevant; people do not live and spend in the past or in other countries, and what they earn must be evaluated in terms of the needs and wants identified as desirable by the mass media and the rest of American culture. Undoubtedly an advertising man or a college professor who earns $15,000 is in the richest 1 per cent of all the people who ever lived, but this fact does not pay his mortgage or send his children to school. And if *he* has economic problems, they are a thousand times greater for the poor, who have much the same wants and hopes, but must make do with $3,000 a year or less.

The extent of economic inequality is also indicated by the fact that the richest

5 per cent of Americans earn 20 per cent of the nation's income; but the bottom 20 per cent earn only 5 per cent of the income. Although this distribution has improved immeasurably since America's beginnings, it has not changed significantly since the nineteen-thirties. In other words, the degree of economic inequality has not been affected by the overall increase in incomes or in gross national product during and after World War II.

There are other kinds of economic inequality in America as well. For example, most good jobs today require at least a bachelor's degree, but many families still cannot afford to send their children to college, even if they are not poor. Job security is also distributed unequally. College professors have tenure and are assured of life-time jobs; professionals and white-color workers earn salaries and are rarely laid off, even in depressions; factory workers, service workers and migrant farm laborers are still paid by the hour, and those not unionized can be laid off at a moment's notice.

Economic inequality goes far beyond income and job security, however. Some executives and white-collar workers have a say in how their work is to be done, but most workers can be fired for talking back to the boss (and are then ineligible for unemployment compensation). Generally speaking, most work places, whether they are offices or factories, are run on an autocratic basis; the employee is inherently unequal and has no more right to determine his work, working conditions or the policy of his work place than the enlisted man in the Army. He is only a cog in a large machine, and he has about as much influence in deciding what he will do as a cog in a machine. Our schools are similarly autocratic; neither in college nor in elementary and high school do students have any significant rights in the classroom; they are unequal citizens who must obey the teacher if they are to graduate.

The poor suffer most from these inequalities, of course. They hold the least secure jobs; they are least often union members; if they are on welfare, they can be made penniless by displeasing the social workers in charge of their cases. And being poor, they pay more for everything. It is well known that they pay more for food (sometimes even at supermarkets) and for furniture and other consumer goods; they also pay more for hospital care, as a recent study in New Haven indicates. They even pay more when they gamble. Affluent Americans can gamble in the stock market, where it is difficult to lose a lot of money except in the wildest speculation. The poor can afford only to play the numbers, where the chance of a "hit" is about 1 in 600, and if they prefer not to participate in an illegal activity, they can play the New York State Lottery, where the chance of winning is only about 1 in 4,000.

Political inequality is rampant, too. Although the Supreme Court's one-man, one-vote decision will eventually result in voting equality, the individuals who contribute to a candidate's election campaign will have far more political influence than others.

Ordinary citizens have few rights in actual practice; how many can afford to argue with policemen, or hire good lawyers to argue their cases, or make their voices heard when talking to their elected representatives? Last year's ['68] political conventions indicated once again that the rank-and-file delegates (including those named by political bosses or rigged state conventions) have little say in the choosing of Presidential candidates or platforms. Even the person who is included in a sample of the now-so-important public-opinion polls cannot state opinion if the pollster's questions are loaded or incorrectly worded.

Economic Level Key to Equality

Finally, there are many kinds of inequality, autocracy and lack of autonomy of which most Americans are not even aware. In many cities, for instance, high-speed mass-transit lines rarely serve poorer neighborhoods and really good doctors and lawyers are available only to the wealthy.

In a large and complex society, inequality and the lack of control over one's life are pervasive and are often thought to be inevitable by-products of modernity and affluence. We are learning, however, that they are not inevitable—that there can be more equality, democracy and autonomy if enough people want them.

In the past, when most people earned just enough to "get by," they were interested mainly in higher incomes and did not concern themselves with equality or autonomy in their everyday lives. For example, the poor took—and still will take—any jobs they could get because they needed the money to pay for the week's food and the month's rent. Working-class and lower-middle-class people were, and are, only slightly more able to choose; they take whatever job will provide the most comfortable lives for themselves and their families. But in the upper-middle class, the job is expected to offer personal satisfactions, and upper-middle-class people gravitate to the jobs and careers that provide more equality and autonomy. The huge increase in graduate-school enrollments suggests that many college students want the personal freedom available in an academic career; their decreasing interest in business careers indicates that they may be rejecting the autocracy and lack of autonomy found in many large corporations.

Today, as more people approach the kind of economic security already found in the affluent upper-middle class, they are beginning to think about the noneconomic satisfactions of the job and of the rest of life; as a result, aspirations for more equality, democracy and autonomy are rising all over America.

Some manifestations of "the equality revolution" are making headlines today, particularly among students and blacks. Whatever the proximate causes of college protests and uprisings, the students who participate in them agree on two demands: the right to be treated as adults—and therefore as equals—and the right to participate in the governing of their schools. Though the mass media have paid most attention to the more radical advocates of these demands, equality and democracy are sought not just by the Students for a Democratic Society but by an ever-increasing number of liberal and even conservative students as well.

Similar demands for equality and democracy are being voiced by the young people of the ghetto. Only a few years ago, they seemed to want integration, the right to become part of the white community. Today, recognizing that white America offered integration to only a token few and required with it assimilation into the white majority, the young blacks are asking for equality instead. When they say that black is beautiful, they are really saying that black is equal to white;

when the ghetto demands control of its institutions, it asks for the right to have the same control that many white neighborhoods have long had.

Many other instances of the equality revolution are less visible, and some have not made the headlines. For example, in the last two generations, wives have achieved near equality in the family, at least in the middle class; they now divide the housework with their husbands and share the decision-making about family expenditures and other activities.

Children have also obtained greater equality and democracy. In many American families, adolescents are now free from adult interference in their leisure-time activities.

Religion Moves to Democracy

Man's relationship to God and the church is moving toward greater equality, too. The minister is no longer a theological father; in many synagogues and Protestant churches, he has become the servant of his congregation, and the unwillingness of many Catholics to abide by the Pope's dictates on birth control hides other, less publicized, instances of the rejection of dogma that is handed down from on high. The real meaning of the "God is Dead" movement, I believe, is that the old conception of God as the infallible autocrat has been rejected.

In the years to come, the demand for more equality, democracy and autonomy is likely to spread to many other aspects of life. Already, some high-school students are beginning to demand the same rights for which college students are organizing, and recipients of public welfare are joining together to put an end to the autocratic fashion in which their payments are given to them. Public employes are striking for better working conditions as well as for higher wages; teachers are demanding more freedom in the classroom and—in New York—the right to teach where they choose; social workers want more autonomy in aiding their clients, and policemen seek the right to do their jobs as they see fit, immune from what they call "political interference." The right of the individual to determine his job is the hallmark of the professional, and eventually many workers will seek the privileges of professionalism whether or not they are professional in terms of skills.

Eventually, the equality revolution may also come to the large corporations and government agencies in which more and more people are working. One can foresee the day when blue-collar and white-collar workers demand a share of the profits and some voice in the running of the corporations.

Similar changes can be expected in the local community. Although the exodus to suburbia took place primarily because people sought better homes and neighborhoods, they also wanted the ability to obtain greater control over governmental institutions. In the last 20 years, the new suburbanites have overthrown many of the rural political machines that used to run the suburbs, establishing governments that were responsive to their demands for low taxes and the exclusion of poorer newcomers. In the future, this transformation may spread to the cities as well, with decentralized political institutions that respond to the wants of the neighborhood replacing the highly centralized urban machines. New

York's current struggle over school decentralization is only a harbinger of things to come.

The Revolution Will Spread

Consumer behavior will also undergo change. The ever-increasing diversity of consumer goods represents a demand for more cultural democracy on the part of purchasers, and the day may come when some people will establish consumer unions and cooperatives to provide themselves with goods and services not offered by large manufacturers. Television viewers may unite to demand different and perhaps even better TV programs and to support the creation of UHF channels that produce the types of quality and minority programming the big networks cannot offer.

It is even possible that a form of "hippie" culture will become more popular in the future. Although the Haight-Ashbury and East Village hippies have degenerated into an often-suicidal drug culture, there are positive themes in hippiedom that may become more acceptable if the work-week shrinks and affluence becomes more universal; for example: the rejection of the rat race, the belief in self-expression as the main purpose of life, the desire for a more communal form of living. In any case, there is no reason to doubt that many people will want to take advantage of a "square" form of the leisurely hippie existence—now available only to old people and called retirement—while they are still young or middle-aged.

These observations suggest that the future will bring many kinds of change to America, producing new ideas that question beliefs and values thought to be sacrosanct. Who, for example, imagined a few years ago that the ghetto would reject the traditional goal of integration or that college students would rise up against their faculties and administrations to demand equal rights? Thus, nobody should be surprised if in the next few years adolescents organize for more freedom in their high schools or journalists decide that their editors have too much power over their work.

These demands for change will, of course, be fought bitterly; protests will be met by backlash and new ideas will be resisted by old ideologies.

Today many argue that college students are still children and should not be given a voice in college administration. Undoubtedly, the defenders of outmoded traditions will argue sincerely and with some facts and logic on their side, but processes of social change have little to do with sincerity, facts or logic. When people become dissatisfied with what they have and demand something better they cannot be deterred by facts or logic, and the repression of new ideas and new modes of behavior is effective only in the very short run.

But perhaps the most intense struggle between new ideas and old ideologies will take place over America's political philosophy, for a fundamental change is taking place in the values which guide us as a nation. In a little-noticed portion of the "Moynihan Report," Daniel P. Moynihan pointed out that the civil rights struggle, which had previously emphasized the achievement of liberty, particularly political liberty from Jim Crow laws, would soon shift to the attainment of equality, which would allow the "distribution of achievements among Negroes roughly comparable to that of whites."

Moynihan's prediction was uncannily accurate with respect to the civil rights struggle, and I would argue, as he does, that it will soon extend to many other struggles as well and that the traditional belief in liberty will be complemented and challenged by a newly widespread belief in the desirability of equality.

Since America became a nation, the country has been run on the assumption that the greatest value of all is liberty, which gives people the freedom to "do their own thing," particularly to make money, regardless of how much this freedom deprives others of the same liberty or of a decent standard of living. Whether liberty meant the freedom to squander the country's natural resources or just to go into business for oneself without doing harm to anyone else, it was the guiding value of our society.

Today, however, the demand for liberty is often, but not always, the battle cry of the "haves," justifying their right to keep their wealth or position and to get more. Whether liberty is demanded by a Southern advocate of states' rights to keep Negroes in their place or by a property owner who wants to sell his house to any white willing to buy it, liberty has become the ideology of the more fortunate. In the years to come, the "have-nots," whether they lack money or freedom, will demand increasingly the reduction of this form of liberty. Those who ask for more equality are not opposed to liberty *per se*, of course; what they want is sufficient equality so that they, too, can enjoy the liberty now virtually monopolized by the "haves."

The debate over liberty vs. equality is in full swing, and one illuminating example is the current argument about the negative income tax and other forms of guaranteed annual incomes for the underpaid and the poor. The advocates of guaranteed annual incomes want greater equality of income in American society; the opponents fear that the liberty to earn as much as possible will be abrogated. However, neither side frames its case in terms of equality or liberty. The advocates of a guaranteed annual income rely on moral argument, appealing to their fellow Americans to do away with the immorality of poverty. The opponents charge that a guaranteed annual income will sap the incentive to work, although all the evidence now available suggests that professors and other professionals who have long had virtually guaranteed annual incomes have not lost their incentive to work, that what saps incentive is not income but the lack of it.

Being poor makes people apathetic and depressed; a guaranteed income would provide some emotional as well as economic security, raise hopes, increase self-respect and reduce feelings of being left out, thus encouraging poor people to look for decent jobs, improve family living conditions and urge their children to work harder in school. A guaranteed annual income may reduce the incentive to take a dirty and underpaid job, however, and at the bottom of the debate is the fear of those who now have the liberty to avoid taking such jobs that less-fortunate Americans may be given the same liberty.

In the years to come, many other arguments against equality will develop. We have long heard that those who want more equality are radicals or outside agitators, seeking to stir up people thought to be happy with the way things are.

This is clearly nonsensical, for even if radicals sometimes lead the drive for more equality, they can succeed only because those who follow them are dissatisfied with the status quo.

Another argument is that the demand for more equality will turn America into a society like Sweden, which is thought to be conformist, boring and suicidal, or even into a gray and regimented society like Russia. But these arguments are nonsensical, too, for there is no evidence that Swedes suffer more from ennui than anyone else, and the suicide rate—high in all Scandinavian countries save Norway—was lower in Sweden at last counting than in traditionalist Austria or Communist Hungary and only slightly higher than the rate in *laissez-faire* West Germany or pastoral Switzerland. And current events in the Communist countries provide considerable evidence that the greater economic equality which some of these countries have achieved does not eliminate the popular desire for freedom and democracy.

But perhaps the most frequently heard argument is that the unequal must do something to earn greater equality. This line of reasoning is taken by those who have had the liberty to achieve their demands and assumes that the same liberty is available to everyone else. This assumption does not hold up, however, for the major problem of the unequal is precisely that they are not allowed to earn equality—that the barriers of racial discrimination, the inability to obtain a good education, the unavailability of good jobs or the power of college presidents and faculties make it impossible for them to be equal. Those who argue for earning equality are really saying that they want to award it to the deserving, like charity. But recent events in the ghettos and on the campuses have shown convincingly that no one awards equality voluntarily; it has to be wrested from the "more equal" by political pressure and even by force.

Many of the changes that make up the equality revolution will not take place for a generation or more, and how many of them ever take place depends on at least three factors: the extent to which the American economy is affluent enough to permit more equality; the extent to which America's political institutions are able to respond to the demands of the unequal, and—perhaps most important— the extent to which working-class and lower-middle-class Americans want more equality, democracy and autonomy in the future.

If the economy is healthy in the years to come, it will be able to "afford" more economic equality while absorbing the costs of such changes as the democratization of the workplace, increased professionalism and more worker autonomy. If automation and the currently rising centralization of American industry result in the disappearance of jobs, however, greater equality will become impossible and people will fight each other for the remaining jobs. This could result in a bitter conflict between the "haves" and the "have-nots" that might even lead to a revolution, bringing about formal equality by governmental edict in a way not altogether different from the Socialist and Communist revolutions of the 20th century. But that conflict between the "haves" and the "have-nots" could also lead to a right-wing revolution in which the "haves," supported by conservatives among the "have-nots," would establish a quasi-totalitarian government that would use force to maintain the existing inequalities.

Although the likelihood of either a left-wing or a right-wing revolution is probably small, even a gradual transformation toward greater equality is not likely to be tranquil. More equality for some means a reduction in privilege for others, and more democracy and autonomy for some means a loss of power for others. Those who have the privilege and the power will not give them up without a struggle and will fight the demand for more equality with all the economic and political resources they can muster. Even today, such demands by only a small part of the black and young population have resulted in a massive backlash appeal for law and order by a large part of the white and older population.

Moreover, whenever important national decisions must be made, American politics has generally been guided by majority rule or majority public opinion, and this has often meant the tyranny of the majority over the minority. As long as the unequal are a minority, the structure of American politics can easily be used to frustrate their demands for change. The inability of the Federal Government to satisfy the demands of the Negro population for greater equality is perhaps the best example. In the future, the political structure must be altered to allow the Government to become more responsive to minority demands, particularly as the pressure for equality grows.

Whether or not such governmental responsiveness will be politically feasible depends in large part on how working-class and lower-middle-class Americans feel about the equality revolution. They are the ruling majority in America, and if they want more equality, democracy and autonomy, these will be achieved— and through peaceful political methods. If the two classes remain primarily interested in obtaining more affluence, however, they will be able to suppress demands for equality by minorities, especially those demands which reduce their own powers and privileges. No one can tell now how these two classes will feel in the future, but there is no doubt that their preferences will determine the outcome of the equality revolution.

Still, whatever happens in the years and decades to come, the equality revolution is under way, and however slowly it proceeds and however bitter the struggle between its supporters and opponents, it will continue. It may succeed, but it could also fail, leaving in its wake a level of social and political conflict unlike any America has ever known.

What I have written so far I have written as a sociologist, trying to predict what will occur in coming generations. But as a citizen, I believe that what will happen ought to happen, that the emerging demand for more equality, democracy, and autonomy is desirable. Too many Americans, even among the nonpoor, still lead lives of quiet desperation, and the good life today is the monopoly of only a happy few. I think that the time has come when unbridled liberty as we have defined it traditionally can no longer be America's guiding value, especially if the right to liberty deprives others of a similar liberty. But I believe also that there is no inherent conflict between liberty and equality; that the society we must create should provide enough equality to permit everyone the liberty to control his own life without creating inequality for others, and that this, when it comes, will be the Great Society.

QUESTIONS FOR DISCUSSION AND DIALOGUE

1. What is so different about most social protest in the 1970's contrasted to earlier American social protest? What is so significant about the difference? Discuss.
2. By economic comparisons with people in other countries and by economic comparisons with Americans in the past, Americans today are, in general and statistical terms, much better off. Why then the fear, loneliness, frustration, anger, and hatred we have been reading about and experiencing?
3. Review Gans' discussion of how equality and democracy are developing in the following groups: Wives, Children, Church, Poor, Public employees, Consumers, "Square hippies." Do you think this is as much an important trend as Gans seems to think? Discuss.
4. Do you agree with Gans that guaranteed annual incomes would not decrease or destroy the incentive to work? If yes, how much should the guaranteed annual income be? If no, how will those without jobs, income, security, and self-respect obtain them? Discuss.
5. After rethinking the major ideas of Gans' article, do you agree with his conclusion that there need be no conflict between liberty and equality? When has there been conflict? What do your answers suggest about the future of the United States? (How much is enough?)

The World Still Moves Our Way
Eric Sevareid

> Eric Sevareid is optimistic about the future of the United States, and he claims many of the "contemporary intellectuals" are wrong in thinking this is a "sick society." Rather, according to Sevareid, it is "a deeply unsettled and bewildered society" because of the rate of change the United States has recently experienced. The "premise and the point about America. . . is a great lifting of the massive center, of the 'ordinary' people." The stakes of the future in the country Sevareid is describing are certainly different from those of George Wald's description! (Chapter Two, Article 7.)

There are those who say the dream is dead or dying, poisoned by self-interest, rotted by surfeit and indifference, maimed by violence. The great aspiration is ended, they tell us, and America is now only another crowded nation, not even able to maintain order; a Power, but not a society, not a culture. We have gone, almost directly, they would have us believe, from primitiveness to decadence, a far poorer record than that of Rome.

The fireworks of this July 4 ['69] which may well illuminate the scene, again, of whole urban blocks consumed by flames, from the Molotov cocktail, not the holiday sparkler—will give further force to this cry of the Cassandras.

But the cry is as old as the nation. It was sounded in Jefferson's time, when the states seemed ready to drift apart; in Lincoln's time, when they split apart; in Roosevelt's time, when, by the millions, husbands shuffled in soup lines; in Truman's time, when the Russians and Chinese were supposedly reordering the earth and Communist traitors were supposedly infesting the Government.

But this is not It—this is not our Armageddon, not the great day of judgment on America. For America is change, and the changes have come, often enough, in convulsive spasms. This country is the vast experimental laboratory in human relations for the twentieth century; it is, in a sense, defining and creating the twentieth century for much of the world.

Unless it is seen in this light, America cannot be understood at all. If many of our contemporary intellectuals, especially those communing with one another in New York City, almost a separate nation in spirit, do not understand it, this is partly because they do not understand themselves. As they attest in innumerable books, they do not know who they are. It may be news to them that the overwhelming majority of Americans *do* know who they are, do *not* feel alienated from their country or their generation.

This is not a "sick society." It is a deeply unsettled and bewildered society, and the reason is not merely the extraordinary changes in this last generation but the speed of these changes. It is the *rate* of change that is new. The life of Americans today resembles that of, say, Grant's time, less than life in Grant's time resembled life in ancient China. The nation is not overpopulated, but the population has shifted out of balance. In the last 20 years alone, 18 million people, including, of course, the Negroes, have moved into the urban centers. This second industrial-scientific revolution has jammed us together, polluted much of our air and waters, smeared ugliness over much of our countryside, obliged us to work within greater economic units and increased the tensions of daily living.

Two other revolutions have been taking place in concert with the new industrial-scientific revolution. One is the communications revolution, which brings every social evil, every human tragedy and conflict immediately and intimately within everyone's ken. The other is the educational revolution, which adds millions every year to the ranks of those moved to add their investigation, articulation or actions to the processes of problem-solving and problem-creating.

We are not becoming less democratic but more democratic. It is not our individual freedom that is in jeopardy, in the first instance, but our public order. It could be argued that we are moving away from representative government in the direction, at least, of direct democracy, by no means an unmixed blessing. For the immediate future, the problem is not only the indifference or "apathy" of the much-abused middle class or any other group. It is also the problem of too many untrained cooks in the kitchen.

Many current phenomena to the contrary notwithstanding, Americans are the most natural workers-together in the world. We say we live by the system of individual enterprise, while we are the supreme cooperative society. Totalitarian countries say they are cooperative societies, while their regimes must coerce their people to work. It is absurd to believe that the races of men who turned an empty, forbidding continent into the most efficient engine of production and distribution ever seen, who created the first *mass* democracy with essential order and essential freedom will not solve the problems of crowding, poverty, pollution and ugliness. The solutions will create new problems, after which there will be new solutions, then new problems, and so our life will go on. Time is life. Were human problems ever totally solved, change would come to a stop, and we would begin to die.

American cynics and Cassandras see neither their own history nor the rest of the world with clarity. Violence? We have *always* had a high tolerance level for violence. Abraham Lincoln worried about what he called "the increasing disregard for law which pervades the country; the growing disposition to substitute the wild and furious passions, in lieu of the sober judgment of courts; and the worse than savage mobs, for the executive ministers of justice."

It is even to be doubted that crime is more prevalent than it was in the nineteenth century. Historian Arthur Schlesinger, Jr., reminds us that a century ago, every tenth person in New York City had a police record.

Alienated and irreverent youth? To a degree, youth is always alienated and to a degree ought to be. More than 2,000 years ago, Plato wrote that in a democracy, the father "accustoms himself to become like his child and to fear his sons. . . . The schoolmaster fears and flatters his pupils. . . the young act like their seniors, and compete with them in speech and action, while the old men condescend to the young. . . ." This happens because democratic life carries the in-built impulse to wish to please and accommodate to others.

The alarm over drug-taking is also exaggerated. There is far less use of dangerous drugs today than a half century ago, before narcotics control, when about one American in every four hundred was an addict of some harmful drug, ten times the present rate.

Americans, of course, are not spiritually geared to the past but to the future. It is a reflection of what John Steinbeck, speaking of the on-pushing, haggard "Okies" in the dust-bowl years, called the "terrible faith," that we are constantly seized with concern for our children more than for ourselves. Yet it is not possible to see our society in perspective without these backward glances to what we once were, with the consequent realization that we are using different scales of measuring well-being today.

At the turn of the century, a newborn could expect to live about to the age of 50; today, the expectancy is about 70. Once, a mother had sound reason to fear giving birth; today, death in childbirth is regarded as intolerable. Once, a full high school education was the best achievement of a minority; today, it is the barest minimum for decent employment and self-respect. Once, the timber and mining barons stripped away the forests and topsoil wholesale; today, these companies are confronted by their communities at every other move.

One could cite hundreds of similar examples of how our standards of expectancy have risen, as they should, along with our standard of life. The truth is that we Americans are perfectionists, which simply means that we were not, are not and never will be satisfied either with the quantities or the qualities in our life.

By the year 2000, we will look back upon these present years not only as one of America's periodic convulsions but as a rather backward period. By then, the typical American family will have an income of around $20,000 a year or more; the typical American adult will have had at least two years of college, with far broader intellectual and aesthetic horizons. By then, the old urban centers will have been rebuilt, and many millions will live in satellite "new cities," part-urban, part-rural. The incurable diseases like cancer and arthritis will be under far better control.

The present explosion in books, theater, music and art will have transformed tastes and comprehension to an enormous degree. And already, according to the Englishman C. P. Snow, something like 80 percent of the advanced study of science in the Western world is going on in the United States of America. This is the heart reason for the "brain drain" from abroad to the U.S., not merely the higher pay. The facilities, the action, the creative excitement are increasingly here. None of this guarantees a single new Shakespeare, Rembrandt, Beethoven or Einstein, because genius is not developed (though even this may occur one day through selective breeding and cell transplant).

What it does guarantee is a great lifting of the massive center, of the "ordinary" people. This is the premise and the point about America—ours is the first organized dedication to *massive* improvement, to the development of a *mass* culture, the first attempt to educate *everyone* to the limit of his capacities. We have known for a long time that this can be done only through the chemistry of individual freedom. Soviet Russia is just now beginning to discover this for itself. I am unable to understand the thrust of the sufferings and strivings of Western man over the last thousand years save in terms of this kind of achievement.

The popular passion of Americans is not politics, baseball, money or material things. It is education. Education is now our biggest industry, involving more people even than national defense. The percentage of children in kindergarten has doubled in a rather short period; the percentage of youth in college climbs steeply upward. Today, even a Negro boy in the South has a better statistical chance of getting into college than an English youth. And there are about 44 million full- and part-time *adult* students pursuing some kind of formalized learning on their own!

Intelligent foreigners nearly everywhere understand the mountainous meaning of all this for the world as well as for America. They know that much of the world will be transformed in the American image, culturally if not politically. They know that struggle is really all over—it is the Western way of living and doing, our way and the way of Europe combined, that the world wants. It is North America and West Europe that make up the "in" world; Russia and China are still the outsiders trying to enter.

Communism already appears irrelevant, essentially passe. The more the Communist regimes educate their people, the more complex their life will become. They will struggle with the complexities the Western world confronts already, and they will discover that authoritarian direction from the top cannot cope with them. Only the essentially liberal society can manage twentieth-century life, even in practical terms. They will learn, as we have always known, that the effective, the lasting revolution lies in the West, particularly in America.

Why, then, are we in such a state of uproar in this year of Our Lord, and why is much of the world upset about the America of today? Because, as a philosopher once said, "nothing that is vast enters into the life of mortals without a curse," and America is struggling to rid itself of one old curse and one new one. The old curse is the Negro slavery Europeans fastened upon this land long ago, which continues in a hundred psychological, social and economic, if not legal, forms. The Negro Passion of today is a revolution within the continuing American revolution, and the one absolute certainty about it is that it is going to succeed, however long and distracting the agony for everyone. It will succeed not only because it has justice with it (justice has been suppressed before) but because there is a deep evangelical streak in the American people, a true collective conscience, and it has been aroused.

Racism exists in almost all societies on this globe, virulently so, incidentally, in Black Africa. It may be that race prejudice—the psychologists' "stranger hatred"—is an instinct tracing from our animal origins, and therefore ineradicable. Yet man is the only animal *aware* of his instincts; the only animal, therefore, capable of controlling, if not eliminating, his instincts. New law, enforced, compels new behavior. Behavior repeated daily comes to seem normal, and attitudes change. Illusions tend to vanish. The idea that a difference in skin color is an essential difference is an illusion. I am struck by an observation of McGeorge Bundy of the Ford Foundation. He said discrimination will end, partly because this college generation regards racial equality as natural, whereas the older generation regards it only as logical.

The twentieth-century war over racial injustice is now in its virulent stage. The nineteenth-century war in its virulent stage lasted four years. This one will last much longer because it is fought on a thousand narrow fronts, like guerrilla war, and because no grand climacteric is possible. But it is not going to "tear this country apart" or "burn America down" or anything of the sort. A tiny percentage of extremists among only 12 percent of the American population can do much, but they cannot do that.

The new curse has come with America's new military power. A form of Parkinson's Law operates here. The greater the power, the more the men who associate with it, extoll it and find needs, real or sophistical, for its use. The use of available, flexible force becomes easier than hard thought; and the worst aspect of the curse is the gradual, almost unconscious identification of power with virtue. John Adams said, "Power always thinks it has a great soul and vast views beyond the comprehension of the weak. . . ."

We have fallen into this trap with the Vietnam intervention. For the first time, we have misused our power on a massive scale. But it does not mean that we are a "Fascist" or aggressive people, any more than the racial mess means that we are a hating or oppressive people. Vietnam is not typical; it is a mistake, now recognized as such by most serious thinkers in this country. If millions of people in Europe (every province of which is soaked in blood) stand aghast at what we have done and reproach us bitterly, one unarticulated reason is that they *expect* the United States to act with humaneness and common sense. They do not shout advice to Russia and China, whatever their misdeeds, for the same reason that the crowd in the bullring does not shout advice to the bull but to the bullfighter.

The reassuring thing is not merely that we will get out of this trap and undo the damage as best we can but that we will do so because our own people demand it, not because the enemy is too strong, not because of foreign criticism. We could, if we would, lay North Vietnam totally waste. The American conscience will not permit it. We may not win a military victory in Vietnam, but we will win a victory in our own soul.

No—the humaneness of the American people is still here. The new problems have piled up too rapidly for our brains and our institutions to cope with at anything like the same rate, but the will for justice is as strong as ever—stronger, in my own belief, because thought and expression are freer today than ever before. This is why the Negro revolution has come now—not because conditions of life became worse, save for some, but because of a climate of free expression. In just such periods of great intellectual freedom have nearly all revolutions been generated.

It is a remarkable fact that great numbers of very ordinary people in distant lands understand all this about America better than some of our own intellectuals. If, by some magic, all barriers to emigration and immigration around the world were lifted tomorrow, by far the single biggest human caravan would start moving in one direction—our way.

One day recently, I asked a Cuban refugee why most Cubans like himself wanted to come to the United States rather than go to Latin American countries with the same language and the same general culture. Was it just the thought of greater economic opportunity?

"No," he said, "many of us would have an easier time, economically, in a Latin country. It's just that we feel better here. We can feel like a human being. There seems to be something universal about this country."

This is living testimony, not abstract argument, from men who know the meaning of America in their bones and marrow. Of course, it is the truth. Of course, the dream lives on.

Let those who wish compare America with Rome. Rome lasted around a thousand years.

QUESTIONS FOR DISCUSSION AND DIALOGUE

1. Do you think Sevareid's optimism about the United States is justified? Discuss. (For contrast, George Wald's article in Chapter two gives a very pessimistic point of view.)
2. As Sevareid discusses it, why are "many of the contemporary intellectuals, especially those communing with one another in New York City, almost a separate nation in spirit" when they see the United States as a "sick society"? (The reader might wish to refer back to Stewart Alsop's article, Chapter Three, Article 5, on the "New Snobbism.")
3. Why does Sevareid claim that "Communism already appears irrelevant"? Discuss.
4. How does the author explain "The new curse" of America's new military

power, and the Vietnam "trap" the United States has fallen into? Do you agree with him? Discuss.

Excerpts from 1976 Agenda for Tomorrow
Stewart Udall

What does a nation do after it has solved the perplexing problems of production? In this excerpt from *1976 Agenda for Tomorrow,* former Secretary of the Interior Udall considers the new problems and challenges for Americans. These problems and challenges are of quality and balance rather than quantity. Udall frames two questions for the future of the United States, and hopes Americans will concern themselves much less with the first one than the second one: 1. "Can it be made, mass produced, and sold at a profit?" 2. "Beyond its salability, will it work for man and with nature for the future?"

The two chief failures that confront us as we approach our bicentennial—a failure to build livable cities and a failure to eradicate racism—are failures to establish genuine democracy. We have amassed awesome destructive power, but our cities are a mess. We have acquired the material trappings of great wealth, but have still to exhibit the wisdom that will build good will between groups. Yet the mark of a mature civilization is always made in the twin realms of culture and human understanding. Do we have the determination, the wisdom, and the will to redirect the revolution of science and technology that has produced this power and wealth and to use our combined gifts to transform life in this country? This is the crucial question.

We cannot answer in the affirmative unless we first realize the dangerously small dimensions of our existing efforts and expectations. Two decades of "urban renewal" have improved less than one per cent of the urban blight in this country. Today we have ten million substandard units of housing. Postwar public-housing and slum-clearance projects have not kept pace with rising demand for low-cost housing and the rapid obsolescence of jerry-built structures of earlier years. Our lenient local tax and enforcement policies, moreover, still reward inaction by the owners of slums. The remedies we have applied to our urban ills have largely consisted of dabbing disinfectant on selected sores, not in the bettering of the lives of all citizens. Even the most successful exercises in downtown renovation—in such cities as Hartford, Baltimore, San Francisco, Philadelphia, and Fresno—stand today only as glistening ornaments in teeming seas of decay. It is a discouraging commentary on our ingenuity that we waited until the mid-1960's to try out, on much too small a scale, such promising ideas as President Johnson's rent-supplement and "Model Cities" programs. We must now recognize that piecemeal approaches to renovation have failed to meet the fundamental challenge. They are invariably inefficient, often inequitable, and have all the shortcomings of patchwork repair.

Plans of action of a large scope are needed to reach and take full advantage of economies and to upgrade the quality of life in all of our cities. The task is less to renovate than to re-create. More than slum clearance is involved. There are gilded as well as slum ghettos. Given the will, we can turn our drab urban landscape into a spiritually nourishing as well as physically satisfying environment, not only in a broken Newark or a gutted Detroit, but also in ugly cities, towns, and villages that stretch from New York to Memphis and on to Los Angeles. . . . . . . We need a strategy and a plan that, while giving first priority to slum eradication, will have a further range of priorities to transform our communities and our lives. There is in our country still too much bigotry and too little altruism for even the piecemeal program prescribed by the Kerner Commission to gain the support it will need for full implementation.

The experience of the 1960's tells us that "wars" on poverty and slums will continue to receive halting, underfunded support unless we have the imagination to attack these ills in the much larger context of expansive aims and goals capable of regenerating the whole nation. We must view these ills as a crisis of opportunity. The considerable problem now is to broaden and go beyond the Kerner Commission's recommendations, to include the whole nation, and thereby to enlist the interest of all Congressmen and every citizen. More piecemeal plans geared to quantitative conventional programs—more jobs, better schools, improved welfare, accelerated housing—will not arouse the nation. We need a dream of excellence and betterment to involve and excite every citizen.

We have not succeeded in this century in devising William James' moral equivalent of war because we have never dared to think and act on a scale that would involve each individual and every community across the land. Franklin Roosevelt turned the Great Depression into an opportunity to build sorely needed public works, to replant forests, to harness the hydroelectric power of our great rivers. Unhappily, these depression-combating programs had to give way to wartime priorities, then to post-war catching up on consumer goods and an unplanned rush of construction and production that has left every city in this land from New York to Nome with its poor, its slums, its outworn public services, its social diseases, its disordered environments.

We need now, not a call to cure specific diseases, but a plan to make all cities cathedrals for everyday existence. We need:

a plan that envisions full employment as the humane use of human beings, not merely more jobs;

conditions that will create social health and shrink the need for welfare, not merely "improved" administration of "increased" welfare programs;

balanced cities, not merely more housing;

liberation from the congested prison of private wheels by the creation of fast and quiet public transportation.

A sound political base, not altruism, should be relied on to accomplish these things. The watchwords of the program should be "opportunity" and "quality". To meet the art-of-the-possible test of politics, our approach must tackle rural as well as urban renewal, and be as interested in the revitalizing of small towns as in the renovation of the largest megalopolis. It should expend as much creative thought on the refurbishing of middle-sized cities as on the reconditioning of New York or Chicago, and contemplate the erection of many comely new towns as well.

Were we to decide that urban revival will be our dominant ambition for the remaining years of this century, this establishment of a national priority would not be without precedent in our history. The federal government made agriculture its first priority during most of our history. It granted huge slices of the public domain to railroad promoters to improve our systems of transport, and smaller slices to the land-grant colleges. Priority was later given to the restoration of the Tennessee Valley when it lay in ruins. In the 1940's first priority went to winning the war; in the 1950's, to highway-building; and in the 1960's the space mission to the moon was our big adventure.

Pilot programs and peripheral "wars" on social problems will never suffice as a moral equivalent of war, however. We need a task so spacious, a goal so intimate yet universal, that our people will be unified by the endeavor it compels. We need a plan that will enlist all segments and cities of America, and become the most exciting national enterprise since the founding of the republic. . . .

QUESTIONS FOR DISCUSSION AND DIALOGUE

1. Do you think you could consider the problems Udall is writing about as problems with the scope of a "moral equivalent of war"? Why or why not? Discuss.
2. Some might challenge Udall's suggestions for such deep reforms as too idealistic and impractical. After all, it is often said, "Politics is the art of the possible". How does Udall answer this kind of question? Do you agree? Why?
3. Reread the last paragraph. Do you agree with Udall here? Discuss.

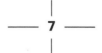

Fighting to Save the Earth
from Man

Time

In this excerpt from a *Time* article modern ecological problems are discussed both in a general and a political context. Concerns similar to those of Udall in the previous excerpt from his book are reflected here. *Time* poses an interesting and meaningful question by asking whether these concerns will unify or further polarize the United States.

The great question of the '70s is: Shall we surrender to our surroundings or shall we make our peace with nature and begin to make reparations for the damage we have done to our air, to our land and to our water?

State of the Union Message

Nixon's words come none too early. The U.S. environment is seriously threatened by the prodigal garbage of the world's richest economy. In the President's own boyhood town of Whittier, a part of metropolitan Los Angeles, the once sweet air is befouled with carbon monoxide, hydrocarbons, lead compounds, sulfur dioxide, nitrogen oxides, fly ash, asbestos particulates and countless other noxious substances. The Apollo 10 astronauts could see Los Angeles as a cancerous smudge from 25,000 miles in outer space. Airline pilots say that whisky-brown miasmas, visible from 70 miles, shroud almost every U.S. city, including remote towns like Missoula in Montana's "big sky" country. What most Americans now breathe is closer to ambient filth than to air.

The environment may well be the gut issue that can unify a polarized nation in the 1970s. It may also divide people who are appalled by the mess from those who have adapted to it. No one knows how many Americans have lost all feeling for nature and the quality of life. Even so, the issue now attracts young and old, farmers, city dwellers and suburban housewives, scientists, industrialists and blue-collar workers. They know pollution well. It is as close as the water tap, the car-clogged streets and junk-filled landscape—their country's visible decay, America the Ugly.

Politicians have got the message. Late last year, Congress easily passed Senator Henry M. Jackson's National Environmental Policy Act and appropriated $800 million to finance new municipal waste-treatment plants. Senator Gaylord Nelson plans to introduce an amendment to the U.S. Constitution that will guarantee every citizen's right to a "decent environment." Last month, the Governors of New York and California devoted much of their "state of the state" speeches to environmental matters; campaigns later this year will reverberate with antipollution statements. Says Senator Edmund S. Muskie: "In the past, we had to fight against all kinds of political pressure, public apathy and ignorance. Now the wind is blowing at our back."

The New Jeremiahs

The real problem is much bigger than the U.S. By curbing disease and death, modern medicine has started a surge of human overpopulation that threatens to overwhelm the earth's resources. At the same time, technological man is bewitched by the dangerous illusion that he can build bigger and bigger industrial societies with scant regard for the iron laws of nature. French Social anthropologist Claude Levi-Strauss compares today's human condition to that of maggots in a sack of flour: "When the population of these worms increases, even before they meet, before they become conscious of one another, they secrete certain toxins that kill at a distance—that is, they poison the flour they are in, and they die."

Ultimately, both men and maggots need the help of an emerging science of survival—ecology. In the U.S., a tiny band of ecologists has achieved sudden prominence: Rene J. Dubos (Rockefeller University), LaMont C. Cole (Cornell), Eugene P. Odum (University of Georgia), Paul R. Ehrlich (Stanford), Kenneth E. F. Watt (University of California at Davis), and a few others. In terms of public recognition, perhaps the outstanding figure in the field is Barry Commoner of Washington University in St. Louis . . . who has probably done more than any other U.S. scientist to speak out and awaken a sense of urgency about the declining quality of life. Last week he addressed 10,000 people at Northwestern University, where young activists staged the first of a series of major environmental teach-ins that will climax in a nationwide teach-in on April 22. In varying degrees, the once sheltered ecologists have become ardent advocates of seemingly radical views. They sometimes sound like new Jeremiahs. They do not hesitate to predict the end of the world, or at least the end of a life with quality. Yet they hold out hope too. "We are in a period of grace," says Commoner. "We have the time—perhaps a generation—in which to save the environment from the final effects of the violence we have done to it."

Web of Life

Ecology is often called the "subversive science." Only 70 years old, it avoids the narrow specialization of other sciences—and thus appeals to generalists, including people with a religious sense. Ecology is the systems approach to nature, the study of how living organisms and the nonliving environment function together as a whole or ecosystem. The word ecology (derived from the Greek root *oikos,* meaning "house") is often used in ways that suggest an attitude rather than a discipline. Anthropologists and psychiatrists have adapted it to their work. Poet Allen Ginsberg declaims it like a revolutionary slogan. But few yet grasp its subtle meanings—as Senator Ted Stevens of Alaska proved last summer. Arguing for fast development of his state's oil-rich North Slope, Stevens referred to his dictionary. "Ecology," he declared, "deals with the relationship between living organisms." Then he added triumphantly: "But there are no living organisms on the North Slope."

Stevens missed the whole point: the arctic ecosystem is full of life (including Eskimos) but is so vulnerable to pollution that the North Slope threatens to become a classic example of man's mindless destruction. The intense cold impedes nature's ability to heal itself; tire marks made in the tundra 25 years ago are still plainly visible. What most worries ecologists, in fact, is man's blindness to his own utter dependency on all ecosystems, such as oceans, coastal estuaries, forests and grasslands. Those ecosystems constitute the biosphere, a vast web of interacting organisms and processes that form the rhythmic cycles and food chains in which ecosystems support one another.

The biosphere . . . is an extraordinarily thin global envelope that sustains the only known life in the universe. At least 400 million years ago, some primeval accident allowed plant life to enrich the atmosphere to a life-supporting mixture of 20% oxygen, plus nitrogen, argon, carbon dioxide and water vapor. With uncanny precision, the mixture was then maintained by plants, animals and bacteria, which used and returned the gases at equal rates. The result is a closed system, a balanced cycle in which nothing is wasted and everything counts. For example, about 70% of the earth's oxygen is produced by ocean phytoplankton —passively floating plants and animals. This entire living system modified temperatures, curbed floods and nurtured man about 5,000,000 years ago. Only if the biosphere survives can man survive.

To maintain balance, all ecosystems require four basic elements: 1) inorganic substances (gases, minerals, compounds); 2) "producer" plants, which convert the substances into food; 3) animal "consumers," which use the food; and 4) "decomposers" (bacteria and fungi), which turn dead protoplasm into usable substances for the producers. As the key producers, green plants alone have the power to harness the sun's energy and combine it with elements from air, water and rocks into living tissue—the vegetation that sustains animals, which in turn add their wastes and corpses to natural decay. It is nature's efficient reuse of the decay that builds productive topsoil. Yet such is the delicacy of the process that it takes 500 years to create one inch of good topsoil.

The process is governed by distinct laws of life and balance. One is adaptation: each species finds a precise niche in the ecosystem that supplies it with food and shelter. At the same time, all animals have the defensive power to multiply faster than their own death rates. As a result, predators are required to hold the population within the limits of its food supply. The wolf that devours the deer is a blessing to the community, if not to the individual deer. Still another law is the necessity of diversity. The more different species there are in an area, the less chance that any single type of animal or plant will proliferate and dominate the community. Even the rarest, oddest species can thus be vital to life. Variety is nature's grand tactic of survival.

The Domino Theory Applied

Man has violated these laws—and endangered nature as well as himself.

When a primitive community ran out of food, it had to move on or perish. It could harm only its own immediate environment. But a modern community can destroy its land and still import food, thus possibly destroying ever more distant land without knowing or caring. Technological man is so aware of his strength that he is unaware of his weakness—the fact that his pressure upon nature may provoke revenge.

By adding just one alien component to a delicate balance, man sometimes triggers a series of dangerous changes. Nature immediately tries to restore the balance—and often overreacts. When farmers wipe out one pest with powerful chemicals, they may soon find their crops afflicted with six pests that are resistant to the chemicals. Worse, the impact of a pesticide like DDT can be vastly magnified in food chains. Thus DDT kills insect-eating birds that normally control the pests that now destroy the farmers' crops. The "domino theory" is clearly applicable to the environment.

In South Africa, for example, a campaign was waged against hippopotamuses. Deemed useless beasts that merely cluttered up rivers, they were shot on sight. Result: the debilitating disease called schistosomiasis has become as great a public-health hazard in certain areas as malaria was 50 years ago. As usual, the missing links in the chain of events were discovered the hard way. It turns out that hippos keep river silt in motion as they bathe. When they heave themselves up riverbanks to dry land, they also go single file and act like bulldozers, making natural irrigation channels. Without the animals, the rivers quickly silted up; without the overflow channels, periodic floods swept like scythes over adjacent lands. The altered conditions favored a proliferation of schistosomiasis —carrying water snails.

Such harsh intrusions on wildlife constitute only one way in which man abuses nature. Another is through his sheer numbers. From an estimated 5,-000,000 people 8,000 years ago, the world population rose to 1 billion by 1850, 2 billion about 1930, and now stands at 3.5 billion. Current projections run to 7 billion by the year 2000. Neo-Malthusians like Stanford Population Biologist Paul Ehrlich grimly warn that the biosphere cannot sustain that many people. As Ehrlich puts it: "There can only be death, war, pestilence and famine to reduce the number."

Davy Crockett Goes to Jail

Ecologist LaMont Cole raises the crowding problem. Since 80% of the population is likely to live in cities occupying only 2% of the land, the sheer density of people will strain what might be called the urban ecosystem. Asks Cole: "Are we selecting for genetic types only those who can satisfy their aesthetic needs in congested cities? Are the Davy Crocketts and Kit Carsons who are born today being destined for asylums, jails or suicide?"

Barry Commoner believes that under present conditions the earth can hold between 6 billion and 8 billion people. After that, environmental and food-supply problems may become insurmountable. Commoner notes that humans tend to view the procreation of several children as a kind of guarantee of immortality. "What makes human populations turn off?" he asks. "If a father knows that his sons will survive, perhaps he will not feel the need for so many successors." But Commoner's principle that greater material security might stop population growth requires a dramatic rise in the world standard of living—hardly a bright prospect. Moreover, ecologists are not hopeful that a "green revolution" can increase farm harvests enough to feed twice as many people. "Undeveloped countries cannot afford to mechanize their farming production," argues Eugene P. Odum. "The fancier a seed we give them, the more artificial care it needs, along with tractors and gasoline."

Modern technology is already pressuring nature with tens of thousands of synthetic substances, many of which almost totally resist decay—thus poisoning man's fellow creatures, to say nothing of himself. The burden includes smog fumes, aluminum cans that do not rust, inorganic plastics that may last for decades, floating oil that can change the thermal reflectivity of oceans, and radioactive wastes whose toxicity lingers for literally hundreds of years. The earth has its own waste-disposal system, but it has limits. The winds that ventilate earth are only six miles high; toxic garbage can kill the tiny organisms that normally clean rivers. . . .

QUESTIONS FOR DISCUSSION AND DIALOGUE

1. Reread the second paragraph in this article. Do you think the "gut issue" of the environment will unify or further polarize the United States during the '70's? Discuss.

2. Reconsider the response you gave to question two about Udall's excerpt—Since politics is "the art of the possible" are the environmental reforms many call for unlikely to be realized politically in the light of what this article says about politics and the environment? Does this article make you more or less optimistic than Udall's article about political—environmental reform? Discuss.

3. Discuss this quote from the article: "No one knows how many Americans have lost all feeling for nature and the quality of life." Have you lost this feeling? How many do you think have?

—— **8** ——

Correcting Society's Specific
Defects No Longer Enough
to Meet Changes
John W. Gardner

John Gardner, former Secretary of Health, Education and Welfare, offers alternatives to the rigidifying, tearing down, or collapse of American society's institutions. "Continuous renewal" is the key to the "imaginative redesign of our institutions." This renewal process can be realized by implementation of nine attributes which Gardner specifies. His conclusion challenges the Americans as "We the people" to "return this nation to a path of confidence and well being. . . You and I can do these things. No one else can do them for us."

John W. Gardner is chairman of the National Urban Coalition and former Secretary of Health, Education and Welfare. This article was adapted from a recent address he gave as he accepted Caltech's first annual Robert A. Millikan Award at the Ambassador in Los Angeles. The award—created on the 100th anniversary of the birth of Dr. Millikan, a Nobel laureate who led the institution to its present academic position—will to be presented annually, said Caltech President Lee A. DuBridge, to a person who has "so shaped his conduct as to promote the well-being of mankind."

I'm going to try to suggest how we might think more clearly about the difficult matter of social change.

We must first dispose of the notion that social change alters a tranquil status quo. Today there is no tranquility to disrupt. The disruption has occurred, and one of the purposes of social change is to find new solutions that will preserve old values. When the spring dries up the farmer seeks a new source of water—not for love of novelty but to bring himself back into balance with his environment.

Our status quo has been knocked head over heels by the revolutions in science and technology, in transportation, in communication and the processing of information, in industry, agriculture and education, in demography and biomedical affairs.

The swift pace of these revolutions makes it desperately necessary that our institutions be adaptable. When they are not, the sweep of events isolates them and dramatizes their anachronistic character. Even institutions that are fairly young (as history goes) find themselves woefully out of date. The rush of change brings a kind of instant antiquity.

And it isn't enough just to change institutions. Some of today's college-age critics have a feeling that if they could tear down existing institutions, better ones would surely rise. But history is an endless reiteration of the tearing down (or collapse) of institutions and their replacement by institutions essentially no better. As an institution builder man has a notable gift for making the same mistake over and over.

Source of Error: Ignoring Flaws in Human Nature

One source of such repeated mistakes is to ignore flaws in human nature that survive all social transformations. Man's inclination to tyrannize over his fellow man, his impulse to prejudice, his greed, his lust for power—all must be held in check by culture and by social institutions. Some of our young critics imagine that somehow those traits will disappear when their bright new world dawns. But they will not disappear. If we jettison procedures developed over centuries to protect us from the rapacity of our fellow man, we shall regret it bitterly.

A second reason men make the same mistake over and over is that they fail to recognize certain tendencies intrinsic in human institutions. All social institutions decay and rigidify and tend sooner or later to smother individuality. This is particularly true of modern, highly organized societies, capitalist or communist. Many of the attributes most galling to critics of our own system are equally characteristic of every modern large-scale society and will be increasingly so. If we are to alter those attributes for the better, we shall have to be very knowing indeed about the design of human institutions.

A first step toward a sound philosophy of institutional redesign would be to break our habit of concentration exclusively on the routine repair of institutions.

The mechanic faced with a defective carburetor can put it back in working order and stop there. Or, if he is a very gifted mechanic, he may sit down and design an improved unit, less subject to breakdown. If he is still more imaginative, he may think of a whole new means, simpler and more efficient, for mixing air and fuel in the proper proportions for combustion.

More and more, at this critical time in our history, we must undertake imaginative redesign of institutions. And there has been ample evidence of such inventing and innovating on the social front. Among the consequences: the Bill of Rights, the Land Grant College, the county agent, the Federal Reserve System.

Spirit Is Imprisoned by the Decay of Institutions

If we are serious about such redesign, then we must address ourselves to one of the central and universally neglected aspects of the problem: the decay of human institutions.

As they decay they imprison the spirit, thwart the creative impulse, diminish individual adaptability and limit the possibility of freedom. As the institutions grow increasingly resistant to criticism, the critics grow increasingly hostile. And the stage is then set for one of the most familiar contemporary dramas—violent collision between angry critics and sluggish institutions.

That human institutions require periodic redesign (if only because of their tendency to decay) is not a minor fact about them or easily overlooked. Taking the whole span of history, there is no more obvious lesson to be learned.

How curious, then, that in all of history, with all the immensely varied principles on which societies have been designed and operated, no people has seriously attempted to build a society to take into account the aging of institutions and to provide for their continuous renewal. Why shouldn't we be the first society to do so?

One of the reasons people interested in improving the society never examine the requirements of continuous renewal is that they are preoccupied with specific evils that must be corrected. I don't blame them. So am I. That's what I work on every day of my life, and I would not seek to divert anyone from the attacks on poverty, discrimination, inadequate housing, unemployment, faulty education and all the other problems that urgently need our attention.

But somehow, sooner or later, someone must dig deeper. Each reformer comes to his task with a little bundle of desired changes. The society is intolerable, he asserts, because it has specifiable defects. The implication is that if appropriate reforms corresponding to those desired changes are undertaken, the society will be wholly satisfactory and the work of the reformer done.

That is a primitive way of viewing social change. The true task is to design a society (and institutions) capable of continuous change, continuous renewal, continuous responsiveness to human need. We are creating new problems as fast as we solve the old ones. Our society must be a good problem-solving mechanism. It is not so today.

In addition, our ideas of what is a good society evolve and change over the years. If our institutions are capable of continuous renewal, then we can move by successive approximations toward the society we want.

The individual is the ultimate source of social renewal. It follows that the self-renewing society will be one that fosters creative, free and self-renewing individuals. The authentic nightmare for modern man is not communism or capitalism, or a conquering tyrant or an oppressive class or the Machine. It is the beehive model of society—a society in which the total system perfects itself as the individual is steadily dwarfed.

All modern technological societies, whatever their ideology, are moving toward ever larger and more embracing systems of organization, toward ever greater specialization of function on the part of individuals, toward ever greater dominance of the system's purposes over individual purposes.

Social critics tend to believe that the smothering of individuality is a consequence of intentional decisions by people at the top. (Right-wingers blame government leaders; left-wingers blame corporate leaders.) The hostility of the critics, right wing or left, to the people at the top, governmental or corporate, is strengthened by a wholly nostalgic conception of power and how it is exercised. They see them as people who are free to shape events quite to their will, but that is a wholly unreal notion of how a modern, intricately organized system works.

The modern leader himself is always in some measure caught in the system. The system determines how and when he will exercise power. And if present trends continue this will become more rather than less so. The queen bee is as much a prisoner of the system as any other in the hive.

Now let me list the attributes of a society capable of resisting this trend, capable of fostering creative individuals, capable of renewing itself:

1—Pluralism. The creative society will be characterized by variety, alternatives, choices and multiple foci of power and initiative.

We have had in this society a high degree of just such pluralism. But it would be folly to ignore the fact that logic of modern, large-scale organization, governmental or corporate, squeezes out pluralism and moves toward one tightly articulated system of power. We must work against that trend. In our own society, this means, in practical terms, a concern for the vitality of local leadership, for the strength and autonomy of state and local government, for the vigor and creativity of the private sector and for various kinds of decentralization.

2—Release of individual potential. The society capable of continuous renewal will be one that develops to the fullest its human resources, that removes obstacles to individual fulfillment, that emphasizes education, life-long learning and self-discovery.

In these matters our record is uneven—brilliant in some respects, shameful in others. We have worked hard and accomplished much toward combating the conditions that stunt human growth and thwart individual promise. But we have allowed our black citizens and some other minorities to live in conditions that make a mockery of our ideals. And we are still far from having created, for either black or white, an educational system that produces self-discoverers and life-long learners.

Removal of the barriers to individual fulfillment involves far more than education, of course. We must be certain that no individual suffers a life-long physical handicap because his family could not afford early medical attention. We must enable blind, deaf and crippled children to live useful lives. We must combat all the destroyers of individual promise—alcoholism, mental illness, and so on.

3—Internal communication. A society that is capable of continuous renewal will have excellent internal communications among its diverse constituent elements.

In my judgment we do not have that today. We are drowning in a torrent of communication, but most of it is irrelevant to this particular need. Grave gaps in communication still exist between the businessman and the working man, between white and black, between young and old, between conservative and liberal, between public and private sectors. They are not wholly out of touch. But they do not normally engage in the kind of open and constructive dialog that would permit each to understand the other's values and assumptions.

Communication in a creative society must be more than a flow of messages; it must be a means of conflict resolution, a means of cutting through the rigidities that divide and paralyze a community.

4—Dissent. The creative society must provide for dissent, for the emergence of alternatives to official doctrine or widely accepted assumptions. It must provide for honest appraisal of the disparity between existing conditions and widely professed ideals.

Expressed Dissent Lacks Awareness of Complexities

Despite assertions to the contrary by social critics, our society rates very highly in sheer volume of expressed dissent. At times it is almost deafening. But we are still quite short of technically expert, knowing dissent on many of the highly complex matters that affect our lives. And we have still not discovered how to counteract the process by which every organization filters the feedback on performance in order to screen out data it doesn't want to face up to. And when we learn how to lick that one, we'll have made a considerable gain.

5—Participation. In order to have a vital society we must have as high a degree of participation by the individual as we can manage.

Personally, I do not believe that the urge to participate actively in the shaping of one's social institutions is a powerful human motive. On the contrary, it appears to me to be notably weak and undependable. But we must fan that uncertain flame.

Why? I shall suggest two reasons—one having to do with the perils of this moment in history and the other essentially timeless.

This is a moment when men, here and around the world, have in some measure withdrawn faith in their institutions. They are questioning, reexamining. At such a time, there can be nothing more healthy, nothing more healing, than for men to participate directly in reshaping the institutions that no longer enjoy their confidence. It is the only way that confidence will be reestablished. And there is today a healthy impulse toward such participation. People do want to have their say. They want to feel that they count, that they're "connected."

The timeless reason is that participation preserves the vitality of institutions and nurtures a healthy relationship between the individual and society. When people for whatever reason (oppression, laziness, complacency) cease to take part in their institutions, the institutions themselves decay at an accelerating rate.

But if we are to make participation possible we must restore the sense of community and restore the vitality of local leadership. It is only at the local level that the average citizen will ever enjoy the opportunity to participate.

And we need to develop further "the service idea" inherent in the Peace Corps, VISTA and similar programs. People who are serving a meaningful cause no longer feel "unconnected." Life gains significance.

6—Leadership. A society capable of renewal will have a plentiful supply of relevant leadership.

On this score we are in poor shape. The specialization of modern society channels virtually all executive and analytical talent into professional and specialist channels and away from the kinds of public and generalist leadership that we so badly need today.

A self-renewing society does not need leaders to tell it what to do; it has grown beyond paternalistic leadership. But it does urgently need leaders to symbolize its values, to clarify issues, to help sift priorities and, most of all perhaps, to keep hope alive—hope that we can find our way through the troubles of the day, despite confusion and cross-purposes, despite our own folly, despite the bitterness of conflict.

7—Conflict resolution. The society capable of continuous renewal will have developed effective means of resolving human conflict to deal with the fierce antagonisms that divide and often immobilize a society.

I do not regard this as an impossible goal. It is really only in the past 15 or 20 years that we have given any attention at all of a systematic or analytical nature to the resolving of human conflict. And we have learned a great deal—far more than we have applied to date.

It is not the fact of conflict itself that threatens a society. Conflict is a fact of life. What endangers the adaptability of a society are the consequences of violent, prolonged and savage conflict—deeply embedded hatreds, devastating break-downs in communication and the rigidity of entrenched defensive positions.

8—Values. A society capable of renewal must have deeply rooted values. If it believes in nothing, there is no possibility that it can generate the high level of motivation that renewal demands. The values must not only be compatible with the process of renewal, they must be worthy of a great civilization.

We are fortunate in that respect. Freedom, justice, equality of opportunity, the worth and dignity of the individual—these are values that are supremely compatible with social renewal. Our problem is not to find better values but to be faithful to those we profess.

9—Morale. A society capable of continuous renewal will have morale, conviction, confidence.

We have in some measure lost confidence. It is not easy to say how we shall regain it, since morale and confidence are emergent characteristics which cannot be summoned up by order. It is my belief that our loss of confidence is traceable to a variety of factors: the severity of internal conflict, the failure of leadership, the incapacity of society, at least in the recent past, to solve obvious and grave problems, a visible disparity between the values we profess and the practices we tolerate. If this is true then the restoral of confidence may take some time.

Confidence May Return with Beginning of Progress

The one hopeful possibility is that if we begin to make some progress in rolling back our troubles, our confidence may surge back. The return of confidence doesn't depend on achieving ultimate goals. It does depend on seeing light at the end of the tunnel.

It's going to require great courage and commitment and steadiness of purpose to get us moving in the right direction. It's going to require a great burst of national energy . . .

A considerable part of that burst of energy will have to go toward tackling the tough substantive problems, such as the rebuilding of the cities and tackling the problems of poverty and discrimination. But we're also going to have to think about how we can design this society to be a better problem-solving mechanism.

It can be done. We can create the first society in history that is capable of continuous renewal. But not by just letting events take their course. We have to build into the system the characteristics that we want.

The logic of large-scale organization tends to squeeze out pluralism and participation. We must preserve them. The self-affirming characteristics of all human organizations tend to suppress dissent. We must foster it. All human institutions tend to decay. We must design ours for renewal.

This free society begins with you. It mustn't end with you. I'm not proposing new duties. I'm calling you back to old duties. You remember the preamble to the Constitution: "We the people of the United States, in order to form a more perfect union, establish justice, insure domestic tranquility, provide for the common defense, promote the general welfare, and secure the blessings of liberty, for ouselves and our posterity. . . "

'We the People'

Great phrases, but the greatest of all is "We the people of the United States." Not we the public officials of the United States, not we the certified experts in public administration, not we who happen to have time to think about these things when we're not busy running our businesses or practicing our professions; just we the people.

Now we have just elected a new President. No matter how gifted he may prove to be, he cannot save us from ourselves. He cannot function effectively unless we are actively and intelligently at work on our problems. No matter how accomplished our public servants may be, the inner mystery of democracy will always involve that old and good idea—we the people.

You and I, and others like us, acting in our own communities around the nation, can pull this fragmented society together. We can recreate an America in which men speak to one another in trust and confidence, sharing common objectives, working toward common goals. We can return this nation to a path of confidence and well-being. We can design a society capable of continuous renewal. You and I can do these things. No one can do them for us.

QUESTIONS FOR DISCUSSION AND DIALOGUE

1. Outline John Gardner's numbered list of attributes in a society which resists the smothering of individuality and instead fosters creative individuals and self renewal. Do you agree with the necessity for these attributes? Discuss.
2. Discuss the implications that Gardner's use of the queen bee and hive analogy have for the Americans, their politicians and parties, and nonpolitical influentials. Do you agree with Gardner here that "The queen bee is as much a prisoner of the system as any other in the hive"?
3. What in the United States today seems to indicate Americans can generate the continuous renewal of American institutions as Gardner suggests it? What seems to indicate Americans can not succeed at this? On balance, do you think the United States will or will not pay attention to Gardner's suggestions? Why?

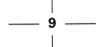

Message for a Revolutionary Generation: You Can Remake This Society

John W. Gardner

This part of the book concludes with John Gardner speaking directly to the "Revolutionary Generation" which most of you reading the book comprise. He says you can do "Plenty" to change things that need change in this society. Gardner also warns against the rhetoric and action of "playpen revolutionaries, imprisoned by their own tactics in the only world that will tolerate them." The stakes are no less than renewing American society by preserving the institutions which deserve preservation, while changing in such a way that human potential is released.

This spring, I received a letter signed by three undergraduates at a major university. They said, "We don't like the fanaticism, the coercive tactics and the ego games of the extremist leaders. But we think things have to change in this society. What can we do?"

I have had the same inquiry—"What can we do?"—from many young people. The quick answer is "Plenty!"

But first, you are right to say there are things that must be changed. Our nation is in deep trouble. There are intolerable injustices to be corrected, outworn institutions to be overhauled, new solutions to be found—and you can't live placidly as though you hadn't noticed.

If we are to root out the evils, deal with the swift pace of change, meet new conceptions of human need and preserve the vitality of this society, our institutions must undergo quick, far-reaching adaptation.

As young people, you are well fitted to renew human institutions. You have the necessary freshness of vision. You have the necessary impatience. And you are not yet entrapped in custom.

But if you are to benefit from those assets, you are going to have to think hard about the realities of social change. The extremist student leaders have devised some theatrical and destructive games that provide the thrill of conflict (and great ego inflation for the leaders themselves) but accomplish virtually nothing in the way of real social change. The extremists are dependent for their success on the permissive atmosphere of academic life. For all their talk of changing the world, they are playpen revolutionaries, imprisoned by their own tactics in the only world that will tolerate them.

The weaknesses of most political action by youth, here and throughout the world, have been inexperienced and futile assaults on the wrong targets, aimless and destructive bursts of anger and violence, and the willingness of many to be exploited by irrational, narcissistic and cynically manipulative leaders. Over and over, we have seen that violence and coercion do not lead forward to constructive change but backward to repressive countermeasures.

What are the alternatives for you? To my mind, they are many and exciting. The best proof that they exist may be found in last year's ['68] political campaigns.

Those of you who served as campaign workers committed yourselves to disciplined endeavor to cope with the world on its own terms. In doing so, you left an indelible mark on the year 1968. You may have started something that will change everything.

What I propose is that you now bring your enthusiasm and commitment to a very specific set of tasks that *must* be carried through if this nation is to measure up to the challenge ahead: 1) *reform of the major parties;* 2) *reform of the electoral process;* 3) *reform of state and local government.*

What you have seen in the past year must have whetted your interest in the machinery of party politics and the workings of the electoral process. Some of you have been so repelled or discouraged that you have given up both on the parties and the process. But others, perhaps most of you, are not discouraged because you sense that you have really set some changes in motion. Few professional politicians would have predicted that the Democratic convention of 1968 would outlaw the unit rule not only at the national convention but down to the state and local levels. Few would have believed the convention would require that delegates be chosen under procedures open to the public. Yet those revolutionary steps were taken—and you played a major role.

At the local level, thanks in part to your efforts, new candidates with fresh views appeared in many places. Incumbents were forced to reassess their positions on important issues, including the war. Local party chairmen were in some instances replaced. School boards have been forced to reexamine their policies.

That is only a taste of what can come. You know how badly a fresh breeze is needed. You know that we need to shake up the means by which the parties manage their affairs, choose their delegates, run their conventions. You know what peril for democracy lies in the skyrocketing expenses of political campaigns. You understand how archaic are the processes of the electoral college.

Similarly, you have gotten at least a glimpse of the critical need for reforming state and local government. You care about the idea of participation, and you know that most participation must necessarily be at the grass roots, a level dominated by antiquated and creaky political machinery. State and local governments are ripe for major changes. You can have a major hand in bringing about those changes.

Here are some of the activities young people could engage in (and I would include many age levels and many kinds of people: ghetto youth with natural leadership capacities but not much education, college undergraduates, graduate students, young professionals, teachers and businessmen):

Sign up for work in your own party; write (Lawrence O'Brien) or (Robert Dole), chairmen, respectively, of the Democratic and Republican national committees, and ask what plans they have for involving young people in party work. (They have such plans.)

Run for elective office, or do volunteer staff work for someone running for office.

Enter government service at state or local levels.

Help design and participate in publicly or privately financed internship programs that will enable young people to get a taste of public life before entering it as a career.

Form a local group to study in depth the social problems that confront your community, and present your findings to appropriate legislators and administrators.

Insist on participation by youth in civic organizations concerned with social problems. Say to civic leaders, "You don't like it when we take unconventional action; then give us a piece of the conventional action."

Do volunteer work for organizations dedicated to good government, and recruit others of your age group to do likewise; if you find no organization that suits your purposes, form your own.

Form a local youth organization to study the processes of state and local government, to discover practical means of improving it and to take action.

These suggestions stress state and local politics, but I'm not suggesting you forsake the national arena. Every member of Congress has roots "back home," has ties with local party machinery and worries about what his constituents say. You can reach him.

College and university professors of government can help you explore the realities of the world you hope to change, through courses for credit, field projects and extracurricular action. Law school professors can advise you on model-state legislation, conflict of interest, new instrumentalities for citizen action and so on.

Mayors, governors, state legislators and members of Congress can give you counsel on the workings of government. (I know that only a few such public figures will have the adventurousness—or is it shrewdness?—to do so, but a few may be enough!)

All civic organizations should make a point of bringing young people into the heart of their activities. Foundations should provide funds for action-oriented research and programs.

I propose that you form local organizations to pursue these matters. I do not wish to suggest the form the organizations should take, because your purposes will vary. Some of you will wish to work through the Young Democratic or Young Republican organizations. Others will be inclined to form new organizations.

Just the fact of your participation in local politics and government will in itself have a powerful and beneficial effect. It will be good for the community and good for you. But mere participation is *not* the goal. You could enter the system, adjust to it perfectly, end up at the top—and leave us exactly where we are now. The purpose is *not* just to enter the system. The purpose is to change it for the better. Your elders have shamefully neglected the task of improving state and local government. You can correct that.

The object is the redesign of institutions, the renewal of society. It will take all the intelligence and energy and shrewdness you can bring to bear. But the stakes are high.

The object is to win—not to make yourselves feel noble, not to indulge your anger, not to pad your vanity but to renew the society.

Human institutions can be changed, if you care enough to work at it, if you care enough to study the machinery you want to change and find the points of leverage.

At this critical point in our history, we can less and less afford to limit ourselves to routine repair of breakdowns in our social processes. More and more, we must undertake the imaginative redesign of those processes. We see in all clarity that many of our institutions are ill-fitted for the tasks the modern world presses on them; yet they stubbornly resist change, even in the face of savage attacks by those who would destroy them.

Unless we are willing to see a final confrontation between institutions that refuse to change and critics bent on destruction, we had better get on with the business of redesigning our society.

You can renew this society. But not in a fit of impatience and not without effort. You must be discriminating critics of your society, seeking to identify, coolly and precisely, those things about it that thwart or limit human potentialities, and therefore need modification. And so must you be discriminating protectors of your society, preserving those features that strengthen the individual and make him more free. To fit yourselves for such tasks, you must be sufficiently serious to study your institutions, sufficiently dedicated to become expert in the art of modifying them.

The time is ripe for constructive and far-reaching improvement in our institutions. No one person, obviously, can do it alone. But young people all over the country, working together, might produce just the leaven, just the stimulus, just the lift of spirit that this nation needs to move on to the next stage of development.

QUESTIONS FOR DISCUSSION AND DIALOGUE

1. Gardner emphasizes the need for youthful concern and reform efforts in state and local government. Can you list two or three such specific areas of concern in your state or your community? Discuss.
2. Which of the activities proposed for young people do you think have the most merit? Which would you be most inclined to join in? Why?
3. In your own words and after reflecting on the major ideas of this chapter, just what are the most important things at stake that will be determined by politics in the 1970's? Do you intend to play a personal role? How? Why?

——— **CHAPTER SIX** ———

The Political Scientists'
Perspective

Up to this point, there has been little deep and technical rigor in the structure and content of this book. Nevertheless, this relatively simplistic approach will prove fertile if it succeeds in organizing the issues of politics in such a way that attention is focused on the fundamental questions of political structure and dynamics. If the structure and content of these first five chapters have conveyed a sense of excitement and a degree of meaning about politics which inspire further inquiry and deeper commitment to the ideals of American politics, this book has served its basic purpose.

At this point, for the student interested in a deeper and more technical level of empirical and theoretical inquiry into politics, an article has been selected from an academic political science journal that deals with a subject area already covered by readings in this book, but in a different fashion. At first glance, the beginning student of politics will likely be overwhelmed by the language and style of the article. However, upon further reading and after reflecting back to many of the less "scholarly" articles in the first five chapters, it becomes apparent that the subject is still politics. The difference in this article is that political science professionals rather than "The Americans," "The Students," "The Politicians and Their Parties," are at work with the presidential election of 1968. These particular "Non Political Influentials" demonstrate by this study that when political scientists, as contrasted with the above groups, view politics there are some important differences. There are also some important similarities.

At the outset, it is necessary for the reader to be aware that each political science journal is controlled by a board of editors which dictates a particular style and content. Consequently, it is to be expected that some journals will emphasize empirical (behavioral) techniques, while others will reflect a more traditional flavor. (The reader might wish to review Brown's article in Chapter Four on this point.) Of course, there are journals dealing with both approaches. Therefore, an acquaintance with the policies of the various journals is necessary for the committed student of politics.

In reading this article, or other political science journal articles, it will prove helpful for the reader to first read the concluding page, (or, the "Abstract" if one is provided). This should be followed by a quick glance at the middle pages in order to determine the type of data used in developing the article. Finally, the article itself should be read with great care exercised in discriminating among the facts, ideas, and opinions which are being presented.

—— 1 ——

Continuity and Change in American Politics: Parties and Issues in the 1968 Election

Philip E. Converse
Warren E. Miller
Jerrold G. Rusk
Arthur C. Wolfe

Without much question, the third-party movement of George C. Wallace constituted the most unusual feature of the 1968 presidential election. While this movement failed by a substantial margin in its audacious attempt to throw the presidential contest into the House of Representatives, in any other terms it was a striking success. It represented the first noteworthy intrusion on a two-party election in twenty years. The Wallace ticket drew a larger proportion of the popular vote than any third presidential slate since 1924, and a greater proportion of electoral votes than any such movement for more than a century, back to the curiously divided election of 1860. Indeed, the spectre of an electoral college stalemate loomed sufficiently large that serious efforts at reform have since taken root.

At the same time, the Wallace candidacy was but one more dramatic addition to an unusually crowded rostrum of contenders, who throughout the spring season of primary elections were entering and leaving the lists under circumstances that ranged from the comic through the astonishing to the starkly tragic. Six months before the nominating conventions, Lyndon Johnson and Richard Nixon had been the expected 1968 protagonists, with some greater degree of uncertainty, as usual within the ranks of the party out of power. The nominating process for the Republicans followed the most-probable script rather closely, with the only excitement being provided by the spectacle of Governors Romney and Rockefeller proceeding as through revolving doors in an ineffectual set of moves aimed at providing a Republican alternative to the Nixon candidacy. Where things were supposed to be most routine on the Democratic side, however, surprises were legion, including the early enthusiasm for Eugene McCarthy, President Johnson's shocking announcement that he would not run, the assassination of Robert Kennedy in the flush of his first electoral successes, and the dark turmoil in and around the Chicago nominating convention, with new figures like Senators George McGovern and Edward Kennedy coming into focus as challengers to the heir apparent, Vice President Hubert Humphrey.

No recent presidential election has had such a lengthy cast of central characters, nor one that was kept for so long in flux. And under such circumstances, there is an inevitable proliferation of "what ifs?" What if Lyndon Johnson had decided to run again? What if Robert Kennedy had not been shot? What if George Wallace had been dissuaded from running, or had remained simply a regional states-rights candidate? What if Eugene McCarthy had accepted party discipline and closed ranks with Humphrey at the Chicago convention? What if Hubert Humphrey had handled the interaction with Mayor Daley and the Chicago demonstrators differently?

Strictly speaking, of course, there is no sure answer to questions of this type. If the attempt on Kennedy's life had failed, for example, an enormous complex of parameters and event sequences would have been different over the course of the campaign. One can never be entirely confident about what would have happened without the opportunity to live that particular sequence out in all its complexity. Nonetheless, given sufficient information as to the state of mind of the electorate during the period in question, plausible reconstructions can be developed which do not even assume that all other things remained constant, but only that they remained *sufficiently* constant that other processes might stay within predictable bounds. And answers of this sort, if not sacrosanct, carry substantial satisfaction.

One of our purposes in this paper will be to address some of these questions, as illuminated by preliminary analyses from the sixth national presidential election survey, carried out by the Survey Research Center of the University of Michigan.[1] An effort to develop answers gives a vehicle for what is frankly descriptive coverage of the 1968 election as seen by the electorate. At the same time, we would hope not to miss along the way some of the more theoretical insights which the peculiar circumstances of the 1968 election help to reveal. In particular, we shall pay close attention to the Wallace campaign, and to the more generic lessons that may be drawn from this example of interplay between a pair of traditional parties, potent new issues, and a protest movement.

I. The Setting of the Election

The simplest expectation for the 1968 election, and one held widely until March of that year, was that President Johnson would exercise his option to run for a second full term, and that with the advantages of incumbency and the support of the majority party in the land, he would stand a very good chance of winning, although with a margin visibly reduced from his landslide victory over Barry Goldwater in 1964.

We will probably never know what role public opinion may have actually played in his decision to retire. But there is ample evidence that the mood of the electorate had become increasingly surly toward his administration in the months preceding his announcement. When queried in September and October of 1968, barely 40% of the electorate thought that he had handled his job well, the rest adjudging the performance to have been fair to poor. A majority of Democratic and Independent voters, asked if they would have favored President Johnson as the Democratic nominee had he decided to run, said they would not have. Affective ratings elicited just after the election for all the prominent political figures of the campaign showed Johnson trailing Robert Kennedy in average popularity by a wide margin, and lagging somewhat behind Humphrey and Muskie as well, among other Democrats (see Table 2). Given the normal head-start that a sitting president usually enjoys in such assays of opinion, Johnson completed his term amid a public bad humor matched only in recent elections by the cloud under which Harry Truman retired from the presidency in 1952. It is correspondingly dubious that Lyndon Johnson could have avoided the embarrassment of defeat had he set his sails for another term.

Indeed, the pattern of concerns exercising the voters and turnover in the players on the presidential stage combined to produce a shift in popular preferences between 1964 and 1968 which was truly massive. It is likely that the proportion of voters casting presidential ballots for the same party in these two successive elections was lower than at any time in recent American history. Among whites who voted in both elections, a full third switched their party. Almost one Goldwater voter out of every five turned either to Humphrey or to Wallace four years later (dividing almost 3 to 1 for Wallace over Humphrey); at the same time, three in every ten white Johnson voters switched to Nixon or Wallace, with Nixon the favorite by a 4-to-1 ratio. A full 40 percent of Nixon's votes came from citizens who had supported Lyndon Johnson in 1964! Much of this flood, of course, came from Republicans who were returning home after their desertions from Goldwater.

Nevertheless, Democrats and Independents who had voted for Johnson and then turned to Nixon four years later made up nearly half of *all* the remaining vote switches, more than matching the combined flow of Johnson and Goldwater voters who supported Wallace, and almost equalling the total Wallace vote. The Johnson-Nixon switchers easily outweighed the flow away from Goldwater to Humphrey and Wallace, and the Republican presidential vote rose from 39% to 43% in 1968 as a consequence. At the same time, the loss of more than a quarter of the total Johnson vote to Wallace and Nixon was scarcely offset by the trickle of votes from Goldwater to Humphrey, and the Democratic proportion of the vote across the land dropped a shattering 19 percentage points from more than 61 percent to less than 43 percent.

Such a massive drain from the Democratic ranks establishes a broader parallel with 1952, for in both cases an electorate professing to be of Democratic allegiance by a considerable majority, had arrived at a sufficient accumulation of grievances with a Democratic administration as to wish it out of office, thereby producing what we have labelled elsewhere a "deviating election."[2] Indeed, the frantic motion of the electorate in its presidential votes between 1964 and 1968 may be ironically juxtaposed against the serene stability of party identifications in the country, for the overall proportions of self-proclaimed Democrats, Independents and Republicans have scarcely changed over the past twenty years, much less in the past four. Of course this juxtaposition calls into question the predictive value of party identification, relative to other kinds of determinants of the vote, and we shall undertake a more intensive discussion of this matter presently. For now, however, let us simply point out that while the inert distribution of party loyalties cannot by definition explain the complex flows of the presidential vote between 1964 and 1968, it was handsomely reflected in the 1968 congressional elections, as it has been in virtually all of the biennial congressional contests of the current era. Despite widespread dissatisfaction with Democratic performance, the Republican proportion of seats in the House rose only a minute 1 percent, from 43 in 1966 to 44 percent on the strength of the Nixon victory. Even at more local levels, the continuing dominance of Democratic partisanship across the nation is documented by the results of thousands of races for state legislative seats. Prior to the election, Democrats controlled 57.7 percent of all legislative seats. After the election, which saw contests for some or all seats in 43 states, Democratic control had dropped from 4,269 seats (or 57.7%) to 4,250 seats (57.5%).[3]

In view of such continued stability of partisanship, it is clear we must turn elsewhere to account for the remarkable changes in voting at the presidential level between 1964 and 1968. The classic assumption is, of course, that such change must spring from some flux in "short-term forces"—the impact of the most salient current issues, and the way in which these issues interlock with the leadership options, or the cast of potential presidential figures in the specific year of 1968. These terms obviously best define the setting of the 1968 election.

When asked on the eve of the presidential election to identify the most important problem facing the government in Washington, over 40% of the electorate cited the war in Vietnam. The salience of this issue provided another striking parallel with 1952. In both presidential elections, widespread public discouragement with the progress of a "bleeding war" in the Far East, seen as initiated by a Democratic administration, was a major source of indignation.

But the Vietnam issue did not, of course, stand alone. Offering vivid testimony to another bitter current of controversy was a simple, though little-noted, pattern in the popular presidential vote itself: while some 97% of black voters in the nation cast their ballots for Hubert Humphrey, less than 35% of white voters did so. Thus the presidential vote must have been as sharply polarized along racial lines as at any time during American history.[4] One major irony surrounding this cleavage was the fact that it was the comfortable white majority that was agitating to overturn control of the White House, while the aggrieved black minority was casting its vote as one in an effort to preserve the partisan status quo.

Indeed, this irony is compounded when the role of the Vietnam issue is jointly taken into account. We have indicated above that the public was deeply impatient with the Johnson administration, in part because of the handling of the war.

Blacks stood out as the major demographic grouping most exercised about the entanglement in Vietnam. They were more likely than whites to opine that the government should never have undertaken the military commitment there. They also were more likely to feel that American troops should be brought home immediately, a position not generally associated with the Johnson administration. Nonetheless, as Table 2 (below) will document, Negro enthusiasm not only for Hubert Humphrey but for Lyndon Johnson as well remained high to the very end. It seems quite evident that when black citizens were making decisions about their vote, Vietnam attitudes paled into relative insignificance by contrast with attitudes toward progress on civil rights within the country; and that where such progress was concerned, the Johnson-Humphrey administration was seen as much more friendly than the other 1968 alternatives.

Because of the near-unanimity of the black vote, many of our analyses below have been focussed on differences within the white vote taken alone.[5] At the same time, this treatment must not be allowed to obscure in any way the deep imprint of racial cleavage on the election outcome. The additional "between-race" variance in the vote, concealed when data are presented only for whites, remains extreme, and is a faithful reflection of the crescendo to which civil rights tumult had risen over the four preceding years. It should be kept in mind.

To say that Vietnam and civil rights were dominant issues for the public in 1968 is not equivalent, however, to saying that voter positions on these issues can account for the large-scale voting change we have observed for whites between 1964 and 1968. As the comparisons provided by Table 1 suggest, changes in public thinking about strategic alternatives in Vietnam or civil rights outcomes over this period were rather limited. Where Vietnam was concerned, opinion was somewhat more crystallized in 1968 than in 1964 but there had been no sweeping shift of sentiment from hawk to dove in mass feeling. On civil rights, the drift of white opinion had been if anything toward a more liberal stance, and hence can hardly explain a vote which seemed to vibrate with "blacklash." Thus public positioning on these two central issues taken alone seems no more capable of illuminating vote change from 1964 to 1968 than the inert partisan identifications.

What *had* changed, of course, was the public view of the success of Administration performance in these areas. As we have discussed elsewhere, throughout the 1950's citizens who felt the Republicans were better at keeping the country out of war outnumbered those who had more confidence in Democrats by a consistently wide margin, much as the Democratic Party tended to be seen as better at keeping the country out of economic depression. In 1964, however, the pleas of Barry Goldwater for an escalation of the Vietnam War in order to produce a military victory served to frighten the public, and rapidly reversed the standing perception: by the time of the November election more people felt the Democrats were better able to avert a large war.[6] But this novel perception was transient. President Johnson himself saw fit to authorize an escalation of bombing in Vietnam almost immediately after the 1964 election. By the time of the 1966 congressional election, the balance in popular assessments had already shifted back to the point where a slight majority chose the Republicans as more adept in avoiding war. By 1968, exasperation at the handling of the war had increased

TABLE 1: Comparison of Attitudes on Current Vietnam Policy and Racial Desegregation, 1964 and 1968, for Whites Only

"Which of the following do you think we should do *now* in Vietnam?"
1. Pull out of Vietnam entirely.
2. Keep our soldiers in Vietnam but try to end the fighting.
3. Take a stronger stand even if it means invading North Vietnam.

Northern Democrats

	Pull Out	Status Quo	Stronger Stand	Don't Know, Other	Total
1964	8%	25	29	38	100%
1968	20%	39	35	6	100%

Northern Republicans

1964	8%	19	38	35	100%
1968	20%	39	36	5	100%

Southern Democrats

1964	8%	25	28	39	100%
1968	17%	36	38	9	100%

Southern Republicans

1964	10%	18	42	30	100%
1968	15%	29	48	8	100%

"What about you? Are you in favor of desegregation, strict segregation, or something in between?" (This was the fourth question in a series asking about others' attitudes toward racial desegregation.)

Northern Democrats

	Desegregation	Mixed Feelings	Strict Segregation	Other	Total
1964	31%	50	17	2	100%
1968	38%	45	14	3	100%

Northern Republicans

1964	32%	51	13	4	100%
1968	35%	50	10	5	100%

Southern Democrats

1964	12%	35	52	1	100%
1968	18%	45	30	7	100%

Southern Republicans

1964	15%	44	40	1	100%
1968	15%	60	20	5	100%

sufficiently that among people who felt there was a difference in the capacity of the two parties to avoid a larger war, the Republicans were favored once again by a margin of two to one.

To the bungled war in Vietnam, the white majority could readily add a sense of frustration at a racial confrontation that had taken on increasingly ugly dimensions between 1964 and 1968. Although national opinion had evolved in a direction somewhat more favorable to desegregation, largely through the swelling proportions of college-educated young, some persistently grim facts had been underscored by the Kerner Commission report in the spring of the year: forbidding proportions of the white citizenry outside of the South as well as within it had little enthusiasm for the redress of Negro grievances to begin with. And even among whites with some genuine sympathy for the plight of blacks, the spectacle of city centers aflame had scarcely contributed to a sense of confidence in the Administration handling of the problem.

From Vietnam and the racial crisis a corollary discontent crystallized that might be treated as a third towering issue of the 1968 campaign, or as nothing more than a restatement of the other two issues. This was the cry for "law and order" and against "crime in the streets." While Goldwater had talked in these terms somewhat in 1964, events had conspired to raise their salience very considerably for the public by 1968. For some, these slogans may have no connotations involving either the black race or Vietnam, signifying instead a concern over rising crime rates and the alleged "coddling" of criminal offenders by the courts. More commonly by 1968, however, the connection was very close: there were rally cries for more severe police suppression of black rioting in the urban ghettos, and of public political dissent of the type represented by the Vietnam peace demonstrations at Chicago during the Democratic convention.

In view of these latter connotations, it is not surprising that people responsive to the "law and order" theme tended, like George Wallace, to be upset at the same time by civil rights gains and the lack of a more aggressive policy in Vietnam. Therefore it might seem redundant to treat "law and order" as a third major issue in its own right. Nevertheless, we have found it important to do so, even where the "order" being imposed is on black militants or peace demonstrators, for the simple reason that many members of the electorate reacted as though the control of dissent was quite an independent issue. This becomes very clear where support for blacks and opposition to the war are accompanied with a strong revulsion against street protest and other forms of active dissent. And this combination occurs more frequently than an academic audience may believe.

One would expect, for example, to find support for peace demonstrations among the set of people in the sample who said (a) that we made a mistake in getting involved in the Vietnam War; and (b) that the preferable course of action at the moment would be to "pull out" of that country entirely. Such expectations are clearly fulfilled among the numerous blacks matching these specifications. Among whites, however, the picture is different. First, a smaller proportion of whites—about one in six or seven—expressed this combination of feelings about Vietnam. Among those who expressed such feelings it remains true that there is relatively less disfavor vented about some of the active forms of peace dissent that had become customary by 1968. What is striking, however, is the absolute division of evaluative attitudes toward peace dissenters among those who were themselves relative "dove," and this is probably the more politically significant fact as well. Asked to rate "Vietnam war protestors" on the same kind of scale as used in Table 2, for example, a clear majority of these whites who themselves were opposed to the Administration's Vietnam policy located their reactions on the negative side of the scale, and nearly one-quarter (23%) placed them at the point of most extreme hostility.

Even more telling, perhaps, are the attitudes of these same whites toward the peace demonstrations surrounding the Democratic convention at Chicago, for in this case the protestors were given undeniably sympathetic coverage by the television networks. Keeping in mind that we are dealing here with only those whites who took clear "dove" positions on Vietnam policy, it is noteworthy indeed that almost 70% of those giving an opinion rejected the suggestion that "too much force" was used by Chicago police against the peace demonstrators, and the *modal* opinion (almost 40%) was that "not enough force" had been used to suppress the demonstration.[7]

It should be abundantly clear from this description that the white minority who by the autumn of 1968 felt our intervention in Vietnam was a mistake and was opting for a withdrawl of troops turns out to fit the campus image of peace sentiment rather poorly. Such a disjuncture between stereotypes developed from the mass media and cross-section survey data are not at all uncommon. However, as certain other aspects of the election may be quite unintelligible unless this fact has been absorbed by the reader, it is worth underscoring here. This is not to say that the more familiar Vietnam dissent cannot be detected in a national sample. Among whites resenting Vietnam and wishing to get out, for example, a unique and telltale bulge of 12% gave ratings of the most extreme sympathy to the stimulus "Vietnam war protestors." Now this fragment of the electorate shows all of the characteristics expected of McCarthy workers or the New Left: its members are very young, are disproportionately college-educated, Jewish, and metropolitan in background, and register extreme sympathy with civil rights and the Chicago convention demonstrations. The problem is that this group represents such a small component (one-eighth) of the 1968 dove sentiment on Vietnam being singled out here that its attitudes on other issues are very nearly obscured by rather different viewpoints held by the other 88% of the dove contingent. On the larger national scene, in turn, those who opposed Vietnam policy and were sympathetic to Vietnam war protestors make up less than 3% of the electorate—even if we add comparable blacks to the group— and law and order were not unpopular with the 97 per cent.

In the broad American public, then, there was a widespread sense of breakdown in authority and discipline that fed as readily on militant political dissent as on race riots and more conventional crime. This disenchantment registered even among citizens who apparently were sympathetic to the goals of the dissent on pure policy grounds, and everywhere added to a sense of cumulative grievance with the party in possession of the White House. Thus the "law and order" phrase, ambiguous though it might be, had considerable resonance among the

TABLE 2: Average Ratings of Major 1968 Political Figures
by a National Sample, November-December, 1968

	Total Sample	Non-South		South	
		White (N's of 785-843)	Black (N's of 54-64)	White (N's of 315-340)	Black (N's of 55-66)
Robert Kennedy	70.1	70.4	94.1	60.5	91.2
Richard Nixon	66.5	67.7	53.0	67.8	56.6
Hubert Humphrey	61.7	61.2	86.1	53.4	85.8
Lyndon Johnson	58.4	56.6	81.9	53.7	82.7
Eugene McCarthy	54.8	56.5	59.1	49.8	54.0
Nelson Rockefeller	53.8	54.4	61.6	50.7	53.5
Ronald Reagan	49.1	49.6	42.9	50.0	41.8
George Romney	49.0	50.4	48.3	45.6	50.2
George Wallace	31.4	27.7	9.4	48.2	13.2
Edmund Muskie	61.4	62.7	71.0	54.7	68.9
Spiro Agnew	50.4	50.9	37.7	52.9	42.4
Curtis LeMay	35.2	33.6	21.1	48.9	22.9

voters, and deserves to be catalogued along with Vietnam and the racial crisis among major issue influences on the election.

While the 1968 situation bore a number of resemblances to the basic ingredients and outcome of the 1952 election, the analogy is far from perfect. In 1952, the public turned out to vote in proportions that were quite unusual for the immediate period, a phenomenon generally taken to reflect the intensity of frustrations over the trends of government. It is easy to argue that aggravations were fully as intense in 1968 as they had been in 1952, and more intense than for any of the elections in between. Yet the proportion turning out to vote in 1968 fell off somewhat from its 1964 level.[8]

Of course any equation between indignation and turning out to vote does presuppose the offering of satisfactory alternatives, and there was somewhat greater talk than usual in 1968 that the candidate options in November were inadequate. Certainly the array of potential candidates was lengthy, whatever the actual nominees, and our account of the short-term forces affecting the electorate would be quite incomplete without consideration of the emotions with which the public regarded the dramatis personae in 1968. Just after the election, respondents in our national sample were asked to locate each of twelve political figures on a "feeling thermometer" running from zero (cold) to 100° (warm), with a response of 50° representing the indifference point. Table 2 summarizes the mean values for the total sample, as well as those within relevant regional and racial partitions.

Numerous well-chronicled features of the campaign are raised into quantitative relief by this tabulation, including Wallace's sharply regional and racial appeal, Muskie's instant popularity and near upstaging of Humphrey, and the limited interest that McCarthy seemed to hold for Negroes compared to other Democratic candidates. At the same time, other less evident comparisons can be culled from these materials, although the reader is cautioned to keep in mind that these scores refer to the period just after the election, and not necessarily to the period of the spring primaries or the summer conventions.[9] This may be of particular importance in the case of the ratings of Eugene McCarthy. When respondents were asked before the election which candidate from the Spring they had hoped would win nomination, over 20 percent of Democrats and Independents recalling some preference mentioned McCarthy. However, many of these citizens gave quite negative ratings to McCarthy by November, so it appears that some disenchantment set in between the primaries and the election.

The question of timing poses itself acutely as well where Robert Kennedy is concerned.

Taken at face value, the data of Table 2 imply that aside from the tragedy at Los Angeles, Kennedy should have been given the Democratic nomination and would have won the presidential election rather handily. Yet how much of this massive popularity is due to some posthumous halo of martyrdom? It seems almost certain that at least some small increment is of this sort, and that the harsh realities of a tough campaign would have eroded the bright edges of Kennedy appeal. Nevertheless, both in contested primaries and poll data of the Spring period, as well as in the retrospective glances of our autumn respondents, one cannot fail to be impressed by the reverberations of Kennedy charisma even in the least likely quarters, such as among Southern whites or among Republicans elsewhere. And rank-and-file Democrats outside the South reported themselves to have favored Kennedy for the nomination over Humphrey by two-to-one margins, and over McCarthy by nearly three-to-one. Clearly a Kennedy candidacy could not have drawn a much greater proportion of the black vote than Humphrey received, although it might have encouraged higher turnout there. But there is evidence of enough edge elsewhere to suggest that Robert Kennedy might have won an election over Richard Nixon, and perhaps even with greater ease than he would have won his own party's nomination.[10]

As it was, Humphrey received the mantle of party power from Lyndon Johnson and, with Robert Kennedy missing, captured the Democratic nomination without serious challenge. At that point he faced much the same dilemma as Adlai Stevenson had suffered in 1952: without gracelessly biting the hand that fed him, how could he disassociate himself from the unpopular record of the preceding administration? In 1952, Stevenson did not escape public disgust with the Truman administration, and was punished for its shortcomings. The 1968 data make clear in a similar manner that Humphrey was closely linked to Lyndon Johnson in the public eye through the period of the election. For example, the matrix of intercorrelations of the candidate ratings presented in Table 2 shows, as one would expect, rather high associations in attitudes toward presidential and vice presidential candidates on the same ticket. Thus the Humphrey-Muskie intercorrelation is .58, the Nixon-Agnew figure is .59, and the Wallace-Lemay figure is .69. But the highest intercorrelation in the whole matrix, a coefficient of

.70, links public attitudes toward Lyndon Johnson and those toward Hubert Humphrey. Humphrey was highly assimilated to the Johnson image, and his support came largely from sectors of the population for which the administration had not "worn thin."

When we consider the relative strength of Kennedy enthusiasts as opposed to loyal Humphrey-Johnson supporters among identifiers with the Democratic Party within the mass public, the line of differentiation that most quickly strikes the eye is the noteworthy generation gap. As we have seen above, Kennedy supporters enjoy a marked overall plurality. However, this margin comes entirely from the young. For Democrats under thirty, only about one in five giving a pre-convention nomination preference picks Humphrey or Johnson, and Kennedy partisans outnumber them by nearly three to one. Among Democrats over fifty, however, Humphrey-Johnson supporters can claim a clear plurality.[11] The "wings" of the Democratic Party that emerged in the struggle for the nomination had an "old guard" and "young Turk" flavor, even as reflected in a cross-section sample of party sympathizers.[12]

This completes our summary of the setting in which the 1968 election took place. We have seen that despite great continuity in party loyalties and a surprising constancy in policy positions of the public, there was an unusual degree of change in partisan preference at the presidential level by comparison with 1964. This change occurred in part as a response to increased salience of some issues, such as the question of "law and order," and in part because of the way in which contending leadership cadres had come to be identified with certain policies or past performance. The Democratic party lost, as quickly as it had won, its perceived capacity to cope with international affairs and the exacerbating war in Vietnam. Hubert Humphrey, long a major figure in his own right, could not move swiftly enough to escape his links with a discredited regime.

Let us now pursue some of the more obvious analytic questions posed by the general discontent among voters in 1968, and by the Wallace movement in particular. We shall first consider influences on the actual partitioning of the vote on Election Day, and then examine some of the attitudinal and social bases underlying the outcome.

II. Hypothetical Variations on the
Vote Outcome

Impact of the Wallace Ticket. There were signs of some concern in both the Nixon and Humphrey camps that the success of George Wallace in getting his name on the ballot might divert votes and lower their respective chances of success. Nixon was more alarmed by the prospective loss of the electoral votes in the Deep South that Goldwater had won in 1964, while Humphrey was alarmed in turn by intelligence that Wallace was making inroads outside the South among unionized labor that had been customarily Democratic since the New Deal. At the very least, the Wallace ticket was responsible for the injection of unusual uncertainty in a game already replete with unknowns. Now that the dust has settled, we can ask more systematically how the election might have been affected if Wallace had been dissuaded from running.

Numerous polls made clear at the time of the election that Wallace voters tended to be quite disproportionately nominal Democrats, and data from our sample are congruent with this conclusion, although the differences were more notable in the South than elsewhere. For the South, 68% of Wallace voters considered themselves Democrats, and 20% Republicans.

Outside the South, proportions were 46% Democratic and 34% Republican. Yet these proportions taken alone do not address in any satisfying fashion what might have happened if Wallace had not run. In the first place, these partisan proportions among Wallace voters do not differ very markedly from those which characterize the regional electorates taken as a whole. Indeed, as we shall see, the overall association between partisanship and attitudes toward Wallace (the rating scale) shows Republicans slightly more favorable across the nation as a whole, although this fact is faintly reversed with blacks set aside, and the main lesson seems to be that the "true" correlation is of utterly trivial magnitude (.05 or less). More important still, however, is the obvious fact that Democrats voting for Wallace were repudiating the standard national ticket, as many as a third of them for the second time in a row. If Wallace had not run, we can have little confidence that they would have faithfully supported Humphrey and Muskie.

It is clear that the crucial datum involves the relative preferences of the Wallace voters for either Nixon or Humphrey, assuming that these preferences would have been the same without Wallace and that these citizens would have gone to the polls in any event. This information is available in the leader ratings used for Table 2. In Table 3 we have arrayed the total sample according to whether Humphrey or Nixon was given the higher rating, or the two were tied, as well as by the respondent's party identification. Within each cell so defined, we indicate the proportion of the vote won by Wallace, and the number of voters on which the proportion is based. The latter figures show familiar patterns. Of voters with both a party and a candidate preference, more than four-fifths prefer the nominee of their party. And while Democrats are in a majority, it is clear that the tides are running against them since they are suffering the bulk of defections.

It is interesting how the Wallace vote is drawn from across this surface. While the numbers of cases are too small to yield very reliable estimates in some of the internal cells, it is obvious that Wallace made least inroads among partisans satisfied with their party's nominee, and showed major strength where such partisans were sufficiently disgusted with their own party nominee actually to prefer that of the opposing party. Conceptually, it is significant that these protestors included Republicans unenthusiastic about Nixon as well as the more expected Democrats cool to Humphrey. Practically, however, Nixon Democrats so far outnumbered Humphrey Republicans that while Wallace drew at nearly equal rates from both groups, the majority of his votes were from Democrats who otherwise preferred Nixon rather than from Republicans who might have given their favors to Humphrey.

This in turn provides much of the answer to one of our primary questions. While the data underlying Table 3 can be manipulated in a variety of ways, all

**TABLE 3: Distribution of the Wallace Vote,
by Traditional Parties and Candidates**

		PARTY IDENTIFICATION		
		Democratic	Independent	Republican
Rating of Two Major Candidates	HUMPHREY over NIXON	4% (347)	26% (23)	21% (24)
	Tied	24% (79)	9% (11)	6% (17)
	NIXON over HUMPHREY	26% (132)	15% (53)	7% (314)

The percentage figures indicates the proportion of all voters in the cell who reported casting a ballot for Wallace. The number of voters is indicated between parentheses.

reasonable reconstructions of the popular vote as it might have stood without the Wallace candidacy leave Nixon either enjoying about the same proportion of the two-party vote that he actually won or a slightly greater share, depending on the region and the detailed assumptions made. In short, unless one makes some entirely extravagant assumptions about the mediating electoral college, it is very difficult to maintain any suspicion that the Wallace intrusion by itself changed the major outcome of the election.

Impact of the McCarthy Movement. If he was ever tempted at all, Eugene McCarthy decided against mounting a fourth-party campaign for the presidency. At the same time, he withheld anything resembling enthusiastic personal support for Hubert Humphrey. In view of his devoted following, some observers felt that McCarthy's refusal to close party ranks after Chicago cost the Democratic nominee precious votes, and conceivably even the presidency.

In order to understand the basis of McCarthy support at the time of the election, it is useful to trace what is known of the evolution of McCarthy strength from the time of the first primary in the spring. It will be recalled that McCarthy was the sole Democrat to challenge the Johnson administration in the New Hampshire primary. With the aid of many student volunteer campaign workers, he polled a surprising 42% of the vote among Democrats, as opposed to 48% drawn by an organized write-in campaign for President Johnson. Although he failed to upset the president in the vote, most observers saw his performance as remarkably strong, and a clear harbinger of discontent which could unseat Lyndon Johnson in the fall election. This reading was plainly shared by Robert Kennedy, who announced his own candidacy for the nomination four days later, and probably by Johnson himself, who withdrew from any contention less than three weeks later.

Sample survey data from New Hampshire at the time of the primary show some expected patterns underlying that first McCarthy vote, but also some rather unexpected ones as well. First, the vote among Democrats split toward Johnson or McCarthy in obvious ways according to expressions of satisfaction or dissatisfaction with Administration performance in general and its Vietnam policy in particular. The McCarthy vote in New Hampshire certainly reflected a groundswell of anger at the Johnson administration, and an expression of desire for a change which was simply reiterated in November. Surprisingly, however, in view of McCarthy's clear and dissenting "dove" position on Vietnam, the vote he drew in New Hampshire could scarcely be labelled a "peace vote," despite the fact that such a conclusion was frequently drawn. There was, of course, some hard-core peace sentiment among New Hampshire Democrats that was drawn quite naturally to McCarthy. Among his supporters in the primary, however, those who were unhappy with the Johnson administration for not pursuing a *harder* line against Hanoi outnumbered those advocating a withdrawal from Vietnam by nearly a three to two margin! Thus the McCarthy tide in New Hampshire was, to say the least, quite heterogeneous in its policy preferences: the only common denominator seems to have been a deep dissatisfaction with the Johnson administration.[13] McCarthy simply represented the only formal alternative available to registered Democrats. This desire for an alternative was underlined by the fact that most of the 10 percent of the Democratic vote that did not go to Johnson or McCarthy went to Nixon as a write-in candidate on the Democratic ballot.

The entry of Robert Kennedy into the race did provide another alternative and, as we have seen, a very popular one as well. He made major inroads into the potential McCarthy strength, and by the time our autumn sample was asked what candidate of the spring would have been preferred for the Democratic nomination, 46% of those Democrats with some preference cited Kennedy first while only 18% mentioned McCarthy. Nevertheless, even this 18% cannot be thought of as constituting hard-core McCarthy support at the time of the actual election, since almost two-thirds of this group had turned their attention elsewhere, giving at least one of the other presidential hopefuls a higher rating than they gave McCarthy in the responses underlying Table 2. The remainder who reported McCarthy as their preconvention favorite and awarded him their highest ratings just after the election, make up some 6% of Democrats having some clear candidate preference, or 3% of all Democrats. Along with a handful of Independents and Republicans showing the same reiterated McCarthy preference, these people can be considered the McCarthy "hard-core."

While it is this hard-core whose voting decisions interest us most, it is instructive to note where the other two-thirds of the pre-convention McCarthy support among Democrats went, over the course of the campaign. If these migrations are judged according to which presidential aspirant among the nine hopefuls of Table 2 was given the highest rating in November, one discovers that a slight plurality of these erstwhile McCarthy backers found George Wallace their preferred candidate in the fall. Slightly smaller groups favored Kennedy and Nixon, and a scatter picked other Republicans like Reagan and Rockefeller, despite their own Democratic partisanship. Very few of these McCarthy Democrats—about one in seven—migrated to a preference for Hubert Humphrey. Where the actual presidential vote was concerned, the choice was of course more constrained.

Since the McCarthy movement was commonly thought of as somewhat to the left of Humphrey and the administration, while Wallace was located rather markedly to the right, a major McCarthy-to-Wallace transfer of preferences may seem ideologically perplexing. Were McCarthy supporters so furious with the Humphrey nomination that pure spite overcame issue feelings and led to a protest vote for Wallace? Although there were rumors of such a reaction at the time, our data suggest a somewhat simpler interpretation. We have already noted the attitudinal heterogeneity of McCarthy voters in New Hampshire. Those in our autumn sample who recall a preconvention preference for McCarthy are similarly heterogeneous. Indeed, on some issues of social welfare and civil rights, preconvention McCarthy supporters are actually more conservative than backers of either Humphrey or Kennedy.

This heterogeneity declined markedly, however, as the size of the McCarthy group eroded over the summer to what we have defined as the hard-core. If we compare the attitudes of that hard-core on major issues with those of the professed early backers of McCarthy who subsequently supported Wallace, the differences are usually extreme. The McCarthy-Wallace group was against desegregation, in favor of an increased military effort in Vietnam, and was highly indignant with the situation where "law and order" was concerned (see Table 4). People supporting McCarthy to the bitter end took opposite positions on all of these major issues. Similarly, the winnowing down of the McCarthy support operated very sharply along demographic lines. Among non-Southern white Democrats who reported a preconvention McCarthy preference, for example, the hard-core that remained enthusiastic about McCarthy through to the actual election were 60% of college background, whereas, of those whose ardor cooled, only 18% had had any connection with college.

In short, then, it is evident again that among Democrats particularly, McCarthy was an initial rallying point for voters of all policy persuasions who were thoroughly displeased with the Johnson administration. When the Wallace candidacy crystallized and his issue advocacies became more broadly known, that portion of the discontented to whom he spoke most directly flocked to him. Hence it seems very doubtful that Humphrey would have won many votes from this group even if McCarthy had lent the Vice President his personal support in a whole-hearted fashion. The main motivation of this group was to register its disgust with incumbent leaders concerning civil rights advances, timidity in Vietnam and outbreaks of social disorder. It may well be that by September, with the far more congenial candidacy of Wallace available, Senator McCarthy would already have become a relatively negative reference point for this two-thirds of his early support, especially if he had joined forces with Humphrey. Therefore if we are to search for votes withheld from Humphrey because of the kinds of discontent McCarthy helped to crystallize, they are much more likely to be found among the McCarthy hard-core.

We persist in looking for such withheld votes, not simply because of rumors they existed, but also because there are rather tangible signs in the data that they

TABLE 4: Issue Differences Among Whites Preferring McCarthy
as the Democratic Nominee, According to November
Preferences for McCarthy or Wallace

		McCARTHY "HARD CORE"[a]	VOTED WALLACE[b]
"Are you in favor of desegregation, strict segregation, or something in between?"	DESEGREGATION	79%	7%
	IN BETWEEN	21	50
	SEGREGATION	0	43
		100%	100%
		(24)	(14)
"Do you think the (Chicago) police (at the Democratic Convention) used too much force, the right amount of force, or not enough force with the demonstrators?"	TOO MUCH FORCE	91%	0%
	RIGHT AMOUNT	9	50
	NOT ENOUGH	0	50
		100%	100%
		(23)	(12)
"Which of the following do you think we should do now in Vietnam: pull out of Vietnam entirely, but try to end the fighting, or take a stronger stand even if it means invading North Vietnam?"	PULL OUT	50%	7%
	STATUS QUO	50	7
	STRONGER STAND	9	86
		100%	100%
		(24)	(13)

[a]This column is limtied to whites whose pre-convention favorite was Eugene McCarthy and who continued to give him their top rating after the November election.

[b]It is to be emphasized that this column includes *only* those Wallace voters who said that in the spring of 1968 they had hoped Eugene McCarthy would win the Democratic nomination. This fact explains the small case numbers. However, in view of the relative homogeneity of respondents in the table—all are whites who reported a pre-convention McCarthy preference and most happen in addition to be nominal identifiers of the Demoractic Party—the disparities in issue position are the more impressive.

were present in 1968. Such votes could take any one of four major alternative forms: they could be located among citizens who went to the polls but did not vote for the president; they could be reflected in votes for minor party candidates; they could involve staying at home on election day; or they could take the form of votes spitefully transferred to Humphrey's chief rival, Mr. Nixon. Easiest to establish as "withheld votes" are the first two categories. Although their incidence is naturally very limited, both types can be discerned in the sample and do occur in conjunction with strong enthusiasm for McCarthy. Projected back to the nation's electorate, perhaps as much as a half-million votes are represented here, lying primarily outside the South. This is only a faint trace when sprinkled across the political map of the nation, however, and taken alone would probably have made little or no difference in the distribution of votes from the electoral college.

It is more difficult to say that specific instances of abstinence from any voting in 1968, or "defection" to Richard Nixon, reflect an abiding loyalty to McCarthy that Humphrey could not replace, and would not have occurred but for the McCarthy intrusion. There is a faint edge of non-voting that looks suspiciously of this sort, but it is again very limited: most ardent McCarthy fans were too politically involved to have thrown away a chance to vote at other levels of office. Far more numerous are the defections to Nixon on the part of voters of liberal and Democratic predispositions, who reported sympathy toward McCarthy. Here, however, it is difficult to be confident that McCarthy made any necessary contribution to the decision equation: the situation itself might have soured these people sufficiently, McCarthy or no. Nevertheless, when one begins to add together putative "withheld votes" from the preceding three categories one does not need to factor in any very large proportion of these defectors to arrive at a total large enough to have provided Humphrey with a tiny majority in the electoral college, without requiring any gross maldistribution of these new-found popular votes outside the South.

We should reiterate, of course, that any such hypothetical reconstructions must be taken with a grain of salt. If McCarthy had embraced Humphrey on the final night in Chicago, not all of his most fervent supporters would necessarily have followed suit, and Humphrey would have needed most of them for a victory. Or if Humphrey had entered more dramatically to the McCarthy wing in terms of Vietnam policy after the election, he might have suffered losses of much greater proportion to Wallace on his right, for there is simply no question but that Democrats sharing the circle of ideas espoused by Wallace outnumbered the Democrats attuned to McCarthy by a very wide margin —perhaps as great as ten to one. Moreover, it is appropriate to keep in mind our earlier suggestion that the Wallace intrusion hurt Nixon's vote more than Humphrey's: if we now remove Wallace as well as McCarthy from the scene, the net result might remain a Nixon victory.

However all this may be, it seems probable that the entire roster of prominent Democratic candidates—McCarthy, Wallace, Kennedy, McGovern—who were in their various ways opposing the administration, must have contributed cumulatively to Humphrey's problem of retaining the loyalty of fellow Democrats in the electorate. Certainly the failure of liberal Republican leaders to rally around the Goldwater candidacy in 1964, itself an unusual departure from tradition, had contributed to the Republican disaster of that year. 1968 provided something of a mirror image, and the result was an inordinate movement of the electorate between the two consultations.

III. The "Responsible Electorate" of 1968

In describing the current of discontent that swirled around the Democratic party and the White House in 1968, we indicated that disgruntled Democrats rather indiscriminately supported McCarthy in the earliest primaries, but soon began to sort themselves into those staying with McCarthy versus those shifting to Nixon or Wallace, according to their more precise policy grievances on the major issues of Vietnam, civil rights, and the problem of "law and order." By the time of the election, the sorting had become remarkably clean: in particular, differences in issue position between Wallace supporters and what we have called the McCarthy hard core are impressive in magnitude.

Even more generally, 1968 seems to be a prototypical case of the election that does not produce many changes of policy preferences but does permit electors to sort themselves and the candidates into groups of substantial homogeneity on matters of public policy. This trend over the course of the campaign calls to mind the posthumous contention of V.O. Key, in *The Responsible Electorate,* that the mass electorate is a good deal less irrational, ill-informed or sheep-like than it had become fashionable to suppose. He presented empirical materials to develop a counter-image of "an electorate moved by concern about central and relevant questions of public policy, of governmental performance, and of executive personality."[14] He argued that in a general way voters behaved rationally and responsibly, or at least as rationally and responsibly as could be expected in view of the pap they were frequently fed by contending politicians, while recognizing in the same breath that contentions of this unequivocal nature were necessarily overstatements.

To our point of view, Key's general thesis represented a welcome corrective on some earlier emphases, but his findings were hardly as discontinuous with earlier work as was often presumed, and the "corrective" nature of his argument has itself become badly exaggerated at numerous points. We cannot begin to examine here the many facets of his thesis that deserve comment. However, several features of the 1968 campaign seem to us to demonstrate admirably the importance of the Key corrective, while at the very same time illustrating vividly the perspective in which that corrective must be kept.

It is obvious, as Key himself recognized, that flat assertions about the electorate being rational or not are of scant value. In New Hampshire, as we have observed earlier, Democrats exasperated at Johnson's lack of success with the Vietnam war voted for Eugene McCarthy as an alternative. The relationship between this disapproval and the vote decision is exactly the type of empirical finding that Key musters in profusion from a sequence of seven presidential elections as his main proof of voter rationality and responsibility. In the New Hampshire case, however, we might probe the data a little farther to discover that more often than not, McCarthy voters were upset that Johnson had failed to scourge Vietnam a good deal more vigorously with American military might, which is to say they took a position diametrically opposed to that of their chosen candidate. This realization might shake our confidence somewhat in the preceding "proof" of voter rationality. But then we push our analysis still another step and find that many of the New Hampshire people fuming about Vietnam in a hawkish mood voted for McCarthy without having any idea of where he stood on the matter. Hence while they may have voted directly counter to their own policy preferences, they at least did not know this was what they were doing, so the charge of irrationality may be a bit ungenerous. In the most anemic sense of "rationality," one that merely implies people have perceived reasons for their behavior, these votes perhaps remain "rational."

However, when we reflect on the rather intensive coverage given by the national mass media to Eugene McCarthy's dissenting position on Vietnam for many months before the New Hampshire primary, and consider how difficult it must have been to avoid knowledge of the fact, particularly if one had more than the most casual interest in the Vietnam question, we might continue to wonder how lavishly we should praise the electorate as "responsible." Here, as at so many other points, pushing beyond the expression of narrow and superficial attitudes in the mass public to the cognitive texture which underlies the attitudes is a rather disillusioning experience. It is regrettable that none of the data presented in *The Reponsible Electorate* can be probed in this fashion.

Key was interested in showing that the public reacted in a vital way to central policy concerns, at least as selected by the contending political factions, and was not driven mainly by dark Freudian urges, flock instinct, or worse still, the toss of a coin. With much of this we agree wholeheartedly. In addition, to put the discussion in a slightly different light, let us imagine, in a vein not unfamiliar from the literature of the 1950's, that voting decisions in the American electorate might be seen as a function of reactions to party, issue and candidate personality factors. Let us imagine furthermore that research suggests that these determinants typically have relative weights in our presidential elections of 60 for the party factor, and 40 divided between the issue and candidate determinants. The exact figures are, of course, quite fanciful but the rough magnitudes continue to be familiar. Since classical assumptions about voting behavior have attributed overweening weight to the issue factor, it is scarcely surprising that investigative attention shifts heavily away from that factor to the less expected party and candidate influences. If the issue factor draws comment at all, the finding of greatest interest is its surprisingly diluted role.

It is at this point that the Key volume exerts its most useful influence. Key points out that there *is*, after all, an issue factor, and he develops an analytic format which dramatizes the role that issue reactions do play. This dramatic heightening is achieved by focussing attention on voters who are shifting their vote from one party to the other over a pair of elections. If we set for ourselves the explanatory chore of understanding why the change which occurs moves in the direction it did, it is patently evident that the party factor—which merely explains the abiding finding that "standpatters" persistently outnumber "changers" by factors usually greater than four—is to be set aside as irrelevant. If this in turn leaves candidate and issue factors sharing the explanatory burden, our sense of the relative importance of the issue factor is, of course, radically increased, even though it is our question that has changed, rather than anything about the empirical lay of the land. Key was quite explicit in his desire to explain movement and change in the electorate, rather than voting behavior in a more general sense, and there is no gainsaying the fact that from many points of view it is indeed the change—marginal gains and losses—which forms the critical part of the story of elections.

In our analyses of such changes in the national vote over the course of presidential elections in the 1950's and 1960's we have been impressed with the magnitude of the effects introduced as new candidates focus on different issues of public policy, and as external events give particular candidate-issue intersections greater salience for the nation.[15] However, 1968 provides an opportunity to examine relative weights of party, candidate and issue factors under more varied circumstances than United States presidential elections usually proffer. We have talked above for illustrative purposes as though there were "standard" relative weights that would pertain for these three factors in some situation-free way. This is of course not the case: we can imagine many kinds of elections which would vastly shift the weights of such factors, if indeed they can be defined at all.

The Wallace movement is a good case in point. By Key's definition nobody who voted for Wallace could have been a "standpatter": all must be classed as "changers." Therefore party identification as a motivating factor accounting for attraction to Wallace is forced back to zero, and any variance to be understood must have its roots distributed between Wallace's attraction as a personaltiy and the appeal of the issue positions that he advocated.[16]

In point of fact, the Wallace candidacy was reacted to by the public as an *issue* candidacy, a matter which our data make clear in several ways. For example, about half of the reasons volunteered by our respondents for favorable feelings toward Wallace had to do with positions he was taking on current issues; only a little more than a quarter of the reactions supporting either of the two conventional candidates were cast in this mode. Still more noteworthy is the relative purity of the issue feelings among the Wallace clientele where the major controversies of 1968 were concerned. Among the *whites* who voted for one of the two major candidates, only 10% favored continued segregation rather than desegregation or "something in between;" among Wallace voters, all of whom were white, almost 40% wanted segregation. Where the issue of "law and order" was concerned, a substantial portion of the voters felt that Mayor Daley's police had used about the right amount of force in quelling the Chicago demonstrations. However, among white voters for Nixon or Humphrey, the remainder of the opinion was fairly evenly split between criticizing the police for using too much force or too little, with a small majority (55%) favoring the latter "tough line." Among Wallace voters, the comparable ratio was 87-13 favoring a tougher policy. Or again, 36% of white voters for the conventional parties felt we should "take a stronger stand (in Vietnam) even if it means invading North Vietnam." Among Wallace voters, the figure was 67%. Much more generally speaking, it may be observed that all Wallace voters were exercised by strong discontents in at least one of these three primary domains, and most were angry about more than one. Wallace was a "backlash" candidate, and there is no question but that the positions communicated to the public and accounted for his electoral support in a very primary sense. The pattern of correlations between issue positions and the vote for these "changers" would support Key's thesis of a "rational" and "responsible" electorate even more impressively than most of the data he found for earlier elections.

Another way of organizing these preference materials helps to illuminate even more sharply the contrast between the bases of Wallace support and those of the conventional candidates. It will be recalled that all respondents were asked to give an affective evaluation of each of the three candidates taken separately, along with other aspirants. If we examine the pattern of correlations between issue positions and the ratings of Humphrey, Nixon and Wallace, we capture gradations of enthusiasm, indifference and hostility felt toward each man instead of the mere vote threshold, and we can explore the antecedents or correlates of the variations in sentiment toward the individual candidates.

Where the ratings of Wallace given by whites are concerned, patterns vary somewhat South and non-South, but substantial correlations with issue positions appear everywhere. In the South, the most generic question of civil rights policy shows a relation of .49 (gamma) with Wallace reactions; the most generic question on "law and order" shows a .39; and the central Vietnam policy question shows a relationship of .30. Party identification, however, shows a relation of only .04. Other ancillary questions probing more specific aspects of policy feelings in these areas vary around the most generic items somewhat, but tend to show fairly similar magnitudes of relationship. Outside the South, patterns are a little less sharp but remain unequivocal. Instead of the above correlations of .49, .39 and .30 in the main issue domains, the figures are .25 (civil rights), .27 (law and order), and .25 (Vietnam). The relationship of party identification to Wallace ratings among whites, however, is .01. Thus it is true in both regions that party identification is entirely dwarfed by any of several issue positions in predicting reactions to Wallace among whites, and in terms of "variance accounted for" the differences between issues and party would best be expressed in terms of *orders of magnitude*.

Differences that are almost as sharp turn up in the relationships surrounding the ratings of Nixon and Humphrey. Here, however, everything is exactly reversed: it is *party* that towers over all other predictors, and the central 1968 issues tend to give rather diminutive relationships. Thus comparable correlations (gammas) between partisanship and candidate ratings all run between .36 and .44, varying only slightly by region and man. Where Nixon is concerned, the average correlation values for issue items in the three main domains emphasized in the 1968 election never get as high as .10, and fall as low as .01, with the central tendency about .05. Where Humphrey is concerned, somewhat higher issue values are observed, varying between .05 and .25 according to the region and the domain. Moreover, there is another issue domain not hitherto cited in which average values over three items for Humphrey considerably outstrip the Wallace correlation in both North and South. Significantly, this is the domain of items concerning governmental social welfare activities that one might associate with the period running from the New Deal through the 1950's.[17] Nevertheless, averaging correlations across all of these issue domains (the obsolescing as well as the three most salient in 1968) suggests that party identification still accounts for three to five times as much variance in Humphrey ratings as does the average issue among the 18 issues posed in the study. These correlation patterns are summarized by region in Table 5.

TABLE 5: Correlations Between Issue Positions, Partisanship
and Affective Ratings of the Major Candidates

(Whites Only) [a]

ISSUE DOMAIN:	NON-SOUTH			SOUTH		
	Humphrey	Nixon	Wallace	Humphrey	Nixon	Wallace
A. Civil Rights (6 or 7 items) [b]	.17	.09	.27	.24	.08	.41
B. Law and Order (2 items)	.25	.05	.27	.19	.01	.35
C. Vietnam (2 items)	.05	.03	.23	.14	.02	.26
D. Cold War (4 items)	.12	.11	.15	.16	.05	.28
E. Social Welfare (2 or 3 items) [b]	.22	.20	.09	.26	.13	.10
F. Federal Gov't Too Powerful? (1 item)	.37	.18	.17	.49	.13	.15
SUM: 18 issue items	.19	.10	.20	.22	.07	.31
SUM: Three Major 1968 Issue Domains (A, B, C)	.16	.07	.26	.22	.07	.37
PARTISANSHIP: (3 items)	.47	.47	.04	.39	.36	.03

[a]Cell entries are average absolute values of gamma ordinal correlations between items of the types listed in the rows and affective ratings of the candidates noted in the columns.

[b]An item having to do with the role of the federal government in aid to local education was considered a social welfare item outside the South, but a civil rights issue within that region.

Such dramatic comparisons between types of support for Wallace on one hand and the conventional candidates on the other may be perplexing to the casual reader who is keeping the thesis of V.O. Key in mind. After all, it is the pattern of Wallace support that shows the kind of strong issue orientation Key sought to demonstrate, whereas evaluations of both Humphrey and Nixon seem to show a strong factor of traditional party allegiance suffocating most issue concerns into relative obscurity. Yet the span of time Key's data covered limited him almost completely to observation of races of the routine Humphrey-Nixon type. Did these earlier two-party races look more like the Wallace patterns for some unknown reason?

The answer, of course, is very probably not. However, if we set the Wallace phenomenon in 1968 aside and limit our attention in the Key fashion to two contrasting groups of "changers" between the 1964 and 1968 election (Johnson to Nixon; Goldwater to Humphrey) we can show correlations with issue differences which look very much like those presented in cross-tabulations by Key for earlier elections: some strong, some weak, but nearly always "in the right direction." There are, to be sure, other problems of interpretation surrounding such correlations that one would need to thrash out before accepting the Key evidence fully.[18] But our principal point here is the simple one that even with Wallace analytically discarded from the 1968 scene, the rest of the 1968 data seem perfectly compatible with the data Key used. The only reason there may seem to be a discontinuity, then, is due to the different nature of the question being asked by Key which, by focussing on marginal change from election to election, effectively defines party loyalty out of the explanation and correspondingly opens the way for greater orienting weight for issues.

It is because the change in vote division from election to election is so critical that V.O. Key's contribution is a welcome corrective. On the other hand, the configurations of 1968 data we have summarized here help to put that contribution into perspective. The patterns of Wallace support show how empirical data *can* look when issues play a strongly orienting role. The contrasts between these patterns and those generated by routine two-party politics may help to suggest why investigators have tended to be more impressed by the feeble role of issues than by their strength.

The lessons to be drawn are several. One is a simple point of methodology. It has been suggested upon occasion in the past that relationships between issue positions and voting choice turn out to be as pallid as they usually are because investigators fail to ask the right questions or word them in confusing ways. We feel that improvement in these matters is always possible. However, we have seen that exactly the same issue items which continue to look pallid in accounting for assessments of Humphrey and Nixon blaze forth into rather robust correlations where Wallace is concerned. Hence we conclude that poor item choice scarcely accounts for past findings.

Another lesson is more substantive. Some past findings have been to our mind "overinterpreted" as implying that issues are poorly linked to voting preferences because of innate and hence incorrigible cognitive deficiencies suffered by the mass electorate in the United States.[19] Merely the Wallace data taken alone would suffice to show, exactly as Key argued, that the public can relate policy controversies to its own estimates of the world and vote accordingly. The fact that it does not display this propensity on any large scale very often invites more careful spelling out of the conditions under which it will or will not.

It seems clear from the 1968 data that one of the cardinal limiting conditions is the "drag" or inertia represented by habitual party loyalties: as soon as features of the situation limit or neutralize the relevance of such a factor, issue evaluations play a more vital role. Much research has shown that partisanship is fixed early in life and tends to endure. As the individual moves through the life cycle, old political controversies die away and new ones arise toward which at least some individuals crystallize opinions. While the parties try to lead this new opinion formation among their faithful, and probably succeed on a modest scale, there are many independent sources of such opinion for the citizen. The average citizen either does not know his party's position well enough to be influenced on many matters, or if he knows, frequently resists the influence. As a result, policy opinions are very loosely or anachronistically linked to party preference at any point in time. But in the moment of truth in the polling booth, party allegiance seems the most relevant cue for many voters *if conditions permit it to be used.*

Another type of condition which mediates the links between citizen position on issues and voting choice is the "objective" degree of difference between parties or candidates with respect to policy controversy, or the clarity with which any objective difference gets communicated to the populace. In every United States election there are accusations from one quarter or another that the two conventional parties provide no more than "tweedledee" and "tweedledum" candidates. However, these accusations as aired in the public media rose to something of a crescendo in 1968 from both the Wallace and the McCarthy perspectives. And even as measured a source as the *New York Times* noted wrily that it would take no more than the deletion of two or three codicils to make the official 1968 campaign platforms of the Democratic and Republican parties into utterly undistinguishable documents. If the main discriminable difference between Humphrey and Nixon began and ended with the party label then it would certainly not be surprising that the public sorted itself into voting camps by party allegiance and little more, save where Wallace was concerned. In this case, the public would be limited to exactly that "echo chamber" role which Key ascribed to it.

As a matter of pure logic, nobody can deny that policy differentiation between parties is likely to be a precondition for meaningful relationships between policy feelings and partisan voting decisions. Our only problem here is to evaluate whether the party/issue data configurations surrounding Humphrey and Nixon are the obvious result of some lack of policy difference peculiar to 1968, or represent instead some more abiding feature of presidential voting in the United States. Unfortunately, there is no obvious way to arrive at an objective measurement of "degree of party difference." Perhaps the closest approximation is to ask the public how clear the differences appear to be. Nevertheless, since some people invariably feel party differences are big and others feel they are non-existent, even this approach leaves one without reference points as to "how big is big" where reports of this kind are concerned, except inasmuch as trends in such reports can be observed over periods of time. In this light, it can be said while reports of "important differences" between the Democrats and the Republicans were slightly fewer in 1968 than in 1964 (the year of Goldwater's "choice, not an echo"), they show a reasonable parity with such reports for 1952 and 1960. Hence in the public eye, at least, differences between what the major parties stand for were not lacking in unusual degree in 1968.

It may be useful to note that whereas we have labelled the Wallace effort in 1968 an "issue candidacy" from the point of view of the electorate, we have not said that it was an ideological candidacy from that same point of view. From other viewpoints of political analysis, it was of course just that: a movement of the "radical right." Moreover, with occasional exceptions, data on issue positions show Wallace voters to differ from Humphrey voters in the same "conservative" direction that Nixon voters do, only much more so. Therefore by customary definitions, not only the leadership of the radical right, but the rank-and-file espoused clearly "rightist" positions of a sort which were frequently extreme, on highly specific questions of public policy.[20]

Yet there was an element of ideological self-recognition present among Goldwater voters in 1964 that was simply lacking among Wallace voters in 1968. One measure of ideological location which we use involves the respondent in rating the terms "liberal" and "conservative." If the respondent gives the highest possible score to the stimulus "liberal" and the lowest possible score to "conservative," he is rated as the most extreme liberal, with a score of 100. In the reverse case, the extreme conservative receives a score of zero. At 50 are clustered individuals who either do not recognize these terms, or give the same affective rating to both.[21] In 1964 there was a rather considerable relationship between such a measure and response to Goldwater, in the expected direction. In 1968, the same scale showed only a very limited correlation with reactions toward Wallace (gammas of .13 and .09 among whites within the South and outside, respectively). Indeed, as Table 6 shows, in both political regions of the country Wallace voters were more favorable to the "liberal" label than Nixon voters! Thus while Wallace supporters were entirely distinctive in their "backlash" feelings on public policy, they were much less ideologically attuned to a left-right spectrum than their Goldwater predecessors.

Although Wallace supporters did not seem anywhere nearly as distinctive in terms of ideological measures as they did on specific issues, they did show some moderate trends in terms of other more generic political attitudes. In particular, various measures bearing on discontent with the responsiveness and probity of government show correlations with ratings given by whites to Wallace, and are related but with opposite signs to ratings of the "establishment" candidates, Humphrey and Nixon. Since Wallace was more of a mainstream candidate in the South than in the rest of the country, it might be thought that his appeal in that region might depend less strictly on this syndrome of political alienation than it would elsewhere. However, these relationships are stronger and more pervasive in the South, and seem only weakly mirrored in other parts of the nation. Within the South, white attitudes toward Wallace are quite sharply associated with our scales of political efficacy and cynicism about government. People drawn to Wallace tended to feel they had little capacity to influence government, and expressed distrust of the morality and efficiency of political leadership. These correlations reach a peak on items where the referent is most explicitly "the federal government in Washington," and it is plain that Southern voters felt more or less attracted to Wallace in the degree that they responded to his complaints that Washington bureaucrats had been persistently and unjustly bullying the South with particular respect to civil rights. Since there is no methodological need for it to be true, it is of particular interest that ratings of Humphrey show as substantial correlations in the opposing direction, in the South and other regions as well: people responding warmly to Humphrey had quite sanguine views of government.

TABLE 6: Ideological Responses of White Voters for Different
Presidential Candidates in 1964 and 1968[a]

	1964		1968		
	Johnson	Goldwater	Humphrey	Nixon	Wallace
NON-SOUTH	51.8	39.9	51.8	43.4	44.9
SOUTH	49.6	35.9	49.5	40.7	41.9

[a]The cell entry registers the mean value shown on the ideological scale described in the text for white voters for each of the candidates listed. A high value indicates that liberalism is held in relative favor; a low value means that conservatism is preferred.

All told, then, a sense of political alienation was a rather visible correlate of a sorting of the citizenry away from the conventional candidates toward Wallace, as was certainly to be expected and necessary if terms such as "blacklash" are relevant. At the same time, it is worth keeping the apparent temporal sequences clear. The data suggest that Southern whites have become alienated with government because prior attitudes, particularly racial ones, have been contradictory to national policy for nearly twenty years. Thus there is a readiness to condemn government on a much broader front, and Wallace appealed in obvious ways to this readiness in the South. Outside the South Wallace also articulated the same array of specific grievances and received a clear response. However, the evidence suggests that any resonance he might have achieved in terms of a more generic condemnation of government, while present, was relatively limited.

IV. The Social Bases of Wallace Support

A variety of facts already cited about the Wallace movement of 1968 makes clear that while there was some modest overlap in support for Goldwater in 1964 and Wallace in 1968, it was at best a weak correlation and the Wallace clientele differed quite notably from Goldwater's. Thus, for example, almost exactly half of our 1968 Wallace voters who had participated in the 1964 election reported that they had voted for Johnson. Or again, we have seen that the majority of Wallace voters, like the electorate as a whole, was identified with the Democratic party, while it is obvious that most Goldwater voters were Republican identifiers. Similarly, we have just noted that the Wallace movement had a much less clear ideological focus among its sympathizers than marked Goldwater supporters in 1964.

This discrepancy in clientele may seem perplexing. After all, in the terms of conventional analysis in political sociology both candidates were "darlings of the radical right." Yet the limited degree of overlap between Goldwater and Wallace voters is confirmed in equally impressive fashion when one compares their social backgrounds or even their simplest demographic characteristics. Among Goldwater voters, for example, women both South and non-South showed the same slight majority they enjoy in the electorate; Wallace voters in the South showed a similar balance, but elsewhere were rather markedly (almost 60-40) male. The Goldwater vote had been much more urban, while the Wallace vote was relatively rural and small-town, particularly in the South. Outside the South, the age distribution of Wallace voters departed markedly from that shown by Goldwater in 1964, with the proportion under 35 being about twice as great and that over 65 only half as large.

The well-publicized appeal of Wallace to the unionized laboring man is clearly reflected in our data: outside the South, the proportion of white union members preferring Wallace over the other major candidates was more than three times as great as it was within households having no unionized members (19% to 6%); even in the South, where other appeals were present and the unionization of labor is more limited, the contrast between the preferences of union members and non-union households remains dramatic (52% to 28% giving top preference to Wallace over the conventional candidates). Indeed, in both regions the occupational center of gravity of Wallace popularity was clearly among white skilled workers. Nationwide, only about 10% of the Wallace vote was contributed by the professional and managerial strata, whereas persons of these occupations had given Goldwater almost half of his vote (46%). Needless to say, the proportion of unionized labor supporting Goldwater was very low. Along with these class differences, marked discrepancies in educational background can be taken for granted. In the South, one-third of Wallace's support came from whites with no more than grade school education, while the national figure for Goldwater was 13%. The proportion of voters of college experience backing Goldwater was about double that found voting for Wallace either in the South or elsewhere.

All of these comparisons help to underscore the major disparities in the social bases of support for Goldwater and Wallace, despite the apparent common policy ground of the relatively extreme right. While one should not lose track of the fact that there was a small and systematic overlap in clientele, it is abundantly clear that neither candidate exhausted the potential support for a severely conservative program in matters of civil rights, law and order or Vietnam. In a very real sense, it can be seen that Wallace was a poor man's Goldwater. As we suggested at the time, Goldwater pitched his campaign on an ideological plane which rather escaped some members of the electorate who might otherwise have found his positions congenial.[22] Wallace's perfectly direct appeal to citizens of this latter description, along with the undercurrent of populism alien to the Goldwater conservatism, apparently sufficed to put off some of the Arizona senator's more well-to-do supporters.[23] The Goldwater support was drawn from a relatively urbane and sophisticated conservatism; Wallace appealed to many similar instincts, but the style was folksy and tailored to the common man.

In a significant way, too, Wallace remained a regional candidate despite his discovery that he could win more than scattered votes in the North and his consequent presence on every state's ballot. Over half of his popular votes came from the states of the Confederacy. Everything, from his lack of political experience at a federal level to his marked Southern accent, suggested a parochial relevance that had rarely been salient where Goldwater was concerned. While electoral maps leave no doubt as to the regional nature of the response, sample survey data show that even these visible effects have been diluted by inter-regional migration. Thus, for example, while much has been written about the Wallace appeal in various European ethnic communities of northern cities, little has been said about the "American ethnic group" of southern white migrants, most of whom are blue-collar and frequently in a position to take special pleasure in the spectacle of a Southern compatriot coming north to give the Yankees what for. Our data indicate that Wallace drew over 14% of the vote from these migrants, and less than 7% otherwise outside the South. On the other hand, the significant stream of migration of Yankees into the South, the political implications of which we have described elsewhere,[24] provided something of a barrier to further Wallace successes. Heavily Republican in a non-Southern sense and now constituting better than one-seventh of white voters in the region, these migrants were even less interested in voting for Wallace than were Southern whites in the North, and gave the former Alabama governor only 10% of their vote while their native Southern white colleagues were casting almost one vote in every three for him.

Table 7 summarizes the affective ratings given Wallace by our respondents according to the region in which they grew up as well as their current region of residence. It is rather clear that the region of socialization is a more critical determinant of these assessments of Wallace than is the region of current residence. Moreover, it is easy to show that regional differences in correlates of Wallace preference also follow lines of socialization rather than those of current residence. For example, we have noted that Wallace's appeal to women outside the South was rather limited. For white women of Southern background living outside the South, the response was much as it was in the South. Setting the migrants aside, the sex ratio among white Wallace enthusiasts outside the South is even more sharply masculine.

It is not our purpose here to do more than briefly summarize the social and demographic correlates of Wallace preferences, for numerous other essays are being prepared to treat the subject in detail. However, one correlate which has frequently surprised observers deserves more extended discussion, both because of its practical significance and because of its high relevance to some of the theoretical issues uniquely illuminated by the 1968 election. We speak of the relationship between the Wallace movement and the generational cleavages so evident at other points in data from the presidential campaign.

TABLE 7: Reactions of Whites to Wallace by Region
of Socialization and Residence

| | | RESPONDENT NOW RESIDES . . . | | |
		Outside the South	Within the South	TOTAL
RESPONDENT	Outside the South:	26.2[a]	26.5	26.2
		(757)	(51)	(808)
GREW UP . .	Within the South:	34.7	50.0	48.5
		(53)	(281)	(334)
	TOTAL:	26.7	46.3	
		(810)	(332)	

[a]Cell entries are mean values of ratings on a scale from 0 (hostility) to 100 (sympathy) accorded to George Wallace by white respondents of the types indicated.

It would seem self-evident that Wallace's primary appeal to traditional and even obsolescing American values, as well as his caustic treatment of the rebels of the younger generation, would have brought him votes that were even more heavily clustered among the elderly than those drawn by Goldwater in 1964. We have already noted that Wallace took issue positions that were communicated with unusual clarity, and that these positions determined in unusual degree the nature of his clientele. On almost every issue of nearly a score surveyed, the position characteristic of Wallace voters in our sample is also the positon associated with older citizens, where there is any age correlation at all. Hence it is somewhat surprising to discover that among white Southerners there is actually a faint *negative* correlation between age and a Wallace vote. And it is perplexing indeed to discover that outside the South voting for Wallace occurred very disproportionately among the young. For example, Wallace captured less than 3% of the vote among people over 70 outside the South, but 13% of those under 30, with a regular gradient connecting these two extremes. One of the major ironies of the election, then, was that Wallace made his appeal to the old but mainly received the vote of the young.

However, a whole cluster of empirical theory has grown up in recent years which, without any particular knowledge of the Wallace platform, would predict that such a third-party candidate would draw votes primarily from the young in just this way. It is established, for example, that repeated commitments of votes to a political party tend to increase the strength of psychological identification with that party, and it is an immediate corollary that voters of the older generation are more fixed in their party loyalties than are relatively new voters.[25] It follows with equal logic that when some new candidate or *ad hoc* party arises to challenge the conventional parties of a system, it should have relative difficulty making headway among the older generation, even though it might have natural appeals to such voters.

We have never had a chance to test this somewhat non-obvious expectation, although reconstructions of the fall of the Weimar Republic have always suggested that voters for the Nazi Party in its culminating surge were very disproportionately drawn from the youngest cohorts of the German electorate. Therefore the age distribution of Wallace support has been of uncommon interest to us. When issue appeals of a rather vital sort conflict with long-established party loyalties, as they must have in Wallace's case for many older voters, which factor is likely to exert most influence on the voting decision? The apparent difficulties older people had in voting for Wallace, particularly outside the South where he was a less "legitimate" Democrat and hence a less conventional candidate, seem to provide a rather clear answer.

However, if this interpretation is correct a variety of ancillary effects should be discernible in the 1968 data. For example, if prior party identification is truly the critical source of resistance to a Wallace vote simply because of the disloyalty implied, the prediction that the young would vote more heavily for him need not mean the young have any monopoly on admiration for him. Indeed, one could almost predict that the older generation should have shown more warmth of feeling toward Wallace per vote allotted him than would be true of the younger generation, simply because of the "artificial" inhibition on the vote represented by greater loyalty to a conventional party. Moreover, since strength of identification is measured explicitly in this study, it is of importance to show that it does indeed vary positively as in times past with age; that such identification with a conventional party is indeed negatively associated with voting for Wallace; and that the tendency of young persons to vote for Wallace did co-occur with weak conventional loyalties.

All of these empirical expectations are borne out, and usually in rather handsome fashion. First, while the young voted more heavily for Wallace, the correlation between age and affective rating of him as a political figure is nonexistent. Second, the old in 1968 were, as always, much more strongly identified with one of the two conventional parties than the young. Third, defection from a conventional party to vote for Wallace was indeed strongly related to degree of party identification, particularly outside the South:[26] the probability of a Wallace vote doubles there as one moves each step from strong through weak to "independent" or leaning identifiers. And finally, when strength of partisanship is controlled, the sharp inverse correlation between age and a Wallace vote outside the South is very nearly wiped out; within the South where it was a somewhat ragged relationship to begin with, it completely disappears or if anything, shows a slight reversal as though Wallace might in fact have had some extra drawing power for the older voter, aside from the complications posed by other allegiances.

This nest of relationships holds more than detached clinical interest in several directions. The reader concerned about the future of the Wallace movement as an electoral force on the American scene is likely to be interested in the fact that the clientele was young rather than aging. In one sense this is a pertinent datum and in another it is not. It is unquestionable that a Wallace candidacy in 1972 has a brighter future than it would have if its 1968 legions were dying out of the population. Nonetheless, the whole thrust of our argument above is that the Wallace movement is not in any special good fortune to have drawn young voters: this will be true of virtually any new party entering the lists in an old party system, and but for the habits which kept older voters with the conventional parties, the initial Wallace vote would probably have been significantly larger. Still more to the point, we would hazard that the future of the Wallace movement as a third party will be determined more by Wallace's personal plans and the organizational aspirations of his entourage on one hand, and by the evolution of events affecting national frustrations on the other, than by the age level of its 1968 voters.

Nevertheless, the youthful nature of Wallace's clientele provides a further irony to the backdrop of generational cleavage reflected in the 1968 campaign. For while such a cleavage was genuine and intense, as some of our earlier data have witnessed, one of the most important yet hidden lines of cleavage split the younger generation itself. Although privileged young college students angry at Vietnam and the shabby treatment of the Negro saw themselves as sallying forth to do battle against a corrupted and cynical older generation, a more head-on confrontation at the polls, if a less apparent one, was with their own age mates who had gone from high school off to the factory instead of college, and who were appalled by the collapse of patriotism and respect for the law that they saw about them. Outside of the election period, when verbal articulateness and leisure for political activism count most heavily, it was the college share of the younger generation—or at least its politicized vanguard—that was most prominent as a political force. At the polls, however, the game shifts to "one man, one vote," and this vanguard is numerically swamped even within its own generation.

This lack of numerical strength is no intrinsic handicap: any cadre of opinion leadership is small in number. However, it must successfully appeal to some potential rank and file, and it certainly cannot risk becoming a negative reference point for large numbers of people if it expects to operate in a medium involving popular elections. In part because of collegiate naivete concerning forms of dissent that maintain sympathy,[27] and in part because the public image of constructive efforts by the many can be so rapidly colored by a few whose needs are mainly to antagonize as much of society as possible, this vanguard became a negative reference point for most Americans. The result at the election thus had a different coloration from what went before: McCarthy did not run and Wallace captured a proportion of the vote which was historically amazing. Indeed, it was probably the political stodginess of the older generation so decried by campus activists which kept the vote of "people over 30" within the channels of the conventional parties and prevented the Wallace vote from rising still higher. Certainly it is true that in several major metropolises of the United States where party loyalty has been nullified in primary election settings in the spring of 1969, candidates of relative Wallace coloration have surprised observers with their mounting popularity.

There can be no question but that dramatic and persistent displays of dissent on the campuses between 1964 and 1968 helped to place question marks around "consenual" national policies which might otherwise have continued to be taken for granted by most of the citizenry. At the same time, disregard for the occasional junctures of electoral decision when the mass public has some say in the political process may mean that a battle was won but a war was lost. For some few, this *politique de pire* is quite intentional, being thought to help "radicalize" the electorate in ways that can be controlled and manipulated. For most student activists, however, success in raising questions is of little value if one is helping in the same stroke to elect "wrong people" to answer them. And quite apart from the nature of the leadership elected in 1968, it is obvious to any "rational" politican hoping to maximize votes in 1970 or 1972 that there are several times more votes to be gained by leaning toward Wallace than by leaning toward McCarthy.

If these facts were inevitable consequences of "raising the issues" from the campuses, the dilemma would be severe indeed. It is not clear to us, however, that any intrinsic dilemma is involved. Much of the blacklash expressed in the 1968 voting received its impetus less from irreconcilable policy disagreement—although on civil rights there is more than a modicum of that—than from resentment at the frequency with which the message of dissent from the campuses was clothed to "bait" conventional opinion. In the degree that the feelings and opinion reflexes of the common man, including age peers of lower circumstances, were comprehended at all by campus activists, they tended to be a subject for derision or disdain. Strange to say, such hostile postures communicate with great speed even across social gulfs, and are reciprocated with uncommon reliability. Fully as often, of course, there was simply no comprehension of the dynamics of public opinion at all.

Whether one likes it or not, the United States does retain some occasional elements of participatory democracy. A young and well-educated elite-to-be that is too impatient to cope with this bit of reality by undertaking the tedium of positive persuasion may find its political efforts worse than wasted.

[1]The 1968 national sample survey (N = 1559) was made possible by a grant from the Ford Foundation, whose support we gratefully acknowledge. A total of 1559 citizens of voting age were interviewed, most of them both before and after Election Day. The preliminary nature of this report is to be emphasized, since the data on which it is based had not been fully cleaned at the time of

writing. When the study is released through the Inter-University Consortium for Political Research, interested analysts may discover small discrepancies from the statistics reported here. Readers should also remember that all sample statistics are subject to varying amounts of sampling error in relation to the number of cases on which they are based.

[2]A deviating election is one in which the party commanding the identifications of a majority of the electorate is nonetheless voted out of power temporarily. See A. Campbell, P. Converse, W. Miller, and D. Stokes, *The American Voter* (New York: John Wiley, 1960), Chapter 19.

[3]*Congressional Quarterly,* November 22, 1968, p. 3177.

[4]The percentage difference of 62% in candidate preference between blacks and whites is substantially larger than class differentiation or other social cleavages and partisanship within the United States in recent history or for democracies of Western Europe.

[5]Such segregation is indicated simply because of the fact that within the black vote in 1968 there is next to no meaningful "variance" to be "accounted for." When categories of "Nixon voters" and "Wallace voters" are presented, they are necessarily "lily-white" in composition. Therefore when "Humphrey voters" are contrasted with them, it is confusing if differences may be totally a function of the large admixtures of blacks in the Humphrey support, as opposed to differences which would stand up even with comparisons limited to whites.

[6]See "Voting and Foreign Policy," by Warren E. Miller, Chapter 7 in James N. Rosenau (ed.), *Domestic Sources of Foreign Policy* (New York: The Free Press, 1967).

[7]A separate analysis, carried out by a colleague in the Survey Research Center Political Behavior Program and using the same body of data from the SRC 1968 election study, suggests, moreover, that many voters who thought the police used too little force deserted Humphrey in the course of the campaign while the minority who objected that too much force was used voted more heavily for the Democratic nominee. See John P. Robinson, "Voter Reaction to Chicago 1968," Survey Research Center (1969), mimeo.

[8]The decline was only on the order of 1-1/2 percent nationally, but the overall figures are somewhat misleading. Enormous efforts devoted to voter registration projects among Southern blacks between 1964 and 1968 appear to have paid off by increasing voter participation in that sector from 44% to 51%. Perhaps in counterpoint, Southern whites increased their turnout by 2%, thereby inching ever closer to the national norm. Thus the decline in turnout was concentrated outside the South, and there approached the more substanial drop of 4%. Even this figure is misleading, since whites outside the South showed a 3% loss in percentage points of turnout, while nonwhites declined by almost 11 percentage points! See *Current Population Reports,* "Voter Participation in November 1968," Series P-20, No. 177, December 27, 1968. Although such turnout figures, apart from the more general mobilizing of Southern blacks, are consistent with a proposition that whites were more eager to "throw the rascals out" than blacks, and that among whites, Southerners had the fiercest grievances of all, there is no hiding the fact of anemic turnout in most of the country in 1968. Interestingly enough, the decline from 1964 was uniformly distributed across the entire spectrum of party allegiances from loyal Democrats to strong Republicans.

[9]The reader should also keep in mind several other things about Table 2. The "South" here refers, as it will throughout this paper, to the Census Bureau definition of the region that includes 15 states and the District of Columbia. Hence such border states as Maryland or West Virginia are included along with the deeper southern states of the old confederacy. Presumably, for example, George Wallace's rating among whites of a more hard-core South would be correspondingly higher. Secondly, it should be remembered for some of the lesser candidates that respondents knowing so little about a candidate as to be indifferent to him would end up rating him "50°." Thus it would be questionable to conclude from Table 2 that LeMay was more popular than George Wallace, except in a very limited sense. Actually, three times as many respondents (nearly one-third) left LeMay at the indifference point as did so for Wallace. Thus lack of visibility helped to make him *less unpopular.* But among those who reacted to both men, LeMay was less popular than Wallace. Similarly, Wallace's low rating must be understood as a compound of an admiring minority and a hostile majority. The variance of Wallace ratings is much greater than those for other candidates, even in the South.

[10]Just after the decision of Robert Kennedy to run and before Lyndon Johnson's withdrawal, the Gallup poll showed Democrats favoring Kennedy as the party's nominee by a 44-41 margin.

[11]Interestingly enough, the same generational cleavages among Southern white Democrats occur at an earlier age than those elsewhere. In that region, Humphrey-Johnson preferences hold a plurality in all age cohorts over 30, despite the fact that Kennedy support has an edge of better than three to one among those under 30 (N of 34), perhaps because the latter group has less of a memory of the fury in the deep South at the Kennedy family prior to the assassination of President John Kennedy in Dallas in 1963.

[12]Although there is some slight tendency for pre-convention supporters of McCarthy to be relatively young, the distribution by age is more homogeneous than expected, and much more so than is the case for Kennedy. It is possible that young people supporting McCarthy as the only alternative to the Administration switched more heavily than the middle-aged to Kennedy when he announced his candidacy.

[13]See also the account for New Hampshire by Louis Harris, "How Voters See the Issues," *Newsweek,* March 25, 1968, p. 26.

[14]V. O. Key, Jr., *The Responsible Electorate: Rationality in Presidential Voting, 1936-1960* (Cambridge, Mass: Belknap Press, 1966), pp. 7-8

[15]Donald E. Stokes, "Some Dynamic Elements of Contests for the Presidency," this Review, LX (March, 1966), 19-28.

[16]This is not to say that it would be inconceivable for identification with one of the two traditional parties to correlate with preference for some third-party candidate. For example, it is possible that most of the voters for Henry Wallace's Progressive Party in 1948 were identified with the Democratic Party. However, it is clear that in such an instance "party loyalty" would have been a rather spurious name for the motivating factor. In the case of George Wallace, even this kind of spurious correlation is absent, except insofar as his Democratic origins and the invisibility of his American Independent Party label made it easy for Democrats to support him. Indeed, in the context of this argument it will be fascinating to discover whether Republicans and Democrats invoked different images of Wallace's party location in order to satisfy their need for consonance while voting for a man who reflects their own issue commitments.

[17]Another domain of issues surrounding the "cold war" as it confronted the nation in the 1950's with controversies over foreign aid and trade with communist countries shows only modest correlations with the candidate rankings, and Nixon and Humphrey ratings show more of a parity with the Wallace correlations, although in an absolute sense the latter continue to outrun the former sharply in the South and mildly elsewhere. See Table 5.

[18]These include such considerations as that of the casual direction underlying the observed relationships; or known and systematic biases in recollection of a presidential vote four years later; or the superficiality of the issues that show such patterns, as opposed to issues thought basic by sophisticated observers; or blatant misinformation supporting the issue positions registered; or a tendency for the less informed to "shift" more quickly than the better informed, with position on any given issue held constant, etc.

[19]We much prefer an interpretation which hinges on a general inattention which is endemic because information costs are relatively high where little information is already in hand, and the stakes are rarely seen as being very large. While such a "condition" is likely to persist in mass electorates, there is nothing about it which is immutable given the proper convergence of circumstances.

[20]This was not true across every issue domain. The most notable exception was in the area of social welfare issues such as medicare and full employment guarantees, on which issues Wallace voters were significantly more "liberal" than Nixon voters, and almost matched the liberalism of Humphrey voters. This admixture was of course familiar in Wallace's frequent appeals to the underdog and the working man, in the tradition of Southern populism.

[21]For reasons discussed elsewhere, a rather large proportion of the American electorate—nearly half—is found at this point of ideological neutrality.

[22]P. Converse, A. Clausen, and W. Miller, "Electoral Myth and Reality: The 1964 Election" this Review, 59 (June, 1965), 321-336.

[23]It is quite possible, however, that some of this support might have moved to Wallace had the Republican Party nominated anybody but Nixon or Reagan, among the main contenders.

[24]A. Campbell, P. Converse, W. Miller, and D. Stokes, *Elections and the Political Order* (New York: John Wiley, 1965), Chapter 12.

[25]Philip E. Converse, "Of Time and Partisan Stability," *Journal of Comparative Politics* (issue to be announced).

[26]The South shows somewhat diluted patterns here, compatible with the likelihood that for at least some Southern Democrats, a vote for Wallace was not conceived as a defection.

[27]The American public seems to have a very low tolerance for unusual or "showy" forms of political dissent. Responses to an extended set of items in the 1968 study on the subject are appalling from a civil libertarian point of view. At the most acceptable end of the continuum of "ways for people to show their disapproval or disagreement with governmental policies and actions" we asked about "taking part in protest meetings or marches *that are permitted by the local authorities*" (italics not in original question). Less than 20% of all respondents, and scarcely more than 20% of those giving an opinion, would approve of such subversive behavior, and more than half would disapprove (the remainder accepted the alternative presented that their reaction "would depend on the circumstances"). In view of such assumptions, the overwhelmingly negative reaction to the Chicago demonstrations despite sympathetic media treatment (cited earlier) is hardly surprising.

QUESTIONS FOR DISCUSSION AND DIALOGUE

1. Identify the major propositions presented by Converse, et.al. which account for continuity and change in American politics. What type of evidence was used in validating these propositions?
2. Converse, et.al. maintain that had Robert Kennedy lived, he would have received his party's nomination and won the presidential election. What evidence was used to justify this proposition? Do you think the evidence justified this conclusion? Why or why not?
3. According to Converse, et.al. what were the major facts facilitating the emergence of the third party movement of George C. Wallace?
4. Refer back to the Seyom Brown article in Chapter 4. Do you see a different approach to political science being utilized in this article you have just read on the 1968 presidential election contrasted to the approach emphasized in Brown's article? Which article is more inclined to "measure" and "categorize"? Which article is more inclined to "philosophize" and "interpret"? Which do you think is of more political value? Why?
5. Refer back to the articles about the 1968 presidential election in Chapter 3. How would you contrast the tone of these articles to the tone of this article in a professional political science journal? Which kinds of articles would you consider more valuable? Discuss.

———— **Epilogue** ————

The 1970 Elections and
American Political Perspectives
Louis Reichman

By the early 1970's the Americans of Chapter One could find little to fundamentally alter their hopes or fears. The 1970 off-year election that was looked
upon as an important "ideological victory" by Vice-President Spiro Agnew was
labeled a "fantastic Democratic win" by Chairman of the National Democratic
Committee Lawrence O'Brien. Both could back up their claims with circumstantial evidence.

From the Republican point of view the emphasis should be on the fact that
the average loss of House of Representative seats for the presidential party in an
off-year election during the twentieth century was thirty-five, and the average loss
of Senate seats was four. Since the Republicans lost only nine House of Representatives seats and actually gained two Senate seats (three, if New York's Conservative Party winner James Buckley who had stated he would support President
Nixon's policies, is counted) what else could this be called other than Republican
victory?

From the Democratic perspective their victory claims could be backed up by
the following facts:

> The number of Democratic governors increased from eighteen to twenty-
> nine.
> The control by the Democratic Party of both houses of the state legisla-
> tures increased from twenty to twenty-four states. This is extremely signifi-
> cant because the state legislatures will begin drawing the new U.S.
> congressional district boundaries and state legislative district boundaries in
> early 1971.

While the Republican Party stressed the support of Republican conservatism indicated by the above figures, the Democratic Party claimed its brand of liberalism was backed by the election results. Republicans tended to interpret the voters' verdicts as an expression of reaction against Democratic permissiveness on the "law and order" issue, and reaction against Democratic financial irresponsibility as well as foreign policy incompetency. On the other hand, Democrats stressed the failure of large Republican expenditures (nationwide the Republican Party spent five times more money than the Democratic Party in the 1970 election), and the futility of the unprecedented presidential and vice-presidential campaigning.

Some of the major Non Political Influentials reflected the grayness of the 1970 elections in the following terms: *U.S. News and World Report* (November 16, 1970, P. 16) wrote of the returns which

> baffled political experts and left party leaders in a maze of uncertainties. In the aftermath, each side tended to emphasize what it wanted to read into the election results.

Time (November 16, 1970, P. 17) surmised that

> From the swirl of contrary trends, ticket-splitting, upsets and dissimilar contests, one result seemed certain: most voters in most places opted for calm, for reasonableness, for a cessation of domestic hostilities.

Newsweek (November 16, 1970, P. 30) reported the election results as the culmination of

> an autumn of rare partisan bitterness, and when it came mercifully to an end . . . the Silent Majority didn't show up—not at least, in Mr. Nixon's column.

More long-range American political perspectives have been developing in the early 1970's. In general terms the "Left," "Center" and the "Right" considered the American political scene in contrasting yet overlapping ways.

In the "Center" Richard Scammon and Ben Wattenberg (*The Real Majority,* 1970, Coward-McCann) gauged the American voters as moderately well-intentioned, moderately well-informed moderates who do the best they can by averaging out the politicians' stands on social, economic, and foreign policy issues. These "Real Majority" voters are "unyoung," "unpoor," and "unblack." Liberal and radical philosophical and civil rights views and proposals find little or no support among them. Support is found, however, for practical economic governmental measures which control inflation, protect against unemployment, and generally enhance a healthy economic climate. Support is lost when politicians cross their practical economic liberalism over into permissiveness on the social issues—failure to take strong enough stands on "law and order," on drug control, on anti-pornography, and on campus militancy. As self-described "Independent Democrats," Scammon and Wattenberg draw the obvious conclusions for Democratic candidates in the early 1970's. They claim that President Nixon's Vietnamization policy has muted the foreign policy issue. Thus, the debate is between stands and performances on the economic and social issues. And this debate will be won or lost far away from the distractions of ideological and philosophical considerations.

On the "Left" observers such as Louis Harris claim that

> "The extraordinary political fact of America in the early 1970's is that politically we are a collection of warring minorities with no Real, Silent, Middle America, Conservative, Centrist, Liberal or other kind of majority presently operative. There is increasing evidence that the first principle of the old politics, embodied in Roosevelt's New Deal, of putting many groups, races, religions and regions under one permanent party tent may not work any more." (*Time,* November 16, 1970, P. 18)

Harris and other more "Left" ward interpreters emphasize the kind of political —economic—social combination of youth, the minorities, and the poor under the leadership of well-educated, resourceful, shrewd, and wealthy liberals such as those who were influential in the Kennedy and McCarthy movements and in obtaining reform of the Democratic Party.

The "Right," well represented by Kevin Phillips in his book *The Emerging Republican Majority* (1969, Arlington House), draws different conclusions and implications from political America in the early 1970's:

> What this young lawyer-turned-political technician forecasts is a political future that will be increasingly Republican and increasingly conservative ... Phillips adds Nixon's ('68) razor-thin plurality to George Wallace's ten million votes and concludes, in political parlance, that's where the ducks are. If the Republican Party can appeal to those voters who cast ballots for Nixon and Wallace, then, says Phillips, the future will be Republican. According to his analysis, the new Republican majority will emerge in the South, in California, and in the "Heartland" (by which Phillips means all twenty-five states without coastlines or seaports except Vermont). Meanwhile, the Democrats, he believes, will be left as the minority party of the electorate in the Northeast and the Pacific Northwest, as well as of the blacks. (*Saturday Review,* September 13, 1969, P. 31. Book Review of Kevin Phillips' *The Emerging Republican Majority* as reviewed by Mark Levy)

Whether the student of modern American politics leans "Center," "Left," or "Right," the challenges of differing perspectives is as fascinating as it is confusing. Hopefully some of the pieces of the American political puzzle fit together better now that the student has concluded *American Politics and Its Interpreters.* Although the gaps necessarily loom prominently for the beginning student of American politics, they are better pieced together with the aid of the political interpreters, many of whom have been sampled on these pages. In the final analysis, however, the most important political interpretation and activity rests with you and your citizen peers throughout America.

QUESTIONS FOR DISCUSSION AND DIALOGUE

1. Which do you think is more justified by the 1970 election returns, Republican or Democratic optimism? Why?

2. Briefly summarize the "Center," "Left," and "Right" interpretations of modern American politics as reviewed in this reading. Which do you think comes closest to capturing modern American political reality? Why?

INDEX